Options for a New Britain

Options for a New Britain

Edited by

Varun Uberoi, Adam Coutts,
Iain McLean and David Halpern

palgrave
macmillan

First published 2009 by
PALGRAVE MACMILLAN

Palgrave Macmillan in the UK is an imprint of Macmillan Publishers Limited,
registered in England, company number 785998, of Houndmills, Basingstoke,
Hampshire RG21 6XS.

Palgrave Macmillan in the US is a division of St Martin's Press LLC,
175 Fifth Avenue, New York, NY 10010.

Palgrave Macmillan is the global academic imprint of the above companies
and has companies and representatives throughout the world.

Palgrave® and Macmillan® are registered trademarks in the United States,
the United Kingdom, Europe and other countries.

ISBN-13: 978–0–230–57485–4   hardback
ISBN-10: 0–230–57485–8   hardback
ISBN-13: 978–0–230–57486–1   paperback
ISBN-10: 0–230–57486–6   paperback

This book is printed on paper suitable for recycling and made from fully
managed and sustained forest sources. Logging, pulping and manufacturing
processes are expected to conform to the environmental regulations of the
country of origin.

A catalogue record for this book is available from the British Library.

A catalog record for this book is available from the Library of Congress.

10   9   8   7   6   5   4   3   2   1
18   17   16   15   14   13   12   11   10   09

Printed and bound in Great Britain by
CPI Antony Rowe, Chippenham and Eastbourne

This book is dedicated to the memory of Gavin Cameron
(1969–2007)

Contents

List of Tables, Figures and Boxes

Tables

Figures

Boxes

Foreword

This book is a timely follow-up to *Options for Britain* (1996). It provides a survey of the successes and the failures of British Government policy over the last 12 years as well as a series of analyses of the possible options awaiting an incoming government in 2009 or 2010. It is the sort of book that should stimulate the fresh thinking required to address the challenges facing Britain and the world over the coming decades.

Indeed, one such challenge was dramatically signalled in the first weeks of September 2008 with the collapse of Lehman Brothers and the unprecedented bankruptcy of other large banks and financial institutions around the world. Another challenge is the growth of the global population which is increasing at a rate equivalent to that of the British population every year. In order to secure and enhance the well-being of the 9 billion inhabitants that are expected by the middle of the century, new approaches are required to build structures of global decision-making to enable us to efficiently manage the limited resources of the planet. Our creaking and outmoded international agencies, developed to face post World War Two circumstances, will need to be revamped to face these contemporary challenges. The United States, Europe and Japan need to take on board the emergence of the new powers like China, India and Brazil while also acknowledging the need for rapid economic growth amongst the poorer countries – particularly those of sub-Saharan Africa. Our greatest collective challenge, in the face of food, energy, mineral, water and disease crises is to move from economic dependence on fossil-fuels to low carbon economies. These challenges must, and will, pre-occupy many of us over the decades to come.

They certainly pre-occupied me during my time in government, although I had none of the advantages of the authors of *Options for Britain*. Parachuted into government from a career in science (not science policy), everything in this strange new environment had to be picked up as I went along. But the outbreak of what became the world's biggest Foot-and-Mouth Disease (FMD) epidemic in February 2001 placed me on a very steep learning curve. A key lesson surrounds the responses of the civil servants to the crisis. As the outbreak occurred, officials in the Ministry for Agriculture, Fisheries and Food tried to resolve the problem using the same means that were employed during the last UK FMD epidemic in 1967. They behaved almost as if farming practices had not changed and as if science and technology had not developed over the intervening 35 years. But in real time, working around the clock, I laboured with the expert community to determine an effective new strategy to overwhelm the epidemic. But here was a revelation. The remarkable developments in our scientific knowledge that have taken place around the world, largely within universities, and public research establishments, are seldom available to policymakers in government.

This experience led me to develop a new in-depth Foresight process as a horizon-scanning tool for government. It was initially used to gauge Britain's long-term needs in relation to flooding and coastal management issues. Working with over a hundred scientists, engineers and economists we planned how Britain's needs would change to cope with the long-term hazards that were mostly driven by climate change. It became clear from our Foresight Report that global action to mitigate future climate change was urgently required if the UK was to be able to effectively manage the impacts to its population. This was before the well publicised Stern Report in 2006 and a new flood management programme was thus implemented. The Foresight process was extended to eight other programmes and will hopefully remain in place over the coming years to serve the need for in-depth, robust, evidence-based approaches to cross-departmental government issues. However, there is a long way to go before this approach becomes embedded in government procedures. Future Prime Ministers and Secretaries of State should, in my view, demand detailed scenario analyses which bring in the wider expert communities before tackling large-scale new ventures. Indeed, the post 9/11 actions in Afghanistan and particularly Iraq were situations where scenario building might well have highlighted the possibility of overwhelmingly damaging outcomes.

This Foresight process thus reflected my belief that the expertise of the wider research community can and should influence the thoughts of policymakers and *Options for a New Britain* is another example of how this can be done. It brings together researchers to assess what has happened since the election of New Labour in 1997 and what challenges an incoming government, regardless of political persuasion, might face. A broad range of domestic and international policy issues are covered, many of which are now affected by the global social and economic context. At the very least, these kinds of exercises can help prevent policymakers making costly mistakes and at most they can help us navigate our way to better futures, both for those in the UK and for the rest of the world.

David King
University College, Oxford

Preface

In 1993 four young British public policy researchers at Oxford University assembled a group of eminent contributors to publish *Options for Britain: A Strategic Policy Review* (Halpern et al 1996). It was common knowledge that a change of UK government was likely soon. The incumbent Conservatives had been in power since 1979. They had won four general election victories in a row. However, the government headed by John Major was riven by very public disagreements about the European Union. More damagingly, its reputation for economic competence – always one of the Conservatives' secret weapons, for as long as the opinion poll companies have been asking the question – was shattered the day that the pound was forced out of the European Monetary System, the precursor to the Eurozone, on 'Black Wednesday' in September 1992. In fact by 1996 the UK economy was starting to show distinct benefits from Black Wednesday, but the electorate gave the Conservatives no credit for that.

However *Options* was not intended as a partisan manifesto for the expected Labour government, which duly did win a landslide victory in May 1997. The editors wrote:

All too often, pre-election debates become captured by one or two 'key issues' that in retrospect don't seem very 'key' at all. For example, the 1992 election involved considerable debate about the resources available to the National Health Service, yet the fact is that the objective commitments made by the parties differed very little. Similarly, promises about tax were considered to be a major issue at the time, but in retrospect now look rather flat. Unfortunately, such false debates tend to obscure the very real policy options that are available and that need to be discussed. (Halpern et al 1996: ix)

Contributors – all of them specialists in one or other area of UK public policy – were asked to provide an evidence-based briefing for an incoming government, of any political complexion, in their area of expertise. The evidence assembled by the *Options* team was extensively used by Labour ministers and their advisers in the ensuing Labour governments. We like to think that it would have been equally useful if the Conservatives had won in 1997.

All four of the 1996 editors continued to be active both as academics and as policy analysts. David Halpern became Chief Strategist at the Prime Minister's Strategy Unit before leaving government in order to be free to edit the present policy volume. He is now Research Director at the Institute of Government which is a new venture that aims to support and help improve government through research into the issues which matter to senior decision-makers. Stewart Wood became a lecturer in politics at Oxford University, on secondment after 2001 to Chancellor of the Exchequer Gordon Brown. It was originally hoped that he would become one of the editors of this book. However his contract with Gordon Brown was renewed when Mr Brown became Prime Minister in summer 2007, and Stewart was therefore ineligible to be an editor. He has remained interested in this project, and we thank him for his help. Stuart White is also a lecturer in politics at Oxford University, and current director of its Public Policy Unit, under whose wing this book shelters.

In 1996, when the original *Options for Britain* was published, it owed much to an outstanding young economist called Gavin Cameron. Not only did the book benefit, but so did the rest of the editorial gang of four, from working on the project with him.

Gavin became Reader in Economics at Oxford University, and ran a successful housing policy website. It is a matter of great sadness that he is not here to see this successor volume. He died on 9 September 2007, from complications related to cystic fibrosis. Born in 1969 of Scottish lineage (he looked magnificent in his kilt), he was diagnosed with cystic fibrosis as a boy. At that time the life expectancy of CF sufferers was 10. Gavin's survival was due to an iron constitution and equally iron determination. He was intensely proud to win the Cystic Fibrosis Academic Achiever of the Year Award in 1997. Having obtained a first-class degree before he was 21, he worked briefly in government before spending the rest of his life in academe. He was one of the leading applied economists of his generation and would have made an important contribution to the housing chapter of this book, as indeed he already had to UK public debate. At the time of his death he was a reader in economics and dearly-loved fellow of Lady Margaret Hall, Oxford. This book is dedicated to his memory.

After the general election of 2005, our thoughts turned to repeating the exercise. Prime Minister Tony Blair soon signalled that he would not serve for the whole length of the 2005 Parliament, so it was certain that there would be a new administration – of the same or a different party. When we started planning this volume, we hoped to have it out in time to advise Tony Blair's successor. The inevitable delays of grant-getting mean that it will be out in time to advise Gordon Brown's successor, who may or may not be Gordon Brown, after the UK general election that is due in 2009 or 2010.

We are very grateful to the funding agencies that have made this successor volume possible. The lead funder is the Economic and Social Research Council (ESRC) under grant no. RES-177-25-0003. This was an 'ESRC Venture' meaning that the initiative came from the ESRC, but our application was peer-reviewed in the normal way. The ESRC later gave us supplementary funding in order for this book to be ready in time for the Festival of Science in March 2009.

We are also extremely grateful for funding from the Gatsby Foundation, Oxford University's Department of Politics and International Relations, the Gwilym Gibbon Fund of Nuffield College, Oxford, and the John Fell Fund of Oxford University.

We have had an active Advisory Committee containing public policy experts of all political persuasions and none. Some expressed the fear that, as two of the editors of *Options* went on to work for the Blair/Brown governments (one as a civil servant and one as a special adviser) this book would be excessively Blairite and/or Brownite. We hope there was never any danger of that, but if there was our Advisory Committee kept us on the straight and narrow. The political party most heavily represented at the events we held while developing the ideas of this book was the Conservative Party. Our contributors, likewise, come from multiple points of the political compass, and some of them from no known point. Where chapter authors have a known political affiliation (which is no crime, but neither was it a requirement), we made a point of having each relevant chapter read, and sometimes co-authored, by an expert from a different political standpoint from that of the original author.

Therefore this has been a truly collegiate project. We thank all our chapter authors who have toiled away for no reward save the joy of knowing that they have contributed to the public good of policy discussion. Many people whose names do not appear in the Notes on Contributors also contributed. Among those who have read and commented on chapter drafts, we thank Asheem Singh, Dave Allen, Lord David Sainsbury, David Levy, Giles Wilkes, Ilian Iliev, Mike Kelly, Richard Berthoud, Roy Griffiths, Samantha Callan and Nasar Meer.

We held two successful conferences, one at Nuffield College, Oxford (which hosted the original *Options* project), and one at the Centre for Research in the Arts, Social Sciences and Humanities, Cambridge, the latter kindly co-sponsored by the *Cambridge Journal of Economics* (Brendan Burchell and Ron Martin), *Political Quarterly* (Andrew Gamble) and the History and Policy group (Simon Szreter). At these conferences, chapter authors presented their drafts, which were subjected to lively and incisive discussion. We thank all those who attended either conference, especially the following discussants who made substantial contributions of their own. From the Oxford conference we thank Adam Swift, Alan Walker, Andrew Harrop, Chris Ham, Dann Finn, Danny Dorling, David Miller, David Willetts, Fran Bennett, Gillian Crosby, Hilary Graham, Jim Bennett, Malcolm Dean, Mark Carroll, Nick Canning, Sally Prentice, Stephen Aldridge, Steve Wilcox, Tim Newburn and Will Cavendish. From the Cambridge conference we thank Alan Hughes, Chris Nash, David Good, David Newbery, Jonathan Brearley, Michael Woolcock, Mike Kitson, Nadim Shehadi, Pat Thane, Paul Ingram, Ron Martin, Shailaja Fennell, Simon Caney and Simon Szreter. Though their names do not appear on the list of contributors, this book owes its breadth to them. We also thank the kind and helpful staff at Nuffield College, Oxford and St Catharine's College, Cambridge as well the staff at the Centre for Research in the Arts, Social Sciences and Humanities.

Ideas from this book have been presented at numerous other conferences and events. Each of the editors has been involved in public policy events in his own area. For instance, IM is a member of the Independent Expert Group advising the Calman Commission of the Scottish Parliament on options for the future financial arrangements between the UK and Scotland. Neither the IEG nor the Commission is responsible for any opinions expressed in this book.

In the fog of war and party conflict, the continuities of public policy are sometimes lost. In all areas, policy options are constrained by the facts. We have tried to give the best available data, where possible from official sources or reliable survey organizations. Therefore we hope that this book will be a modest help to an incoming government of any political complexion.

VU, AC, IM, DH
Oxford

Introduction

In 1996, a team of policy experts, including two of the present editors, published *Options for Britain: A Strategic Policy Review* (Halpern et al 1996). The four editors of *Options* were all young academics with interests in public policy, in the UK and beyond. In 1996, a UK general election was due within a year, which was widely expected to (and in the event did) lead to a change of government. However, the motives behind *Options* were not partisan. The editors believed that facts and data were vital, but also that the task facing an incoming government was not predetermined:

> It has ... become fashionable ... to believe that governments are powerless to make real changes in the economy or society ... The most that can be done, it is often argued, is to tinker with the slimmest margins of change. Yet cross-national, econometric and sociological analyses suggest that governments can do a great deal ... the question is not whether we *can* affect our social and economic future, but whether we have the imagination and the political will to do so. (Halpern et al 1996: ix)

Twelve years on, we endorse that. A lot has indeed changed in British politics; some of it due to conscious choices by the Labour governments first elected in 1997, but much of it driven by external shocks such as the terrorist attacks on the USA on 11 September 2001 and the world economic shock of 2008.

In 1996 we surveyed the main areas of domestic policy, with additional chapters on UK devolution, on Europe, and on representational reform. We were probably too parochial. We said nothing about the world beyond Europe. But the shocks of 2001 and 2008 (and not only those) have reminded everybody that we have only one globe to share. Global environmental threats, especially that of global warming, are remarkably low profile in the 1996 volume. The issue of immigration is also strikingly low profile in comparison to the public concern and political profile it took on in the decade that followed.

In this introduction we preview, first, the policy areas we covered in 1996; next, those which are new to this volume. Finally we revisit the 1996 themes that we have not repeated, explaining why not.

Both in 1996 and now, we start with the economy. The health of the UK economy sets the boundaries for all other policy options. If the economy grows, policymakers can decide how to set the balance between cutting taxes and improving services. If it shrinks, Governments may have to cut services and improve taxes. In 1996, we argued that 'the immediate prospects for growth are good, and that continued growth at a 2.5–3% rate should be feasible', but worried that an incoming government might not be able to maintain the 'competitive level of the pound'. There was some risk that inflation would start to creep up; even if not, the expected recovery might be 'joyless' because disposable spending would rise more slowly than GDP per head (Currie, in Halpern et al 1996: 29–38).

In this book we have two chapters on the economy. Nicholas Crafts discusses microeconomic policy and the productivity agenda. Martin Weale discusses prosperity and productivity. Crafts notes that in 1997 Labour broke decisively with its past. It did not seek to promote national champions nor to protect lame ducks. Rather, Labour depended on what Gordon Brown in 1994 had called 'post-neoclassical endogenous growth theory'. He was roundly derided, the former Conservative frontbencher Michael Heseltine saying 'It's not Brown's: it's Balls' in a schoolboy reference to Ed Balls, Brown's economic adviser in opposition and for many years in government. At the time of writing, Mr Balls is Secretary of State for education.

From 1997 until 2007 the joke was on the Conservatives. In the private sector, Crafts shows, Labour did promote endogenous growth. It did not attempt to pick winners (in other words, attempt to guess the next big thing better than the market can). Microeconomics is about the factors influencing individual economic agents such as firms, consumers, and employees. The Treasury, under Brown and Balls, insisted that the five drivers of productivity were investment, innovation, skills, competition, and enterprise. Microeconomic policy was aimed at improving these.

Labour did not take the 'easy' route to improving GDP per hour worked, namely to exclude the least productive workers from the workforce. This approach has been associated with some large European economies, including France and Germany. Rather, Chancellor Brown had a moral commitment to maximizing the proportion of the workforce in work (derived from his reading of Adam Smith – see McLean 2006). Crafts writes:

> The attractive feature of UK productivity performance since 1997 is that it has assimilated significant increases in employment without seeing a reduction in labour productivity growth thereby raising the rate of growth of real GDP per person. (below, p. 18)

The Blair and Brown governments welcomed globalization as a driver of productivity growth. A notable feature was the openness of the UK to mass immigration from the new EU countries of central and Eastern Europe during the period.

However, Crafts is more critical in some policy areas, suggesting scope for further microeconomic improvements for an incoming UK government. Public sector productivity has probably improved only sluggishly if at all (there are issues of measurement here). Land-use planning is stuck in a 1947 world of command and control, a point also made by Nickell in relation to housing policy (see below). Relaxing this would probably give an incoming government its least-cost option for improving GDP per head.

Martin Weale looks at the big picture. GDP has grown since 1997, but how much of that was driven by what we now know was an unsustainable credit-fuelled consumer boom? Weale points out that the UK's record of capital accumulation from 1997 to 2007 was poor, and may be even more vulnerable during the current downturn. Weale speculates about the likely effects, as far as possible in a chapter that had to be prepared in the first week of confirmed recession.

One 1997 innovation, discussed in the Constitution chapter, is worth mentioning here: functional independence for the Bank of England, coupled with a decision by Chancellor Brown to publish credible commitments to restrain government deficits. His 'Golden Rule' stated that over the economic cycle government would borrow only to invest (not to fund current consumption); and his 'Sustainable Investment Rule' stated that net government borrowing would not exceed 40% of GDP. This regime worked very well for 10 years but is in trouble in 2008. A future government of any complexion is likely to retain Bank independence but as Simon Wren-Lewis points out we will have to revisit the fiscal rules and there is some limited room for manoeuvre as is shown in Box 2.1.

After these opening chapters, we arrange our policy discussions in roughly descending order of the size of the various functions of government, as categorized by international statistical agreement. The largest single function of government is 'social protection', followed by health and education. Education and science were linked in one government department for most of our period, though there has been a recent shuffle such that children and schools are in one department and higher education, research, and science in another. It therefore makes sense for us to take education and science in adjacent chapters. Then follow other domestic functions – smaller in budget but not in political or policy importance. These include law and order, housing, transport. We have taken defence (a big budget item) and foreign affairs (a small budget item) together, followed by diversity and extremism, and media (very small in budget, but with large public visibility). The book is then finished by our chapter on the constitution – trivial in budget terms but obviously vital in setting the options open to future governments. There has been huge constitutional change since 1997, more than we (or anybody else) anticipated in 1996.

Social protection includes both cash transfers to individuals (such as pensions, unemployment benefit and incapacity benefit) and the provision of social services. In 1996 we had chapters on unemployment, the welfare state, and family change. We thought it should not be difficult to reduce unemployment, providing we avoided blind alleys we then identified as 'cunning demand-side policies ... reducing labour supply ... cutting employment protection ... profits sharing and related pay structures' (Nickell, in Halpern et al 1996: 67). Rather, an incoming government should target the long-term unemployed, and the unskilled; improve education and training for the bottom half of the ability range; reform benefits to maintain the advantage of working over not working; and encourage employers to coordinate their labour market operations. On welfare policy, we discussed the growth in income inequality in the UK, which was most notable in the 1980s, and the difficult trade-off between universal benefits (expensive) and targeted benefits (which can lead perversely to high marginal rates of taxation as people move out of poverty and cease to qualify). We looked at trends in family formation and break-up. Married couples have been delaying the start of their families; but there was an increase in pregnancy among (mostly low income, low education) teenagers. Divorce and increasing longevity had both led to a sharp increase in single-person households. We noted the interaction between family structures and patterns of crime, unemployment, and housing demand.

In this book, Peter Kenway particularly focuses on the Labour government's poverty-reduction policies on children. Furthermore, Labour followed the Adam Smith–Gordon Brown route of insisting that work was the best way out of poverty. Hence the national minimum wage (which most commentators believe has worked, in a modest way) and tax credits (not so successful because of administrative costs and glitches). Kenway regards Labour's 'Sure Start' programme (subsidized childcare centres for under-fives) as successful and notes that commentators across the political spectrum welcome the principle of means-tested anti-poverty measures. The main problem now seems to be in-work poverty. The recent focus on means-tested benefits leads directly to Kenway's most uncomfortable observation: that those emerging from poverty face

> an effective marginal [tax] rate above 70%. For those receiving Housing Benefit or Council Tax Benefit, this rate can be as high as 95%. (below, p. 62)

How that high marginal tax rate might be reduced is a large question as is the question that Jo Blanden considers: social mobility. By comparing the life chances of two big cohorts of British children as they get older – those born in 1958 and those born in 1970 – it seems that there is no increase in social mobility in the UK, and there may even be a decline. (The figures have to be treated with care because of fuzziness in the data.) She implies that social immobility is deeply rooted in the structure of UK society (Strategy Unit 2008).

Martin Evans and Susan Harkness discuss worklessness, which, as they point out, is a broader concept than unemployment as it includes those out of the workforce for other reasons such as sickness, being a full-time carer or being a student. They point out that the structure of employment has become strongly gendered – more so, perhaps, than in 1996. Manufacturing employment has continued to fall; the growth has been in services and public administration – in the public sector and predominantly female. Labour has prioritized 'making work pay'; the national minimum wage has played a part in this. One downside is that, as benefits for the unemployed have become harder to get and with more conditions attached, so the incentives for a second family member to work in a household where there is already one working member have become very weak. Evans and Harkness recommend that an incoming government should be more relaxed than in the past about short-term temporary – and perhaps 'cash in hand' – jobs at the bottom of the occupational ladder.

Our 1996 analysis of options in health policy explained how from its inception in 1948 until the mid-1970s the National Health Service was divided into three sectors: centrally planned hospitals; self-employed GPs; and a (weak) local authority sector responsible for public health. The Conservatives elected in 1979 promised an NHS that was both more decentralized and more strongly managed. When this did not prevent a financial crisis in the winter of 1987–88, the government turned rather to the idea of 'internal markets'. NHS purchasers were separated from NHS providers. The former, such as GP practices, bought services from the latter, such as acute (i.e. general) hospitals, for their patients. In 1996 it was too early to judge the success of this experiment. On coming to office in 1997, Labour announced that it would abandon it. That proved short lived. Furthermore, the concept of rationing is inherent in the NHS, financed as it is out of general taxation rather than out of either public or private insurance. Financing the NHS in any other ways is outside the range of practical political options for an incoming UK government of any complexion. Where does that leave us?

John Appleby and Adam Coutts remind us that one of Labour's main promises in 1997 was to 'End the Tory internal market'. Before long, the party had substituted a Labour internal market. By 2002 the government proposed to 'introduce stronger *incentives* to ensure the extra cash produces improved performance. Primary Care Trusts will be free to purchase care from the most appropriate provider – be they public, private or voluntary' (below, pp. 90–1). Under Labour, the proportion of GDP devoted to health care has risen massively; health outputs have improved, but at a disappointing rate, and little at all in the area of ICT (always an intractable problem for governments). Productivity per unit input has declined. Nevertheless, in England waiting lists and waiting times have shortened massively. In Wales, Scotland, and

Northern Ireland which forwent the pain of NHS reform, waiting times have not shortened at the same rate (Greer 2004). Overall, health outcomes have improved, but they have worsened for some conditions, including diabetes (which is linked to obesity). Health inequalities have stubbornly failed to improve. Although smoking and unhealthy diets have declined, they have declined as much or more among the rich as among the poor, and therefore the relatively worse health of the poor remains a feature of the landscape.

Under future governments demand for health care will continue to increase, especially as the proportion of very elderly citizens continues to soar. On the supply side, new treatments and technologies will continue to offer hope to patients and put pressure on resources. Labour has created agencies (such as NICE – the National Institute for Health and Clinical Excellence, whose acronym has drifted away from its title) to distance politicians from the inevitably unpopular choices that result, but politicians find it very hard to avoid being sucked in. To improve health, government should perhaps concentrate on improving lifestyles – and if they could crack the nut of improving the lifestyles of the poorest, they might achieve the long-wished goal of reducing health inequality.

On education, in 1996 we noted that the UK performed poorly on some international league tables. It had low pre-school participation and weak results especially in mathematics and science, although results were improving as the then Conservative government put increasing stress on targets and grades. Among rich countries, the UK had one of the lowest proportions of teenagers staying in education after the compulsory school-leaving age. The UK also had a weak record at intermediate-level training for skilled occupations. However, the UK had successfully expanded the proportion of the age-group entering higher education. Other problems identified in 1996 were the poor quality of teaching, especially in subjects where it was hard to recruit teachers; an uncoordinated maze of qualifications; weak provision for lifelong learning and training; and a perverse funding formula which sometimes offered more funds per pupil in rich areas than in poor areas of England. We did not consider the Scottish education system, which had always done things differently to England.

Devolution has indeed led to a natural experiment, where policies on education, health, and the other devolved services – which add up to most domestic policy – have begun to diverge in the four countries of the UK. In the tight word-limit for this book, we have had limited room to address this issue, though it is discussed in a special linked issue of *Political Quarterly* which will discuss this and other intergovernmental issues. We have not forgotten the Scots, Welsh or Irish. As one of us is Scots and another half-Scots, we would never dare to.

On education, Alison Wolf reviews the changes made since 1997 and the issues still facing an incoming government. She notes that Labour inherited a regime of 'centralized control plus parental choice' – and kept it in place, sidelining formerly-powerful interests such as local authorities and teachers' unions. She notes that a number of *Options I* suggestions were pursued by Labour ministers. Of the problems and priorities identified in 1996, she notes that early years education has vastly expanded. Labour ministers are particularly proud of their 'Sure Start' programme to expand early years provision in poorer parts of England, though Wolf is sceptical whether it has actually broken the cycle of deprivation – indeed markedly less positive in this respect than Peter Kenway in relation to employment (see above). Labour ministers have intensified the target-driven standards programme they inherited from the Conservatives, with mixed results. Some improvement is genuine; some a result of gaming. Goodhart's Law states, in its original form, 'any observed statistical regularity will tend to collapse once pressure is placed upon it for control purposes' (Chrystal and Mizen 2001). C.A.E. Goodhart, who gave it its name, was thinking of the efforts of governments to control the money supply by targeting a particular measure of it. But the lesson is much more general. If schools are rewarded for achieving a certain benchmark and punished for failing to meet it, then they will strain every nerve to achieve *that particular* benchmark. As Wolf drily notes, the phrase 'GCSE *or equivalent*' is especially significant for the government's own self-imposed targets and for schools (below p. 125).

The gaps between the best and worst schools have remained stubbornly wide and, as with health, these gaps probably owe more to pupils' environment than to anything schools do. In Wolf's opinion, the most successful New Labour education policy was one that actually contradicted a manifesto promise. The Higher Education Act 2004 was bitterly contested in and out of Parliament, and passed only on the votes of Scottish Labour MPs whose constituents were unaffected by its most controversial section. It introduced student fees, initially capped at £3,000 a year, and an income-contingent loan to pay both those fees and some maintenance costs. In Wolf's view this has rescued English universities from decades of underfunding and helped them to maintain their world-class position. On intermediate skills and Further Education, however, Wolf rates Labour's initiatives much more harshly, suggesting a powerful lesson for the role played by the educational customer and market in HE in contrast, and its absence in FE.

Wolf concludes with a menu of options for an incoming government. Unsurprisingly, they relate closely to things that previous reformers (including the authors of *Options I*) have pressed unavailingly on governments. She considers that centralized targetry has run its course and recommends a system where funds follow the pupil – much as health reformers have tried to make funds follow the patient. Barriers to entry for new schools should be lowered, and governments should try to reintroduce the incentives or 'vouchers' for sub-university students to stay in education and power a more responsive sector.

In 1996 we did not have a separate chapter on science and technology policy. We should have done. As it turned out, it was one of New Labour's successes. Jonathan Grant and Joachim Krapels recur to Brown's (or Balls') post-neoclassical endogenous growth policy. Brown and Balls recognized that scientific research was a public good, which the market would undersupply. Under New Labour, real expenditure on science grew by 63%, largely overseen by a committed (and unpaid) science minister, Lord Sainsbury. Unlike with education, there is objective international evidence of the quality of British science in publications per researcher and citations per paper. Concerns remain around the balance of British students and school-leavers qualified to do world-class science in particular subjects, though this is partly offset by a 'brain gain' from other countries.

Grant and Krapels refer to a centuries-old tug of war between scientists and government. Scientists want to be given money without strings for pure research. Governments want to set research priorities. '[N]either position is tenable' (below, p. 148). Scientists must expect public auditors to be interested in how public money is used. Governments cannot expect to know better than scientists where the next advance in science will come. There are signs that this battle is being fought to a draw, with the research councils becoming less prescriptive on what scientists should do, while scientists accept that some audit of their activities is reasonable.

Technology transfer from universities to spin-out companies has been broadly successful, though the equivalent 'spin-outs' of knowledge to the public and social sectors have been less so. Nevertheless Grant and Krapels are among the few of our chapter authors who can say 'if it ain't broke, don't fix it' in their recommendations to policymakers. Among possible options, however, are a greater use of government procurement policies to advance science and a more consistent support of scientific evidence in policymaking. They point to the example of how health research is transferred and applied in Canada as a possible model that we might borrow from in other areas. Perhaps other areas where an incoming government could make more robust use of science include genetically modified organisms and nuclear power (in both cases, compared to the safety of *not* using them).

From the heights we turn to the depths, or at least from science to crime. In 1996 we opened by noting that 'Crime is inescapably, and rightly, a political issue' (Halpern et al 1996: 207). We noted the perennial problem of judging the 'true' level of crime when different measures tell very different stories. Crime reporting is another victim of Goodhart's Law. Crime had risen since the 1950s; but beyond doubt, Britain in 1996 was much safer than in the eighteenth and nineteenth centuries. It was also well known that most crime was committed by young men – about half of all crime that could be traced to an offender was committed by men under 21. Crime was heavily associated with illegal drug use, though that association proves nothing about causation. We argued that the best long-term measure against crime was a set of social norms in support of the law. It was not easy to see how these might be deliberately induced. Crime policy was (and is) peculiarly vulnerable to populist sloganeering. The slogan 'Prison works' (associated with Conservative Home Secretary Michael Howard) is true to the extent that prisoners can't normally commit further crimes; however, at any one time few criminals are in prison, and increasing the prison population by 25% would produce a fall in recorded crime of only 1%.

Mike Hough (one of the authors of the 1996 chapter on 'crime and criminal justice') and Julian Roberts now note that some things have changed radically, and others not at all, in this policy domain. One issue that has not changed is the dilemma for policymakers:

[T]he next government will have to choose between populist criminal justice policies or a more nuanced – and hence less politically attractive – approach to responding to crime and disorder. (below, p. 156)

A smart government could (and perhaps should) do both. Crime is down since 1997, though most people believe it is rising. A smart government should clearly address those crimes that both have a high media profile and are a serious threat to public peace. The two circles overlap but are not the same. Knife crime among socially excluded young males is an issue of grave public concern, though it directly affects relatively few, while chaotic and persistent drug-induced lifestyles arguably affect far more people, such as through the acquisitive crime they drive, but tends to have a much lower public profile. Hough and Roberts imply that a third tabloid preoccupation, city-centre binge drinking, is more a public health than a crime issue, the social order aspects of which could be addressed by local authorities robustly using their licensing powers.

Any government must address the fact that the prisons of England and Wales, despite a massive expansion in their size, are full. Hough and Roberts recommend clearer and more binding sentencing guidelines, perhaps combined with greater use of early release. To address the gap between perception and reality, they stress the need for trustworthy independent crime statistics. The public tend to believe the tabloids, and they completely disbelieve government ministers. This can be galling when it is the latter who appear to be telling the truth. One machinery-of-government move that has occurred since 1997 is the greater independence of official statistics. However much ministers enjoy spinning statistics to fit their story, their long-term interest lies in not being allowed anywhere near them. This observation applies to many policy domains, perhaps nowhere more so than with crime.

In 1996 we identified the main problems of housing policy as 'encouraging unsustainable levels of home ownership ... creating dependency [among social housing tenants] on Housing Benefit and fierce disincentives to work ... concentrating and segregating poor and disadvantaged households on council estates' (Best, in Halpern et al 1996: 273). We warned against stimulating the housing market. We stressed the need to restore the private rented sector with public support. Surprisingly (from a 2008 perspective) little was said about land-use planning.

Stephen Nickell opens by pointing out that the real price of houses for owner-occupation doubled between 1997 and 2008. On the supply side, housebuilding has nowhere near kept up with the increase in the number of households: a problem that will only have got worse with the 2008 credit crunch and shut-down of the building industry that has deepened since Nickell's chapter was written. The number of households continues to increase faster than the population, with more family breakdowns and single pensioners in the population. Furthermore,

> real incomes are steadily growing and ... richer people tend to demand more housing services. The historical evidence suggests that the income elasticity of demand for housing exceeds the price elasticity of demand. In other words, as real incomes rise, house prices will rise more rapidly than incomes even if there is a perfect match between house building and population growth. (p. 173 below)

On the demand side, real interest rates have been at a historic low and there was a bubble (now burst) in the buy-to-let market. The 2008 crunch will worsen the housing market further. Although prices are falling rapidly, that is no consolation to first-time buyers because mortgages have become hard to get. And new construction in the market sector has stalled. Nickell sees the long-term problem as being the unaffordability of housing for new entrants, which implies 'a large transfer of wealth from the young and the poor to the old and the wealthy' (p. 175). The main solution, he suggests, is to revive market housing which will relieve the pressure on social housing. Like Crafts, Nickell sees land-use planning as the principal villain in this melodrama. As local authorities no longer control business rates, they have lost the incentive to be pro-development. Those who would benefit from releasing land for housing do not yet live in the area. Everyone acts rationally, including through NIMBYism and voting in local elections, but the net result is far from optimal. Nickell's solution is deceptively simple – local authorities must (once again) receive an incentive to unlock the planning gain that will accrue if they permit large-scale housebuilding, especially in the South of England, where demand is most acute. This is one of the awkward truths that this book has uncovered. Like some others, this truth is moderately well known among public policy specialists, but you look in vain for discussion of it in most political manifestos or media (even heavyweight media) treatises.

In 1996 we treated transport and the environment together. We noted that there was substantial but erratic public concern with transport-generated threats to the environment, but that nobody wanted to curb their use of transport in a way that would actually help (Taylor and Taylor, in Halpern et al 2006). *Options I* argued that the most urgent environmental priorities at the time were to reduce urban air pollution (probably relatively easy, e.g. by encouraging cycling) and to reduce the need for new roads (tougher). *Options I* also noted and endorsed the policy of the Royal Commission on Environmental Pollution to double fuel prices by 2000. When that target was actually reached, a populist revolt against fuel taxation caused the government to abandon its policy, inherited from the Conservatives, of deliberately increasing fuel taxation faster than inflation (McLean 2008). It has not been reinstated. Transport policy – both today and then – presents some tough choices. *Options I* advocated urban road pricing as a 'first best' policy option, though this faced issues both around technical feasibility and public acceptability. Since we wrote, this has been introduced in London, rejected in Edinburgh, and was recently under discussion in Manchester. We did not expect Mancunians to vote for it. They did not. We, the public, have proven ourselves over and over again to be cheap-talk environmentalists.

In this book, Richard Wellings first notes how Labour took on even more ambitious pollution-reduction targets than we anticipated in *Options I*, where we failed to anticipate just how rapidly global warming would move to be *the* environmental issue. Labour quickly adopted Kyoto global warming targets (discussed below) and committed itself in 2000 to a transport policy that would lead to rapid reductions in greenhouse gas emissions. This policy has comprehensively failed. CO_2 emissions from transport have remained stable – perhaps praiseworthy in itself, but not even close to the pollution-reduction targets Labour set itself.

Part of the public's cheap-talk environmentalism is to say, whenever they are asked, 'Let there be more buses and trains'. If a government provides those, the public then fails to use them in a way that makes any serious impact on pollution. Although passenger rail travel has soared, it is still a trivial proportion of passenger travel, and one which absorbs the lion's share of passenger travel public expenditure (one reason for this being the collapse of Railtrack after the Hatfield crash of 2000). Meanwhile air travel has soared because of the eruption of low-cost carriers, a development we failed to anticipate in 1996. This is good for the UK economy and for people's travel plans, but bad for the environment.

On policy options, Wellings speaks a truth that usually dare not speak its name. The only feasible policy intervention with much chance of success in the short run is road pricing. Every serious transport expert knows that; the editor and readers of the *Daily Mail* do not. A future UK government needs a Secretary of State for Transport as robust as the much-reviled Ken Livingstone, Mayor of London from 2000 to 2008, who introduced the only successful road pricing scheme in the UK. Ken for Secretary of State? (Our suggestion, not Wellings'.)

As noted above, in 1996 the chapter on 'Britain in the World' focused heavily on the European Union. At the time, this issue was particularly pressing, with substantial matters to decide (such as the looming option of euro entry) yet with John Major's Conservative administration split down the middle between Europhobes and Europhiles. This time – after 11 September 2001, the start (but not the end) of two difficult and unpopular wars, terrorist attacks in London and Glasgow, a global economic crisis, and several other domestic policy issues with global tentacles – it is necessary to say something more extensive about the UK in the world. We do so principally in three chapters: 'Energy, Climate Change and the Environment'; 'Britain's Role in the World'; and 'Diversity and Extremism'.

On climate change, Federico Gallo and co-authors describe global warming and energy security as two of the greatest challenges facing mankind today. By using a holistic, first-principles approach, they identify the fundamental causes of the problem: we are using the wrong technologies to sustain the growing levels of consumption of a vast population. This situation is unsustainable, and there is evidence that we may be already hitting many natural limits of our finite planet. Fortunately these twin problems may share a common solution – i.e. reducing our environmental footprint – and the authors, based on an analysis of the fundamental causes, propose a number of policy options. They call for the UK and the world to account for the social cost of carbon using some mixture of monetary and non-monetary policies. However, in order to fully solve the problem, we will need to seriously improve our energy efficiency and perhaps reassess our levels of consumption. Climate change is a global problem and requires a global solution: although the UK cannot solve this problem alone, it has an opportunity to play a leading role in the solution.

Malcolm Chalmers brusquely summarizes UK foreign policy under Major as insular and mercantilist (below, p. 219). Whatever it has been since 1997, it has not been either of those things. One unsung achievement has been a much greater concentration on foreign aid, especially to the poorest countries. Chalmers lays stress on the role of Tony Blair as a humanitarian interventionist in Kosovo and Sierra Leone. However, when the multilateralist Blair allied with the unilateralist George Bush, these things resulted in the swamp of Iraq. Chalmers is quite forgiving of the Blair administration on Iraq, warning against 20-20 hindsight. However, he warns that the emerging superpower China is more likely to take a 'national interest' than a 'humanitarian intervention' perspective on world politics.

Unlike the Bush administration, the UK government does not regard Islamist terrorism as an existential threat, but nevertheless regards it as more serious than previous terrorist threats to the nation. For Chalmers, this means that defence policy must continue to focus on Afghanistan and Pakistan. Domestically Varun Uberoi and Shamit Saggar focus on the relationship between extremism and the current rise in hostility towards

British Muslims. The former and the latter are seen as intricately linked and the most salient current challenges that relate to governing Britain's increasingly diverse citizenry. At the time of *Options I* there was no chapter on the policy issues that relate to this area, but since then a lot has happened. Asylum seekers (always 'bogus' in the tabloid press) continued to dominate public discourse about migration until well into the period when a greater number of migrants from EU accession countries had entered the UK. A 'points system' for immigrants that gives priority to the highly skilled but doesn't apply to those who come from the accession countries is the most recent innovation that the authors allude to. They also chart the seeming dismissal and then acceptance of 'Britishness' as an area that public policy should focus on and the UK government's multiple but incoherent responses to the London terrorist bombs of 2005. Clearly, governments need to reduce the feelings of alienation and sense of social isolation among certain young UK Muslims, but how? Uberoi and Saggar show which groups are most at risk of radicalization and thus which groups any incoming government must focus some attention on. They also allude to the difficulties that government faces in this area because it is un-trusted by the very communities that it needs to gather intelligence from, and a means is suggested to help address this issue. Likewise they suggest a way that we can learn more about what attracts some British Muslims to and subsequently repels some of them from violent Islamism.

In 1996 we said nothing about media policy. Since then, the massive expansion of mobile phone penetration and wireless broadband have undermined the traditional pattern of media regulation. Damian Tambini paints a picture of a government struggling to keep up with the pace of technical change. Tambini nevertheless sees the creation of a unified media regulator, Ofcom, as a key change – more important than most of the fluff that passes for a discussion of media policy. To date, the digital switchover of terrestrial TV capacity, which releases bandwidth for other uses, has been a quiet success. Tambini raises questions of the respective roles of the state and the market in communications. The next UK government will have to get beyond endless discussions about the future of the BBC (fascinating though these are to the entire national media, almost all of whom either work for the BBC or would like to). Important though these discussions are, the next government needs clear-headed debate as to how far (if at all) there is market failure in communications in the UK. That outranks the fate of Andrew Gilligan or Jonathan Ross, probably the two biggest media rows since 1996.

Our final chapter concerns the constitution. In 1996 we examined the case for devolution, suggesting a formula for partial devolution – to Scotland, Wales and London – as well as making the case for mayors in local government (Bogdanor, in Halpern et al 1996). We also had a chapter examining the case for alternative forms of representational reform (Plant, in Halpern et al 1996).

The devolution chapter turned out to be a loose blueprint for that which followed – including urging caution for attempts to extend devolution to a wider set of regions; but subsequent action on representational reform, at least in relation to the House of Commons, was far more limited – though Plant's warning about the importance of seeing constitutional reform in the round still holds true.

By 2008, devolution had entered its long-awaited second phase with none of the three devolved territories (Scotland, Wales, and Northern Ireland) under the unified control of the UK governing party. But unfinished business of devolution remains, as Guy Lodge and Roger Gough explain. The two most unfinished pieces of business are the financial arrangements for the devolved territories and the nature of their representation in Parliament. In shorthand, these two are known as the 'Barnett formula' and the 'West Lothian Question' – WLQ to its devotees.

The Barnett formula is fatally wounded. As we write, both the Scottish and Welsh parliaments have appointed committees to review it, and one of us (IM) is a member of the first and expert witness to the second. Although the replacement of Barnett is unknown as we go to press, the direction of travel is towards greater fiscal autonomy for Scotland, and perhaps for all three devolved territories.

It has been said half in jest that the solution to the WLQ is a large Conservative majority. The WLQ addresses the anomalies of asymmetric devolution: *why should a question that affects only territory X be decided by the votes of MPs from not-X*? The most prominent example under Labour has been the Higher Education Act 2004, whose provisions for student fees applied only to students at English universities, but which was passed only on the votes of loyal Scottish and Welsh Labour MPs. If a future UK government, of either main party, rules with a narrow majority in the Commons, the question will recur. Lodge and Gough discuss some suggestions to deal with this knotty problem. These could involve the tempting but difficult idea that has become known as 'English votes on English laws', or EVOEL to its devotees. Under EVOEL, Scottish (etc) MPs would not be able to vote on questions which do not affect Scotland (etc). EVOEL is popular with the public and the Conservative Party, but Lodge and Gough explore some of its problems.

As influential as devolution has been, the incorporation of the European Convention on Human Rights into domestic law in 1998 has been arguably even more fundamental. It has led to huge changes in judicial behaviour but not universal political acceptance. Lodge and Gough explore what might lie behind the sloganeering that a 'British Bill of Rights' should either supplement or replace the Human Rights Act 1998.

One broken election pledge has been a promise of a referendum on proportional representation for the House of Commons. Now that PR systems are in place for all the devolved territories, London, and Europe, this is less of a stand-alone issue than it seemed to be in 1996. There has also been a flowering of 'alternative' democratic innovations, with uncertain impacts and relationships to the 'traditional' mechanisms of democracy. Parliament should be considered as a unit. The electoral system for the Commons should be complementary to that for an elected upper house. A 2008 White Paper set out options for an elected upper house, to be implemented only after a general election (to prevent it being blocked by the Lords). That is unfinished constitutional business for the next elected government.

In 1996 we included a chapter on tax policy. We have not done so this time. A massive inquiry, better resourced than us, is under way at the Institute of Fiscal Studies, under the chairmanship of Nobel laureate Sir James Mirrlees. With our limited resources and tight word limit, we have not tried to second-guess Sir James. His progress will be reported on the IFS website, currently at http://www.ifs.org.uk/mirrleesreview/publications.php. Watch that space.

We have attempted to give a précis of our chapters. We hope that the reader is intrigued enough to read on.

1
Microeconomic Policy and the Productivity Agenda

Nicholas Crafts

Introduction

Productivity growth matters because it underpins long-run growth in living standards. Producing more GDP from the same inputs of capital and labour means that there is more value added to be distributed as profits and/or wages. Over the long run, real wages and labour productivity grow at a similar rate. It is well-known that labour productivity is lower in the UK than in many other advanced countries and that this productivity gap has been quite persistent. It is not surprising, therefore, that, for several decades, governments of both parties have sought to improve productivity.

New Labour, in particular, has made the productivity agenda high profile and it has been a major concern of HM Treasury as well as the Department for Business Enterprise and Regulatory Reform (BERR) and the Department for Trade and Industry (DTI). Certainly, one way to justify this is that government has a role in correcting market failures that are reflected in lower productivity. It should, however, be noted right at the outset that a policy criterion based on economic efficiency would not seek to maximize labour productivity per se but rather to equate the marginal benefit (extra output) from employment with its marginal cost (the value of the worker's time).[1]

In opposition as Shadow Chancellor, Gordon Brown made a much-derided reference to 'post-neoclassical endogenous growth theory'. In office, insights from modern growth economics have been central to the way that New Labour's productivity policy has been framed. The main thrust of this approach is that growth of output and productivity depends on investment both in capital equipment and in education and training, and also on innovation. Decisions to invest and to innovate respond to economic incentives such that well-designed policy can raise the growth rate a bit. This implies that government

16

needs to pay attention to direct tax rates, to undertake investments that complement private sector capital accumulation, to support activities like R&D where social returns exceed private returns, and to facilitate competitive pressure on management to adopt cost-effective innovations. These ideas are clearly reflected in the '5 Drivers' of productivity performance which were articulated initially in HM Treasury (2000b).[2] These are investment, innovation, skills, competition, and enterprise.

In the 1970s, Old Labour governments thought in terms of industrial policy which was conceived in terms of intervention to promote either key industrial sectors or manufacturing as a whole through investment subsidies, state ownership, encouragement of mergers, protectionist policies etc. A notable difference since 1997 has been that Labour policy has downplayed the special role of manufacturing and has discarded overt protectionism and dirigisme. In part, this reflects changes in ideas but it also chimes with the realities of the evolution of the structure of the economy in which over 75% of GDP is in services and less than 20% in manufacturing. Arithmetically, at least, the key to strong productivity performance lies in the services sector. And, in fact, the most important contribution to Britain's relative economic decline in the century prior to the 1980s was lagging productivity in market services (Broadberry 2006).

Although higher productivity may seem attractive, the politics of achieving it may be quite challenging. A central aspect of technological progress is 'creative destruction', i.e. the exit of the old replaced by the entry of the new. The pursuit of higher productivity through policies such as trade liberalization also creates losers as well as gainers. Realizing the potential productivity gains from privatization typically involves job losses. The common theme here is that, while there are net gains for the economy as a whole, these do not translate into votes whereas the losses of the downsized producer groups are highly visible, matter a lot to the individuals involved, and have adverse implications for vote-seeking politicians.

It is also important to recognize that there are trade-offs involved in designing policies to enhance productivity and that how far such policies should be pursued is a matter of value judgements. For instance, some of these questions arise in the context of fiscal policy where improving incentives to invest and to innovate may have consequences in terms of the distribution of income – a classic example of a possible conflict between equity and efficiency.

Obviously, many aspects of government policy have impacts on productivity performance. The focus of this chapter is relatively narrow and considers microeconomic policies which have mainly been under the auspices of HM Treasury and BERR in the recent past. The key areas to be reviewed are competition, regulation, taxation and trade policy.

Productivity performance

It is useful to distinguish between real GDP per person and real GDP per hour worked. The latter is a measure of labour productivity while the former reflects differences in demography, labour force participation and unemployment as well as output per unit of labour input.

With regard to real GDP per person, as Table 1.1 reports, there was an increase of about 0.6 percentage points per year in the growth rate in 1997 to 2007 compared with the Conservative years 1979 to 1997, and growth since 1997 has been faster than in France, Germany or the United States. The corollary is that by 2007 the level of real GDP per person was higher in the UK than in France or Germany and the change in relative positions since 1979 is really quite striking.

Trends in real GDP per hour worked have been somewhat different, as Table 1.1 also shows. Its growth is virtually the same in 1997–2007 as in 1979–97 but the UK's relative position in terms of productivity levels has improved. The difference between relativities in terms of GDP per hour worked and per person arises from the fact that employment to population ratios and annual hours worked are higher in the UK. Increasingly over time, the French and German labour markets have tended to exclude relatively low productivity workers. Making a correction for these distortions would take about 8 percentage points off the measured labour productivity gap (but increase it by about 3 percentage points vis-a-vis the United States) so that a truer picture of the productivity gap may be that it had fallen to about 5% versus France in 2007 but was still about 18% versus the United States (cf. Table 1.2).

The attractive feature of UK productivity performance since 1997 is that it has assimilated significant increases in employment without seeing a reduction in labour productivity growth thereby raising the rate of growth of real GDP per person. The government's approach to productivity has clearly sought this as an outcome rather than seeking to improve headline numbers by excluding low-productivity employment. On the reasonable assumption that the marginal benefit of additional employment has exceeded marginal cost, this is economically efficient.

Table 1.3 reports the results of a growth accounting exercise for the marketed sector of the economy, that is, leaving aside output of the public sector which is not paid for by the user. Growth of labour productivity has been faster in the marketed sector than for GDP as a whole but it is noticeable that for the UK post-1995 there was a slowdown. Growth accounting is a technique to decompose the growth of labour productivity into contributions from capital per unit of labour, labour quality (education and skills) of the labour force, and total factor productivity (TFP) growth. TFP growth represents the contribution from improvements in efficiency and in technology.[3]

Table 1.1   Real GDP per Person and per Hour Worked

(a) Levels (UK = 100)

(i) Real GDP per Person

	1979	1997	2007
France	113.7	103.6	95.9
West Germany	115.9	107.1	
Germany		95.6	87.1
USA	142.7	141.1	133.0

(ii) Real GDP per Hour Worked

	1979	1997	2007
France	118.9	119.4	112.9
West Germany	121.1	128.5	
Germany		103.0	95.6
USA	139.9	117.0	114.7

(b) Rates of Growth (% per year)

(i) Real GDP per Person

	1979–97	1997–2007
France	1.37	1.71
West Germany	1.45	
Germany		1.55
UK	1.90	2.49
USA	1.84	1.90

(ii) Real GDP per Hour Worked

	1979–97	1997–2007
France	2.39	1.73
West Germany	2.71	
Germany		1.53
UK	2.37	2.28
USA	1.36	2.08

Note: Levels comparisons are at purchasing power parity.
Source: The Conference Board (2008).

Table 1.2   Adjustments to Labour Productivity Gap for Labour Market Distortions, 2004 (percentage points)

France	−7.9
Germany	−8.3
USA	+3.0

Note: Normalized so that adjustment in UK = 0.
Source: Bourles and Cette (2006).

Compared with France and Germany, the UK has experienced faster growth of labour productivity in the marketed sector sustained by stronger contributions from each of labour quality, capital intensity and TFP. It is, however, noticeable that the latter two, and especially TFP growth, were weaker than pre-1995. The UK was unable to match the performance of the United States in the 'new economy' phase which benefited from a relatively large sector making Information Communication and Technology (ICT) items and re-organization of sectors making intensive use of ICT, such as retailing. This is reflected in Table 1.3.

Table 1.3   Sources of Labour Productivity Growth in the Marketed Sector (% per year)

	Real GDP per Hour Worked	Due to Capital per Hour Worked	Due to Labour Quality	Due to TFP
France				
1980–95	2.4	1.1	0.5	0.8
1995–2004	1.9	0.8	0.4	0.7
Germany				
1980–95	2.5	1.1	0.2	1.2
1995–2004	1.5	1.0	0.1	0.4
UK				
1980–95	3.4	1.5	0.3	1.6
1995–2004	2.7	1.3	0.5	0.9
USA				
1980–95	1.5	0.6	0.2	0.7
1995–2004	3.2	1.3	0.3	1.6

Source: Derived from O'Mahony and Robinson (2007).

Growth accounting can also be conducted in terms of levels which allow a view of the cumulated effect of differences in capital accumulation and TFP growth over the long run. Table 1.4 reports that the UK labour productivity gap with France and West Germany is largely accounted for by a shortfall of capital, reflecting the cumulative effect of lower investment over many years, while about half of the gap with the United States is attributable to capital and just slightly less than this to TFP. Labour quality is not responsible for a very high fraction of any of these gaps, with a highest share of 22%.

Table 1.4 Decomposition of Comparative Labour Productivity Levels, 2000 (%)

	France/UK	West Germany/UK	USA/UK
Capital	82.6	69.6	51.9
Labour Quality	17.4	22.0	1.6
TFP	0.0	8.3	46.5

Source: Broadberry and O'Mahony (2007).

Table 1.5 looks at the marketed services sector. It should be recognized that these estimates are less reliable than those for the marketed sector as a whole and the methods used in this research are not the same as for Table 1.1. Nevertheless, the message that the UK still has quite a large productivity gap in market services is worth heeding. A recent estimate by OECD (2007d) suggests that 60% of the labour productivity gap between the UK and the United States comes from a few services sectors, namely, retail and wholesale distribution, business services and the financial sector. However, it should also be noted from Table 1.5 that the recent contribution of productivity growth from market services has been much stronger than in France or Germany. This has been based in particular on sectors like retailing which are intensive in the use of ICT.

Table 1.5 Comparative Productivity Performance in Market Services

(a) Real GDP per Hour Worked, 2003 (UK = 100)

	Market Services	Wholesale Trade	Retail Trade	Transport & Communications
France	141	155	161	105
Germany	162	215	156	81
USA	159	167	169	137

(b) Contribution of Market Services to Labour Productivity Growth, 1995–2004 (percentage points per year)

France	0.6
Germany	0.2
UK	1.6
USA	1.8

Note: Comparison of levels for distributive trades is for 2002 and for transport & communications is for 2004.

Sources: Inklaar et al (2007), Timmer and Ypma (2006), van Ark et al (2008) and Ypma (2007).

Nevertheless, Tables 1.3 to 1.5 taken together suggest that, despite encouraging recent signs, there are still some weaknesses in UK productivity with scope to catch up other countries. In particular, the UK has weaker TFP growth than the United States since the mid-1990s while levels of labour productivity in the important marketed-services sector leave something to be desired.

Productivity policy since 1997

When Labour won a landslide victory in the 1997 election, it was possible to wonder whether in government it would revert to 'Old Labour' policies. The answer to this question soon became apparent and was a resounding 'No'. 1970s-style policy was conspicuous by its absence in that there was no nationalization programme, no move to subsidize manufacturing investment, no return to high marginal rates of direct tax, no major reversal of industrial relations reforms, no return to protectionsim, and no pro-active industrial policy based on a 'super DTI' and a National Investment Bank. Overall, there was certainly no desire to re-instate the de facto policy veto held by the trade unions that had characterized that period. Implicitly, the Thatcher supply-side reforms had been accepted.

In fact, since 1997 there has been a new emphasis on competition policy as central to improving productivity performance. This is consistent with developments in economic theory and associated empirical evidence. Competition is seen as an antidote to principal–agent problems (bad management) in firms with weak shareholders and entry threats are seen as a good way to encourage firms to be innovative to protect their profits. The evidence is that downward pressure on mark-ups of price over cost promotes both investment and innovation (Griffith and Harrison 2004; Griffith et al 2006). The classic example in the UK of tougher anti-trust policy leading to significant improvements in productivity gains is that of the 1956 Restrictive Practices Act (Symeonidis 2008).

Taken together the 1998 Competition Act and the 2002 Enterprise Act represent a radical change in UK competition policy. The former introduced prohibitions of anti-competitive behaviour and abuse of dominant positions while the latter instigated a 'substantial lessening of competition' test for mergers. The changes represent a move to a rules-based system with ministerial discretion removed, pro-active powers for the competition authorities, criminal penalties for infringements and civil actions for damages. This makes competition policy much tougher by eliminating the 'public-interest' defences allowed to business and by providing serious sanctions rather than the previous 'please stop it' approach to dealing with abuse of market power.

HM Treasury lists 'enterprise' as a key driver of productivity performance. Here a major emphasis of policy has been to reduce the burden and costs of regulation. Again, economic analysis provides a rationale for this. Compliance costs can be thought of as representing the diversion of resources from productive activity. The Better Regulation Task Force (2005) estimated that these amount to 10–12% of GDP annually (comprising 3–4% GDP for 'administrative costs' and 7–8% GDP for 'policy costs'). Potentially much more serious may be disincentives that regulation imposes on investment and innovation by reducing expected returns and slowing down the diffusion of new technology (Crafts 2006). One route by which regulation can be shown to have adverse effects is by raising entry barriers (Cincera and Galgau 2005).

Business and government have very different views on the state of regulation. The British Chambers of Commerce regularly publish estimates of the cost to business of new regulation and their latest 2008 estimate is that the cumulative total since 1997 is £66 billion. The government points to the fact that in assessments by international agencies the UK is rated as having a regulatory environment that is very business friendly; for example, the rating in World Bank (2008) for the UK is 6th best in the world compared with a ranking of 3 for the United States, 20 for Germany, and 31 for France. The government has recently seemed to give more weight to reducing regulatory costs. The Legislative and Regulatory Reform Act in 2006 replaced the largely ineffective Regulatory Reform Act of 2001 and a White Paper on revising planning rules makes explicit reference to the desirability that planning policy be formulated with a view to promoting productivity. At this stage, however, it would be difficult to call any of these proposals radical change.

The endogenous growth literature indicates that structure and rates of taxation are relevant to productivity outcomes because they affect expected returns to investment and innovation. The standard argument is that high marginal direct tax rates, especially on corporate income, have a negative impact while consumption taxes are neutral. There is much less agreement on the magnitude of any negative effects but they are generally thought neither to be completely trivial nor massive. Kneller et al (1999) suggest that an increase of 1 percentage point in the distortionary taxes to GDP ratio on average reduces the growth rate by 0.1 percentage point.

There has been a small increase in the tax burden overall in recent years and the share of distortionary taxes is now a bit higher than in the mid-1990s but expenditure on social transfers has risen only modestly (Table 1.6). The Labour government has not increased the top marginal rate of direct income tax but in 2002 imposed a 1 percentage point increase in National Insurance contributions for these taxpayers. The statutory rate of corporate tax has been reduced from 33% to 28% continuing a trend which has seen the rate fall from 52% in the early 1980s. The main rate of value added tax (VAT) and the VAT tax base (with many items of consumption attracting no VAT) have remained unchanged until Chancellor Alistair Darling announced an emergency 13-month cut of the standard rate by 2.5 percentage points in the November 2008 pre-budget statement.

The main novelty in tax policy has been the introduction of the R&D tax credit in 2000 which can also be justified using growth economics. A careful study of its possible impact suggested that it would be cost effective and might raise TFP growth by 0.3 percentage points per year in the long run (Griffith et al 2001). The lags in the impact of this policy are believed to be quite long and, as yet, R&D expenditures as a share of GDP are no higher than in the mid-1990s.

Table 1.6　Distortionary Taxes and Social Transfers

(a) Distortionary Tax Revenues (% GDP)

	1980	1995	2005
France	30.0	31.2	32.9
Germany	27.3	26.8	24.7
UK	24.9	22.7	25.4
USA	21.7	22.9	22.5

(b) Social Transfers (% GDP)

	1980	1995	2003
France	20.8	28.3	28.7
Germany	23.0	26.6	27.3
UK	16.6	20.4	20.6
USA	13.3	15.4	16.2

(c) Statutory Corporate Tax Rates (%)

	1981	1995	2008
France	50.0	36.7	34.4
Germany	60.0	56.8	29.8
UK	52.0	33.0	28.0
USA	49.7	40.0	39.0

Note: 'Distortionary' taxes as defined in Kneller et al (1999) and are basically direct taxes on incomes.
Sources: Eurostat (2008), OECD (2007b, 2007c, 2008b).

Modern economics sees the potential for reductions in trade barriers to improve productivity performance by increasing investment, innovation and efficiency through reductions in the price of capital goods, increase in market size and intensification of competition. Although the evidence on the impact of trade liberalization on growth is not unambiguous, on balance, it points towards sizeable positive effects at least in terms of raising productivity levels.

The influential paper by Frankel and Romer (1999) concluded that an increase of 1 percentage point in the ratio of trade to GDP means that real GDP goes up by at least 0.5% and perhaps as much as 2% with the effects coming both through more investment and higher TFP. A similar analysis by Badinger (2005) concluded that economic integration since 1950 had raised income levels in the EU countries as a whole, and in the UK itself, by about 26%.

The stance that New Labour adopted from the outset was that the driving force of economic change is globalization and that the right approach was to accept this and to work with it. The measures of barriers to foreign trade and investment constructed by OECD and reported in Table 1.7 reflect this; in 2003 only Belgium and Iceland had lower barriers. Similarly, the UK has relatively low levels of subsidies to domestic producers; state aid for industry and services was only 0.16% of GDP in 2006 compared with an average of 0.41% across the EU15 countries (European Commission 2007).

Table 1.7 Barriers to Foreign Trade and Investment (0–6)

	1998	2003
France	1.5	1.0
Germany	0.9	0.8
UK	0.6	0.4
USA	1.1	0.7

Note: Low scores signify lower barriers.
Source: Conway et al (2005).

Evaluating productivity policy

The OECD has undertaken a substantial empirical investigation of competition and product market regulation policies. Some of the results are reported in Table 1.8. Part (a) reports their evaluation of the UK's competition policy and law and shows comparisons with peer group countries where the lower the score the better the policy is rated. The UK scores well and it is quite clear from the criteria that this would not have been the case prior to 1998 so the implicit evaluation is that there has been a big improvement in the UK competition policy framework stemming from the new criteria, the granting of independence to the competition authorities, and the introduction of penalties for violations. That said, the OECD indicator gives a disappointing score to mergers policy (= 4.2/10) and to enforcement (5.7/10) where for comparison the US scores 0.5/10 in each case.

This indicator is relatively new and there are no studies of its predicted productivity impact. However, the OECD also publishes a measure of Product Market Regulation (PMR) defined as an index to reflect the extent to which the regulatory environment is conducive to competition; this is reported in part (b) of Table 1.8. Here the UK's score in recent years has been the best in the OECD and improved slightly over the period 1998 to 2003. The estimates for earlier years are not constructed on a comparable basis but suggest that the UK experienced a relatively aggressive phase of liberalization prior to 1998. The evidence of lower mark-ups in the UK also supports this point. Empirical studies show that high PMR scores inhibit TFP growth (Nicoletti and Scarpetta 2003) and reduce the contribution that market services, especially those intensive in the use of information and communications technology, make to labour productivity growth (Nicoletti and Scarpetta 2005).

Table 1.8   Competition Policy Indicators

(a) Competition Law and Policy Indicator (0–10)

	OECD CLP Indicator	Scope of Law & Enforcement	Independence of Competition Authorities
France	3.93	4.50	2.50
Germany	3.58	3.50	1.75
UK	3.03	4.00	0.00
USA	2.38	2.33	2.50

(b) Product Market Regulation (0–10)

	1978	1998 (1)	1998 (2)	2003
France	10.00	7.17	4.17	2.83
Germany	8.67	4.67	3.17	2.33
UK	8.00	2.33	1.83	1.50
USA	6.17	2.67	2.17	1.67

(c) Price-Cost Margin in Non-Manufacturing

France	1.26
Germany	1.25
UK	1.16
USA	1.19

Note: Low scores are better.
Sources: Conway et al (2005), Conway and Nicoletti (2006), Hoj (2007), Hoj et al (2007).

This suggests that the UK stance on product market regulation has been favourable for productivity performance compared with that in many other European countries. One very important caveat needs to be recognized, namely, that the OECD measure does not take account of the land-use planning system. Early in the life of the Labour government, a high-profile report to HM Treasury (McKinsey Global Institute 1998) identified planning rules as a key obstacle to competition and productivity improvement in the service sector.

This seems to be particularly important for retailing where the productivity gains from larger stores and the replacement of low productivity by high productivity outlets have been retarded. The restrictions on building out-of-town stores introduced in 1996 are estimated to have reduced TFP growth in retailing by 0.4% per year or about one-eighth of the total slowdown in TFP growth post-1995 reported in Table 1.3 (Haskel and Sadun 2007).

Land-use planning is an aspect of regulation that creates massive allocative inefficiency and reduces labour productivity both by making land unduly expensive and by restricting city size which means that agglomeration economies are forgone (Leunig and Overman 2008). Cheshire and Sheppard (2005: 660) conclude that 'controlling land supply by fiat has generated price distortions on a par with those observed in Soviet-bloc countries during the 1970s and 1980s'. The key symptoms of this allocative inefficiency are huge discrepancies in the price of land designated for alternative use, especially in the South of England, and very high urban land values in successful cities. The implication is an implicit regulatory tax rate of around 300% which make office space in cities like Leeds and Manchester much more expensive than even New York and San Francisco (Cheshire and Hilber 2008).

All these points were noted by the Barker Review (2006) which concluded that there were substantial adverse impacts on productivity and recommended inter alia that government review the Green Belt policy and take action to remove the disincentives to development that local councils face. With such large gains to be had from a more efficient policy there clearly could be strong local support for relaxation of the planning rules if voters obtained a substantial share of them. The subsequent White Paper on planning (CM 7120, 2007) steadfastly refused to go down these paths presumably because they are judged to be vote losers.

By contrast, in employment protection the UK has had a regulatory stance which is conducive to productivity growth. The index reported in Table 1.9 is designed to reflect regulation as a tax on employment adjustment including difficulty of dismissal and severance costs. This shows that Labour has continued the relatively low levels of employment protection inherited from

Table 1.9 Employment Protection (0–10)

	1973–79	1988–95	2003
France	6.05	7.05	7.00
Germany	8.25	7.60	5.60
UK	1.65	1.75	1.75
USA	0.50	0.50	0.50

Note: Low score equates to low employment protection.
Source: Nickell (2005).

the Conservatives. This has aided the more rapid diffusion of ICT in Britain compared with continental Europe because the productivity payoff to ICT depends on re-organization of work practices and upgrading of the labour force as the empirical estimates in Gust and Marquez (2004) show. The message is that it is better to offer social protection to workers rather than jobs.

Indeed, it seems overall that the Labour government has introduced little deregulation even though there are reasons to worry about regulatory disincentives to investment and innovation. Even the current drive to reduce administrative compliance costs (rather than what might seem more appropriate, namely, to target total regulatory costs) has been diluted by acceptance of the idea that many of these costs are for actions business would anyway undertake. A recent survey by the National Audit Office (NAO) found that over the previous year only 2% of businesses said compliance had become easier and only 1% said compliance took less time compared with 30% who said it was more difficult and 40% who said it took longer (NAO 2008). It may be that there are good reasons to fear government failure in deregulation of a kind that Sir Humphrey would easily recognize (Ambler and Chittenden 2007).

Recent OECD research has concluded that an effective, revenue-neutral, growth-oriented tax reform would entail reductions in corporate tax rates financed by increases in consumption taxes (Johansson et al 2008). The implication of this analysis is also that, if increases in government outlays as a share of GDP are seen as desirable, then the growth-efficient way to finance them is through indirect taxation. In fact, as Table 1.6 reported, the rapid growth of public spending in the UK since 2001 has been funded in part by increases in the direct tax burden.

As noted above, the statutory rate of corporate tax has been reduced from 33 to 28% since 1997. This has, however, largely been funded by reducing capital allowances with the result that the effective average tax rate is only about 2 percentage points lower than in the early 1980s (Devereux 2007). But it is reductions in the effective tax rate which seem to matter far more for raising productivity growth. The OECD study finds that a reduction of 5 percentage points in the average effective corporate tax rate raises the average labour productivity growth rate by about 0.1 percentage points over the next ten years (Johansson et al 2008).[4]

New Labour has not really followed the OECD recipe for faster growth through restructuring fiscal policy, although, prima facie, there is considerable scope to do so. The most obvious route would be by increasing the base on which VAT is collected by applying VAT to at least some items which are currently zero-rated. The current UK VAT regime implies that revenue is only about 48% of that which would be obtained if the standard rate was applied to all consumer expenditure. This is quite low by international standards and compares with about 60% in Ireland and nearly 100% in New Zealand (Johansson et al 2008). Using the estimates in HM Treasury (2007d), extending the VAT base to Irish proportions would generate enough revenue to allow the effective corporate tax rate to be reduced by 6 percentage points while imposing the standard rate of VAT on everything but food would allow a reduction of 12 percentage points, sufficient according to the OECD study to raise average labour productivity growth by about 0.25 percentage points over ten years.

The obvious reasons for not extending the VAT base as a way to fund a larger public sector or as a way to reduce taxes that are more adverse to growth are presumably that it is a vote loser and/or that its distributional effects are seen as unacceptable. The Institute for Fiscal Studies (2004) suggests, however, that this last reason may not be as powerful as is sometimes thought and points out that zero-rating is not a particularly effective tool for achieving purely distributional goals.

It should also be noted that there is a productivity problem in the public sector which implies that the tax burden is higher than it needs to be to achieve the present level of outcomes. Afonso et al (2005) estimated that, if the UK attained the highest international standards of efficiency in the use of public expenditure, it could achieve the same results spending 16% less (about £80 billion). A similar result (15%) for the education sector alone was reported by Sutherland et al (2007). Greater effectiveness in addressing these inefficiencies could have lowered the distortionary tax burden without reducing the quantity or quality of public services.

Inefficiency and weak productivity performance in the public sector should be understood in terms of the absence of market disciplines and pervasive principal–agent problems. These problems weaken incentives to reduce costs, to innovate and to put in sufficient effort.[5] The government has sought to address these issues mainly through performance targets but there is little evidence to suggest that this has been successful (Propper and Wilson 2003). The classic private-sector antidote to principal–agent problems is competition either for or in the market. There are limits on how far this is relevant for the public sector, in particular, given the difficulties of ensuring that quality is maintained (Grout and Stevens 2003). Nevertheless, it seems important to explore whether the role of competition in provision of public services should be expanded.

Barriers to trade are reduced when trade costs fall. Trade costs are, of course, increased by explicitly protectionist policies such as tariffs but in the typical OECD country other trade costs are much more important (Anderson and van Wincoop 2004). These include transport costs and border-related trade barriers which include information and transaction costs together with costs arising from using different languages and different currencies. The implication is that the UK could reduce trade barriers significantly by adopting the euro. The assessment carried out by the government in 2003 recognized this point and concluded that trade with the euro area would rise by up to 50% over 30 years and this would raise real GDP per person by between 5% and 9% with the upper estimate more likely (HM Treasury 2003).

If this estimate is correct, then, as Cottarelli and Escolano (2004) pointed out, the welfare gains would surely dominate any losses from giving up monetary policy independence and this would seem to clinch the economic case for joining the single currency. Subsequent research has suggested that the expected increase in trade is much lower than the early studies drawn on in 2003; rather than 50%, 10–20% is more plausible (Baldwin 2006). Even so, this might imply an increase in real GDP of up to 3.5% and a boost to the average growth rate over 30 years of 0.05–0.1% per year. This is still likely to be enough to provide a strong case, although it might be argued that there would be larger net benefits from joining the euro at some future date if downside risks are thereby reduced. In any event, this appears to be another case where the politics is less attractive than the economics.

Overall, the government's approach to productivity policy has a reasonably sound basis in economic analysis. There have, however, been missed opportunities. The government's pursuit of the productivity agenda in terms of microeconomic policies has been much less whole-hearted than a reader of HM Treasury (2007b) might suppose. The political economy of a more vigorous approach has not appealed to a government that was unwilling to face down the fuel tax protesters. The relatively decent productivity performance since 1997 owes a good deal to not squandering the legacy from the Conservative period and the interaction of this inheritance with the opportunities of the ICT era.

Policy issues

The preceding discussion has highlighted several major challenges for policymakers who are serious about improving the UK's productivity performance. These are

- Incentivizing improved public-sector productivity
- Re-structuring the tax system
- Radical reform of the planning laws
- Re-opening the debate on euro membership.

These are issues that have been neglected no doubt because they have been thought to be too difficult politically but which will surely become more pressing in the context of an ageing population and a globalizing world. The choices which are made will depend on value judgements about trade-offs and the political clout of potential losers from policy reforms as well as imperfect empirical evidence on likely consequences.

A key question to be answered is how large should the public sector be and how is the tax burden to be met? Growth in the share of GDP accounted for by government outlays has adverse implications for the rate of productivity growth if government fails to ensure a satisfactory rate of productivity growth within the public sector and/or if it is funded by distortionary taxes. This is a risk that the UK is running but with very little public debate. With regard to addressing principal–agent problems and improving productivity in the public sector, it seems clear that an urgent task is to review the role and design of performance targets and to consider how far it is desirable to increase competition in the supply of public services.

From the perspective of designing a tax structure conducive to faster productivity growth, it would seem desirable to reduce the proportion of direct taxes and raise that of indirect taxes in total tax revenues. This would also alleviate the potential impact of larger public spending on growth. There seems to be a strong case for reforming VAT and, in particular, imposing standard rate on many of the zero-rated items. There are some distributional implications that might need to be addressed in terms of additional aspects of a policy package. It appears to be generally accepted, however, that this is a no-go zone in terms of British politics. At the same time, it will be important, especially in a context of increased international capital mobility, to consider reductions in the effective rate of corporate tax. Perhaps the tax system should look more like that in Ireland?

With regard to regulation, a major issue is how to reform the planning system. It should be clear that the status quo is no longer an option, that the present regime has a huge cost in allocative inefficiency and forgone productivity, and that it is also a serious obstacle to the sectoral and spatial adjustments that are necessary to profit from the opportunities of the new global economy. The government commissioned the Barker Review which made all this clear but appears to have no ideas on how to build a coalition in favour of reform. Can anyone else do better or is this an area where the politics is just too difficult?

In the area of trade policy, the issue to which it is important to return is the question of whether to adopt the euro. The productivity implications of joining are positive and it may well be that the option of waiting is becoming less valuable. The economic logic of the analysis performed by HM Treasury in 2003 is that it is at least appropriate to re-examine the issue from time to time and that the economic case for joining may have then already been quite strong. It would be unfortunate if the apparently-entrenched euroscepticism of the British electorate continues to preclude any serious discussion of this topic.

Finally, it might be thought that politicians would be justified in giving a low priority to improving productivity. After all, it appears that increases in income do rather little to add to happiness in countries as rich as the UK (Blanchflower and Oswald 2004). That, however, would be a mistake. Higher productivity, both in the public and the private sectors, is the basis for increasing the set of choices available to society and underwriting more leisure or better healthcare. The indirect payoff in terms of the quality of life certainly does matter.

Notes

1. This implies that the efficient level of employment is where the marginal product of labour equals the supply price (opportunity cost) of labour. Lower levels of employment which might, for example, occur if a high minimum wage were imposed would deliver higher labour productivity but would preclude some employment for which marginal benefit exceeded marginal cost.
2. The Treasury's formulation of the issues is placed explicitly in the context of endogenous growth economics in Crafts and O'Mahony (2001).
3. Conventional growth accounting only considers 'tangible capital'. In modern economies, 'intangible capital' is becoming increasingly important and refinement of both the national accounts and growth accounting techniques to take account of this is urgently required.
4. The estimate in Johansson et al (2008) is for the impact on TFP growth in the marketed sector. The estimate given here for labour productivity growth in the total economy adjusts both for the inclusion of the non-marketed sector where there is no effect and also for the steady-state impact on the capital to labour ratio.
5. Observed trends in productivity growth in the public sector are worrying, although this may to some extent reflect measurement errors. If TFP growth is estimated using crude volume measures of output (e.g. numbers of pupils taught), then the picture is generally that productivity has been falling. More sophisticated indices of output in education and health which attempt to adjust for quality (e.g. allow for exam grades obtained) suggest productivity may have been flat rather than declining (ONS 2007c, 2008c).

2
Prosperity and Productivity

Martin Weale

Introduction

The period from 1997 to 2007 was one of steady economic growth. Output per person rose at a rate of 2.4% p.a. This translated into a general rise in living standards, and contributed to a feeling of rising prosperity. Britain's long-term decline relative to other European countries was arrested in the 1980s and early 1990s. Since 1997 Britain has gained ground against its large neighbours as well as continuing to close the gap with the United States, as Table 2.1 shows. On the other hand Britain's productivity performance remained disappointing with output per hour worked considerably below the levels achieved in France and the Low Countries and probably also that of Western Germany. From a policy perspective, the government aimed to provide stable demand growth with low inflation and a sustainable fiscal position. Policies to promote growth were focused on the supply side, with the aim of stimulating labour input and productivity growth.

By 2007 the weaknesses of the boom started to become apparent. At least some part of the output growth had been supported on the back of a credit boom interlinked with rising house prices. A tightening of credit markets and an end to the house-price boom seem likely to lead to a period of below-average growth, of uncertain duration. It is perfectly possible that, as a result of this the gains Britain made between 1997 and 2007 will appear more in the nature of a long cyclical upswing rather than a long-term improvement relative to our neighbours.

This chapter presents a detailed analysis of the factors behind Britain's economic record, assessing how far it is reasonable to expect them to continue to support economic growth over the next ten years. The effects of the financial crisis and its implications are discussed.

The growth record

Table 2.1 summarizes how Britain's record compares with other advanced countries over the period 1997–2006 with full data not yet available for 2007. The first two columns of the table show the countries' ranking in terms of output per person, the most widely used indicator of economic performance. The third column shows the annual growth rate of each country's output per person over the same period.

Looking first at the rankings, Britain's overall position has not changed very much, rising from 16th in 1997 to 14th in 2006. This modest change masks its improved position among the large countries. The UK has overtaken

Table 2.1   Rankings of per capita GDP and per capita Growth Rates 1997–2006

	Ranking 1997	Ranking 2006	Growth Rate (% p.a.)
Australia	13	10	**2.2**
Austria	7	9	1.9
Belgium	11	13	1.8
Canada	8	6	**2.4**
Czech Republic	25	24	3.3
Denmark	6	11	1.7
Finland	19	15	3.2
France	18	18	**1.7**
Germany	12	17	**1.4**
Greece	22	21	3.8
Hungary	26	26	4.7
Iceland	5	7	3.2
Ireland	17	4	5.0
Italy	15	20	**1.0**
Japan	9	16	**0.9**
Korea	23	23	3.7
Luxembourg	1	1	4.0
Mexico	30	29	2.0
Netherlands	10	8	1.9
New Zealand	20	22	2.2
Norway	4	2	1.8
Poland	28	28	4.0
Portugal	24	25	1.5
Slovak Republic	27	27	4.0
Spain	21	19	**2.6**
Sweden	14	12	3.0
Switzerland	3	5	1.2
Turkey	29	30	2.2
United Kingdom	16	14	**2.4**
United States	2	3	1.9

Source: Author's calculations from OECD databank.

Germany, Italy and Japan but still lies well behind Canada and the United States. On the other hand, despite the US 'miracle', output per head in the UK grew faster than in the US between 1997 and 2006.

Compared to the period 1970–97 the UK's per capita growth rate has improved by 0.4% p.a. At one level the explanation of this is that, in the period 1970–97 there were a number of accidents which befell the British and the world economy. There were two oil price shocks which were associated with two recessions and the economic mismanagement which led to a third recession around 1990. Thus over the last ten years a coherent argument is that the British economy performed better because it avoided mishaps such as the periods of stagnation which affected, in particular Germany, Italy and Japan.

Drivers of economic growth

From an economist's point of view it is helpful to think of economic output being produced by inputs (factors of production). The standard view is that in broad terms there are two key inputs: labour and capital. An increase in output may therefore take place because more inputs are made available. Working longer hours or retiring later to increase the amount of labour input or building up the capital stock by increasing investment – which can be done only at the expense of consumption – may not seem very attractive ways of delivering increased output. But alternatively output may rise because the efficiency with which labour and capital is used increases. This second growth source is particularly attractive because it does not involve harder work or giving up consumption for investment.

Employment

As Table 2.2 shows, economic growth has been associated with rising employment, at least partly as a result of immigration and a reduction in the unemployment rate. The sharp increase in employment has been associated with a decline in average hours worked per employee.

For both men and women employment rates of people aged 16–64 have risen. Even so, among young adults employment rates have fallen; this reflects the expansion of participation in further and higher education over the period. But perhaps the most striking change has been the increased employment rate of people older than the current state pension age of 60 for women and 65 for men. More generally the period has seen a reversal of the trend towards pre-pension age retirement which had developed in the 1970s and 1980s.

These changes mean that the total number of hours worked has increased by 5.8% over the period 1997–2006, an increase of 0.6% p.a. If instead we look at the number of hours worked per capita, we find that this has increased by

1.8% over the period or 0.2% p.a. Thus a part of Britain's increased income can be attributed to the fact that more people are working longer, but this can explain only a small part of the rise in incomes per head.

Table 2.2   Total Employment and Employment Rates by Age

	Total Employment ('000)	Average Hours Worked per week	Unemployment Rate (%)	Employment Rates (% of population)					
				Men Aged 16–64	Women Aged 16–64	Men Aged 18–24	Women Aged 18–24	Men Aged 65+	Women Aged 60+
1997	26,526	33.2	6.9	77.9	67.5	69.7	63.2	7.4	8
2006	29,233	32.0	5.4	78.8	70	68.3	62.8	9.6	11.3

Source: Labour Force Survey Integrated First Release.

Within this picture it is necessary to pay some attention to the role of immigration. Riley and Weale (2006) suggest that in 2005 immigrants arriving after 1997 earned wages equal to 4.5% of the total wage bill and 3.1% of GDP. The latter figure, averaged over the eight years 1998 to 2005 implies that immigration had a direct impact on the growth rate of 0.4 % p.a. It is not completely correct to compare this figure to the overall growth in hours worked of 0.6% p.a. because there are questions of differences in quality and also of the hours worked per week by immigrants as compared to the native population. Nevertheless, one reasonably concludes that much of the total increase in labour input is attributable to immigration. That immigration raises overall output does not mean that it raises the prosperity of the indigenous population and the House of Lords (2008) suggests it is unlikely to be of significant economic benefit.

Improved education

A separate change which has almost certainly contributed to rising incomes is the fact that the educational attainment of the working-age population has increased, as Table 2.3 shows.

Table 2.3   Qualification Levels of the Working-age Population

Proportion of Working-age Population	No Qualifications	1st Degree or Higher (NVQ Level 4+)
1997	17.4%	21.9%
2006	12.1%	30.1%

Source: Labour Force Survey. See http://www.dfes.gov.uk/trends/index.cfm?fuseaction=home.showChart&cid=5&iid=37&chid=161

Rising educational attainment has the effect of raising the growth rate because earnings increase with educational attainment; there is an underlying presumption that, at any point in time, relative earnings reflect productivity. Indeed Barrell et al (2008) suggest that Britain's outperformance of the large euro-area countries between 1997 and 2006 is largely due to this. The effects of education on earnings are substantial, as the figures shown in Table 2.4 from Mcintosh (2006) show.

Table 2.4 The Impact of Selected Qualifications on Average Earnings 2002

Qualification	Academic Qualifications			Vocational Qualifications		
	1st Degree	2+ A-levels	5+ GCSE A*–C	HNC/HND	NVQ 3–5	BTEC
Men	0.258	0.142	0.246	0.139	0.027	0.045
Women	0.241	0.151	0.221	0.068	0.025	0.067

Note: This table shows the impact of each qualification on the logarithm earnings of full-time employees and are cumulative.
Source: Mcintosh (2006).

These figures are cumulative so that someone who has a first degree after 2+ A-levels and 5+ GCSEs will benefit from all of the increments shown, raising his log earnings by 0.258 + 0.142 + 0.246 = 0.646 or 91% over someone with no qualifications. Mcintosh finds no evidence that returns declined between 1996 and 2002 despite an increase in the proportion of the population which is qualified.

Qualifications premia can be used to produce a quality-adjusted measure of labour input. The EUKLEMS data base[1] shows the quality-adjusted labour input in Britain as having risen by 11.3% from 1997 to 2005 or 0.9% p.a. per capita.[2] This includes both the effect of the increase in hours and the increase in the quality of labour. With hours worked per capita having growth by 0.2% p.a. the effect of rising educational attainment can be set at 0.7% p.a.

Capital accumulation

If growth in labour input – after adjusting for quality – is one driver of economic growth, expansion of the national capital stock is likely to be another main driver. On a per capita basis the stock of produced national capital has increased by 2.1% p.a. per capita. In other words it has not kept pace with economic growth. However, if one looks at the stock of capital excluding housing it has grown by 3.1% p.a. Exclusion of housing is probably sensible because although it accounted for about 45% of the net capital stock in 1997 it makes only a small direct contribution[3] to GDP.

Jorgenson (1989) argues that estimates of this type can, however, be misleading as to the true involvement of the capital stock to output. Changes in the prices of capital goods should be offset by the amount of income that they generate. In particular, high-technology capital such as computers tends to fall in price rapidly; this implies that it makes a much larger contribution to output than does the same amount of capital held as a building.[4] The EUKLEMS data suggest that this has happened and that, when due account is taken of this, the volume of capital services has increased by 4.5% p.a. per capita from 1997 to 2005.

An overall account of rising income

With these estimates of the increase in labour and capital inputs, we can identify the contribution they have made to output growth. The standard way of doing this (Solow 1957) is to add up the percentage increase in each input multiplied by the share of that input in total national income. On average over the period 1997–2005, 63.1% of income was paid in wages and 36.9% of income as the gross return to capital while the economy grew at 2.5% p.a. per capita. This implies that growth in labour input including the effects of rising skill levels contributed 0.6 percentage points to the per capita growth rate and growth of capital services contributed 1.7 percentage points, leaving, after adjusting for rounding errors, 0.3 percentage points unaccounted for.

There are many possible explanations of the factors behind this residual growth. One is that it is due to residual technical progress, perhaps associated with a high level of foreign investment in the United Kingdom (Barrell and Pain 1997). Another explanation is that research and development work, both at home and abroad, plays a major role. A third is that conventional measures of capital ignore 'intangibles' and these have grown in importance over time (Marrano and Haskell 2006). Finally there is the suggestion that education and training are more important than the analysis of earnings suggests, with spillovers raising incomes of people who work with highly educated people but who do not themselves have high levels of education or that they are needed to allow countries to absorb available technologies (Kneller and Stevens 2006).

These issues and the related policy questions are discussed in more detail in Crafts' chapter.

The capacity of policy to deliver rising prosperity

The analysis above provides the background to the supply side policy challenges facing the country. Output per capita can be increased by a mixture of (i) promoting employment, (ii) improving the quality of labour, (iii) adding to the capital stock and (iv) using resources more efficiently. Over the last ten years, the government has tried hard to address the first two challenges. Its contribution to the third has been sporadic at best, while the measures it has taken to address the fourth are discussed in Crafts' chapter. However, the recent financial crisis also raises major challenges and in many ways these are more acute than the traditional supply-side issues.

A backdrop to the analysis is provided by the observation, present in the Government Actuary's population projections.[5] 62.5% of the country's population is expected to be aged 18–65 in 2010, up from 61.4% in 1998. This proportion is expected to fall to 61.6% in 2015 and 60% in 2020. So while growth in output per capita has been supported by a rising share of the population being of working age up till now, that process is reversing. In itself this is likely to take 0.5% off the growth rate of GDP per capita over the period 2010–15 as compared to 1998–2010.

Promoting employment

We note that the number of hours worked has increased by 0.2% p.a. per capita over the period from 1997 to 2006. This increase is probably better described as useful than as highly valuable in terms of enhancing overall income per head[6] – although there is an obvious question how far people see working longer as a desirable route to greater prosperity. They probably do to the extent that average working hours increase because unemployed people find work, but do not if everyone's working day lengthens. Between these there are various intermediate categories, such as reducing the incidence of early retirement and working beyond the state pension age – or encouraging the mothers of school-age children to work.

It is generally recognized that benefit levels affect the duration and extent of unemployment (Krueger and Meyer 2002) and the government introduced Working Family Tax Credits as part of a reform designed to remove the very high marginal tax rates on employment income created by the benefit system as it existed in 1997. Blundell and MaCurdy (1999) suggest that the impact of this was concentrated among single mothers and married women. The government also adopted a range of measures which strengthened the pressure on unemployed people to find jobs. These measures are surveyed by National Audit Office (2007) and generally well reviewed. Dorsett (2007) provides a more detailed and also favourable account of the effects of a particular scheme, 'Pathways to Work', designed to help people drawing invalidity benefit to find work.

These policies have been an important factor behind the rise in average hours worked, as has been increasing participation of people aged between 50 and the state pension age, many of whom draw invalidity benefit. In the 1980s and 1990s, although the state pension age remained unchanged, there had been a trend to earlier and earlier retirement. This was encouraged by the government which saw early retirement as a means of limiting unemployment among younger workers. It was also facilitated by the healthy state of pension funds at that time together with the high level of annuity rates. As annuity rates have fallen and pension funds look less healthy[7] early retirement feels much less affordable today than it did ten years ago, and as a consequence retirement ages have been rising. Separately but probably driven by similar influences, as Table 2.2 also shows, the proportion of people older than state pension age who work has increased.

The fact that these policies have worked in itself reduces the scope for further increases in employment rates by means of similar policies. Nevertheless, both policy and the economic environment are likely to raise the labour supply of people close to or older than the current state pension ages. First of all the government is raising the state pension age for women from 2010, to reach 65 by age 2020 – although the increase in the state pension age, eventually to 68 in 2044 is too far ahead to have much impact on employment over the next five to ten years. Secondly, the government has recently abolished Incapacity Benefit for new claimants and replaced it with the Employment and Support Allowance, designed to help those who would otherwise be claiming Incapacity Benefit to return to work. With 2.4 million people, over 7% of the population, of working age claiming Incapacity Benefit in February 2008, the scope for increasing output by encouraging some of these to return to work is considerable. Thirdly, the recent stock market and house price falls mean that people who had thought they had enough resources to retire are likely now to find that they have to work for longer. Offsetting this, the recession which is now starting is likely to lead to an increase in unemployment. This will have some semi-permanent effect on the employability of people who lose their jobs, even though labour markets are much more flexible than they were.

In terms of promoting employment, the relevant policies are largely continuations of those which are already in place. However, as a response to the likely rise in unemployment the government may need to consider a range of policies to encourage people to return to work. This may involve an extension of the Return to Work Credits, which are currently paid at a rate of £40 per week for one year to people who have been claiming Incapacity Benefit for at least three months, to people who have been unemployed for more than six months. But, as the earlier figures imply, it is unlikely that measures to promote employment can do much more than offset the demographic decline in the ratio of people of working age to the whole population. And, as we have observed, while immigration is a means of raising output, it is much less clear that it is a means of promoting prosperity for the existing population.

Education and labour force quality

The Labour government followed the path of its predecessor in adopting policies designed to raise the educational standard of the labour force. Historically, while the top quartile of the workforce has been well educated, Britain has suffered from a long tail of under-achievers by comparison with its competitors. (See Chapter 6, Wolf.)

Policy has been designed, on the one hand, to raise the number of children staying on into the sixth form and going to university, and on the other hand to facilitate the acquisition of basic skills by adults who do not have them. An important part of the policy with respect to universities has been to introduce fees, initially set at £1,000 p.a. and then raised to £3,000 p.a. This follows from the observation that, while most of the evidence suggests that university education results in a substantial increase in people's earnings, in the absence of fees university places are limited by rationing restricting attendance (Farmer and Barrell 1982).

Looking at qualification rates and changes to participation since 1997, there is something of a mixed message. The proportion of children aged 15 achieving 5+ GCSEs at grade A–C has risen from 45.5% in 1997/99 to 60.8% in 2006/07 and the number with 2+ A-levels or equivalent has risen from 29.6% in 1995/96 to 37.3% in 2005/06 although, as Table 2.5 shows, the proportion of 16–17 year olds studying for A-levels has changed little over the period. Participation in higher education[8] has moved only from 39.2% in 1999/00, the earliest year for which data on this basis are available, to 39.8% in 2006/07 although these figures relate only to English students studying anywhere in the country; the government has a target for this to rise to 50% but with no particular deadline.[9] Some of these participating students do not, of course complete their degrees.

The number of full-time UK domiciled students of all ages graduating with first degrees[10] has risen from 206,000 in 1995/96 to 244,000 in 2006/07; there has also been an increase in numbers completing other undergraduate qualifications from 33,000 to 46,000 over the same period. Since the cohort of 18 year olds is much the same size in 2006/07 as in 1999/00 this points to the increase in numbers of graduates coming largely from students aged older than 30. These will include people who would have taken degrees earlier in life if the 17–30 participation rate had been at its current level.

Thus, although the proportion of the working-age population with graduate qualifications is likely to continue to rise, it also seems likely that unless the proportion of people aged 17–30 participating rises further, the benefits may not be as great as they have been in the past. It follows that, unless some other change takes place, the figure for the proportion of the population with graduate qualifications is likely to rise from the value of 28.1% in Table 2.3 (above) to an eventual proportion of below 39% – after allowing for people who enrol for degrees but do not complete them. Thus, unless some sharp change takes place, the eventual future increase in the proportion of the population with graduate-level qualifications may be no higher than it was in the ten years since 1997; the rate of improvement of skill levels is likely to be lower than it was between 1997 and 2007.

The government set an arbitrary target that 50% of the population aged 18–30 should participate in higher education at some time in this age range. Recognizing that this was unlikely to be delivered through conventional institutions and standards, it has introduced foundation degrees which can be gained in two years of study. While the degree premia shown in Table 2.4 have proved fairly robust to the expansion of the number of graduates, it is difficult to imagine that two-year graduates will benefit from similar premia. The figures shown for HNC/HND qualifications are probably a better guide and the overall impression is that the pace of upskilling to graduate level is likely to slow, either because the rate of upskilling slows or because the premia to the new marginal graduates are smaller than those accruing to other graduates.

Similar points arise over lower level qualifications. The sharp improvement in GCSE and A-level equivalent success rates may mask a decline in standards (see Wolf's chapter). If we look at the type of course followed by 16 year olds, in Table 2.5, it is clear that there has been little change in numbers studying for traditional qualifications since 2000. Wolf (2007a) questions the value of many of the courses which are being taken.

Table 2.5   Percentage of 16 year olds in England in Full-time Education by Course Type

	1995	1997	1999	2000	2001	2002	2003	2004	2005	2006	2007*
A/AS Levels	42.1	42.6	44.0	44.3	44.0	43.6	43.1	42.3	41.9	42.2	42.9
Other Level 3	5.6	5.6	5.9	5.7	5.5	6.1	6.9	7.9	9.6	10.9	11.6
Level 2	13.4	12.2	11.4	10.9	10.5	10.2	10.1	10.5	10.8	11.4	11.0
Level 1	3.0	3.0	2.4	2.4	2.6	3.0	3.3	3.6	4.1	4.4	4.7
Other Courses	1.9	2.1	2.0	2.2	2.1	2.7	3.0	3.2	3.0	2.5	2.8
Total	65.6	64.4	65.8	65.6	64.8	65.5	66.1	67.2	69.2	71.5	72.9

* provisional   *Source:* http://www.dcsf.gov.uk/rsgateway/DB/SFR/s000792/index.shtml

A reasonable conclusion from these trends is therefore that further expansion of post-compulsory education is unlikely to deliver the benefits seen from the expansion of graduate-level education which took place in the 1990s, at least unless there is some major change in the financial benefits associated with particular qualifications. With little recent change in the participation of 17–30 year olds in education, the proportion of the working population with degrees may not rise much above the figure of 37% currently seen for 25–29 year olds.

The Leitch Review of skills needs (HM Treasury 2006b) could be seen as a response to the trends outlined above – and the perception that the scope for raising the proportion of people educated to university level is now limited. Leitch suggested a range of targets for 2020 which, if achieved, would deliver a general upskilling of the UK labour force relative to that implied by current participation rates. These included having 40% of the workforce with degree-equivalent qualifications by 2020. A companion study to the report (Beavan et al 2005) suggests that achieving these targets would add 0.1–0.2% p.a.

to UK growth over the period 2014–20. These calculations are based on the observed impact of skill levels on earnings. But the key point is that it is relative to what would happen if nothing were now done.

The Leitch targets require skill acquisition by adults if they are to be met; they cannot be delivered by plausible increases in participation by school-leavers. For example, even if participation by young people in higher education does increase to 50% by 2010, the average proportion of graduates in the labour force will not rise beyond about 35% unless people older than 30 also take degrees on a large scale. There are, however, a number of questions about whether skills acquired in middle age are as valuable as those acquired when young. Metcalf and Meadows (2008) find that acquisition of basic skills by adults had very little impact on earnings or employment after four years. Blundell, Dearden, Goodman and Read (2000) find poor social returns to male undergraduates who are 21 or older when they start their courses. Egerton and Parry (2001) find very poor private returns to male mature students and suggest that for old mature students they are likely to be negative. For female graduates returns are put at 5–6% p.a. but they inevitably also fall off with age. The introduction of fees of £3,000 p.a. has reduced these private returns and is likely to deter mature students.

It is easy to imagine why returns should be poor. People who acquire skills later in adult life may not find it easy to reorganize their lives to take advantage of the employment opportunities these new skills offer. If they continue in their existing jobs they may not have the opportunity to make the most of their skills which may, in turn atrophy. The Leitch report stresses the involvement of employers in skill upgrading which may reduce these problems to some extent.

Looking at the prospects for the future we find the same unpleasant arithmetic as with policies to promote employment. Beavan et al (2005) suggest that, without any major change, the contribution to economic growth arising from upskilling of the workforce, identified earlier at 0.7% p.a. for 1997–2005 would decline by about 0.1 percentage point per annum in 2010–20. Full implementation of Leitch's proposals would do little more than offset this and, as we have seen, the changes needed to implement them in full are not yet underway. So on balance the rate of growth of prosperity associated with rising education levels will probably decline slightly from recent levels and sharp policy changes are needed if this is to be avoided.

Studies of the economic effects of work-related training are more encouraging. Dearden, Reed and van Reenen (2006) found that a 1% increase in the proportion of workers in an industry undergoing training was associated with an increase in its productivity (value added per hour) of 0.6% p.a. The costs of that training have to be offset against the benefit and questions of causation are not resolved by the study. But a general conclusion is that the aspirations of the Leitch report require the employer link on which Leitch focuses in order to succeed.

Capital accumulation

If the government has been looking for policies to improve the educational attainment of the labour force the same cannot be said about policies to promote accumulation of domestic capital. Gross corporate fixed investment as a proportion of GDP has declined from 11.9% averaged over 1987–96 to 10.9% over 1997–2007, although since the share of depreciation has fallen further, from 8.7% to 7%, so overall net investment as a share of GDP has risen. While it is unlikely that this change can be attributed to specific government policies, it is possible that it may have been a consequence of the fact that the period 1997–2007 was one of unusual economic stability – which, indeed, is now coming to an end. A factor behind this stability may have been the government's macroeconomic framework and in particular the decision to make the Bank of England operationally independent. However, since the international environment was also much more stable than it had been in the 1970s and 1980s, views are likely to remain divided on how far the stability was a consequence of the policy environment rather than simply a property of the international economy.

The UK presents something of an anomaly as far as the return on capital goes. Broadberry and O'Mahony (2004) suggest that about half of the gap in output per hour worked between the UK and France and Germany is attributable to lower levels of capital per worker. If production conditions were similar in all three countries, one might therefore expect that the rate of return would be higher in the UK than in its neighbours. However, Khomen and Weale (2008) find that the rates of return are very similar in France and the UK, leading to the conclusion that low returns to capital are an obstacle to accumulation. The factors behind this are unclear and may include some of the managerial problems identified by Bloom and van Reenen (2007) discussed below.

Looking ahead, one might expect to see the contribution of capital accumulation to economic growth reduced somewhat, at least if the economic environment generally is less benign. Capital accumulation is a complement to labour force growth and rising skill levels. A reduction of either of these would probably mean that the contribution of capital accumulation to growth in GDP per capita would also fall. This is discussed further in the section on the Financial Crisis below. Policy responses which might offset this include a complete reform of Corporation Tax; if full relief were given on business investment, the outcome would be analogous to the government taking an equity stake in businesses, rather than collecting a levy on their profits (Meade Committee 1978) and the impact of the tax on reducing investment would be reduced. Notwithstanding the fact that, as mentioned earlier, investment comes at a cost, this overall would result in an increase in welfare. However, the obstacle to this is that the headline tax rate would increase and the government is likely to be concerned that this might encourage businesses to move abroad even if the effect were to reduce the tax burden on business.

A separate issue concerns policy on the provision of public infrastructure capital. Britain is generally thought to be less well provided in this respect than are many of its neighbours. Logically the willingness of the government to finance such projects should depend on the balance between the costs and the prospective returns rather than be influenced by an upper limit on government borrowing. A reasonable conclusion is that, if projects are being prevented by the government's budgetary rules rather than because the returns they offer seem poor, then public investment should be increased.

Implications of the financial and economic crisis

The period between the summer of 2007 and late 2008 has seen a deepening financial and economic crisis as concerns about losses on some types of US mortgage debt developed into the worst banking crisis to affect the international economy since the early 1930s and the United Kingdom since the start of the Great War. In tandem with this an international recession has developed. While the magnitude of this is not yet clear, the general view is that it will be more like the recession seen in 1980 after the second oil crisis than the much deeper depression of 1929–32.

The crisis has both short-term and long-term implications for Britain's future prosperity and productivity. In the short term declining output is likely to mean static living standards for most of the population but hardship for people who become unemployed. In the longer term the banking crisis means that bank credit is likely to be much less readily available than it was before the summer of 2007. Equally, businesses will find it harder to borrow in financial markets because there is much greater concern about risk levels. Those businesses that can borrow will have to pay more for credit. Risk premia on equities are also likely to increase because investors have learned that the world is not as stable and secure as they had thought.

At present the dominant international disturbance is likely to be the increased charge for risk.[11] If this returns to historically normal levels from the low levels seen in the period before the summer of 2007, Barrell and Kirby (2008) suggest that long-run output in the UK will be reduced by about 2% because investment will be lower. Such a change, equal to about a 0.2 percentage point reduction in the economy's growth rate over a ten-year period, is of similar magnitude to the sort of increase that one might hope judicious policy design would deliver. But if bank lending does not resume for a while the damage may be much greater. HM Treasury (2008b) put the permanent loss of output associated with the current crisis at 4% of GDP although they were probably motivated by the desire not to understate the magnitude of the disruption to economic activity. Either of these figures implies that productivity is likely to stagnate or decline for a year or more, as is usual in recessions (see data for 1975, 1980 and 1990 in O'Mahony 1999: 117, table D), depending on the magnitude of the fall of output.

In the short term the government has responded to the weakening of the economy by means of temporary tax cuts. These are intended to raise growth in output by about 0.5% of GDP in 2009, but it is quite likely that output will nevertheless fall by more than 1% during the year. The policy may well succeed in mitigating the decline in output, but it is subject to both political and economic criticisms. The political criticism is that the government faces the risk that if, despite the measures, output falls by more than the Treasury forecast at the time of the pre-budget report, opposition parties which have opposed the measures will have a good political case that they have been vindicated. The economic concerns are first that the measures rely on the government retaining its credit-worthiness and secondly that fiscal expansion simply transfers resources from the future – with the benefits being offset when taxes rise and the extra debt is serviced or repaid.

The risk of loss of credit-worthiness is difficult to judge, but obviously real. The objection that the policy is simply borrowing from the future can be offset by two points. First of all, the misery of falling output is concentrated on people who become unemployed, while the effects of slower future growth will be more evenly spread. Secondly, in a recession people who would like to work cannot. Tax cuts now mitigate this effect. In more normal times everyone who wants to work can, so the output gained now more than offsets any losses that result from the increased debt.

But in the most recent phase of the crisis credit has become extremely tight indeed, and if things do not improve the outlook for 2009 and beyond is much worse than the figures above suggest. The success or failure of government policies to encourage banks to resume lending on normal terms will be a more important determinant of Britain's overall economic performance over the next few years than will be the supply-side issues discussed above. It may well be that substantial extra provision of public capital to the banks will be needed. Honohan (2008) points out that in an average crisis governments have provided new capital to banks of about 10% of GDP. If the current crisis is average this suggests that about £150 billion will be needed in total, with only £37 billion being provided at the end of November 2008.

In the longer term the key policy challenge the government faces in this context is the redesign of the system of financial regulation to provide a means of managing and dampening credit expansion independently of the interest rate. Goodhart (2008) has suggested that banks' capital requirement might depend on the rate at which their lending increases, as is currently done in Spain. Other questions include whether some types of retail transaction should be regulated – such as maximum loan-to-value limits on mortgages. An obstacle to regulation of institutions is that they may move to lightly-regulated countries; indeed historically light regulation in London has been a key factor behind its success. International agreement will be important if competitive de-regulation is to be avoided.

A separate challenge is raised by the need to restore some sort of credibility to the government's policy for managing the public finances. The policy it had pursued, of balancing the government current account over the cycle, has failed, essentially because in the period from 1997 to 2007 it did not run a surplus large enough to cover the deficits which could arise in a downturn. This of course was because it did not forecast the downturn which began in the spring of 2008. The consequence has been that, in late 2008, it wished both to relax fiscal policy in order to provide an extra stimulus to the economy, and to announce plans to bring the government current account back to balance. One way of enhancing the credibility of its fiscal plans would be to set up some form of independent monitoring of the budgetary position, as described in Box 2.1. However, the current government is unlikely to move in that direction.

Box 2.1   The Future of Fiscal Rules?
Simon Wren-Lewis

When it came into office in 1997, the UK government committed itself to two fiscal rules. The first was the 'golden rule': over the economic cycle, the government will borrow only to invest and not to fund current spending. The second was the 'sustainable investment rule': over the economic cycle, the ratio of net public sector debt to GDP will be set at a stable and prudent level, defined by the Chancellor as no more than 40% of GDP.[a] These rules represented an advance over the simple deficit targets that preceded them, and were also arguably superior to the rules adopted as part of the EU Stability and Growth Pact.[b] The government also began to publish annual projections of the public finances looking 50 years ahead.

After initial years of austerity when it came into office, the government embarked on a programme involving a substantial expansion in public spending. It argued that this was possible while still adhering to its fiscal rules. However, as the rules apply over the course of the economic cycle, it was difficult to check this assertion. During this period the Office for National Statistics also revised its timing of the economic cycle, in such a way as to make it easier for the government to make this claim, a coincidence that did little for the credibility of the rules.

Even without the financial crisis that occurred in the autumn of 2008, it is possible that the government would have had to abandon its fiscal rules. The 2008 recession made that inevitable. The problem is not the recession per se – after all, the rules are designed to smooth out the economic cycle. It is that recent events make previous government assumptions regarding taxes and spending no longer realistic. On top of this, we have the question of how to treat government interventions following the financial crisis, from state ownership of banks to guarantees of various financial assets. In the pre-budget report in November 2008, the government set aside its two fiscal rules.

The UK government is of course not the first to trip up on its own fiscal rules. Several years earlier, the much simpler rules of the euro area's Stability and Growth Pact were broken by a number of countries, and the large fines that should have followed never materialized. The reaction of EU policymakers was to make their

▶

fiscal rules more complex, and more discretionary. Arguably, their ability to constrain governments has decreased as a result.

There appears to be a fundamental problem here. Good fiscal rules are likely to be complex. While cyclical adjustment is an improvement on targets for unadjusted figures, economic cycles are imprecise and messy things. What we are really interested in is long-term trends, which require projections decades ahead. But such long-term forecasts are particularly uncertain, and easily manipulated. While it is important to note the distinction between government investment and consumption, we need to ask further questions, like whether any assets will yield a fiscal return, and if not when will non-pecuniary benefits arise. Can their timing, for example, justify taxing future generations at a higher rate than today's taxpayers?

If fiscal rules become more and more complex, then whether the government is following them becomes less and less transparent. Fiscal rules are meant to discipline governments: to help them resist the ever present temptation to tax less or spend more. The fact that they need this discipline is evident by the substantial and largely unwarranted growth in public debt in the OECD area over the last few decades. It is the problem economists call 'deficit bias'. But if rules become more and more complex, they are easier to fudge by governments, so their disciplinary effectiveness disappears.

This problem with rules had led a number of countries and international institutions to examine the possibility of some form of institutional change.[c] In part the motivation may have come from the perceived success of independent central banks in removing 'inflation bias' in setting monetary policy. However, the solution generally proposed has not been as stark as taking away government's control over fiscal decisions. Instead a number of countries (such as Sweden, Austria and Denmark) have established Fiscal Councils, which are public watchdogs designed to monitor and evaluate the state of the public sector accounts. In October, the UK Conservative Party followed this lead, and proposed setting up an 'Office for Fiscal Responsibility'.[d]

Whether or not a UK Fiscal Council materializes, it is tempting to assume that the outlook for public spending and taxes is grim. The downturn is likely to lead to a very substantial increase in UK public debt, even if the measures taken to avoid a financial crisis turn out to be largely self-financing. The 2008 pre-budget report projects net debt to rise from 40% to nearly 60% of GDP over the next five years. To return to a debt ratio of 40% of GDP will require large cuts in spending or large increases in taxes over the medium term.

However, the existence of a Fiscal Council could make a difference here. There are good economic arguments for treating bygones as bygones when it comes to shocks to the public sector finances. It can be more costly to return debt to some pre-shock level than to fund the interest on permanently higher debt.[e] With the backing of a Fiscal Council, a government could plausibly and credibly avoid the need for large fiscal adjustments once the recession is over. Without a Fiscal Council, such a policy might look like another example of deficit bias.

[a]   For a useful account of these rules, see Emmerson et al (2006).
[b]   This argument is made in Wren-Lewis (2003). For a more thorough and technical discussion, see Buiter (2003).
[c]   See, for example, European Commission (2006) and Kirsanova et al (2007).
[d]   Conservative Party (2008).
[e]   This is a variant on the argument for 'tax smoothing', as explained in Kirsanova et al (2007).

Policy outlook

Even without the effects of the financial and economic crisis it would be a substantial effort to maintain recent rates of growth in output per capita. An important reason for this is demographic; the proportion of people aged 18–65 is set to decline after recent increases. But the analysis above demonstrates how hard it will be to maintain recent momentum, both in terms of raising employment and in increasing skills. Super-imposed on this is the effect of the current financial crisis which is likely to result in a semi-permanent loss of output of 2–4% of GDP with larger losses in output in the shorter term.

There is little to criticize in the general structure of the government's supply-side framework that growth can be enhanced by raising skill levels and promoting innovation, competition and entrepreneurship. Policy with respect to skills is important, but as the analysis above suggests, it will be hard to match the increase in skill levels achieved over the last ten years in the next ten years. Returns to training provided by employers are probably high but the obstacle to this is also well-known. The employer may pay for the training from which a competitor benefits. It is questionable whether the approach set out in the Leitch Review will succeed in generating the employer buy-in which is needed for the policy to work, and a substantial extra effort is probably needed to establish the conditions favourable for employer buy-in.

The British economy has a low capital stock relative to many of its neighbours; while it is a fallacy to look at the benefits of extra capital and ignore the costs of providing it, social welfare probably could be increased if the government were successfully to identify obstacles to investment. While it may be the case that UK businesses make inherently poor use of capital, there is a case for looking at ways of promoting investment taking this as a given. The role of the likely returns on public sector investment should also be examined.

Nevertheless, demand-side influences are going to dominate in their effects in the next few years. Here measures are unlikely to prevent output falling sharply in 2009. It is quite possible that, unless the banking situation improves fairly rapidly, the government will face pressure to make a further fiscal stimulus in 2009. But the desirability of such a move needs to be judged against the risks to the government's credit-worthiness, and it is not clear that such a trade-off can be easily quantified. Measures to restore the functioning of the banking system are likely to prove more important for our prosperity in the next two or three years than are either traditional demand- or supply-side policies.

Notes

1. http://www.euklems.net/data/08i/uk_output_08I.xls

2. There is a risk that the impact may be overstated because a part of the sharp increase in numbers of graduates is the result of mature students graduating. The economic impact of degrees for male mature graduates is found to be lower than that of degrees for 'traditional' graduates (Blundell, Dearden, Goodman and Read 2000; Egerton and Parry 2001). This is not taken into account in the calculations.
3. GDP includes an estimate for the income arising in an industry 'ownership of dwellings'. This is an estimate of rent which could be earned by the national housing stock including the land on which it stands.
4. Albeit for less long. Its economic depreciation is very rapid.
5. http://www.gad.gov.uk/Demography_Data/Population/Index.asp?v=Principal &chkDataTable=yy_singyear&chkDataGraph=&y=2006&dataCountry=uk&sub Table=Search+again
6. But rather more important in reducing the budgetary burden that an inactive population gives rise to.
7. A factor behind the reduced health was the changes to Corporation Tax made in Labour's 1997 Budget. These abolished dividend tax relief for pension funds reducing the return on capital. But the major influence was undoubtedly that stock markets rose fairly steadily in the 1990s and have stagnated or fallen since.
8. http://www.dcsf.gov.uk/rsgateway/DB/SFR/s000780/sfrdius02–2008.pdf. This is the sum of the proportions of people at each age 17–30 entering higher education. About 6 percentage points of the total relate to part-time participation.
9. The target is defined with reference to initial participation. If drop-out rates are substantial the proportion graduating will be appreciably lower.
10. Data from the Higher Education Statistical Authority, http://www.hesa.ac.uk/index. php?option=com_datatables&Itemid=121&task=show_category&catdex=3#quals
11. As represented by the interest rate charged on investment grade (BAA) corporate borrowing relative to that on government debt.

3
Poverty, Inequality and Social Mobility

Peter Kenway and Jo Blanden

Why child poverty?

This chapter is primarily concerned with the subject of child poverty, something which New Labour has pledged to abolish by 2020. Its premise is that whoever is elected at the next general election – and in elections for the devolved administrations since they all, too, support this goal – will strive to honour that pledge. Yet notwithstanding the importance which the political class attaches to this commitment, to focus a discussion of the options for 'social justice and inequality' on 'child poverty' is certainly a brutal reduction in scope. How can it be justified? There are two reasons.

First, even though child poverty remains widespread, the government's strategy for dealing with it shows no sign of being able to deliver further progress; in short, the social justice 'flagship' is becalmed. On top of this is the fact that while the Labour government's goal of ending child poverty marked a sharp break with its Conservative predecessors, most of the Labour government's policies for dealing with poverty are an extension of what has gone before rather than a rupture with it. In that sense, the challenge is no less serious for the Conservatives than it is for New Labour.

Second, 'child poverty' is not an isolated problem. Being as much to do with work as with worklessness, it is directly linked to a host of issues to do with low quality employment. As we shall see, it cannot be separated from poverty among working-age adults. As a result, the problems besetting the child poverty flagship are symptomatic of wider social justice difficulties, and the policy options considered towards the end of the chapter have ramifications that go well beyond child poverty.

The chapter is divided into two main parts. The first part is devoted to an overview of the New Labour strategy in this area, including a description of that strategy; its roots and the support for it; and its record according to the

Box 3.1   **Poverty and Social Mobility**
Jo Blanden

The child poverty agenda is closely related to one of the other main themes of government policy; social mobility. One of the reasons why government is seeking to end child poverty is because limited social mobility means that a poor start in life can have a lasting impact on children's outcomes (HM Treasury 2008a). We might also suspect that the deeper and more widespread poverty is, the harder it is for children to move up the ladder.

Of course for these statements to have any meaning we need a clear definition of what social mobility means to policymakers. Measures of social mobility can be both relative and absolute. In a speech on the subject in 2008, the Prime Minister spoke of a 'mission' to ensure 'that the next generation, whatever their background, should have the opportunity to do better than the last' (Brown 2008). Such a measure of social mobility, in which the outcomes for children are compared with those of their parents, is what academics refer to as 'absolute' social mobility.

If 'doing better' means having more income, then economic growth may be enough for social mobility, provided the fruits of that growth are not shared too unequally across the population. In practice, mere economic growth alone is not the basis for the government's belief in the improved prospects for social mobility of this kind. Rather, the key seems to be the vision, expressed as a recommendation by Lord Leitch's review of skills, that the UK should become one of the top eight countries in the world for skills by 2020, creating wider benefits via both higher productivity and employment (HM Treasury 2006b).

However, the hope that globalization can lead to a shift towards high-skilled employment and away from low-skilled employment has been challenged by some recent research from both sides of the Atlantic which finds increases in employment at both the top *and* bottom of the occupational ladder (Autor et al 2003; Goos and Manning 2007). A further paper argues that at least in the US, the growth in low-skilled service jobs is itself a *reflection* of the growth at the top: more high-paid workers need more low-skilled workers to cook, clean and look after their children (Autor and Dorn 2008).

As a minimum, these findings cast doubt on the idea that globalization, combined with improved skills, will lead to substantial occupational upgrading, with both 'more and better' jobs. In these circumstances, the conditions for 'absolute' social mobility cannot be taken for granted.

In work by economists, social (or intergenerational) mobility tends to be measured relatively by examining the extent to which families move up and down the income distribution. In this approach upward mobility for some implies downward mobility for others: if some sons and daughters move up others must go down. Politicians' fondness for absolute measures of mobility is understandable in that it is essentially a win-win story. By contrast, relative mobility is closer to a zero-sum game (although eased by the general gains afforded by economic growth). However, we may think that the absolute mobility resulting from economic growth is not really what is meant by social mobility. If the goal is to equalize opportunities across family background then a relative measure seems more appropriate.

▶

Increasing relative mobility is a more demanding goal than increasing absolute mobility, requiring a continual narrowing of the gap between the outcomes of children from richer and poorer (or higher and lower class) backgrounds. Reducing child poverty is likely to make it easier for these conditions to be met. If more children are deprived this means they have further to catch up with their more privileged peers. The UK is often compared unfavourably with the high mobility Nordic countries; which are also notable for their low inequality and consequent low rates of child poverty. However, a story that explains differences in social mobility across countries only by differences in child poverty may be missing an important part of the story. Though preliminary investigation shows strong relationships both between inequality and mobility and between poverty and mobility, it appears that the link with inequality is stronger (Blanden 2008). If that is the case, this would imply that the promotion of economic mobility would require a narrowing of income gaps at the bottom and the top, something which given the government's relaxed attitude to top-end inequality may be deemed rather more unlikely.

latest official statistics. The second part begins by developing criteria to use to identify possible options, going on to sketch out and justify four such options. This is followed by a short conclusion which argues that what is now needed is a paradigm shift, prompted by the anomaly of in-work poverty.

New Labour's programme to reduce child poverty[1]

The roots of New Labour's approach

New Labour's strategy for reducing child poverty directly, by raising household incomes, can be characterized as comprising four main elements:

- There is stress on shifting parents, especially lone parents, from worklessness to work, backed by the view that work is the best route out of poverty.
- This shift is encouraged – and the claim that work is, indeed, an escape from poverty validated – by the tax credit system, and underpinned by the National Minimum Wage (NMW). The value of social security benefits for working-age adults has been allowed to fall steadily relative to average earnings, rising only in line with income.
- The childcare strategy further supports a shift into work, through both the supply of childcare and the provision of money to pay for it (again via tax credits).
- (Near) universal Child Benefit raises the income of all families with children irrespective of their means.

The only genuinely new element introduced since 1997 is the National Minimum Wage. On its own, the NMW contributes little to the avoidance of child poverty: two adults (with two children) have to work at least 80 hours a week between them at the NMW in order to avoid poverty without the help of tax credits. What the NMW does, however, is to limit the government's financial exposure by preventing unscrupulous employers cutting wages to a point where the employee is entitled to the maximum amount of tax credits.

The heavy lifting, therefore, is performed by a hybrid of two different approaches, both of which go back long before 1997. The first – the belief that income from work would enable people to avoid poverty, as long as it was boosted by extra money for families with two or more children – was a cornerstone of the analysis beneath the Beveridge Report. The Family Allowance, introduced in 1946, provided that extra. Child Benefit (1977) is its direct successor, albeit in much mutated form.[2]

The second approach – the use of means-tested benefits to boost the money of low-income working families – goes back nearly 40 years to the introduction of the Family Income Supplement in 1971. The current arrangements for Child and Working Tax Credit can be seen as its great grandchild, via Family Credit (1988) and Working Families Tax Credit (1999). The linking of the value of working-age social security benefits to prices rather than earnings also dates from the late 1980s, another legacy of the 1986 Social Security Act alongside the introduction of both Family Credit and Income Support.[3]

Although New Labour has certainly pushed this hybrid much further than its predecessors, it has done nothing to disturb the priority of the principles enshrined in the 1986 Act. In particular, both the pre-eminence of means-testing and the up-rating principle for benefits (in line with prices) remain intact. In short, New Labour has sought to reach its social democratic goal using a Conservative route map.

New Labour's record on child poverty

So how has this strategy fared? New Labour's first anti-poverty measures were introduced in 1999. Official statistics are now available up to 2006/07: in effect, eight years of data since the official 1998/99 baseline. Starting with lone parent employment, the proportion employed has risen by a fifth over the period, from 47% in 1998 to 56% in 2007. Though New Labour would wish to go further, this could fairly be deemed a success.[4]

As far as poverty itself is concerned, the 3.9 million children in 'relative' poverty ('after housing costs') in the UK in 2006/07 was 500,000 lower than in the baseline (see endnote 1 for a discussion of how poverty is measured). This fall is only half what is required to reach the government's first milestone – a reduction in child poverty of a quarter, or about 1.1 million – which was supposed to have been reached by 2004/05. However, this net fall of 500,000 reflects a larger fall, of some 800,000, up to 2004/05, followed by a rise in the latest two years, of some 300,000.[5]

What lies behind this reversal in fortunes? More detailed data show that the problem lies with 'in-work' poverty, that is, children in families where one or more of the adults are doing paid work.[6] Table 3.1, for Great Britain, shows the number of children in poverty by their family's work status, in 1998/99, 2003/04 and 2006/07. As can be seen, while poverty among children in workless families has continued to fall, 'in-work' child poverty fell from 2.1 million to 1.7 million in 2003/04 (the low point), since when it has risen all the way back to 2.1 million again.

Table 3.1   The Number of Children in Poverty, by the Work Status of the Family, Selected Years, Great Britain (millions)[7]

	Children in Poverty in Working Families	Children in Poverty in Workless Families	'In Work' as a Proportion
1998/99	2.1	2.2	48%
2003/04	1.7	1.9	47%
2006/07	2.1	1.7	55%

Although it is tempting to look for an explanation of 'what went wrong' in 2004, other statistics suggest that the problem is longer standing. The number of working adults in poverty, but *without* dependent children, rose steadily under New Labour, from 1.2 million in 1998/99 to 1.7 million in 2005/06.[8] Similarly, estimates of the number of children in working families who 'need' tax credits has risen from 2.4 million in 1998/99 to 3.0 million in 2005/06.[9] The net effect of all this is that the proportion of all children in poverty whose parents are in in-work poverty now stands at 55%, the highest it has been since at least as long ago as 1979.

Rising above the detail, four things of political significance stand out:

* While the anti-poverty strategy was working fairly well up until about 2005, it has, at best, ceased to do so since then. At worst, things are now going backwards.
* The main problem lies with in-work child poverty, where the net improvement under New Labour is now zero.
* Although progress only ceased in the middle of this decade, the forces driving in-work poverty upwards have been evident since at least the late 1990s.
* The adverse trends in in-work poverty impact working-age adults too, especially those without dependent children.

Breadth of support for the current strategy

One of the more curious features of New Labour's anti-poverty strategy is the way that its dependence on means-testing has come to enjoy the overwhelming support of anti-poverty campaigners, for whom more money devoted to tax credits is seen as the best – frankly the only – way of reaching the government's next (still distant) milestone of halving child poverty by 2010. The most influential report to this effect estimated the cost at between £4 billion and £5 billion, an estimate which has been regularly updated since.[10] On the latest evidence, support for tax credits among campaigners seems unabated.[11]

So long as this strategy continued to deliver steady progress, the consensus that it represented was a source of strength. Now that progress has ended, however, it is a source of weakness, since its very pre-eminence has ensured that other ideas about how to abolish child poverty remain sparse in number and under-developed. This is what makes the current situation so difficult. On the one hand, there is a need for a big shift in strategy – not from left to right, but away from a consensus view with bipartisan roots; and on the other, there is little to go on to suggest what this shift might actually be.

Before leaving tax credits, however, there are two more points to note about them and the strategy of which they are part. The first is that they are on a scale that is broadly commensurate with the scale of the problem, that is, they affect millions of people. If child poverty is to be further reduced, never mind abolished, measures that operate at this scale will be needed, even if they are not enough on their own.

Second, both tax credits and the rules on benefit uprating are designed to work by altering the incentives and disincentives that individuals face when making decisions such as whether to take a new job or not. This 'incentive-building' approach seeks to make work more attractive, assuming that individuals are capable and rational agents. By contrast, a 'capability-building' approach tries to leave people better equipped to flourish in the environment in which they find themselves (see also Chapter 4 on employment policy; and Chapter 6 on education). A substantial example of this 'capability-building' or 'personal improvement' approach in New Labour's anti-poverty programme is 'Sure Start'.

The focus on 'early years'

The main exception to the focus on direct measures to address child poverty is the programme of actions aimed at overcoming the disadvantages that young children in low income households tend, on average, to face. By far the most important of these is Sure Start, which began in 1999, and whose most visible manifestation is a developing network of children's centres to meet the health, education, childcare and wider support needs of under fives and their families (see also Chapter 4).[12] The number of such centres is rising rapidly, from around 1,000 in late 2006 to some 2,900 by March 2008.[13] The target for 2010 is 3,500 corresponding to a centre in every area. Allied to this, though separate, is the policy of providing a free, part-time place for every three and four year old in a nursery, playgroup or pre-schools setting.

With academic evaluations of Sure Start beginning to show positive outcomes[14] it is possible that those looking back several decades hence may conclude that it was the legacy of Sure Start, rather than the direct interventions to alter household incomes, that was actually New Labour's lasting contribution to reducing child poverty.

Except for childcare, which by allowing parents to take paid work may raise income now, the full impact of these centres on child poverty may not be visible until the children benefiting from them today have themselves become parents, in other words, some time in the 2020s. The fact that the ultimate effects of such a programme are long in the future cannot be held against it. But if the current policy mix contains direct measures with a short-term effect and indirect ones that take a generation, what is supposed to happen in the meantime?

This tension highlights an area where New Labour's strategy has been striking for what it has not done, namely, to improve the prospects of young adults with the fewest qualifications. By 'young adults', we mean those aged 16 and over (or 18 and over if still in full-time education) and under 25 – that is, a mixture of late teenagers and those in their early 20s. All of these people, it should be noted, were still children in 1999 when Blair made his pledge to abolish child poverty.

The bald poverty numbers for this group are striking enough: almost 1½ million (of whom just 200,000 are lone parents) living in poverty.[15] Even more striking are the statistics on qualifications and employment, and the connections between them for those at the bottom:

- Among 16 year olds, 10% got fewer than five GCSEs at any level in 2006/07, a proportion only slightly down on 1999/00.[16] Among 19 year olds, a quarter were not qualified to NVQ2 or equivalent in 2006 while one in twelve had no qualifications at all. These proportions too are unchanged since the late 1990s.[17]
- Among those in their late 20s, the risks of adverse labour market outcomes in the future associated with poor qualifications are quite stark. For example, among 25 to 29 year olds with no qualifications, 20% lack but want work while 70% of those in work are low paid. For those with only low GCSEs, these risks are 20% and 40%.[18]

Like tax credits, New Labour's focus on early years enjoys widespread support. Yet the neglect up until recently of those leaving childhood with the fewest qualifications – or indeed those 16 and 17 year olds who are neither in employment, education nor training (NEETs) – means that even if Sure Start turns out to be a wonderful success, a whole generation will have gone by before its beneficial impact on the deeper causes of child poverty – that is, in the capacities and capabilities of parents – starts to be felt.[19]

Criteria for possible options

A cursory reading of what can be seen as the main policy documents of both government (*Ending Child Poverty: Everybody's Business*) and opposition (the report of Duncan Smith's Social Justice Policy Group, *Breakthrough Britain*, to the Conservative Party) confirms that there is already a plethora of policies, actual and proposed, which to a greater or lesser extent are relevant to child poverty.[20] There is not space here to subject these policies to detailed scrutiny. (See Box 3.2 for a brief overview.)

Box 3.2   **Family Policies**
Samantha Callan

Tony Blair informed the 1995 Labour Party conference that a strong country could not be morally neutral about the family. New Labour assumed power upon a manifesto pledge to 'uphold family life', building on earlier proposals to strengthen the family to reduce the crime rate. The first ever consultation paper on the family, *Supporting Families*, published in November 1998, attempted to map out a coherent government strategy to increase support for families. Based on three simple principles, that

- children must come first,
- children need stability and security,
- and families raise children, not government,

it was foundational in inaugurating the National Family and Parenting Institute (NFPI), the helpline, ParentLine Plus, and Sure Start. However, significant attention was placed on strengthening the couple relationship. Marriage was treated as the best model for family life (whilst acknowledging that single and unmarried parents could also raise children well) and measures to prevent its breakdown were prominent (consistent with the overall thrust of the Family Law Act 2006).

However these marriage-enhancing elements gave way, both in terms of funding and government rhetoric, to a far more exclusively child-focused approach. Women ministers resisted any emphasis on marriage and, by 2003, the *Every Child Matters* green paper was skewing policy towards improving outcomes for and safeguarding children (following the death of Victoria Climbié) by

- supporting parents in their role,
- ensuring necessary intervention takes place through an integrated, accountable and well-trained service infrastructure.

The maturation of the imperative to effect a vast improvement for children's material well-being and its follow-through into family policy finds expression in a reworking of Sure Start's aims in 2003 to increase the availability of childcare for all children and support parents in their aspirations towards employment.

▶

Echoes of the policy emphasis ten years earlier on harnessing the innate power of a strong family to reduce crime could also be seen in the government's Respect Action Plan in 2006 which vowed to expand national parenting provision and establish a new National Academy for Parenting Practitioners.

Where are we now?

Childcare availability *has* greatly increased, but many areas are now reporting underutilization of places. In 2008 child poverty reductions are disappointing, not least because 60% of all poor children are in couple families. Adults living together experience a well-documented tax credits penalty when their receipts are equivalized with those of lone parents. Family breakdown has increased year on year, with Millennium Cohort Study analysis showing that 73% of all dissolutions involving children under five involve non-married parents. Children's emotional well-being does not on the whole appear to have improved: waiting lists for mental health services are growing (over 10% of children have mental health problems), drug and alcohol use have increased for all ages and report cards like the 2007 UNICEF study place the UK at the bottom of 21 OECD countries, below three former communist states.

In terms of future trends, the ideologically unfavourable marriage support pillar of *Supporting Families* seems likely to be revisited, given repeated calls for a full-blown strategy to support the couple relationship and reiteration of the social and personal benefits of marriage in signalling commitment and stabilizing relationships. Extending parents' choice in childcare to enable those who want to look after their very young children themselves also seems to be gaining policy traction in addressing concerns about the mental health of children. Both of these departures could be part of a new *relational* emphasis in family policy, a pendulum swing away from the focus on improving material outcomes and addressing *behaviour*.

Or we could have more of the same, with both parents increasingly expected to work and the onus placed on better training for childcare practitioners to ensure that children's emotional needs are met. (The fit of this approach with likely high unemployment is questionable.) Similarly, if family breakdown continues to be treated as inevitable, support for the couple relationship might be drained off into services to facilitate functional co-parenting post-separation.

In an ideal, fiscally unconstrained world of course, attention would be beneficially and coherently paid to all of these areas: doing all that is possible to give parents time with their children when they most want it and engendering stability – whilst acknowledging the realities that many parents want to work and may find it impossible to sustain a couple relationship.

Nevertheless, if we are to proceed in any kind of manageable way, reaching conclusions that do not appear wholly arbitrary, we need some criteria to help identify the kinds of policy that are likely to be needed in order to approach the goal of ending child poverty.

On the basis of the analysis of the record to date, we suggest that there are two criteria which any strategy, or overall approach, must meet. They are:

- first, that the approach addresses in-work poverty; and
- second, that the approach addresses the overall 'environment' of incentives, disincentives and opportunities within which individuals make their decisions.

The argument for the first criterion rests directly on the analysis of the New Labour record. In summary, it is the failure to reduce in-work poverty that has brought the previously successful approach to a halt. While the reversal in fortunes is quite recent, the underlying adverse trend is long standing. Finding a way to reduce in-work poverty is the priority.

The argument for the second criterion proceeds from the observation that if even a very general policy like tax credits, operating directly on incomes, can only dent child poverty, how plausible is it that an alternative strategy, which depends on 'improving' or capability-enhancing literally millions of people, can do better? For a start, can it be pursued on a large enough scale? Even if it can, doesn't it overlook the point that since part of the value of personal improvement (e.g. an extra qualification) lies in the advantage that confers over someone else, such that the advantage may disappear if everyone 'improves'? Similarly, while personal strengths and weaknesses may very well explain why one person is poor and another is not, it does not follow that such characteristics can explain why some people are poor. Ultimately, something in the wider social and economic environment has to change if poverty is to be abolished. Improved incentives and opportunities are almost certainly necessary, but not *sufficient*.

Against these criteria, the two documents referred to above fare rather differently. As far as the first criterion is concerned, the government document does clearly acknowledge the problem of in-work poverty and suggests that it may now enjoy the same status as the problem of poverty arising from worklessness. By contrast, the Social Justice Policy Group report commits itself firmly to the view that 'work is the key route out of poverty for virtually all working households.[21] To this author at least, such a confident assertion is reminiscent of the early days of New Labour – for example, see *Opportunity for All* (1999) – before the difficulty of the task had sunk in, and certainly before the evidence of both the extent and persistence of in-work poverty had been appreciated. Its failure even to acknowledge the problem, never mind admit its centrality, must be judged a serious shortcoming.

By contrast, the Conservative document does set greater store by the idea of altering the wider incentives and disincentives facing individuals, not only in relation to employment but to important family and personal choices too. This may be not only to do with the report's broad scope, but also that this type of idea has typically tended to find more favour among Conservatives. It is notable that in this report, the role of incentives is deployed as much in the chapter on family breakdown as it is in the chapter on economic dependency and worklessness.

The absence of any comparable idea in the government document is striking. If there is a dominant motif in emergent government thinking in this area it is the idea of 'progression', which includes working more hours, or staying in a job longer, or getting a better job on the back of improved skills. As we will explain below, all these ideas make sense. Yet there is no sense either of the barriers that might confront people who want to 'progress', nor of whether 'progression' on its own can be remotely sufficient. It is as if, having placed so much faith in tax credits, New Labour has now given up entirely on the idea that further measures of that type have any part to play.

Four options

Against that background, we now suggest four options which, we believe, are in accord with the criteria set out above. These should be understood, at least in the first instance, as being complementary to the other policies of the kind just discussed. They are also complementary to one another. The four are:

- to cut 'taxes' for low income working families;
- to restore out-of-work adult benefits to levels that allow a minimum standard of living, for example via a revival of the 'entitlement-based' approach to social security;
- to replace the current arrangements for childcare funded by means-tested benefits, with a system of free, universal childcare;
- to alter the poverty goal and/or change the way that poverty is measured.

Cutting taxes at the bottom

One of the more striking aspects of New Labour's anti-poverty strategy is that while it has relied so heavily on tax credits, it has neglected the wider tax and social security systems of which they are part. The most egregious example of this was the abolition in 2008 of the 10 pence starting rate of income tax, something which the government itself had introduced in 1999 in order, in the Treasury's words, to improve 'work incentives by allowing individuals to keep more of what they earn'.[22] At least one result of this episode is that it has raised the question of whether the tax system could be used as part of an anti-poverty strategy, with two related but distinct objectives in mind.

The first objective is to reduce the amount of tax that low income, working households pay. More than half of both children and working-age adults in poverty belong to working families.[23] Almost all of them will be paying tax and it is certain that some of them (without dependent children) will have an income below the poverty line by an amount that is less than the combined national insurance, income tax and council tax that they are paying.[24] Of these people it can actually be said that they are being 'taxed into poverty'. Of the rest, it can certainly be said that tax is making their situation worse.

The second objective is to reduce the very high 'marginal effective tax rates' that many of these households face. Anyone earning more than about £100 a week loses 31 pence of every *extra* pound of gross earnings to national insurance and income tax. But anyone in a household receiving tax credits (above the near-universal family element) also stands to lose a further 39 pence as a result of the 'taper' which reduces the amount of tax credit as income goes up. Taken together, this means an effective marginal rate above 70%. For those receiving Housing Benefit or Council Tax Benefit, this rate can be as high as 95%.

In one sense, higher marginal rates are an inevitable consequence of means-tested in-work support. If the 'poverty line' really marked a threshold where life on one side of it was dramatically different from life on the other, such rates could still be justified as the price that had to be paid for taking people over the threshold. But in modern Britain, that is not the case: all sorts of factors – including credit, debt, savings, support from friends and family, the durability of many household goods etc – mean that *no* threshold can have that status. In these circumstances, the capacity to improve one's income *further*, via overtime, a pay increase or a small second job (in effect, the government's idea of progression) ought to be an important part of the story – a similar conclusion to that reached in Chapter 4 on employment. The trouble is the high marginal effective tax rates stand in the way.

A substantial reduction in these marginal tax rates (by say 20%) could only come about as the result of a comprehensive review of how the tax, tax credit and social security systems impact on low income working households. A paper for Sir James Mirrlees' review of a twenty-first-century taxation system, which included an option along these lines, focused on tax credits and benefits and confirms the potential here (Brewer et al 2008).[25] Estimated to cost £9 billion per year, this option would take several years to implement. A substantial reduction, of the scale suggested above, would cost more, take longer and require changes to the income tax system too. While there must always be doubt about how far it is possible to go, there is little doubt about the direction that needs to be followed.

A return to the contributory principle

Relative to earning, out-of-work social security benefits for adults have fallen by a fifth since 1997; anyone dependent on them is in deep poverty.[26] Looking further back, the real value of these benefits (after allowing for inflation) is no higher than it was 25 years ago.

The basic argument for tolerating this situation is that it increases the financial incentive to enter employment. In response to this, two points can be made. First, factors influencing *individual* motivation are necessary but not sufficient to reach any particular *aggregate* level of employment. Since 1999, the overall employment rate in the UK has been stuck between 74% and 75%.[27] As a result, there remain some 3.6 million people of working age, or 10%, in 2007 lacking but wanting paid work.[28] Second, many at the bottom of the labour market actually shuttle back and forth between work and unemployment – or 'labour market churning'. Hence the problem is not just entering work, but of staying there.[29]

A look at this long-neglected issue would involve answering two questions, namely, the level at which benefits might be set and the eligibility conditions that might be attached. While the former will preoccupy the Treasury, it is the latter that is the political concern. Since 'something for something' is the phrase currently in vogue, it must be time to look again at Beveridge's proposals: 'benefit in return for contributions, rather than free allowances from the State, is what the people of Britain desire'.[30]

An immediate application of this principle would be an increase in the value of *entitlement-based* Jobseeker's Allowance (a Beveridgian relic in the current system), that increase being justified on the grounds that those benefiting from it have already contributed towards it. A more general application of the principle would look at what other criteria might meet such an eligibility condition, for example, remaining at home to care for others or taking part in training, apprenticeships or education.

Expanding free childcare to encourage 'all working'

Unlike the first two options which were both about money, the third option counts as 'indirect' in the terms employed in this chapter. In short, it is the suggestion that the UK, or its constituent parts, should move towards the provision of free, universal childcare. It should be said straightaway that such an idea would be controversial. Besides concerns about behaviour and education, which would lead some to argue that society actually does not want parents to spend less time with their children than they do now, there would also be the objection that what was once a liberation – the 'right' to work – is on the point of turning into its opposite, namely a duty to do so. Why, therefore, should this option even be contemplated? The answer is because both equity and effectiveness demand it.

More than four fifths of children in in-work poverty belong to families who are only 'part working'. Alongside those who are self employed, this includes both those families where the working adults had part-time jobs only or, in couple families, where one was working full-time and the other not at all. An obvious implication – and another instance of the New Labour idea of 'progression' – is that to escape poverty the adults in these families should work 'more'. But this raises two questions.

First, what is preventing them? The availability of affordable, quality childcare is part of the answer. A recent government report suggests that New Labour's childcare strategy, which uses tax credits to help parents meet the cost, is not succeeding in providing support for those who need it most. It also finds that earlier progress in extending the use of formal childcare has come to a halt, and that both cost and affordability remain barriers to its use.[31]

Second, why should they work more? At first glance, getting working families to work 'more' may look like a natural progression from the long standing aim of getting workless families to work. When judged by the statistics, however, there is a big difference, for whereas four fifths of children belong to working families, only half of them belong to 'all-working' ones.[32] While it can therefore be said that it is the norm for a child to belong to a working family, it is not necessarily the norm for them to belong to an all-working one. Any suggestion that poor working families should be 'all-working' is to set a different, harder standard for them than for the rest.

The answers to both of these questions point in the same direction. If we want low income, working families to work more, equity requires that we seek to make 'all-working' the norm across society, not just among those on low incomes. That necessitates universal provision. And if that provision is to be affordable, high quality, and fully-utilized, it needs to be free.

There is one more consideration. Although the government has set a target of 80% for the employment rate, that rate has remained stuck between 74% and 75% throughout this decade. To reach 80%, a large number of new jobs are needed: why not in childcare? The childcare workers will need to be highly trained – a profession, rather than workforce – not only to achieve a high quality of provision but also to ensure that the jobs can be well paid, thereby avoiding the ultimate irony of one person's route out of in-work poverty being another person's route into it.

This option has to be set against the counter-arguments of dead-weight costs at the high income end, and the need for childcare to be of especially high quality at the low income end if it is to lead to gains for the children concerned. Additionally, some have argued that it would be better to focus efforts among the more disadvantaged on supporting parents to do a good job at home, rather than pushing their kids into childcare and their parents into low quality work.[33] With strong arguments on both sides, this will be an area of sharp political argument in the decade to come.

Altering the goal or changing the measure

The last option is different again. Both the goal of ending child poverty, and the way this is measured, have barely changed since they were first announced. This stability has served public understanding and has helped establish the importance of the subject, even when the headline results have been disappointing. But in the end, these choices are value-laden, so the start of a new administration would be the time to consider them anew.[34]

In broad terms, there are two types of changes which could be made. The first concerns the subject. New Labour has explicitly identified children, thereby implicitly identifying their parents who live with them too. Through its actions, it has also clearly identified pensioners (see Box 3.3).

Box 3.3 **Poverty and Pensions: Overcoming an Ailing Problem**
Asheem Singh

An ageing problem?

The last ten years have been ten turbulent years for pensioners. Government figures show that average life expectancy in the UK rose by five years for men and four years for women between 1980 and 2000, a good thing, and moreover the often cited government reason for the strain and reevaluated liabilities in the pensions industry. This has been exacerbated in recent years by dwindling stock market returns and moreover the infamous pensions' fund 'raid': Gordon Brown's decision to end the Advanced Corporation Tax in 1997, depriving pension funds of significant income streams.

The principles of reducing poverty rates for children and pensioners were emphasized in 1999 and have received cross-party support. Spending to achieve these goals has often been directed through means-tested programmes, and there has been a related weakening of the link between paid national insurance contributions and benefit entitlements. The trend under New Labour has been to redistribute and they have enjoyed some success, but only some. This section gives a snapshot of that success.

State pension

More than 2 million pensioners have been lifted out of absolute poverty, and 1 million out of relative poverty. Pensioners are now less likely to be poor than younger people. In addition, the savings reward in Pension Credit has tackled the penalty of the 100% marginal deduction rate that many savers faced, increasing the incentives to save for 1.9 million pensioner households who saved for retirement. There have been real terms increases in the size of the weekly state pension, with the pre-budget report of November 2008 raising it to £95.25, with the same report guaranteeing a one-off payment of £60 that Christmas for each pensioner. However, the criticism remains that, relative to spiralling pertinent costs such as fuel costs, even taking into account the winter fuel payment, those rises have been inadequate.

Pension Credit

The Pension Credit was introduced on 6 October 2003 and replaced the Minimum Income Guarantee (MIG). Following the 2008 pre-budget report, the credit provides a minimum income of £124.05 a week for a single pensioner and £189.35 for couples. The pension credit is in two parts. The Guarantee Credit can be claimed by pensioners who are 60 or over, while the Savings Credit can only be claimed by pensioners who are 65 or over and rewards pensioners who have a second pension or modest savings. The credit is a so-called 'passport benefit': those who claim the guaranteed element of the credit should also get help with council tax and housing costs.

As early as 2001, before its introduction, the IPPR criticized the complexity and cost of the pension credit. As recently as 2005, levels of uptake, a key indicator

▶

of complexity and a cause of poverty in itself were relatively low, though in recent years this has been improving.

Winter fuel payment

A winter fuel payment is a tax-free annual payment to help alleviate fuel poverty for people aged 60 or over. The payment is either £125 or £250, depending on your circumstances in the qualifying week (15 to 21 September 2008). For those aged 80 or over who are entitled to a winter fuel payment, the entitlement is either £200 or £400, depending on your circumstances in the qualifying week.

While the winter fuel payment is a welcome recognition of the spiralling costs of fuel and its vital importance during cold months to the very oldest, the supplement provided by the payment in no way matches the amount that fuel costs have risen. Moreover, some have questioned the logic of providing a blanket winter fuel payment to pensioners only, when others are in positions of relative need.

Implications of the credit crunch and direction of travel for future

Aside from the disastrous effects of falling share prices on already stretched pension funds, we have already seen in the pre-budget report a swathe of redistribution that aims to help pension funds. Whatever the merits or otherwise of the fiscal stimulus, any supplement to pensioners in the face of rising fuel prices is welcome.

With both major political parties now enshrining a commitment to social justice in their policies, there is every chance that the New Labour model of redistribution will be welcomed and refined by Conservative policymakers.

One clear direction of travel will be to use up-to-date dynamic methods to model saving and pensions behaviour. Behavioural economic models have been used to model tax regimes at the high end of the income scale, and by some organizations to model benefit regimes for the poorest. An approach that combines social justice and sound money would deploy these sorts of models to produce better outcomes and should form the bedrock of a new approach.

By contrast, it has paid little attention to the remainder – working-age adults without dependent children.

The basic argument for reconsidering the goal is that it is no longer sustainable. As it is, the focus on children to the exclusion of working-age adults has led to a situation in which the maximum value of state child support exceeds the maximum amount payable for adults. That gap will continue to widen. This pattern is far removed from what the official poverty statistics imply about the relative incomes that adults and children need in order for different sized families to have the same standard of living.[35]

More importantly, once we recognize the centrality of 'in-work' poverty, the roots of this large and growing aspect of child poverty are largely the same as the roots of (the rising level of) in-work poverty among adults without dependent children. A switch to a more general poverty target (even if it did not go so far as to pledge anything so bold as an end to adult poverty) would arguably offer a more balanced approach.

The other possible change is to adopt a different measure of poverty. There is, of course, a substantial literature on this subject, including a growing debate about the need to consider 'well-being' in a broader sense than just income.[36] For politicians and policymakers, however, one question matters far more than any others, namely, whether to persist with a 'relative' measure or switch to an 'absolute' one.[37] Anecdotally, the 'absolute' standard would seem to enjoy more popular support and would be easier to deliver, so it would not be surprising if politicians were attracted to it.

In response, two things can be said. First, it should not be thought that an 'absolute' standard is easier to defend. It is actually more arbitrary than the 'relative' standard, being in effect a 'relative' standard at a fixed point in time, and also produces nonsense over a long period of time (e.g. 'most people in poverty in the 1960s by modern standards'). Second, as a recent report from the Rowntree Foundation shows, a well-founded absolute standard would not necessarily lead to a lower poverty line than the current 'relative' measure.[38]

Conclusion

If the exclusive focus on 'child poverty' was a brutal reduction in the subject matter of this chapter, the identification of just four options for child poverty is a further brutal reduction of the view of what needs to be done. Ultimately, the justification for this is the belief that New Labour's strategy is exhausted and that what is now needed is something akin to a paradigm shift. The large ideas sketched out here are an attempt to prompt people towards thinking about what that shift might be.

It is important to be clear, however, that it is not mere exhaustion that demands such a shift, but rather the extent and trajectory of in-work poverty. In Kuhnian terms, this is an 'anomaly' which simply cannot be accommodated within a strategy that is predicated on the idea that work is the route out of poverty. New Labour may finally have adopted various circumlocutions in order to allow it to acknowledge the inevitable; but there is no sign that it has grasped the extent of the challenge posed. The Conservatives, meanwhile, in the shape of Duncan Smith's report, are still in complete denial on this central point.

Talk of paradigm shifts should not obscure the fact that matters of 'normal' administration remain vital too. Sure Start is a good example. On the one hand, it is still a young programme, the basic requirement being to nurture it for several years before its full impact is seen. On the other hand, big issues of implementation and principle remain,[39] such as who should run children's centres (voluntary sector or local government?) or what their ethos should be (top down, government-led, or bottom up, shaped by those who are using them?). Similarly, keeping the tax credit system in good order represents a substantial challenge in its own right.

Putting this more prosaically, whatever options are chosen, a 2010 government will be building on the legacy of New Labour efforts to reduce child poverty. In so far as it has fallen short, Labour has done so because it has overestimated what it was able to do, rather than what it needed to.

Notes

1. All measures of poverty reported here use official statistics and official definitions. In keeping with this, 'poverty' is a *household-level* concept. While most households consist of one or two adults, with or without dependent children, some one in eight also include other adults, usually other family members, mainly grown-up children. 'Child poverty' therefore arises when a household containing (dependent) children is 'in poverty'. Poverty is measured relative to median income, a household being counted as 'in poverty' if its net income (after council tax and income taxes) is less than 60% of *median* household income in the current year. Incomes are 'equivalized' for household size (to allow for the fact that while a family of four clearly needs more money than a single person in order to achieve the same standard of living, they do not need four times as much). For more on these definitions, see appendix 1 of Department for Work and Pensions, 2008, *Households Below Average Income 1994/95 to 2006/07*, via http://www.dwp.gov.uk/asd/hbai/hbai2007/appendicies.asp. This measure of poverty using relative income (that is, relative to the median in the current year) does *not* mean that what is being looked at here is something called 'relative' poverty. Although it is very commonly described as such, it is wrong in principle and betrays a misunderstanding of what poverty is: in short, poverty is measured relative to average income because poverty itself is *inherently* relative, that is, (to quote the pioneering work of Peter Townsend in the 1960s and 1970s) when 'resources are so seriously below those commanded by the average individual or family that they are, in effect, excluded from ordinary living patterns, customs and activities'. As a result, what is being measured is not some lesser thing called 'relative poverty' but poverty itself.

2. The mutation is that whereas Family Allowance (set as five shillings per child per week) was available for second and subsequent children only, Child Benefit is not only available for all children but is also worth more for the first child than for others. This latter feature dates from 1991. Prior to that, that is, from 1978, one year after its introduction as a replacement for Family Allowance, Child Benefit was set at a uniform rate for all children in the family. But until 1999 Child Benefit for children in lone parent families was always about 60% higher than that for children in two parent families. After that, this differential declined rapidly, and was abolished altogether in 2007.

3. See, for example, Joseph Rowntree Foundation, 1994, 'The Effects of the 1986 Social Security Act on Family Incomes', *Social Policy Research* 54: http://www.jrf.org.uk/knowledge/findings/socialpolicy/SP54.asp

4. Source, *Labour Force Survey* via http://www.poverty.org.uk/technical/lfs.shtml

5. The latest Government figures for 2006/07 show that child poverty increased by 100,000 between 2005/06 and 2006/07, after an increase of 100,000 the previous year. Source: DWP, 2008, *Households Below Average Income 1994/95 to 2006/07*,

table 4.3tr, via http://www.dwp.gov.uk/asd/hbai/hbai2007/excel_files/chapters/ chapter_3tr_hbai08.xls

6. For a strategy based on work as the route out of poverty, in-work poverty on the scale observed is extremely damaging. Yet one of the curious features of the discussion of something so conceptually straightforward is the extent to which the idea itself remains contested. It is, for example, quite clear that in-work poverty and low pay (understood as a low rate of pay) are not one and the same thing. Low pay is, after all, a characteristic of an individual worker. Whether that translates into a low household income depends also on the hours that person works, how many people (adults and children) belong to their family, whether anyone else in it works (and if so for how much and for how long), whether the family is taking up the tax credits and any other benefits it is entitled to; what taxes they are paying; and so on. As a result, it is not surprising that the proportion of low paid workers living in poverty has been estimated at just 14% (J. Millar and K.Gardiner, 2004, *Low Pay, Household Resources and Poverty*, Joseph Rowntree Foundation). Consistent with this, more recent analysis, which took as its focus the average hourly pay of all working adults in the household, found that 23% of 'low paid households' were in poverty. However, it also found that 65% of those in in-work poverty belonged to low paid households. When considering how far policies to increase low pay might affect in-work poverty, it is essential to take *both* of these percentages into account. (V. Winckler and P. Kenway, 2006, *Dreaming of £250 a Week: A Scoping Study on In-work Poverty in Wales*, New Policy Institute and Bevan Foundation: http://www.npi.org.uk/reports/in-work%20poverty%20in%20wales.pdf). So while it is perfectly true that the first shows that measures to address in-work poverty via raising low pay will be fairly *inefficient* (since most beneficiaries are not in work poverty), the second shows that such measures will nevertheless be fairly *effective* (since most of those in in-work poverty are low paid). It will be noted, however, that recommendations on low pay do not figure among the options considered in the third section of the chapter.

7. Source: data provided by the Institute for Fiscal Studies. Limited data for Northern Ireland before 2002/03 means that these more detailed statistics are for Great Britain only.

8. Source: *Households Below Average Income*, via http://www.poverty.org.uk/summary/ adults.htm. The coverage is for Great Britain.

9. Source: *Households Below Average Income*, via http://www.poverty.org.uk/summary/ children.htm. The coverage is for Great Britain. This measure of need is made up of those children in working families who are either in poverty (whether or not they receive tax credits) or who escape it by an amount less than the tax credits they receive.

10. D. Hirsch, 2006, *What Will It Take to End Child Poverty? Firing on All Cylinders*, p. 13, Joseph Rowntree Foundation, http://www.jrf.org.uk/bookshop/ eBooks/9781859355008.pdf

11. See, for example, a 2008 call for 'next generation of tax credits to "build on progress"': http://www.cpag.org.uk/press/200508.htm

12. Separate Sure Start programmes are run in Scotland and Wales (as part of Cymorth, the unified children and youth support fund). There are also Sure Centres in Northern Ireland.

13. Hansard, 6 June 2008, co. 1175W (Parliamentary answer by Beverley Hughes, MP), source: http://www.publications.parliament.uk/pa/cm200708/cmhansrd/ cm080606/text/80606w0002.htm#080606139002305

14. See for example, National Evaluation of Sure Start Research Team, 2008, *The Impact of Sure Start Local Programmes on Three Year Olds and Their Families'*. Accessible via: http://www.ness.bbk.ac.uk/impact.asp. It should be noted, however, that this assessment followed an earlier, first evaluation which was not able to be positive: National Evaluation of Sure Start Research Team, 2005, Early Impacts of Sure Start Local Programmes on Children and their Families (report 13), via http://www.surestart.gov.uk/_doc/P0001867.pdf

15. Original source: *Households Below Average Income*, 2003/04 to 2005/06, via http://www.poverty.org.uk/summary/young.htm

16. Original source: Statistical releases from the DCSF (for England) and the National Assembly for Wales (for Wales), via http://www.poverty.org.uk/26/index.shtml. It should be noted that the lack of progress compares unfavourably with the trend for the 'headline' statistic of five GCSEs at grade C or above

17. Original source: Labour Force Survey, via http://www.poverty.org.uk/26/index.shtml. It should be noted that the DCSF dispute the capacity of the LFS to measure these things properly. But while they believe that the LFS understates the (positive) trend in these numbers over time, they also believe that it overstates academic achievement. These matters are discussed more fully on the poverty website (reference as above).

18. Original source: Labour Force Survey, via http://www.poverty.org.uk/31/index.shtml. 'Low pay' is defined here as an hourly rate of pay of £7 or less in 2007.

19. It is true that the Education and Skills Bill going through Parliament in the 2007–08 session (http://services.parliament.uk/bills/2007-08/educationandskills.html) can be seen as partly answering some of these needs, for example, in the duty it imposes on 16 and 17 year olds to continue taking part in education or training, or the duty placed on the Learning and Skills Council to pay the tuition fees for 19 to 25 year olds seeking their first level-three qualification. But some of this is still a long way off: for example the participation duty only comes into effect in 2015, meaning that it does not apply to any child that was alive back in 1999.

20. HM Treasury, DWP and DCSF, 2008, *Ending Child Poverty: Everybody's Business*, http://www.hm-treasury.gov.uk/media/3/F/bud08_childpoverty_1310.pdf; and Social Justice Policy Group, 2007, *Breakthough Britain: Ending the Cost of Social Breakdown*, http://www.centreforsocialjustice.org.uk/default.asp?pageRef=226. It should of course be acknowledged that the proposals in the latter report only have the status of recommendations to the Conservative Party.

21. Social Justice Policy Group, 2007, *Breakthough Britain: Ending the Cost of Social Breakdown*, volume 2, p. 6, via http://www.centreforsocialjustice.org.uk/client/downloads/economic.pdf

22. http://www.hm-treasury.gov.uk/pre_budget_report/pre_budget_report_1999/pbr_1999_press_notices/pbr_pn_ir3.cfm

23. Sources: http://www.poverty.org.uk/summary/children.htm and http://www.poverty.org.uk/summary/adults.htm for adults (between 25 and retirement) and children respectively.

24. See, for example, table 1 in *Memorandum to the Treasury Select Committee by the New Policy Institute: Budget Measures and Low Income Households*, http://www.parliament.uk/documents/upload/BMWrittenEvidence14May08r.pdf

25. M. Brewer, E. Saez and A. Shephard, 2008, *Means-testing and Tax Rates on Earnings*, Paper prepared for the Report of a Commission on Reforming the Tax System for the 21st Century, chaired by Sir James Mirrlees, Institute for Fiscal Studies: http://www.ifs.org.uk/mirrleesreview/press_docs/rates.pdf

26. Source: benefit levels from DWP via http://www.poverty.org.uk/01/index. shtml?2
27. Source ONS Labour Market Statistics (series MGSU).
28. Source: Labour Force Survey via http://www.poverty.org.uk/44/index.shtml?2
29. Source, Juvos cohort, ONS, via http://www.poverty.org.uk/57/index.shtml?2
30. William Beveridge, 1942, *Social Insurance and Allied Services*, para. 21.
31. A. Kazimirski, R. Smith, S. Butt, E. Ireland and E. Lloyd, 2008, *Childcare and Early Years Survey 2007: Parents' Use, Views and Experiences*, Department for Children, Schools and Families, http://www.dfes.gov.uk/research/data/uploadfiles/DCSF-RR025A.pdf. The paraphrased views attributed here to that report are based on the first, second, sixth and eighth paragraphs of the 'conclusions' on pages 18 and 19.
32. Source: analysis of *Households Below Average Income*, 2005/06.
33. See for example, Social Justice Policy Group, 2008, *Breakdown Britain*.
34. As we acknowledged at the very start of this chapter, the focus on child poverty here should not be taken as a sign that poverty is the sum total of government concerns about the disadvantages experienced by children. It is for that reason that we reject the idea that 'child poverty' might be replaced by something called 'child well-being' since although this latter phrase is not, as far as we know, used like this officially, the diverse ensemble of policies currently in place certainly could be described in that way. What this points to, of course, is that the real debate about 'child well-being' is exactly what it should comprise.
35. A ratio of about three to one for a single adult relative to a child, and a ratio of about two to one for any second and subsequent adult relative to a child.
36. See UNICEF, 2007, *Overview of Child Wellbeing in Rich Countries*.
37. It should be noted that these popular labels are thoroughly misleading since both measures are, inevitably and invariably, relative to the modern mode and standard of living. A better pair of terms is 'contemporary' and 'fixed', to distinguish the fact that the former moves year by year in line with average income, whereas the latter does not, being uprated only in line with prices.
38. J. Bradshaw, S. Middleton, A. Davis, N. Oldfield, N. Smith, L. Cusworth and J. Williams, 2008, *A Minimum Income Standard for Britain: What People Think*, Joseph Rowntree Foundation, via http://www.jrf.org.uk/bookshop/eBooks/2226-income-poverty-standards.pdf. For working-age adults, and families with children, this report's standard was around 70% of median income, rather than the normal 60%.
39. For some implementation issues, see, for example, the conclusions in House of Commons Committee of Public Accounts, 2007, *Sure Start Children's Centres*, 38th Report of Session 2006–07: http://www.publications.parliament.uk/pa/cm200607/cmselect/cmpubacc/261/261.pdf

4
Employment, Worklessness and Unemployment

Martin Evans and Susan Harkness

Introduction

In this chapter we set out some of the key trends in employment, unemployment and 'worklessness' over recent decades and then go on to describe some directions for future policy. We start by describing trends in employment since the late 1970s, looking particularly at how changes in demand for labour in different sectors of the economy have differently affected opportunities for male and female employment, and for part-time working. We then go on to look at more recent changes. From the early 1990s to mid-2008 there has been a long period of sustained economic growth and high levels of employment which has pulled more workers into jobs both from unemployment and inactivity. While women have benefited disproportionately from employment growth the statistics on benefit claimants tell a different story. Among the claimant population, the biggest drop in benefit receipt has been among men claiming jobseeker's allowance. However, the claimant population is increasingly female. While there has been some fall in the numbers of lone parents dependent on benefit this has been offset to some extent by an increase in the share of women claiming incapacity benefit.

We conclude by examining the record of New Labour in delivering employment policies aimed at getting the unemployed and inactive into work and looking at possible directions for future policy. Given current high, though now falling, employment levels, efforts to get the remaining claimant population back to work are likely to face significant barriers. This is not only because the remaining out-of-work population have characteristics that make them less able to compete for jobs in the labour market, but also because as the economy enters recession they are likely to face stiffer competition for work from the newly unemployed which may mean that the supply side policy initiatives of the last decade may no longer be sufficient to raise employment among the most disadvantaged.

Trends in employment: the last 30 Years

2008 has seen the slowing down of the sustained economic growth that started in the early 1990s. Indeed, we are now writing at a point where recession looks inevitable, with a quarterly increase in unemployment of over 160,000 people in the summer of 2008 and falls in employment and vacancies (ONS 2008b). We primarily focus this chapter on employment and employment programmes since the 1990s recession, but it is important to put this in the context of the longer term structural changes in the UK economy and employment over the last 30 years. Figure 4.1 shows how employment has grown by gender and industrial sector from 1978 to 2007. This period saw the creation of 4.7 million new jobs, the vast majority of these being female (a net growth of 4 million jobs among women) and in

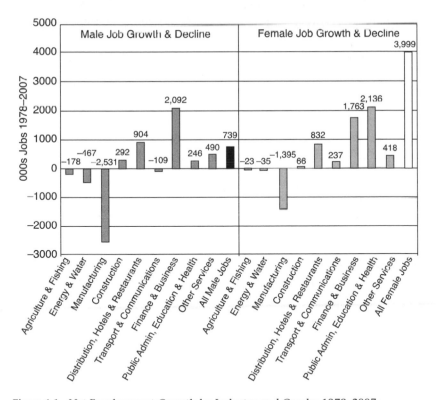

Figure 4.1   Net Employment Growth by Industry and Gender 1978–2007

Source: ONS (2008a), table 2.06 and previous versions.

the service sector. Both men and women saw large losses in manufacturing sector employment, the number of jobs in this sector shrinking by 4 million, reflecting both a contraction in the size of the sector alongside productivity gains. For men, manufacturing job losses were just offset by gains in service sector employment, particularly in the finance and business sector (where 3.8 million jobs were added), leading to a 0.75 million overall gain in employment. Women have gained from employment growth across the service sector, with particularly significant gain in public sector administration, education and health (of 2.2 million jobs in total), an area which for men saw virtually no job growth. It is these strong gendered occupational rigidities that have heavily influenced who has lost and who has gained from job growth over recent decades.

The growing size of the service sector and contraction of the manufacturing sector has strongly favoured female employment, although many of the newly created jobs have been part-time and poorly paid. The increasing prevalence of part-time employment is shown in Table 4.1, with data reported for 1984, 1993 and 2007.[1] Between the two recessionary periods of 1984 and 1993 employment grew by 2% overall, but with very different patterns for men and women – a 7% loss in jobs for men and a 13% gain for women. However, from 1993 to 2007, a period of relative economic growth and prosperity, the total of number of jobs rose by 18% with similar rises for men and women. However, the nature of work has continued to change with part-time work accounting for the majority of new jobs – over half of the newly created jobs are part-time, with particularly strong growth in part-time work among men. The

Table 4.1   Employment 1984, 1993 and 2007 by Part-time Status and Gender

	1984	1993	2007
Employment ('000 employees)			
All	21,000	21,405	25,214
Male	11,832	11,043	12,952
Female	9,168	10,362	12,262
Employment shares:			
part-time as % all employment	23.74%	28.51%	29.45%
part-time as % male	5.35%	9.25%	13.48%
part-time as % of female	47.48%	49.03%	46.32%
Contribution to job growth from:			1993–2007
full-time male			20.9%
full-time female			24.9%
part-time male			29.1%
part-time female			25.1%

Source: ONS (2008a), table 2.03 and previous versions.

relatively poor quality of these jobs, which have been characterized as having poor pay and prospect, and relatively weak growth in full-time jobs, suggests some worrying developments in terms of future job quality and growth.[2] For men in particular, part-time growth is often a signal of underemployment – around one quarter of men work part-time because they have been unable to find a full-time job (compared to just 7% female part-timers).[3]

The UK's employment record between 1994 and 2004 was also impressive from an international perspective with high rates of employment and employment growth relative to the OECD average, sharply falling unemployment and long-term unemployment rates among the lowest in the OECD (OECD 2006). However, inactivity rates among prime-age men in the UK remain higher than the OECD average (8.6% compared to 8%) or the EU15 (7.8%), although labour market participation of older men remained relatively high.[4] Similarly, lone parents continue to substantially under-perform in the UK labour market relative to other countries, a major contributory factor behind the UK's continuing position as having one of the highest numbers of children living in workless households in the EU (Eurostat 2007). Similarly, low-skilled young people continue to fare poorly (OECD 2008d).

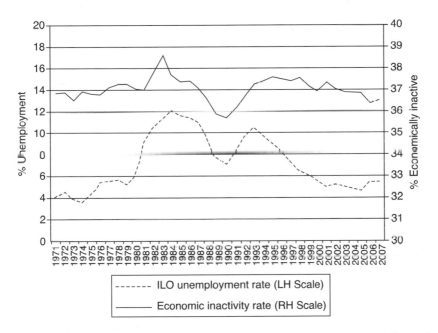

Figure 4.2 Long-term and Recent Trends in Unemployment and Economic Inactivity (All Working Age)

Source: ONS (2008a), tables 2.09 and 2.12 and previous versions.

As employment has grown, albeit less strongly for men than women, unemployment rates have fallen to levels seen in the 1970s of around 5% and are currently close to OECD measures of 'full-employment' (Turner et al 2001). This has been achieved by the sustained economic and job growth seen over the last 15 years which initially resulted in sharply decreasing unemployment, with a more recent flattening out from 2000 and slight rise since 2005. In this context of falling unemployment, it is perhaps surprising that aggregate employment rates have not risen further, particularly for men. The parallel observations of fairly steady levels of male employment alongside falling unemployment appear at first sight an incongruity. To explain this further we need to look away from these to indicators and consider changes in economic inactivity. Figure 4.2 shows how falling unemployment since the mid-1990s was not matched by rising economic activity, suggesting there is something different happening to (un)employment today compared with the post-boom period of the late 1980s. In the following section we endeavour to unpick some of the trends behind this.

The last 15 years

In the previous section we reviewed changes in the job market that have influenced who the winners and losers over the last 30 years are. In this section we focus on more recent changes in employment and non-employment and those that have happened from the mid-1990s onwards. Our attention here centres on those who are not working – both the unemployed and those who are inactive – and the impact of changes in these groups for the numbers of benefit claimants.

In Figure 4.3 we show what has happened to the aggregate unemployment rate since 1993, and the unemployment rates of those under 25 and the over-50s. While the aggregate rate shows a fairly continuous decline from almost 11% to just under 5% over the last 15 years, the picture for young people is somewhat different. For young people the unemployment rate fell sharply from 18% to 10% between 1993 and 2000 but since 2003 youth unemployment has again been rising and is now back to rates similar to those pre-1997, of around 13%. For the over-50s, unemployment is lower than the headline rate and has been falling in tandem with the overall rate.

Of chief concern for policymakers is what has happened to long-term unemployment (of 12 months and over). Figure 4.4 shows trends in the proportions of the unemployed who have been out of work for 12 months or more from 1993 onwards for all the unemployed and for the under-25s and the over-50s. This shows that the over-50s, though facing a relatively low risk of unemployment overall, when they are unemployed face the highest risk of being *long-term* unemployed. In 1993 over half of the unemployed over-50s had been out of work for over a year and, while this proportion has been dropping, this progress has stalled or even reversed since 2002. Young

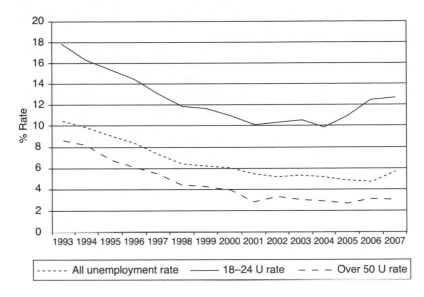

Figure 4.3   Unemployment Rates 1993–2007

Source: ONS (2008a), table 2.09 and previous versions.

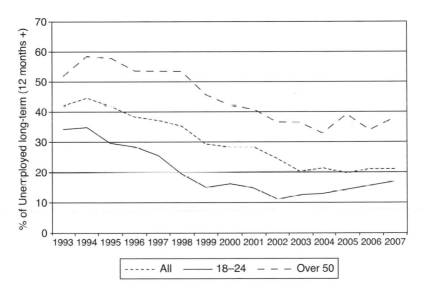

Figure 4.4   Long-term Unemployment (12 months as % of all U) 1993–2007

Source: ONS (2008b), table 2.09 and previous versions.

people on the other hand face the lowest risk of long-term unemployment, although their risk has been growing since 2002.

Of course, the unemployed comprise just a small share of those who are not working. While economic inactivity rates have fallen, just looking at rates of economic inactivity fails to note where this decline has come from and how this has affected the composition of those who remain 'workless'. In order to dig further behind these trends we report changes in the composition of 'worklessness' in Figure 4.5. What is clear from this figure is that, while the numbers of economically inactive remained relatively stable between 1993 and 2007, there have been large reductions in the numbers of women at home looking after the family or home (a 0.6 million fall), particularly from 1997, and rises in both male and female long-term sickness (a combined rise of nearly 0.4 million). There has also been a large rise in the student population and a small rise in the numbers retiring early. There are both geographical and generational dimensions to this rise in worklessnes, in particular among incapacity claimants. Large increases have been particularly concentrated

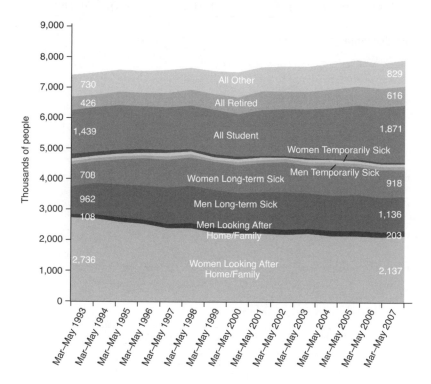

Figure 4.5   Numbers of Economically Inactive by Group, 1993–2007

Source: ONS (2008a), table 2.14 and previous versions.

amongst older men, and within this group on those who are low-skilled and/ or sick and disabled. Geographically, men living in low employment regions (Wales, Scotland and Northern England) are more likely to be inactive than those in regions with relatively high employment (East Anglia, the Southern regions and the Midlands).[5]

Of course economic inactivity is not always a concern for policy: the state's concern is largely focused on the benefit claimant population. Table 4.2 reports changes in the claimant count and the make up of those claims for 1999 and 2007. While the numbers of male and female claimants were roughly equal in both periods, the composition of claimants has seen substantial change over the eight years and differs widely by gender. As we can see, for men the vast majority of working-age benefit claimants are on incapacity benefit (60%), with the next largest share accounted for by those on jobseeker's allowance (21% in 2007, down 9 percentage points since 1999), while just 5% of male claimants make a claim as a lone parent or carer. For women, a large proportion (around 40%) are in receipt of incapacity benefit and a similar proportion claim benefits as lone parents or carers, but fewer than one in ten are in receipt of jobseeker's allowance. Since 1999 there has been a small fall of 6% in the overall size of the claimant count, with the majority of this decline being among males (whose caseload numbers fell by 8.4% compared to a 2.9% fall for women).

Table 4.2   Claimant Count and Composition – Working-age Population ('000s)

%	All Claimants		Male Claimants		Female Claimants	
	1999	2007	1999	2007	1999	2007
Job Seeker	19.9%	14.5%	30.2%	21.5%	9.4%	7.6%
Incapacity Benefit	49.2%	51.5%	59.4%	60.8%	38.9%	42.6%
Lone Parent	17.1%	14.5%	1.7%	1.3%	33.0%	27.2%
Carer	5.8%	7.4%	3.3%	4.4%	8.4%	10.3%
Others	7.9%	12.1%	5.5%	11.9%	10.3%	12.3%
Total	5,432	5,124	2,751	2,520	2,681	2,604

Source: DWP Tabulation Tool (http://www.dwp.gov.uk/asd/tabtool.asp).

These changes in the caseload are illustrated further in Figure 4.6. This shows changes in the out-of-work benefit caseload since 1999, which has experienced a 0.3 million drop in the total number of claimants. The dramatic changes stem from falling numbers of (mainly female) lone parent and (mainly male) job seeker claimants. There has also been a significant drop in the number of men claiming incapacity benefit, although the drop in the overall number of incapacity claims has been offset to some extent by a growing number of claims among women. There has also been a rise in other and carer claims.

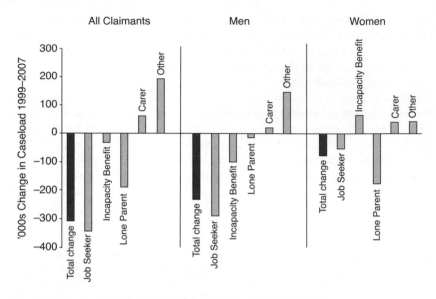

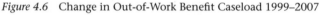

Figure 4.6   Change in Out-of-Work Benefit Caseload 1999–2007

Source: DWP Tabulation Tool (http://www.dwp.gov.uk/asd/tabtool.asp).

As we have seen, the recent long run of economic growth has pulled more workers into jobs from unemployment and inactivity. While women have made stronger gains in employment than men, men have made greater progress in terms of falling out-of-work claims. This is because men have seen large falls in the numbers claiming jobseeker's allowance while those claiming other benefits have been harder to shift off benefits and the focus of most recent policy. The most recent policy reforms, introduced in the 2008 Welfare Reform Act, aim to address this problem with a target reduction of 1 million on incapacity benefit within ten years and a focus on work capability (rather than disability), employment support and measures to encourage a faster return to work after illness.

Recent labour market context and policy developments

Since 1997 the economy has experienced a strong phase of economic growth with high levels of employment. These favourable economic conditions have boosted employment for almost all groups – the notable exception being those with no qualifications – and have benefited those who may, in less favourable circumstances, have found it much harder to find jobs. How has this growth in employment been achieved?

Government policies have, since 1997, focused on promoting employment growth, with particular measures to promote women's employment by improving maternity leave provision and promoting family friendly work and gender equality in employment. The policy legacy of the 1988 Social Security Act, followed in 1997 by the introduction of Jobseeker's Allowance and latterly by New Deals, has tended to divide the workless into three main groups: the unemployed (mostly men), lone parents and carers (mostly women) and the health-restricted (a mixed group – but mostly older and male). Policy has tended to target each of these groups as separate entities, as our discussion of policies in relation to employment below reveals.

Alongside these measures to improve employment service provision for those looking for work, there has been growing conditionality in benefits, a trend signalled in one of Labour's 1997 'five election pledges' to remove the option to claim certain benefits if not actively seeking work or in training. Since 2002 entitlements to benefits have increasingly been linked to attending Work Focused Interviews and more recent policy announcements include a mandatory requirement for lone parents with older children to search for work. Similar obligations are increasingly being applied to those with disability and health limitations.

Most recently, and as yet untested, 'Local Employment Partnerships' have been set up with businesses to encourage employers to recruit from groups that have traditionally found it harder to find work (such as the long-term unemployed) and to provide skills, training and experience. In London the Olympic Delivery Authority has been set up to link the 'workless' with jobs. The supply of labour has also been addressed through a stream of policy measures targeting those out of work. This represents to some extent a new approach as the focus for policy has been widened from 'unemployment' to 'worklessness'. In particular this represents a move to include those with greater employment constraints, such as lone parents or the disabled, which in turn has led to substantial overall growth in the target population for programmes (which now cover a far larger group than the 'unemployed'). Policies targeting these groups initially centred on improving employment service provision. This was achieved through the harmonization of employment and benefit services through the introduction of Jobcentre Plus; the roll out of a series of New Deal programmes, which were mandatory for the unemployed but remain voluntary for lone parents and the disabled; the encouragement of work through the 'Pathways to Work' programmes; and, most recently, moves to introduce competition into employment services provision through privatization.

A final, but crucially important, means by which policy has targeted worklessness over recent years has been an expansion of effort to 'make work pay' and promotion of work as the best form of welfare. This has been achieved through first raising wages at the bottom end of the earnings distribution via the minimum wage. Over and above this there has been a focus on children and child poverty, and thus on parental earnings supplementation. The Working Families Tax Credit replaced Family Credit in 1999, and provided a more generous system of support for low earning families with children. This has subsequently been replaced by the Child Tax Credit and Working Tax Credit, which for the first time introduced an earnings supplement for workers without children. Benefits have however been restricted to those without children who are over 25 and working full-time (unless disabled). There have also been a series of measures designed to hold people in their jobs, with in-work bonuses being introduced for lone parents after their first year in work, and there has been discussion of how such retention schemes may be rolled out to other groups. These improved work incentives have meant that while the real value of out-of-work benefits has risen substantially since 1997 for some groups, such as lone parents, out-of-work benefit rates have still fallen relative to the rewards from working.

Evaluation of recent policy

In broad terms, Labour government policy pursued the combination of capability-building and incentive-enhancing policies recommended by the authors of *Options for Britain I* in 1996 – but did it work? Policy also built on elements put in place by the previous Conservative government, and arguably benefited considerably from a benign international economic environment. The opposition parties have in many respects shadowed, and sometimes anticipated, the policy lines of the government, but they have not been without criticism of important aspects of government policy. In particular, the opposition parties have been harsh critics of the sheer complexity of the benefits system (and especially tax credits), and of the largely unchanged numbers on Incapacity Benefit and NEETs (young people Not in Education, Employment or Training). At the same time, benefits experts have also pointed out subtle flaws, such as the lack of responsiveness of benefits to the rapid fluctuations in earnings that many workers on benefits experience which has led to a growing problem of indebtedness among low income families (Millar 2008). Two other key challenges remain. First, policy has encouraged a high concentration of employment (particularly for lone parents) in poorly paid part-time employment where prospects for career progression and job retention are poor (Evans et al 2004). Second, policy has done relatively poorly at lifting couples with children out of poverty and has encouraged parents to live apart (Brewer 2007). Policy has yet to effectively deal with either of these problems.

While New Labour's record on employment has been strong there can be no doubt that policy has benefited substantially from a benign economic environment (Hills and Stewart 2005). The evaluation evidence on lone parent employment however suggests that the package of policies introduced to promote employment contributed around one-fifth (or 5 percentage points) to overall employment growth (Gregg and Harkness 2003; Francesconi and van Der Klaauw 2007). Yet policy has made a difference and one of the strengths of the Labour government, in relation to employment and benefits policy, has been a commitment to evidence-based policy.[6] The resulting voluminous research on the evaluation of employment programmes is too great to analyse in depth here. In short, policy under Labour began with the introduction of a series of active labour market programmes such as the 'New Deals' that were targeted at different types of claimants (young, unemployed, long-term unemployed, lone parents, disabled and others). Increasingly this categorical approach has made less sense as unemployment drifted down and attention had to shift to those with multiple disadvantages. 'Beyond the New Deal' was a phase used to signify that programmes gradually became more focused on individual circumstances and less on the labels given to people by the system. Part of this process required claimants to be involved in discussions about employment or intention in the first instance and in recent years has introduced a greater element of conditionality – both around being available for work and active job-searching. Claimants with problems of ill-health have had benefit changes that will respond to their employability rather than their incapability of work with the replacement of 'Incapacity Benefit' with an 'Employment Support Allowance' from October 2008. This change will introduce a new expectation that those claiming these benefits should also be engaged in job search, as well as introducing a package of support to help individuals move into employment. For lone parents, changes which will come into force from November 2008 will move them from Income Support to Jobseeker's Allowance when their children reach the age of 12 rather than 16, and this will fall to the age of 7 in 2010.[7] These most recent proposals put out-of-work benefits solely into two categories: Jobseeker's Allowance and Employment Support Allowance (DWP 2008b). The expectation is that by requiring lone parents to engage in job search activities (but with no requirement to take up work) and to provide them with enhanced support to enter employment through training and so on, more lone parents' awareness of work opportunities will be raised and they will be more likely to enter employment. However as the labour market is likely to tighten substantially in 2009 the success of both these reforms may be modest as lone parents fall further behind in a lengthening queue for work.

The majority of welfare-to-work and training programmes, introduced since 1997, have been found to be effective and cost efficient in general (see for instance Dorsett 2008; Adam et al 2008; Griffiths 2007; Cebulla et al 2008; Thomas 2007; Hasluck and Green 2007; White and Riley 2002). The New Deal programmes have worked best in terms of moving participants into sustainable jobs where local labour markets have been tight. Moreover there has been some variation across client groups, with greater success for, for example, programmes aimed at lone parents than the disabled. For young people, the NDYP effectiveness in tackling youth unemployment has varied significantly across different parts of the country with much greater success in both job entry and retention areas and regions with high labour demand.

Alongside these measures to 'push' people into work through welfare-to-work programmes has been an increase in the generosity of in-work benefits and policies to make work pay. The introduction of tax credits and the minimum wage, supplemented by more recent schemes of in-work credits to further boost income from earnings in the first year of employment, have ensured that incentives for job entry have been much improved. The skills agenda has lagged behind, but recent proposals seek to improve access to training and promote retention and advancement at the bottom of the job market (DIUS and DWP 2007) and to implement the Leitch Report (HM Treasury 2006b; but see also the chapter by Wolf in this volume for a critical view).

A broad view of the evaluation evidence of a host of programmes aimed at promoting job growth suggests that current programmes have seen good but modest improvements in boosting job-entry. Results for job retention and advancement are more equivocal, in part because the low-skilled part of the labour market that has been promoted by policy is by its nature vulnerable to the low pay–no pay cycle, or 'labour market churning'. The evidence also suggests that the measures introduced to date have been cost effective with estimated savings to the Exchequer of several billions from lower benefit bills resulting from higher employment (White and Riley 2002), depending on how much credit is apportioned to government programmes versus the wider economic conditions.

Among the client groups for whom the 'best' results have been seen are lone parents, for whom the package of reforms has relied on voluntary participation and making work pay. For the long-term unemployed, partners of the unemployed, and for interventions such as the education option in New Deal for under-25s, the results have been less impressive. For job entry, incentives to start work have had beneficial effects for lone parents; but for second earners in couples, job entry incentives remain weak. The upcoming two-year results from the Employment Retention and Advancement randomized control trial also suggest some positive news and have been fed back into pilot programmes (initially for lone parents) for in-work credits. Finally, delivery of employment programmes will change with the involvement of market organizations for long-term non-employed, with grounds for cautious optimism. The role and success of market and voluntary organizations in providing employment services is well-rehearsed in the USA and Australia, though recent UK experience has yielded mixed results.

The approach as it stands has been very much focused on job entry and reducing levels of worklessness but has been constrained by some of the structural characteristics of the labour market. For example, the low skilled while moving out from non-employment remain at risk of being trapped in a repeated low pay–no pay cycle, and are likely to be in poor quality, often part-time, work with poor prospects for pay and progression. The effect of recent changes to prioritize skills and job retention are as yet unknown. Furthermore the effect of a recession in 2009 may make implementation of these and a continued emphasis solely on the supply side less sustainable. Particular grounds for concern come from evidence that the UK's New Deal programmes have proved far less successful in geographical areas with less tight labour markets, suggesting that their effectiveness may falter in a time of rising unemployment (Martin et al 2001). Of course, as we have already seen, the characteristics of those who are already workless have become progressively worse over time and their ability to compete for jobs is likely to become more constrained in a recession. There is an urgent need for active labour market training programmes such as the New Deal in order to offset and prevent further deterioration in terms of employability and well-being of the worklessness during an economic downturn.

Policy options for incoming government

Moves to make all benefits for working-age people conditional on looking for work appear to have achieved cross-party consensus and are likely to form a fundamental plank of any future employment programmes whatever the outcome of the forthcoming general election. One of the outcomes of such changes will be to raise the numbers counted as 'unemployed' and heralds the likely return of political sensitivity on the level of unemployment.

Even before we consider the potential effects of recession, there are several issues that require consideration about the potential of government to increase employment levels among the workless populations as it stands today in 2008. First, the transaction costs of benefits and other programmes to those who are low-paid and/or out of work must be structurally addressed. There are moves in place to ensure that the multiplicity of claims and agencies are coordinated better in the future with the introduction of single points of contact across the plethora of housing benefits, tax credits, DWP benefits and other agencies (House of Commons Select Committee on Work and Pensions 2007). However, it is crucial that moves to simplification take into account the incentives of organizations, noting that many costs in time and money are to customers rather than the organizations themselves. The inherent systemic transaction costs must therefore be incorporated into funding formulae, operational incentives and performance measurement. To drive improvements in information flows between agencies, system design must consider the role of the claimant offering not only single points of information provision but also underwriting losses that result from poor information handling. This is not 'sexy' policy but a straightforward public management issue that is insufficiently considered or compensated by political rewards at the highest level. Ministers need to be rewarded for running benefits and employment policy well, including addressing its structural problems, rather than being rewarded for changing policy to improve their profile in time for the next reshuffle. But it is crucial that we understand how these structures relate to employment. The workless population tend to be both risk-averse and yet also face relatively greater risk. They are more likely to enter employment with poor working conditions; to be subsequently laid off; and to have income fluctuations when in employment. Reducing the plethora of means-tests and organizations, harmonizing time frames across weekly, monthly, or annual assessments and a greater emphasis on income and risk smoothing is required. Reducing the time required to get back on the unemployment register would be good, particularly for individuals stuck in the low pay–no pay cycle.

Efficiency or employment gains for the workless, such as from single points of information and streamlined transactions, should be the priority in policy change, not efficiency gains for the government or provider per se. In the authors' view, there are real dangers in the extra layer of agencies that accompany the involvement of new 'market providers'. A major problem with market providers as seen in the USA and Australia is that they tend to try to get their 'clients' into jobs as quickly as possible and off their books in order to meet contract targets. The jobs they enter therefore are often low paid and insecure which do not promote labour market sustainability.

The policy shift to the use of workfare programmes is also problematic. These schemes mandate participation in unpaid work activities as a condition of benefit receipt, yet international evidence suggests these schemes need to be matched with other elements of welfare reform (such as job search and time limits). Also a strong labour market is important to their success (Crisp and Fletcher 2008). Private sector and voluntary agencies involved in provision require contracts for performance on employment, job entry and retention but the terms of these contracts will need careful specification to ensure that information flows and brokerage for the claimant are improved.

Second, while the overall improvements in 'making work pay' have been impressive since 1997, there are areas where employment incentives have worsened. The incentives for partners to enter work when there is already one earner are very poor indeed, with effective marginal rates of 70–96% arising from tax and benefit tapers. Extending the in-work credit approach or altering the tapers of tax credits for second earner job entrants requires consideration.

Similarly, for those whose ability or opportunities to work are severely constrained, the current set of disregards for one-off or 'mini-jobs' are extremely poor. A £5 weekly disregard is less than one hour at the minimum wage and makes no sense. It is, in general, important not to set up long-term support for work at the margins for those who are able to work permanently and for considerable hours. But an increasing share of the workless, who increasingly face multiple disadvantages, will benefit from rewards for one-off work, or from small fixed-term jobs of a few days. At the moment the only incentive to take up such work is to do it 'off the books'. This incentive for those on benefits to move into the grey economy, alongside a punitive over-reaction to fraud, needs to be reconsidered if the remaining workless who are at the margins of employment are to be coaxed back into any form of formal labour market engagement. Probity and combating fraud and abuse should continue to be an important aim, but such action should focus on the larger scale and organized end of illegality rather than working at the margins of employment.

But let us return to the issue that currently haunts employment prospects in the foreseeable short-term future: the likelihood of a full recession in 2009. Can the approach to employment policy continue to be solely focused on the supply side if the position of those currently workless, who already have comparatively poor characteristics, is not to fall relatively further behind? Past experience suggests that those most vulnerable include the young, low skilled and older workers. Women, part-time workers and those on temporary contracts are also susceptible to a downturn, and while to date job losses have been concentrated in the construction and financial service sectors, as the recession deepens the effects are extending to other sectors, with service sector employment likely to be particularly hard hit. As we have already seen, the past success of many government programmes has been dependent on a buoyant economy and devising policy to respond to a tougher economic climate is likely to prove challenging.

Notes

1. Note that 1984 and 1993 were similar points in the economic cycle, both were periods of recession with low levels of relative employment.
2. See for example Manning and Petrongolo (2008) for a discussion of the poor quality of part time female jobs.
3. Source: Quarterly Labour Force Survey data, http://www.statistics.gov.uk
4. Source: Centre for Economic Performance (2006).
5. CEP Policy Briefing Paper CEPPA005.
6. As we have seen in other chapters, this commitment to evidence-based policy has not been so strong in some other policy areas.
7. Only those lone parents unable to work through illness or disability will be entitled to claim Employment Support Allowance.

5
NHS, Health and Well-being

John Appleby and Adam Coutts

> 'Health and well-being are measures of the degree to which the society delivers a good life to its citizens.'
>
> (Marmot 2004)

Introduction

On the eve of the 1997 general election, Tony Blair famously declared that there were just 24 hours to save the NHS. Election hyperbole aside, 1997 was not a good year for the NHS and the electorate knew it. Public satisfaction with the NHS was at an all time low. The British Social Attitudes survey (BSA 1997) reported that net satisfaction had reached a low of 15 percentage points, the worst rating since the first survey in 1983. And in what was to be John Major's last year as Prime Minister, UK NHS spending (adjusted for NHS-specific inflation) actually fell by nearly 0.4% for the first time in many years. Waiting lists in England[1] stood at nearly 1.2 million and rising. And, following some success in reducing the number of people waiting over a year, numbers had started to rise. Things, as Labour's 1997 adopted election campaign song had asserted, could only get better.

The questions were and indeed remain, how much better, with what policies and at what cost? New Labour's 1997 manifesto provided some of the answers: waiting lists were to be cut by 100,000; cancer waiting times were to be abolished as was the internal market; there would be standards set for hospital quality and a new public health drive. And the cost? A real (though unquantified) increase in spending each year – to be spent on 'patients not bureaucracy' (Labour Party Manifesto 1997).

Inevitably, after a decade in power and the exigencies of what Harold Macmillan called 'events', New Labour's 1997 manifesto provides only a suggestive historical glimpse of what has actually happened to the NHS and the health and well-being of the nation. With the obvious benefit of hindsight, this chapter provides a critical examination of how well the NHS and other non-health sector policies and interventions have done in terms of delivering health services to improve the nation's health and well-being over the last ten years. We begin by outlining Labour's health policy journey since 1997 before examining and the outcomes of policy over the past decade as well as the key elements which have helped drive policy success and failures. A state of the nation's health and well-being is presented outlining current and future trends in health, health service delivery and usage. In the light of this, we finally propose a number of health promoting policy options for an incoming government, the NHS and the nation's health.

Labour's health policy journey: 1997 to 2007

Set against the charge that, if the Conservatives were re-elected the NHS might well not survive, New Labour's over-arching promise in its 1997 manifesto was a reiteration of its commitment to an NHS free at the point of use with access based on need not ability to pay. Three pledges stood out – particularly in light of the unfurling of policy over the next ten years.

First was the promise to 'End the Tory internal market' including GP fund holding. The idea that separating the purchase from the provision of health care – introduced in the early 1990s under the Conservatives' white paper *Working for Patients* (DoH 1989) – had, according to Labour, achieved little apart from increased transaction costs and bureaucracy. In practice, ending the internal market would not involve a return to pre-Working for Patients days: separation of health care provision from health care planning was seen as a good thing, but competing for contracts and negotiating prices was seen as bad. The objective was '... to restore the NHS as a public service working co-operatively for patients, not a commercial business driven by competition'.

Second, the manifesto pledged to tackle what was seen as the public's number one complaint about the NHS: waiting. Lists would be cut by 100,000 and cancer patients would not have to wait for surgery.

Third, the tricky question of spending in the context of an overall commitment to stick by Conservative public spending plans for the first two years in office was dealt with by an unquantified pledge to 'Raise spending in real terms every year' (Labour Party Manifesto 1997).

This, then, was the start of the policy journey, enshrined in Labour's 1997 white paper, *The New NHS: Modern, Dependable*. For their first two years in power Labour were broadly true to their word and thrust of the white paper. The internal market was, to an extent, dismantled; spending was increased slightly more than previous Conservative plans; and, after initially rising, waiting lists were eventually reduced by 100,000.

In 1999, shortly following the publication of *Saving Lives: Our Healthier Nation* (a revamped and updated version of the Conservatives' *The Health of the Nation* (DoH 1992) the then Secretary of State for Health, Frank Dobson, was replaced by Alan Milburn and a new policy direction soon developed. Late 1999 and early 2000 was in many ways a watershed time for the NHS. Not only was there a new ministerial team in charge, but Labour's pledge to stick to Conservative spending plans was ending and the clamour from the NHS for a boost in funding – not least to cope with meeting an increasing number of centrally-inspired targets – was growing. There was also a feeling (and frustration in government) that the NHS was not delivering improvements fast enough. The political response came – somewhat unexpectedly – in an interview with the Prime Minister, Tony Blair, on the *Breakfast with Frost* programme when the Prime Minister announced an aspiration to increase the percentage of GDP spent on health care in the UK up to the average for EU countries over the following five years. Apart from some quibbling about what this actually meant (spending on private care was included and the target was an unweighted average; Boyle and Appleby 2000), there was no doubt that the pledge would involve a large increase in public spending. The March 2000 budget confirmed the boost to NHS spending up to 2003/04 (HM Treasury 2000a). Significantly, it also heralded the publication of the *NHS Plan* that summer (DoH 2000). Part shopping list and part policy statement, the *NHS Plan* set out new targets for reducing waiting times and health inequalities, increasing NHS staffing, equipment and infrastructure as well as providing the first indications of a new policy direction.

The Plan's diagnosis of the problem with the NHS was that it lacked national standards; that outmoded demarcations between staff groups and services prevented it finding innovative – indeed 'modern' – ways of working; and that there was a lack of clear incentives and levers to improve performance. Such a diagnosis could have been made at almost any time in the history of the NHS – indeed, it had been, in the 1989 white paper, *Working for Patients*. The prescription – in particular over the lack of incentives and levers to improve performance – did not however hark back to the solution of that earlier white paper – the internal market – rather, its proposals centred more on tighter regulation and publication of achievements against targets together with rewards for performance such as limited opt out from the targets regime – 'earned autonomy' – for NHS organizations that had achieved their targets. The *NHS Plan* was the bridging policy document between Labour's manifesto-inspired policy goals and what was to turn out to be somewhat of a looping policy return to solutions originally proposed in *Working for Patients*.

It was not until 2002 and the publication of *Delivering the NHS Plan: Next Steps on Investment, Next Steps on Reform*, that the new direction of travel became clearer. On incentives to improve performance the white paper was very clear. 'Having got the structures right …' – a somewhat presumptive claim given later reorganizations – it went on to state that

… we now need to introduce stronger *incentives* to ensure the extra cash produces improved performance. Primary Care Trusts will be free to purchase care from the most appropriate provider – be they public, private or voluntary. The hospital payment system will switch to *payment by results* using a regional tariff system of the sort used in many other countries. To incentivise expansion of elective surgery so that waiting times fall, hospitals or DTC/surgical units that do more will gain more cash; those that do not, will not. (DoH 2002: 4–5)

It also clarified the choices of hospital open to patients; the implementation of greater autonomy for hospitals through designation of Foundation Trust status under a new independent regulatory regime; and the expansion of the use of the private sector for NHS work, not just as part of a capacity-building programme but to deliberately promote diversity in supply and competition. Potential hard-edged incentives for health care providers through the exercise of patient choice was reinforced through a new activity-based prospective reimbursement system – 'Payment by Results' – which paid hospitals for the patients they treated based on a national tariff derived from the average national cost of specific treatments and operations. There was an evolution in regulatory structures, including morphing of the Commission for Healthcare Improvement into the Healthcare Commission and then into the Care Quality Commission, and a reiterated commitment to move away from micro-management and central control (though, of course, many central targets, particularly concerning waiting times reductions remained in place). Together these represented what Simon Stevens (then adviser on health in No.10) later characterized as the third phase of reform, the 'localist challenge', the first phase having been more money and capacity for providers and the second 'hierarchical challenge' (tough targets, central standard setting, etc).

With the publication of health minister Lord Ara Darzi's *Next Stage Review* (NSR), *High Quality Care for All* (Darzi 2008), a new direction in policy has been established – although, interestingly, one prefigured in one of Labour's early policy consultations published in 1998, *A First Class Service: Quality in the New NHS* (DoH 1998). While the NSR leaves ongoing system reforms in place, it signals a change in emphasis – broadly, away from quantity and towards, eponymously, quality. While one idea of the NSL – polyclinics – received the headlines, in many ways it is the collection of initiatives around public health, the introduction of patient reported outcome measures in hospitals and an emphasis on clinical leadership for example that provides the important messages about a need for the NHS to focus on safe and high quality care.

What has been achieved, and to what extent can this be attributed to the evolving policy framework? Waiting times have, as we will show, reduced substantially (in England) but is this due to the target regime? The technical help supplied by the then Modernisation Agency to the NHS? Simply the access to more resources – staff, beds etc? The extra capacity provided by the private sector through the Independent Sector Treatment Centre (ISTC) programme? In some areas it is possible to attempt an answer, but in many it is not. One significant problem with such policy assessment is that what is being evaluated – patient choice, the reimbursement system for hospitals (payment by results) for example – is still relatively young, with full patient choice (of any hospital in England) only introduced in April 2008.

Did Labour save the NHS? A health impact assessment of a £60 billion investment

The test of New Labour's manifesto commitment to the NHS was to come two years into their first term when the NHS communicated up the line that there was little chance of the NHS achieving even the modest targets the government had set without more money. Here we look at the government's record on NHS funding – its promises and the reality – and summarize the impact on resources, activity, waiting times, public attitudes and public health and health inequalities.

Funding, capacity and activity

Tony Blair's 2000 commitment to boosting NHS spending to match the average of Britain's European neighbours represented a major financial challenge: spending would need to rise by at least 2 percentage points of GDP – from around 5.3% in 1999/2000 to around 7.3%. Together with private spending of around 1.2%, this would then take total health care spend to around 8.5% of GDP, matching the unweighted average spend of the then 15 European Union countries. As Figure 5.1 shows, the boost in NHS spending started in 2000/01.

Together with private spending, as Figure 5.2 shows, successive real increases outpaced the growth in the economy to increase NHS spending from 7% of GDP in 2000 to 8.5% in 2007/08. The 2007 comprehensive spending review spending plans to 2010/11 suggest total health care spend will reach nearly 9% of GDP in 2011 – one pound in every eleven in the economy will be devoted to health care.

Over the decade to 2007/08, the cash increase of nearly £60 billion – an effective real increase of nearly £50 billion – was to provide the financial investment for an unprecedented rise in labour inputs – and, as it turned out, the cost of those inputs. NHS staffing in England, for example, increased by 30% between 1996 and 2006. The number of consultants rose by nearly 60%; GPs by 20%; nurses by 26% and managers and senior managers by 66% (NHS Information Centre, Staff Statistics 2006). Despite this last figure, by 2006, NHS managers still only represented just over 3% of total NHS staff. Overall, these staff increases represented large overshoots on the targets for additional staff set out in the *NHS Plan* (Wanless et al 2007).

Wages rose too. Consultant pay rates increased by between 20% and 25% between 2002 and 2003, with average earnings increasing from around

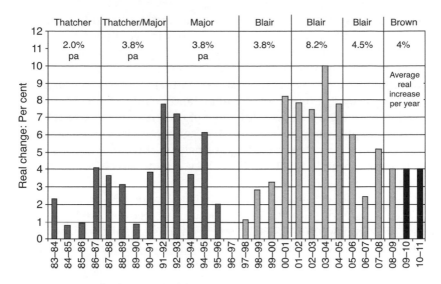

Figure 5.1 Percentage Annual Change in UK NHS Spending

Sources: Author calculations based on: Public Expenditure Survey Analyses (PESA), 2008, http://www.hm-treasury.gov.uk/pespub_index.htm; Department of Health Departmental Annual Reports, 2008, http://www.dh.gov.uk/en/Publicationsandstatistics/Publications/AnnualReports/index.htm

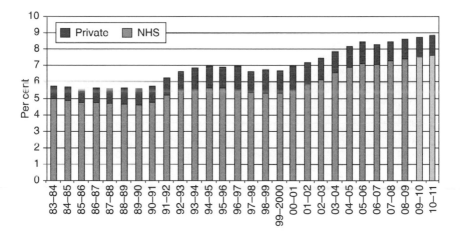

Figure 5.2 UK NHS and Private Health Care Spending as Percentage of GDP

Sources: Author calculations based on: Public Expenditure Survey Analyses (PESA), 2008, http://www.hm-treasury.gov.uk/pespub_index.htm and Treasury GDP deflator data, 2008, http://www.hm-treasury.gov.uk/data_gdp_index.htm

£86,000 to nearly £110,000. GPs' average earnings increased by over 22% between 2003 and 2004, taking average earnings to over £100,000. Overall, between 2002 and 2007, around 43% of the cash increase was absorbed by NHS-specific pay and price inflation (Wanless et al 2007).

Nevertheless, as Wanless et al have shown, virtually all the *NHS Plan* targets for increasing and improving the volume and quality of equipment and general infrastructure were also either met or exceeded (Wanless et al 2007). A notable exception however was the NHS's ambitious plans for modernizing its ICT infrastructure. One of the largest single ICT investment plans in the world (costing around £12 billion) has achieved some successes, but remains off target on its core goals.

Increases in labour and capital capacity enabled the NHS to do more. In England, for example, hospital elective admissions between 1998 and 2006 increased by over 800,000 (15%). Emergency admissions also rose, by nearly a quarter, to 4.7 million. Outpatient and accident and emergency attendances increased by around 10% and 33% respectively.

Productivity

So the rise in inputs was associated with a marked increase in NHS outputs. However, outputs went up slower than inputs particularly from 2001 onwards (reflecting the period covering the boost in spending; see Figure 5.3). Hence productivity fell – by over 10 percentage points between 2000 and 2006. Even

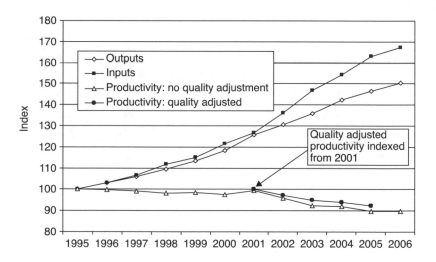

Figure 5.3   Health Care Output, Input and Productivity, 1995–2006

Sources: Office for National Statistics, 2008, Public Service Productivity, UKCeMGA, http://www.statistics.gov.uk/articles/nojournal/HealthCare_290108.pdf

adjusting the productivity figures to try to reflect changes (improvements) in the quality of the outputs produced, productivity still fell.

The failure of the NHS to – at a minimum – maintain its output rise at the level of its inputs meant, for example, that the number of extra elective admissions treated in English hospitals was, at around 800,000, less than half that which could have been treated. The problem, hinted at by Wanless et al when recommending additional spending, was that any significant boost could test the ability of the NHS to effectively absorb such huge amounts. And indeed, this seems to have been the case.

Waiting times

If there was one consistently dominant policy objective over the last decade then reducing waiting times was probably it, and a considerable proportion of the extra investment in the NHS was earmarked to meet this goal (DoH 2008b). In March 1997 the total English NHS inpatient waiting list stood at nearly 1.2 million. A year later it had reached 1.3 million. But from this peak it declined and so too did the numbers of patients waiting over a year. As Figure 5.4 shows, by March 2008, few patients waited more than three months on inpatient waiting lists – a massive change from 1997 when over 1 million waited longer than three months and 13% waited more than nine months.

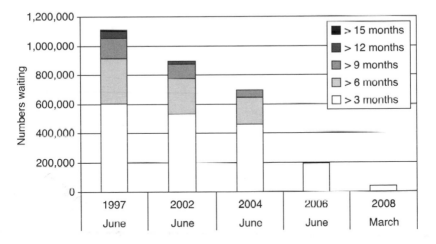

Figure 5.4   English NHS Inpatient Waiting Lists by Timeband

Source: Author calculations based on DoH, 2008, Quarterly Hospital Waiting Time Statistics, http://www.performance.doh.gov.uk/waitingtimes/index.htm

The achievement in reducing waiting lists – now 530,000 compared to over 1.2 million a decade ago – and especially in reducing waiting times (including the median waiting time, now just five weeks compared to nearly twelve in 1997) should not be underestimated. Not only was waiting seen as an intractable problem, it was also viewed as one of the unavoidable rationing devices in a system that had rejected rationing by price on equity grounds. Despite some problems with illegitimate methods for reducing waiting times (NAO 2001, 2002), tactics which continue to take some of the gloss of achieving the government's 18-week maximum target by the end of 2008, the mixture of extra cash, targets, redesign of patient pathways and political and managerial focus tackled the problem.

Waiting times were also reduced in other parts of the system. Waits for outpatients have fallen; the maximum wait of four hours to be seen in an A&E department has been largely met; and maximum waits to see a GP or a specialist as part of the two-week fast track cancer referral programme have also been largely met. None of these successes has been without problems. Apart from some cases of undesirable tactics in reducing inpatient waiting times (NAO 2001, 2002). Some consultants have also complained of distortions to their clinical practice, with pressure to treat less urgent cases ahead of more urgent ones. Despite these and other problems, tackling what was one of the public's major concerns with the NHS has proved a success. With this in mind we now turn to a key barometer of policy success – the attitudes of the public and patients.

Public and patient attitudes

Over the last ten years, the state of NHS has been viewed as one of the most important and critical issues among the British public (see Figure 5.5). On the eve of the 1997 election, a MORI opinion poll of the British population

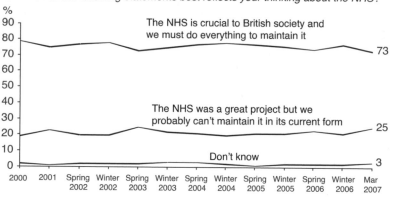

Q. *Which of the following statements best reflects your thinking about the NHS?*

Base: English adults age 16+ (c.1,000 per wave)

Figure 5.5   Public Attitudes to the NHS

Source: Ipsos MORI 2007 survey.

reported that 63% stated the NHS to be the most important issue facing Britain. This figure has fallen to just 15% today, with issues such as crime (47%) and the economy (41%) taking precedence as issues of national concern – albeit probably temporarily in the case of the economy.

Recently Ben Page (2008) and MORI (2008b) reported the highest recorded levels of satisfaction with NHS services, with waiting times the lowest for 40 years. However, there remains a discrepancy between high public satisfaction with the care they receive and their perception that the NHS is in crisis.

Encouragingly, those who have recently been patients report higher satisfaction ratings. More than 90% rated their inpatient care as good, very good, or excellent. Similarly, 74% of those who attended a general practice or local health care centre were completely satisfied that their main reason for attending had been dealt with and only 4% were not satisfied at all (MORI 2008b). In the British Social Attitudes surveys (BSA), those with recent contact with GP services record satisfaction rates of 80% compared with 60% for those without recent contact – a gap of 20 percentage points. The gap for dentists is 39, outpatients 27 and inpatients 26 points (Appleby and Phillips 2009).

BSA surveys show net satisfaction with the NHS overall in 2007 is at its highest level for nearly 25 years. However, there has been a fall in the percentage agreeing that taxes should rise to allow more spending on health and other public services from a peak in 2002 of 63% to just over 40% in 2007, though at least 70% still choose health as their top priority for extra government spending (Appleby and Phillips 2009). Nevertheless, other surveys suggest a degree of dissatisfaction. The Commonwealth Fund found, for example, that 15% of the public agreed with the statement that 'our healthcare system has so much wrong with it that we need to completely rebuild it' and 57% agreed that 'there are some good things in our healthcare system but fundamental changes are needed to make it work' (Commonwealth Fund 2007).

Explaining how the public's satisfaction with the NHS and its services change over time is not easy – not least due to changes in the public's expectations. However, recent experience of the NHS, age and party political identification all seem to contribute. On the other hand, massive reductions in inpatient waiting times do *not* seem to be reflected in improvements in attitudes towards inpatient services, with rates of satisfaction with waiting having remained relatively constant since 2001.

Public health, health inequalities and personal responsibility

As noted in the first *Options for Britain* publication, the Labour Party in opposition made political capital out of the Conservatives' lack of acknow-ledgement and unwillingness to implement the recommendations of the Black report on inequalities in health. When the Labour government came to power in 1997 they acknowledged and focused upon the social and structural determinants of health as proposed in the Black Report and later in the

Acheson Report (1998). Indeed the past decade has witnessed increasing political responsibility both internationally and domestically to tackling inequalities in health (Acheson 1998; DoH 1999, 2000, 2007b; Wanless 2002; WHO 2008). There has been a growing recognition of the complexity and multiplicity of the determinants of these inequalities; their long-term nature; and their entrenchment within wider social structures such as the economy, labour market, neighbourhoods and communities. As Tony Blair commented, these are '... policy areas that are public health policy in disguise'.[2]

With a large proportion of an individual's health being determined by a lifetime's consumption of health, welfare and private goods – in turn determined by income and class (Berkman and Kawachi 2000; Black 2008) – the implied policy actions were not straightforward. Reducing waiting times was clearly NHS business, but reducing gaps in life expectancy between the rich and the poor was altogether a different and more intractable problem, cutting across both government departments and public and private sectors. Nevertheless, across most government departments there was a significant amount of activity related to tackling inequalities via the social determinants of health. These were brought together in a systematic and coherent manner with a cross-cutting review on health inequalities conducted by the Treasury with the participation of 18 government departments and agencies – *The Programme for Action*. These departments entered into 82 commitments aimed at tackling health inequalities including Public Service Agreements covering reduction of health inequalities for infant mortality and life expectancy.

At the same time, there has been a gradual move towards a more liberal agenda of advocating increased personal responsibility for individual health and well-being, and in inducing cultural and behavioural change to achieve policy goals. The *Choosing Health* white paper (DoH 2004) clearly stressed the role of the individual in improving and maintaining health:

> Interventions and policies designed to improve health and reduce health disadvantage should provide the opportunity, support and information for individuals to want to improve their health and well-being and adopt healthier lifestyles. Policy cannot – and should not – pretend it can 'make' the population healthy. But it can – and should – support people in making better choices for their health and the health of their families. It is for people to make the healthy choice if they wish to.

Similarly, the Wanless review (2002) outlined the rights and responsibilities between the individual and government for improving health and well-being as well as advocating a strategy of preventive health care.

As Wanless pointed out, in the absence of 'full engagement', it may be difficult to sustain a universal and comprehensive NHS: the costs of unhealthy behaviours may be unaffordable, and targets, incentives, choices, shorter waiting times and better equipment may not be effective if the population do not adopt healthier ways of living. Indeed, this policy mindset has come to the fore in policies aimed at tackling the three dominant personal vices of the British population – smoking, drinking and over-eating – via public smoking bans, the *National Alcohol Harm Reduction Strategy* (Cabinet Office 2004) and the *Healthy Weight, Healthy Lives Strategy* (DoH 2008c).

It has come to be recognized that 'The government cannot do it alone' (Halpern et al 2004; Knott et al 2007). In order to achieve sustainable lasting outcomes and widespread social improvements, much depends on changes in individual personal behaviour. This means individuals adopting a better diet and taking up more exercise, and, in education, the emphasis is on children's willingness to learn and parents' willingness to help them learn (Knott et al 2007). Policy interventions based on behaviour change can be significantly more cost-effective and preventive than traditional service delivery. For example, altering an individual's diet to one that reduces and prevents the risk of cardiovascular disease is cheaper and more efficient than dealing with the consequences of poor diet with heart surgery. However, one important challenge for behavioural and 'personal responsibility' based interventions is whether higher social groups are more likely to respond to them, thereby improving overall health but leaving the social gap even wider.

A healthy nation?

The overarching objective of health policy over the last decade has been to improve the nation's health and reduce health inequalities. Has it worked?

Health

On most headline measures of health, the last decade has seen improvements in Britain. Overall mortality has declined by 21% for males and 13% for females between 1996 and 2005 (see Figure 5.6). Life expectancy at birth is now at its highest ever level; infant mortality now at its lowest ever level (see Figure 5.7); and cancer survival rates also have shown improvement.

As Wanless et al have noted (2007) there have also been improvements in *premature mortality* (deaths which could have been prevented with the application of existing medical knowledge or where known public health principles had been in force). On the other hand, for some conditions change has been in the wrong direction. For example, there has been a rapid increase in the rates of diabetes. Mortality rates for chronic liver disease and cirrhosis have risen markedly, particularly since the mid-1990s (DoH 2007b). And self-reported measures of health have changed little: there has been virtually no change in the proportion stating their health was good (60%), fairly good (27%) or not good (14%) compared with previous years back to 1998 (ONS 2005).

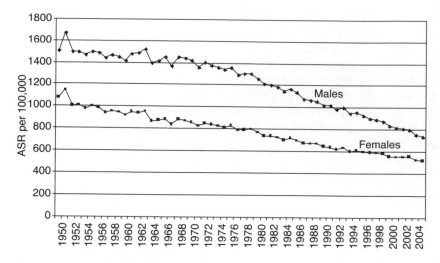

Figure 5.6 Age Standardized Rate per 100,000 All Cause Mortality: Men and Women, 1950–2005

Source: Office of Health Economics, 2008, *Compendium of Health Statistics, 2008* (London: OHE).

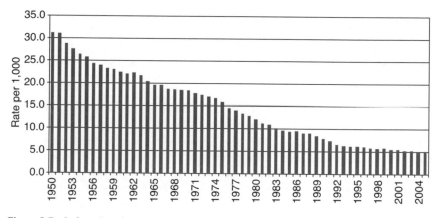

Figure 5.7 Infant Deaths per 1,000 Live Births: England

Source: Office of Health Economics, 2008, *Compendium of Health Statistics, 2008* (London: OHE).

Health inequalities

While in broad terms the health of the British public has improved over the last decade, on the dimensions of equity that are of most concern the *distribution* of health remains somewhat unequally spread. For example, the 'north–south' divide remains, with poorer health in the North of England in comparison to the South in almost all cases. On self-reported health measures, for example, the proportion of men in the North East who assess their health as 'not good' is approaching double that in the South East. And more recently, UNICEF (2007) in their report of *Child Wellbeing in Rich Countries* showed the UK to be the poorest performer amongst OECD nations in terms of children's ratings of their subjective well-being (see Figure 5.8).

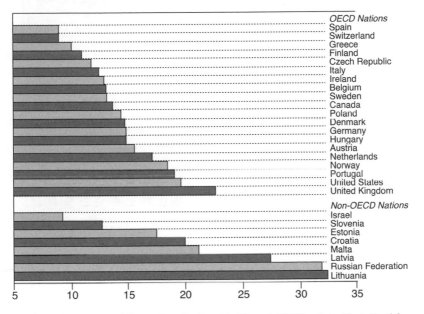

Figure 5.8 Percentage of Young People Age 11, 13 and 15 Who Rate Their Health as 'Fair or Poor'

Source: UNICEF, 2007, *Overview of Child Wellbeing in Rich Countries.*

In all regions from the midlands northwards, female life expectancy is significantly shorter than in the regions to the south. Women in the North East and North West live around two years less than those in the South East and South West. A similar pattern exists for men. Even where government has put energy and resources into tackling two specific measures of health inequality – the socio-economic gap in infant mortality and geographical differences in life expectancy – little has, so far, been achieved. Indeed, on the two specific Public Service Agreement (PSA) measures, inequalities have generally remained unchanged over the last decade (Wanless et al 2007; DoH 2007b).

Determinants of health

Smoking remains one of the most significant single determinants of health and health inequalities. Despite starting to decline in 2002 (see Figure 5.9), smoking still accounts for nearly one in five of all deaths a year, costing the NHS £1.7bn p.a. to treat smoking-related conditions. Between 2001 and 2004 the gap in the proportion of smokers between all adults and routine and manual groups has remained almost unchanged (Wanless et al 2007).

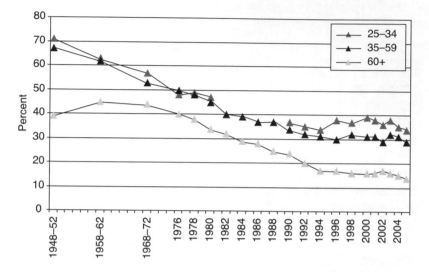

Figure 5.9   Smoking Prevalence: Men

Source: The Information Centre, 2006a, 'Statistics on Smoking', http://www.ic.nhs.uk/pubs/ smokingeng2006

Although obesity is only responsible for around 9,000 (1.8%) premature deaths a year, it is a prime risk factor in type 2 diabetes, heart disease, stroke and some cancers. Moreover, trends in the prevalence of obesity are startling. In 2005, almost a quarter of the adult population was obese – a doubling in 15 years, with England now having the highest proportion of obese people in the EU15. Even more alarmingly, in the decade ending in 2005, the proportion of obese children rose by over 70%.

On another key health determinant – income – changes over the last ten years look encouraging. At an aggregate level, per capita real GDP has increased steadily, rising by over 30% between 1996/97 and 2007/08 (see Chapter 2). There have also been signs (although somewhat mixed) that income distribution has changed in favour of the poor – see Figure 5.10, for example (but see also Chapter 3).

However, Office of National Statistics calculations of the Gini coefficient – a measure of income distribution, which in Figure 5.11 is presented as percentages where a higher percentage implies a more unequal income distribution – suggest that income inequality has, following a large rise up to 1997, remained essentially unchanged up to 2005.

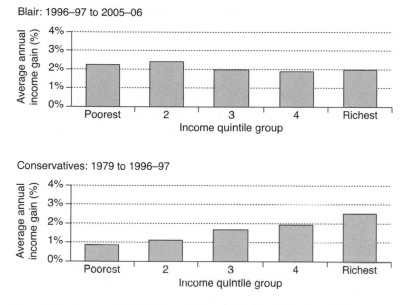

Figure 5.10   Income Distribution 1979 to 1996–97, 1996–97 to 2005–06

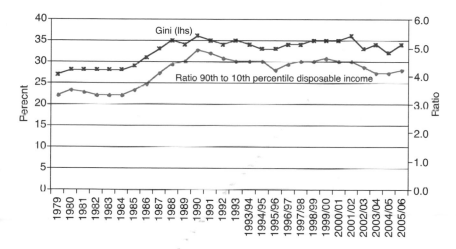

Figure 5.11   Gini Coefficients (%): Disposable Income and Ratio of Income at 90th Percentile to the 10th

Source: Office for National Statistics, 2008, data from http://www.statistics.gov.uk/STATBASE/ ssdataset.asp?vlnk=9638

Future trends and challenges for health and health care

Looking to the future, there are two events which have dominated not just the domestic but the global economy in 2008: the credit crunch and the economic downturn. The impact on the world's financial services sector and government and central bank reactions around the world to the almost complete seizure of wholesale credit markets and the consequent knock-on effects have been unprecedented. Given the massive borrowing by governments not only to support the banking industry but also in an attempt to ameliorate recessionary forces, in the short to medium term it is hard to see public services escaping some the consequences of these actions.

While the macroeconomic environment will undoubtedly dominate economic and fiscal policy over the next few years – and provide a sombre context to public policy in general – there are a number of demand- and supply-side trends and challenges which will inform future policy.

Overall challenges

The first and most immediate health policy challenge – although with some longer-term implications – is the prevailing macroeconomic situation. A combination of falling national output in 2009 – the first time since the early 1990s (see Figure 5.12) – and its implications for tax revenues and huge financial commitments by government in support of the banking industry

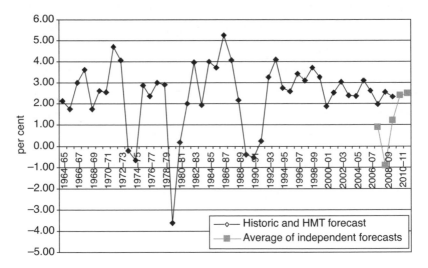

Figure 5.12   GDP: Annual Percentage Change at Constant Prices, 1964/65 to 2012/13

Sources: For independent forecasts: HM Treasury November forecasts from HM Treasury and independent forecasters, http://www.hm-treasury.gov.uk/d/200811forcomp.pdf. Source for historic GDP: http://www.hm-treasury.gov.uk/data_gdp_fig.htm

will mean that funding growth – not just for health, but all public services – beyond the current spending review (2010/11) will be extremely tight.

Given the likelihood of zero or near zero real (in terms of NHS-specific inflation) funding growth from 2011 to 2014 (and as consequence health spending as a share of GDP starting to fall in absolute terms and fall below the recommended spending paths suggested by Derek Wanless' 2002 review of the future of NHS funding), the key challenge for the NHS is how it will make its budget stretch to meet ongoing commitments and targets. The key challenge for government will be the extent to which it can ameliorate the impact of generally straightened financial times on key public services such as the NHS.

The second overarching policy challenge concerns the apparent intractability of closing the gap in health inequalities on almost any dimension of equity of concern. We have already noted that despite efforts over the last decade, even on the government's own target measures little or no progress has been made on reducing health inequalities. Possibly perversely, over the next few years it is likely, given past experience of recessions, that on some measures of income inequality (for example, the Gini coefficient) inequality could either reduce or at a minimum not get worse (Le Grand 2007a). In part this was due to welfare benefits being maintained and incomes amongst the rich falling more quickly and substantially. Nevertheless, the persistent existence of substantial health variations between classes, income and ethnic groups as well as geography remains a 'wicked' problem and challenge to future governments. The challenge that lies within this issue is the extent to which policymakers are prepared to make the reduction of health inequality a priority – and one that will no doubt require sacrifice on other desirable policy aims.

Demand side trends and challenges

On the public's and patients' expectations and values, it seems highly unlikely to expect no change or a reduction in what the public expect from health services. Harder to identify is the size of the impact of any increasing expectations on health care services. However, trends in information and NHS performance, supply-induced demand and (recessions not withstanding) increasing incomes suggest that pressures will increase. On information, the next decade will see a growth in consumer-oriented data about, for example, the performance of the NHS with new and more accurate information on the patient-assessed quality of services and outcomes. Such information will reveal to the public the extent of variations in health outcomes across the NHS, not just at the level of hospitals, but clinicians and clinical teams. A challenge for the NHS and policymakers will not just be how to manage such information but how to manage the consequent public and patient reaction. Rising real incomes are also likely, at a national level, to fuel pressures to spend more on health care as the value attributed to the outputs of the NHS is ranked more highly.

On health, historic trends in the reduction in mortality rates and to a certain extent morbidity (see Figure 5.13) are likely to continue over the next ten years. While the future trends projected in Figure 5.13 must clearly be based on a simplistic and mis-specified model (zero mortality for men and women by 2039 seems unlikely) the point to note is a half century of mortality reductions and the implications for changes in the pattern of population (ill)health and demographic change. For example, increases in life expectancy will mean that demand for informal care from family, friends and community members could rise by 40% by 2022; particularly affecting those without children who are in need of care (one in five of those over 80 by 2041).

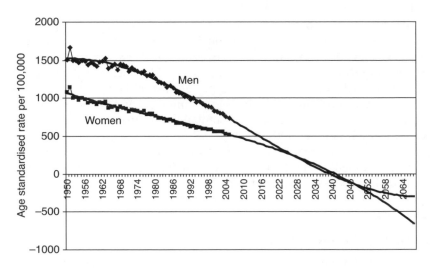

Figure 5.13   Trends in All Cause Mortality, England and Wales, 1950–2068

Source: Author projections based on Office of Health Economics, 2008, *Compendium of Health Statistics, 2008* (London: OHE).

Changes in mortality will be one driver of changes in the demographic structure of the country. Population projections from the Government Actuary's Department suggest that the UK population will grow over the next decade (by around 4.5 million by 2018, see Table 5.1) and thereafter continue to expand to around 85 million by 2081. In addition the composition of the population will change, with a higher proportion of the main users of health and social care services; people aged over 65 will grow from around 16% of the population to nearly 19% in 2018 and then to nearly a quarter by the mid-2030s.

Table 5.1   UK Population Changes 2008–36

| | Share of Age Groups in Total Population | | | | Change in Share 2008–36 | Absolute Change 2008–36 |
	2008	2018	2026	2036		No. ('000)
<20	24.0	23.0	22.9	22.1	–1.9	1,327
20–65	59.9	58.4	55.9	54.5	–5.3	2,905
65–79	11.6	13.3	14.1	15.3	3.6	3,953
>80	4.5	5.3	7.1	8.2	3.6	3,151
Working to non-working age ratio[a]	1.49	1.40	1.29	1.20		
Total UK population ('000)	61,412	65,867	69,260	72,747		11,336

[a] Ratio = (people aged 20–65)/(people aged 0–19 plus 65+)

Source: Author calculations based on Government Actuary's Department, 2008, Projections Database, http://www.gad.gov.uk/Demography_Data/Population/Index.asp?v=Principal&y=2006 &subYear=Continue

The implications for spending may seem obvious but there is considerable uncertainty in making and interpreting projections. For example, taking into account changes in the total composition of the UK population (not just the elderly) and applying current NHS spending on each age group, as Figure 5.14 shows, the impact of demographic change on NHS spend could

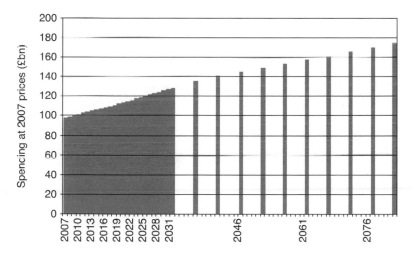

Figure 5.14   Projected Change in UK NHS Spending Arising From All Demographic Change, 2007–81

Source: Author calculations based on Government Actuary's Department, 2008, Projections Database.

be a real increase of around 80% – not insignificant, but not, over 70 years, catastrophic. Given no change in current medical technologies, additional costs due to changes in population structure over the next ten years could add around £1 billion per annum to NHS spending.

Supply side trends and challenges

As we have shown earlier, many of the central reforms of the NHS over the last decade have, in reality, only been in place for a relatively short period of time. Key questions for health policymakers over the next few years will be how changes such as patient choice, the introduction of competitive forces and changes in the structure of financial incentives through employment contracts and payment methods for hospitals will turn out in practice. To date there is a relative dearth of evidence of, for example, the extent to which competition and contestability have brought benefits to patients in terms of better care and access and to the NHS in terms of more efficient and higher quality provision. Moreover, as Scotland, Wales and Northern Ireland further develop their own approach to policy in health, a challenge to all UK countries' systems will be the extent to which common objectives – shorter waiting times, higher quality care, for example – can be achieved by different policy routes.

Secondly, and related to possible demand-side pressures, the next decade will no doubt see further developments and innovation in medical technology. The challenge for the NHS will be how it deals with a possible growing pressure to adopt technologies that may increasingly push the boundaries of what is currently considered cost effective. One outcome of the recent review by Prof. Mike Richards into top-up payments in the NHS has been a suggestion from NICE, for example, to effectively give more weight to the lives of selected groups in the population in order to allow treatments previously deemed not cost effective to be provided by the NHS (Appleby and Maybin 2008). Such a change raises fundamental issues concerning fairness (and efficiency) which will require some collective agreement.

Finally, with long-term projections of health care spending in the UK suggesting expenditure of between 16% and 18% of GDP by 2068 – double today's levels and similar to current US levels of spending (Dormont et al 2008) – there is the question of not only affordability but *desirability* of spending nearly one pound in five in the whole economy on health care. In the shorter term, the November 2008 pre-budget report (HM Treasury 2008b) indicates that while the current NHS spend set out by the 2007 comprehensive review will, by and large,[3] remain untouched, for the next CSR total public spending – including benefit payments – will average around 1.1% in real terms from 2011/12 to 2014/15. After deducting increases in benefit payments – likely to be more than 1.1% due to the general condition of the economy – real increases for the NHS will be negligible. The implication of this will be a concerted challenge on the health and social care systems to generate higher outputs per input; in other (and cruder) words, more bang per buck.

Future health(y) policy themes

In the twenty-first century, there remains a compelling case for a tax-funded, free at the point of need, National Health Service. This chapter celebrates its successes, describes where there is clear room for improvement, looks forward to a bright future, and seeks to secure it for generations to come through the first NHS Constitution. The focus on prevention, improved quality and innovation will support the NHS in its drive to ensure the best possible value for money for taxpayers (Darzi 2008).

The last decade has seen some significant improvements in the nation's health and well-being. As we have shown, a key policy priority to commit a significant extra share of national wealth to health care has been instrumental – but not the only driver – in enabling the NHS to improve its services – most notably to reduce waiting times. Trends in public satisfaction with the NHS have also improved, as have key indicators of population health. However, we also note some qualifications to these successes – not least the difficulty of attributing changes in health to changes in health care funding and system reform policies. We have also set out some key trends and challenges for the future and here identify five related policy themes for the next ten years:

* NHS funding, productivity and organization
* Adapting to changing health care demands
* Health consequences and response arising from economic recession
* Health inequalities
* Investing in health

The NHS

With the prospect of much reduced funding growth at least for the next six or so years, and a set of system reforms which remain relatively new and to a large extent unevaluated, there are three key policy issues that should be addressed:

* Repeat the 2002 review carried out by Sir Derek Wanless into the long-term funding needs of the NHS primarily with a view to update funding projections based on new data but also in the context of a wider public debate about the public's values and expectations concerning the NHS and consequent commitments to funding.

- Tackle the need to make significant productivity and efficiency gains in the NHS using the successful tactics and strategies employed to reduce waiting times: targets backed by frontline help in achieving gains rather than traditional topslicing of 'efficiency savings' followed by managerial exhortations to improve outputs on reduced budgets.
- Review and evaluate system reforms as a collective and interlinked set of policies – from patient choice to foundation trusts and payment by results – to identify the success or otherwise of changes in terms of quantifiable benefits to patients and to abandon irretrievable policy failures.

The pursuit over the next decade of the thrust of the 'vision' set out by Lord Darzi's *Next Stage Review* in 2008 to improve patient safety and the quality of care sets an important direction for the NHS. However, as ever, finding the practical policies to achieve 'an NHS that gives patients and the public more information and choice, works in partnership and has quality of care at its heart' (DoH 2008d: 1) will require consistent (and persistent) political commitment.

Health consequences of economic recession

With economic output falling and unemployment rising into 2010, (and the known relationship between the economic environment, health and social well-being) health, social care and other government agencies should first assess the impact of economic recession on health and social care needs and then devise a coordinated response. There is a vast amount of empirical evidence to show that unemployment has both psychological and physical health impacts (McKee-Ryan 2005). More recently a study by Stuckler et al (2008) found that banking crises are a significant determinant of short-term increases in heart disease mortality rates.

Health inequalities

Population health has improved, but attributing these changes to health policy (either bearing on health care or the more general determinants of health) is, given historic trends in most population health measures, extremely difficult. Things have got better – but it is not always clear why. But some things remain unchanged. A singular failure in policy has been the apparent intractability of achieving even modest and targeted reductions in health inequalities. What this suggests about the effectiveness of policy or the complexity and long-term nature of the problem remains an important question in need of an answer.

However, the recent government commitment to the thrust of Sir Michael Marmot's report on the social determinants of health (WHO 2008) with the setting up of an independent commission to investigate strategies to reduce health inequalities in England beyond 2010 is welcome. However, policy recommendations arising from this important commission on health inequalities need cross-party commitment and high level political support in terms of actual implementation. There is also a need to establish a degree of public agreement over which inequalities generate most concern and where efforts would be best directed to achieve the most significant successes.

Investing in the social determinants of health

Ultimately, the ongoing policy task that faces any government is decisions about actions and investments that will improve the nation's health. Investment in health care is one route to improving health – and one that needs to be pursued, as we indicate above. However, the health of individuals and of populations has many social and economic determinants and as such requires a multi-layered policy approach. While, for example, the main objective of education policy is to educate and of housing to house people, improving access and outcomes in these and other areas such as employment also has impacts on health. *Options 1* did refer to this and over the last ten years good empirical evidence has emerged to show that non-health sector interventions such as those in housing, employment and transport amongst others can improve health and well-being (see for example, Berkman and Kawachi 2000; Molyneux et al 2006; Vinokur et al 2000). Any programme, intervention, strategy and policy aimed at promoting the health and well-being of individuals and communities must be formulated and delivered within the wider context of government policies such as those addressed throughout this book.

As a first step in drawing out the multiple outcomes of non-health care areas of the economy in order to inform possible alternative investment and policy strategies aimed at improving health, therefore, the possibilities and practicalities of producing a health-oriented satellite account to the national accounts, where the output identified is a measure of health rather than one based on financial transactions, should be explored. Secondly, while Health Impact Assessments (HIAs) of non-health care policy initiatives – for example, those carried out by the London Health Commission (LHC) with the support of the Greater London Authority on a range of policy areas such as housing, transport, spatial development and employment (Cave and Coutts 2006; LHC 2008) – have enabled policymakers to explore alternative decisions to improve health as well as meet core non-health objectives. Health improvement policies would benefit from making HIAs a legal requirement of public policymaking such as that already carried out under Strategic Environmental Assessments (SEAs) in the public planning permission processes.

In addition, further steps are required to establish more meaningful and short-term indicators or markers of how policies affect individual health and well-being. Increasing life expectancy and reducing mortality rates are certainly useful long-term markers but we need to know what the immediate impact is of health care delivery but also of wider social policies such as housing and employment programmes. In policy design and monitoring this will entail measuring factors such as psychological health, depression and psychobiological measures which are far more sensitive and display shorter exposure-effect rates to interventions than say cardiovascular disease.

Conclusion

After more than a decade of continuous economic growth, growth which was instrumental in enabling the political decision to be taken to commit an unprecedented share of national wealth to health care spending, the economic fallout of the calamitous breakdown in financial markets during 2008 will set limits and challenges for health care, health and well-being in the next decade. With such a macroeconomic backdrop, and hence little or no spending growth, moving forward with improving the nation's health and reducing health inequalities will require some creative policymaking. However, as long as the often traditional response – to reorganize health systems – is resisted, and with a renewed focus on the quality rather than quantity of care, as set out in the Darzi *Next Stage Review*, plus a clear focus on producing extra value from every health care pound, even in such straightened financial times, there are significant health gains to be made.

Notes

1. Much of the statistical references in this chapter relate to England only. There is not inconsiderable difficulty in collating either a UK- or British-wide set of figures on, for example, waiting times – even NHS spending.
2. Former Prime Minister Tony Blair, 'Healthy Living: Whose Responsibility?', Our Nations Future Speech, 26 July 2006.
3. In fact, around £1 billion will be clawed back by the Treasury in 2010/11 from the NHS capital budget.

6
Education

Alison Wolf

Introduction

'Ask me my three main priorities for Government and I tell you: education, education, and education.'

This is Tony Blair, of course, in his famous speech to the 1996 Labour Party Conference: the eve of Labour victory and the year of *Options for Britain*. There should, he went on, 'be zero tolerance of failure in Britain's schools'. Instead, under Labour, there would be 'radical improvement and reform for our children', and the government would 'ensure that every primary school child leaves school able to read to the adequate standard. A literacy guaranteed ...'

Education was, and would be, the heart of the economy. 'We are 35th in the world league of education standards today – 35th ... Well give me the education system that is 35th in the world today and I will give you the economy that is 35th in the world tomorrow.' We must spend more, spread it more equally, invest in technology in schools, a 'university for industry ... a national grid for learning ... Just think of it – Britain, the skills superpower of the world. Why not? Why can't we do it?'

The voice is inimitably Blair's. His themes have rippled through education policy in the past decade – skills, standards, technology, 'zero tolerance'. Was he sincere about his 'three main priorities'? And did he and his party come close to achieving their specific ends?

The answers, I think, are 'maybe, at least for a while'; and 'only a few'. This is, of course, better than none, and in one specific area – higher education – Blair overturned his own manifesto commitments to create what will surely be one of his most lasting legacies. But here and elsewhere, the incoming government made a number of enormously unrealistic commitments. In office Labour has been finding out that 'fixing' education is very difficult indeed.

This chapter will start by looking at what Labour inherited in 1997. It will then summarise what seemed, ten years ago, to be the most promising policy initiatives, encapsulated in manifesto pledges, or favoured in the policy consensus of the time, notably *Options for Britain* itself. It will then look at where we are, in 2009. Have hopes been fulfilled? Are things really different? And what next?

Labour's inheritance

The education system that Labour took over in 1997 had been transformed under successive Tory governments, especially in England. (Scottish education has always been entirely separate, and run out of Edinburgh, and this continued to be the case in the 1980s and 90s.) English schools, once run almost entirely by local education authorities, were now subject to a national curriculum of internationally unparalleled detail and length. A system of centrally run testing involved every state school pupil at least four times in their career. LEA powers had been further reduced by giving schools control over their own budgets.

'School choice' now allowed parents to apply to a wide variety of schools. The publication of league tables of schools' test results was intended to help parents choose, and incentivize schools to improve their performance. Funding followed the child to a significant degree, and there was enough spare capacity in many areas for under-subscribed schools to be left with declining student rolls, and budgets. In addition, the 1992 Further and Higher Education Act freed sixth-form and further education colleges from LEA control and created a unitary higher education system by turning the polytechnics into universities.

Labour thus inherited a structure, for schools, of centralized control plus parental choice – and retained it. An early and intentionally symbolic act was the retention, as Chief Inspector of Schools, of the controversial Chris Woodhead, an outspoken critic of 'progressive' education. Ten years on, the main features of the Tory settlement have been reinforced and intensified rather than reversed.

At the same time, Labour inherited a system which was visibly short of funds. Capital expenditure on schools had been squeezed for many years; the real level of funding per student, in a fast-expanding higher education system, had more than halved since 1976. The relatively poor performance of British children in international comparisons had been a major force behind the previous Tory governments' determination to carry out school reform; and these surveys, as well as internal results and research, underlined the huge spread in attainment between the best and worst schools, and a 'long tail' of poor achievement among British children.

One obvious policy response was to spend more money. Blair duly promised to increase the proportion of national income spent on education. He also promised to raise standards in all schools. And he set what was to be the first of many targets. In pursuit of that key standards goal he promised, as his third education 'vow', that 'class sizes will be down in primary schools'.

Once in government, of course, concrete policies have to be found with which to deliver sweeping pledges; and here *Options for Britain* (hereafter *Options I*) is actually a good place to start. A high proportion of the myriad education policies which the Labour governments have introduced, appear in nascent form in its pages – including some, like the 'University for Industry', that came and went so quickly that most people never noticed them at all.[1] Labour came into office without having generated detailed policies internally, and the reports and recommendations of 'friendly' think tanks had commensurate influence. In the case of education, another important source of ideas was the independent National Commission on Education, whose main report appeared in 1993: Josh Hillman, who was research officer at the Commission throughout its existence, was also the author of the education chapter in *Options I*.

Three of the key problems and accompanying priorities for action which *Options I* identified resonate very clearly with Blair's (and the 1997 manifesto's) emphases. They are summarized in Table 6.1 and all involved significant increases in spending and were designed to raise standards 'for all'.[2]

Table 6.1   Key Problems in Education and Training Identified by *Options I*

Key Problems in Education & Training Identified by *Options I*	Proposed Solution
Under-investment in the early years	Shift public investment to nursery and primary education
Wide differentials in school performance	Improve school performance by introducing rigorous headteacher selection and training, improving the physical infrastructure, and boosting literacy and numeracy teaching
Low status and quality of teaching	Increase teacher status and quality through giving them a more focused role, exploiting new technologies and increasing their own continuous learning

More generally, a commitment to targets and measured outcomes characterizes all of Labour's last three terms. In one way, however, education is unusual: namely, the importance and influence on policy of international indicators and comparators. This was obvious in the Blair speech quoted above ('35th in the world!'). The most long-standing attainment studies are run by the IEA (the International Association for the Evaluation of Educational Achievement), which has looked at pupils' performance in a number of key subjects over a period from 1959 to the present (http://www.iea.nl; see also Goldstein 1996). More recently, the OECD has started to run its own surveys, notably the PISA studies of teenagers' attainments. Unexpectedly bad showings on these can send a country into a collective nervous breakdown,[3] and are covered with enthusiasm by the media (Rotberg 2004).

However, the measures which mesmerize policymakers, and exert a powerful influence on decision-making, are not confined to these direct measures of attainment. Since 1992, the OECD has also published a massive yearly compendium of indicators (*Education at a Glance*) comparing all the OECD's member states on a range of measures, largely of 'quantity'. It is assumed, implicitly, that more is always better.

Britain has for many years performed relatively poorly on a number of these quantitative indicators. In the last decade, improving the country's relative and absolute performance on measures such as participation and qualification rates has been central to the conduct of policy, driven by targets and Public Service Agreements in a far more organized and systematic way than under the Conservatives (Barber 2007).

Headline figures and score cards

Blair finished his 1996 speech with a list of 'vows'. The education vows were, as noted above, to increase the proportion of national income spent on education; to reduce class sizes in primary schools; and to raise standards in all schools. The first of these is by far the simplest to measure. It has also been achieved. As Figure 6.1 shows, it has been rising steadily, ever since the

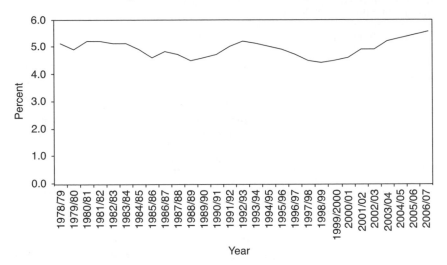

Figure 6.1   Education Spending as % of GDP

Source: Office for National Statistics, *Social Trends 2008*. Data up to and including 1986/87 are based on HM Treasury defined functions; those from 1987/88 are based on the UN Classification of the functions of government (COFOG). Data are public expenditure only. See appendix, part 3: Classification of the Functions of Government (COFOG).

first few 'prudent' years of the late 1990s, to 5.5% – a figure which is well above the previous highs of the early 1980s. In the process it has risen from just under the OECD average (where it remained throughout the 1980s and 90s) to above it.

Reducing average class sizes was the rather limited concrete policy proposed by Blair himself; and sizes are indeed down (see Table 6.2). However, this apparently simple measure in fact introduces one to the endless complexities of measuring, or mandating, educational quality and performance. It seems self-evident to most parents (and most politicians) that smaller class sizes must be good. They are one of the main selling-points of private education, and must, surely, offer more individual attention to each child?

Table 6.2   Class Sizes in English Primary Schools – % of Classes Taught with 31+ Pupils

1977 (all)	1985/6 (all)	1996/7 (all)	2000/1 (all)	2006/7 (Key Stage 1 only)	2006/7 (Key Stage 2 only)
43	26	28	17	2	20

Sources: Glennerster (2002); ONS, *Social Trends 2008.*

However, in a system with some degree of parental choice, the schools with the largest average class sizes are also likely to be the schools that are popular, and vice versa. So if mandating minimum class sizes means denying some children their choice of school, and sending them to an under-subscribed alternative, is that really good for standards? If large amounts of extra money go to over-subscribed schools to bring their classes sizes right down, is that a good use of resources, system-wide?

In fact, research indicates that changes in class size have to be quite substantial to have any major impact, and effects are concentrated among younger children and 'most obvious in the first year of school – the Reception year' (Blatchford 2003: 143). Early commitments to 'no classes over 30' have been scaled back; but as Table 6.2 shows, classes are indeed almost all below 30 for Key Stage 1 (infants). Labour came to power promising 'evidence-based policy', and, here, have acted accordingly. As discussed later, many subsequent policy decisions show no such evidence base.

And so to standards. The policy priorities identified by *Options I*, and by successive Labour manifestos, are all means to the end of 'raising standards'. Indeed, 'standards' are increasingly the only yardstick used in formulating and evaluating schools policy. This is also highly disputed territory. The government cites an array of statistics and measures which appear to indicate major and sustained improvements in performance and results obtained. Critics argue that the measures are misconceived or fallible, the gains overstated, and that some statistics actually indicate a worsening of outcomes.

As Table 6.3 and Figures 6.2 and 6.3 indicate, the period 1997–2006 was one in which there were major quantitative gains on key indicators, especially those relating to formal qualifications. The percentages reaching 'expected' (desired) levels of attainment in the centrally set 'key stage' tests rose, sometimes slightly and sometimes very markedly. So did the percentages attaining formal qualifications at age 16. The percentage of the cohort entering higher education also rose, albeit less markedly (Figure 6.3).

Table 6.3   Pupils Reaching or Exceeding Expected Standards Through Teacher Assessment by Key Stage and Sex

England	Percentages			
	1997		2007	
	Boys	Girls	Boys	Girls
Key Stage 1				
English				
Reading	75	85	80	88
Writing	72	83	75	86
Mathematics	82	86	88	91
Science	84	86	87	90
Key Stage 2				
English	57	70	73	83
Mathematics	63	65	78	78
Science	68	70	84	85
Key Stage 3				
English	52	70	68	81
Mathematics	62	65	78	80
Science	60	63	73	76

Source: Department for Children, Schools and Families.

In comparative terms, however, trends are confusing and messages mixed. For every increase in UK totals, it seems, other countries also moved upwards. The proportion of the adult population with upper secondary level qualifications remains below average for the OECD, as does the proportion of 18 year olds in full-time education. Ministers and policy-makers have become increasingly occupied with the number of science and engineering graduates being produced by Chinese and Indian universities and their supposed threat to UK competitiveness. (HM Treasury 2006b; but see also Lewis 2004 and Bhidé 2008 for an alternative analysis of competitiveness.)

The government was delighted to trumpet the results of the first OECD PISA studies of 15 year olds' attainment, carried out in 2000. These showed English students (largely educated under the Tories) scoring 4th best in the OECD for science, 7th for reading and 8th for mathematics. However, the 2006

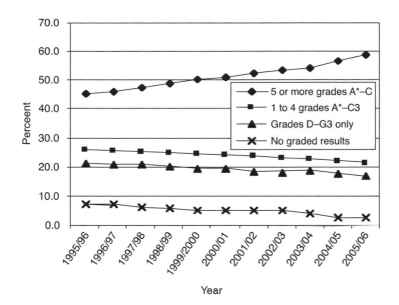

Figure 6.2 GCSE or Equivalent Achievements, by Grade

Source: ONS, *Social Trends 2008*, chapter 3.

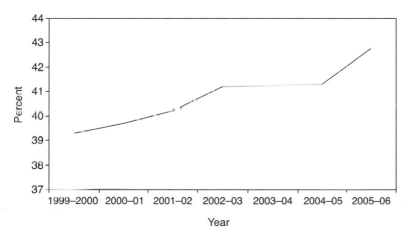

Figure 6.3 Higher Education Initial Participation Rate (HEIPR)

Notes: English domiciled first-time entrants to higher education courses of at least six months duration. Entrants aged 17–30 inclusive expressed as a percentage of the cohort reaching 18 that year.

Source: Statistical First Release DfES: 2005–6 figures provisional, provided in written answer to House of Commons by Bill Rammell, 22 January 2008.

results were far less stellar. They showed a slip to 9th in science, joint 11th in reading and 18th in maths. Most recently, the International Association for the Evaluation of Educational Achievement (IEA) Mathematics and Science study results (TIMMS 2007 – see Mullis et al 2008) cover different ages, a rather different set of countries, and offer a picture which is different again. England appears consistently in the second-to-top group, behind the Asians and level-pegging with, for example, the Netherlands, Hungary and the US. In substantive terms, Year 4 results are substantively better than in previous surveys, Year 8 ones much the same; but that goes for most other countries as well.

It is difficult to make clear sense of this, though individual figures will continue to hurtle back and forth, in a political debate over 'standards' which governments themselves invite. Rather than just counter-pose positive and negative numbers, the next section therefore looks at the major policies which Labour has introduced in attempting to deliver Blair's promise of 'radical improvement'. It takes, as its framework, the three major areas identified by *Options I*, in all of which Labour has indeed been highly active. What impact has this had on the operation of England's education system?

Raising standards? Reform in practice

Early years education

The *Options I* recommendation to focus on pre-school and primary education reflected a consensus among education experts which the intervening years has confirmed and indeed strengthened. In the pre-school years, the developmental gap between children from advantaged and disadvantaged homes widens at a rapid rate. Equally, the attainment of children at the end of primary schooling provides an extremely powerful basis on which to predict their later performance – those who are behind at that point find it very hard to catch up (Feinstein 2003, 2004; Cassen and Kingdon 2007; Astle 2007).

There is some strong evidence that good pre-school programmes can make a difference. As the large, government-funded Effective Provision of Pre-school Education (EPPE) project confirmed, high quality programmes have clear effects that last into primary school, and disadvantaged children stand to gain the most (Sylva et al 2004a, 2004b; see also Goodman and Sianesi 2005).

The evidence is not, however, quite as encouraging as it is often made out to be. Only some programmes have a clear impact on primary school performance; and those where the impact is demonstrably long-term, lasting into teens and adulthood, have tended to be highly structured and quite small programmes run by individuals who combined charisma and depth of scholarship with access to unusually high levels of funding (notably the famous Perry Pre-School Program).[4] Extrapolating from this to all pre-school provision is unjustified. The basic underlying message, however, remains.

High quality programmes produce long-term gains that clearly justify their expense. Conversely, without early intervention, disadvantaged students drop rapidly behind their peers.

Until the mid-1990s, this country, compared to most other European countries, provided relatively little subsidy for pre-school education and childcare. This began to change before Labour's victory, with the introduction of a nursery education voucher scheme by the Major government, responding – as has Labour – both to research and to increased demand from both two-earner families and single parents. The proportion of 3 and 4 year olds enrolled in schools (nursery or primary) has risen steadily over the whole period 1970–2000, peaking at 65% in 2003/04 and currently at 64% (Figure 6.4).

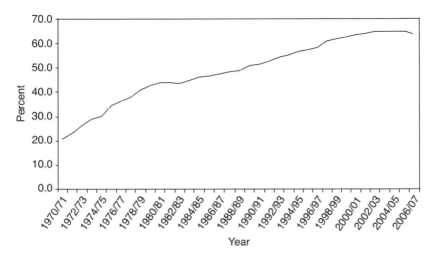

Figure 6.4 Children Under Five in Schools, United Kingdom

Source: Department for Children, Schools and Families; Welsh Assembly Government; Scottish Government; Northern Ireland Department of Education.

Labour has increased public expenditure in the early years sector enormously. In 2005–06 prices, it has more than doubled: from just over £2 billion in 1997–98 to around £5 billion in 2005. Sessional day-care has declined while full-day care has increased (reflecting work patterns rather than research: educationally, part-time provision is as effective as full-time; Sylva et al 2004a). Overall, the use of formal provision has increased significantly in recent years (Astle 2007).

The government's offer is of a universal entitlement to free part-time nursery education, and additional financial support for working parents on low incomes. It is also creating a large number of special children's centres providing high-quality facilities, especially through 'Sure Start', a programme that aims to integrate early education, health and family advice in order to 'deliver the best start in life for every child' (sic). There are over 1,000 Sure Start centres currently, with a target of 3,500 by 2010. And there has been a large increase in the regulation and inspection of childcare and nursery education. These are designed to ensure high quality but seem also to have contributed to a decline in informal parent-organized playgroups and in the number of registered childminders (who look after a few children in an informal home setting).

What is the result? Far more children have experience of formal childcare and preschool than ten years ago, and much of this includes substantial amounts of directed 'educational' activity. But the increase has been most marked for working couples and more affluent families and has been least evident among the most deprived. Although Sure Start was intended to break cycles of disadvantage, there is little evidence to date that it has done so. Early evaluations were generally unfavourable (NAO 2006). More recent data do indicate some improvements across the board for children living in Sure Start areas (for example in parenting behaviour) compared to comparable areas without programmes,[5] although no positive impact was identified for verbal ability (the sole overtly 'educational' outcome in the evaluations; Melhuish et al 2008).

In some ways, the 'early learning' parts of education policy have been typical of Labour's overall approach to education: a determination to help the most disadvantaged, a willingness to spend very large sums of money, and an unshakeable belief in very detailed programme design. The latter is especially apparent in the recent (2008) 'toddler curriculum' or 'Early Years Foundation Stage', comprising no less than 69 'learning goals'. Detailed records must be kept on how each child is progressing on each. Formulation of the curriculum involved extensive consultation with early childhood experts, but the result threatens to encapsulate the last ten years' least appealing features. It is compulsory for *all* formal childcare (whether or not in receipt of government funding); uniform for all children; highly prescriptive, and at odds with many established approaches to nursery education such as Montessori and Froebel.

In other ways, early years education is unusual. The structure of childcare credit rewards – intentionally – parents who are in the workforce. This partly reflects voter and citizen demand, in an age of female workforce participation, and partly the desire of the government to encourage paid employment, especially among poorer and single-parent households. However, in consequence, the huge increases in expenditure which Labour has financed have failed either to close the developmental gap between more and less disadvantaged children, or to benefit the most disadvantaged families to the degree that Labour's aspirations, and the research literature on attainment, would support.

Attacking differentials in school performance: targets and initiatives as default options

The wide differentials in school performance highlighted by *Options I* were in Labour's sights in 1996 (when Blair announced zero tolerance for failure) and have remained so. They also remain stubbornly present. As already noted, there have been substantial increases in the proportions of pupils reaching 'expected' attainment levels on national tests, especially in Labour's first term. This, in turn, fed through more or less automatically into lower gaps in performance, on those measures, among groups of schools.[6] On other measures, however, such as attainment of high A-level grades, or passes in particular high-stakes subjects, no such progress is apparent. Overall, there is little to suggest a significant and systematic decline in the differences among schools, or in the gap between pupils from different backgrounds. But this is not for lack of activity.

The government (like *Options I*) believed that better schools required better infrastructure, better leadership and better literacy and numeracy teaching, and applied itself to all three. It announced a 'Building Schools for the Future' programme to build 200 new schools.[7] It also (again in line with *Options I*) decided to upgrade headteacher quality, creating a new 'National Professional Qualification for Headteachers' (NPQH), originally meant to be compulsory in 2004, and now supposed to become so in 2009. The National College for School Leadership, announced in 1998 and opened in 2002, was an expression of the same belief in leadership skills as the way to improve school performance.

There has been no attempt by government to evaluate rigorously whether having heads with an NPQH, or staff who have attended leadership courses, has tended to improve school performance. However, recent research has cast serious doubt on whether heads' leadership is, in fact, exerting a major influence outside a few exceptional schools (Tymms and Searle in O'Shaughnessy 2007). This may be because current structures make it difficult; but it calls into question the efficacy of the 'leadership' strategy.

Developing leadership has, at least, been a consistent policy thread. Alongside it there has been a relentless stream of much shorter-lived initiatives. No attempt will be made to list them all, but they include Specialist Schools, Excellence in Cities, Education Action Zones, Beacon Schools, the Gifted and Talented Programme, and the Ethnic Minority Achievement programme.[8] More recent (2007) is the ten-year Children's Plan ('designed to make England the best place in the world for children and young people to grow up'). The most visible and consistently implemented initiatives, however, were the first: the primary school Literacy and Numeracy Strategies of Labour's first term.

The strategies encapsulated Labour's approach of taking Conservative policies and doing much more of the same. As noted earlier, the structure of education in this country changed dramatically in the 1980s and 1990s. Reforms introduced a National Curriculum that lays down content in great detail (as has Labour's new 'toddler curriculum'). The Literacy and Numeracy strategy added another layer by providing an extremely detailed and strong steer on precisely how specified content should be taught. Given high-stakes school inspections which used the strategies as reference points, only a few teachers were confident enough not to fall into line.

Tests and targets

Redoubled efforts also characterize the use of testing in schools. The Key Stage tests (SATs) introduced by the Conservatives for 7, 11 and 14 year olds were continued.[9] Schools that failed to achieve target levels of attainment for their pupils faced public shaming and sanctions: being part of a 'National Challenge' list, being put in 'special measures' by inspectors, and losing their senior staff. And it might seem that this 'zero tolerance' has, in fact, paid off. Test scores for 7 and 11 year olds have risen. (See Table 6.3 above.) The number of young people gaining formal examination passes at 16 and 18 increased steadily. In 1995/96 45% of GCSE candidates achieved five grades A–C or the equivalent; in 2005/06 the figure was 59% (see Figure 6.2 above). At A-level, the pass rate rose, and reached 97% last year, with 25% of entries attracting an A grade.

Some of this improvement is almost certainly genuine. Unfortunately, it is increasingly clear that some of it is not.

Teaching to the test

The tests used for Key Stage testing are developed at national level under strict conditions, and provide a reliable indicator in the sense that questions are equivalent in difficulty across years. But much of the improvement that has occurred appears to be in test taking, and answering specific types of question, rather than in the underlying skills that the tests set out to measure. As primary schools grew increasingly sophisticated at analysing test requirements and preparing students for them, scores have improved; of late, they have reached a plateau. The levels that pupils achieve in test questions of an increasingly familiar type often do not translate into supposedly equivalent levels of performance at the start of the next stage of education (Mansell 2007). And, as noted above, international surveys also shed doubt on the pattern of improvement indicated in Key Stage tests.

Non-tested material is neglected. Michael Shayer and his colleagues (Shayer et al 2007; Shayer, forthcoming) compared the performance of upper primary and lower secondary students on tests of scientific understanding in 1976 and 2007. On some measures, today's pupils showed far lower levels of understanding than their exact equivalents in 1976, while on others, the numbers showing high levels of attainment had dropped significantly.

Distortions created by targets are increasingly evident. League tables and targets were both carried over from the Conservatives, but Labour ministers have increased the numbers of targets, and made them more important within the Department (because of Public Service Agreements). At secondary level, the proportion of pupils gaining 'five A–C GCSEs or equivalent' is especially critical for league table rankings and schools' inspection reports. One predictable result has been a great deal of gaming.

The phrase 'GCSE *or equivalent*' is especially significant for the government's own self-imposed targets and for schools. Over the last decade all qualifications offered in institutions receiving public funds have been compulsorily assigned to a 'qualification level'; and all qualifications at that level are then treated as formally equivalent. The process is little understood by the general public but it means that many qualifications 'count' as equivalent to five GCSEs A–C even though they bear no resemblance to GCSEs. Naturally enough, this classification system has led many schools to steer students towards qualifications which are easier to pass, may have little labour market credibility, but count towards the magic target.

The importance of the 'C grade boundary' tends to divert schools' attention away from both high and low attainers; and a further set of perverse incentives was created because, until 2007, the targets made no mention whatsoever of subject content. The five A–Cs (or equivalent) might include English and Maths; or might not.[10] There was no penalty if they did not, no credit if they did. When commentators (such as the BBC) re-calculated the league tables, using only GCSEs and including Maths and English, the tables themselves were transformed, in terms of which schools ranked highest: and the number of students meeting the target plummeted.

'Failing' schools remain, overwhelmingly, those with large numbers of disadvantaged pupils and/or pupils for whom English is not a first language (Marshall 2007). The nature of the school body exerts an independent effect on an individual pupil's attainment, so schools with high levels of disadvantaged pupils are doubly handicapped. And, as already noted, Labour has been unable to achieve any appreciable narrowing of the gap between favoured and less favoured pupils.[11]

Labour's 2005 manifesto announced that, in its first term the party achieved 'record results in primary schools. In our second term we have driven fundamental reform to secondary provision ...' Overall, the evidence suggests a picture which is far more mixed. Improvements have plateaued; and there is good reason to suppose that gaming, teaching to the test and micro-management of the curriculum are now yielding not merely diminishing but negative returns.

The latter part of this chapter considers alternative approaches. However, we need first to consider one additional, high profile and controversial initiative, which was not anticipated in the 1997 manifesto (or, indeed *Options I*): Academies.

The Academies programme emanated not from the Department of Education (under any of its changing identities), but from Number 10, and specifically from Andrew (now Lord) Adonis, Blair's highly influential education adviser.

Unlike the top-down, target-driven approach described above, the core of the Academies programme for secondary schools is greater autonomy. Creation of an academy also involves outside sponsorship, by a wealthy individual, or an association (a charity, or private sector organization) who also has a continuing role in the school's governance.

Academies are situated in low-achieving and deprived areas. The idea is that, by setting up a completely new school – often with new facilities – the culture of low aspirations and attainment can also be changed. In other words, the idea is that autonomy and a fresh start can drive improvement. At the time of writing there are 83 Academies.

The programme has attracted enormous controversy. Like so much else in recent policy, it draws on Conservative precedent; and in this case on a policy strongly attacked by Labour in opposition. One of Labour's first acts on taking power was to abolish the grant-maintained programme under which schools withdrew from LEA control. Now the Academies programme seemed to be reinventing the same approach, albeit specifically for deprived areas.

Academies are indeed conceptually different from other recent education policy, reflecting a divide (or indeed rift) within the party, as well as different institutional bases within government itself. They are also extremely popular with parents. There is ongoing and intense argument over whether the academies – mostly still very new – are raising attainment among their predominantly low-attaining pupil bodies. On balance, the evidence is positive, although the gains are quite modest. (Realistically, what else could one expect?) They also reflect a consistent tendency for Number 10, under Blair, to generate more 'choice-oriented' policies in education than the main departments of state (Astle and Ryan 2008).

Teachers and technologies

Teachers do not figure very much in recent manifestos, other than in pledges to have more of them. The quality of teachers is, nonetheless, central to the quality of schooling – on this all researchers agree; and raising their status was, for this reason, a key recommendation of *Options I*. In office, teachers are also central to any education minister's line of vision. Keeping classrooms staffed is the first and unavoidable priority of the system he or she now heads; and in the last ten years, with a booming economy, teachers have also been in endemically short supply in key subjects.

Here too Labour inherited and absorbed some key Tory policies. It also introduced a number of additional teacher-related policies of its own. Two were prefigured by *Options I* – using technology, and using teaching assistants, to improve quality, productivity and professionalism.[12] The third, performance-related pay, was another product of Number 10's policy unit.

The pre-1997 Tory governments mistrusted the teacher training institutions (all, by then, part of universities), holding them responsible for 'progressive' policies which had undermined educational standards. In 1994 it established the Teacher Training Agency, which centralized and controlled recruitment and training of new teachers. Labour, once again, redoubled Tory efforts, with the TTA (now renamed the Teacher Development Agency) now setting its own skills tests for teachers.[13]

The TTA was not, however, a very effective weapon in the effort to recruit more, good teachers. Higher pay for new teachers in specific subjects has proved rather more useful, though there remain very large numbers of schools without adequate numbers, or even any, teachers qualified in physics, maths and chemistry. (Secondary school language shortages have been 'solved' by allowing students to drop modern languages.) A 'special initiative' of which the government is proud is 'Teach First', which recruits final-year undergraduates in Russell Group universities to teach for two years in low-performing schools. The programme is worthy, admirable, and may have made a genuine contribution to raising the attractiveness of teaching (though recession will achieve that faster). However, the numbers involved to date are a drop in the ocean of the country's teaching workforce.[14]

Labour (and especially its two Prime Ministers) has also been entranced by the idea that technology can revolutionize teaching. It has spent enormous sums on ICT and made it virtually impossible for schools – state or private – to operate without large investments in it. A 'National Grid for Learning' was one of the pledges of the 1997 manifesto, intended to bring a wealth of resources and 'e-learning' into the classroom through one seamless, national portal; but while duly launched, it has since slipped from view.

Unfortunately, evidence that this is money well spent is slight to non-existent. Teachers who are individually committed to intensive IT use can and do create excellent materials and inspiring lessons which are highly-IT dependent. But there is no strong, empirical evidence whatsoever to suggest that intensive use of ICT by schools automatically leads to higher levels of achievement. Indeed, the limited amount of good empirical research that goes beyond descriptive case-studies indicates the opposite (Angrist and Lavy 1999; Machin et al 2007).

Labour has also massively expanded the number of support staff, and specifically teaching assistants, deployed in British schools (see Figure 6.5). Their salaries account for a large and growing part of the school budget; and yet the policy has never been properly evaluated. There are not even any clear data on what teaching assistants do. Some of them are there to assist mainstreamed children with special needs. Some are directly involved in teaching children. Some empty the paint pots.

Ofsted, on the basis of visits to 23 schools, announced in October 2008 that assistants were having a positive impact on achievement (but see Fitzgibbon 1999 for the reliability and validity of such OFSTED studies). However, the EPPI centre, which conducts systematic reviews of research on key topics in education, found no well-conducted reviews linking practice and actual impact at all – studies are instead all about people's *perceptions* of assistants

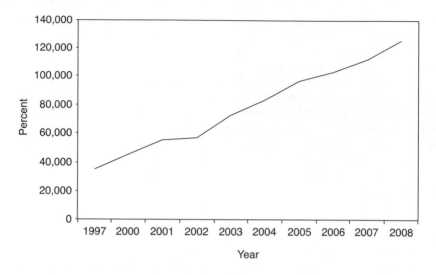

Figure 6.5   Number of Teaching Assistants in Local Authority Maintained Schools, January of Respective Year: England

Source: Statistical First Release, DCSF.

and their role (http://eppi.ioe.ac.uk). In their large-scale study of primary classes, and the impact of class size, Blatchford et al found 'no evidence … that either the presence of Teaching Assistants or their characteristics affected pupil progress' (Blatchford et al 2005: 61).

This absence of evaluation is itself indicative of a more general retreat from the evidence-based policy to which the incoming 1997 Labour government committed itself. About the assistants themselves, one can only remark that, if they are indeed having a major impact on the effectiveness of classroom teaching, one would expect improvements in attainment to have been concentrated in the period after 2003, rather than the reverse.

One other policy relating to teachers is worth attention: performance related pay. Introduced in 1999, it was a classic 'new public management' approach, designed to 'align incentives' rather than handing down orders. The idea was simple: to give more money to better-performing teachers, encourage them to remain in the classroom, and encourage others to improve. It was opposed vehemently by the teachers' unions. This was predictable (unions have an understandable preference for policies which offer benefits to all their members); but their specific criticisms[15] were nonetheless to the point. In particular, they argued that it is very difficult to tell how good a teacher is, since the ultimate measure is students' performance, and this is affected by a very large number of factors outside the teacher's control. Government might claim that pupils' circumstances would be taken into account; in practice the 'best-performing' teachers would appear to be those teaching advantaged, high-performing pupils.

In practice, the scheme's detailed national guidelines for demonstrating specific 'outcomes' meant that almost any teacher willing to put time into form-filling could claim to have met the criteria. Since the money for the increments was additional to pre-existing school budgets, and Heads had little discretion, but a strong incentive to keep their school operating as a team, they duly recommended virtually every applicant for increments, at considerable cost to the Exchequer.

The policy may have helped some schools implement internal 'quality management' more effectively (Marsden and Belfield 2006), and there is some evidence of a small increase in students' GCSE results (in English but not in maths!) as teachers attempted to prove that they had taught successfully (Atkinson 2004). But, especially after the first year, the policy became, in effect, an across-the-board pay rise and a further contribution to teachers' paperwork.

Summary

Education reform has turned out to be far more complex and frustrating a task than it appeared in Opposition. The realities of family background and economic deprivation continue to dominate school outcomes, and the complexities of children's learning have not proven controllable through any cleverly-designed interventions. Meanwhile, two other major areas of educational expenditure and policy have received less money and more intermittent attention. One – higher education – did not even figure in Blair's 1996 speech. The other was to make Britain a 'skills superpower'. The following two sections examine how they have fared.

Reforming the universities

If school policies have been characterized by endless noise and activity, and very modest returns on large expenditures, higher education has been utterly different: a small amount of seismic legislation, and a sector which is more confident, successful and globally admired than was the case in 1997. (See Chapter 7 in this volume.) This is only partly the government's doing. UK universities are independent institutions and owe much of their current success to earning ever-greater proportions of their income directly, with no government involvement. (This trend, in turn, dates back to Thatcher's decision that the government would no longer pay or control the level of overseas students' fees.) Nonetheless, in 1997 this was a sector in decline, facing the likelihood that it would follow many of the continental European systems into chronic under-funding and academic obscurity (Wolf 2002). Today, as the sector's trade body, UKU (UK Universities), is happy to remind us, only the US outranks Britian in leagues of 'top' universities.

Higher education has experienced decades of rapid growth in student numbers but funding from governmental sources had halved in real value per student over the 20-year period up to 1997. The science infrastructure was desperately in need of upgrading and a scientific brain drain was large and evident. Under Lord Sainsbury, Labour began a sustained programme to improve science funding and also corrected the perverse incentives in the dual funding system that has led to chronic underinvestment in capital (see Chapter 7). However, in terms of student funding, there was at first little to signal change from the inherited patterns. Labour introduced flat 'up-front' means-tested and government-set fees, in line with the recommendations of the Dearing Report, commissioned under the previous government but on the understanding of bipartisan support.[16] Otherwise its main contribution was to implement with enthusiasm the Dearing Report's recommendation for a 'Quality Assurance Agency', provoking fury and loathing in the sector as the QAA's inspection teams applied themselves to the room of paper their regime demanded.

Change came because, and when, Blair became convinced that the quality of the sector, and especially of its top institutions, was genuinely under threat. The result was one of the most important legacies of the Blair years: the Higher Education Act of 2004. This was hugely controversial, scraping through Parliament in the face of widespread Labour backbench opposition. It overturned a previous manifesto commitment, was opposed by the Tories for short-term electoral reasons – a position they have now abandoned – and continues to be opposed by the Liberal Democrats (though not by most of their policy thinkers). It was also another policy to emanate directly from Downing Street. It was important partly because it meant a large increase in funding, but also and above all, because it established a genuinely new, long-term and potentially flexible structure for the sector. This is because it institutionalized *both* the principle of student contributions *and* that the individual university, not the government, should decide on the level of fee (albeit with a government-imposed cap).

In essence, the Act introduced mechanisms for charging government-subsidized students (in England, Wales and Northern Ireland) fees which can vary by institution and degree; and for providing them with subsidized loans to meet these fees, which are then paid back only as and when their earnings rise above a certain level. Fees were there already. What the legislation achieved, critically, was to devolve decision-making on fees to individual institutions, and ensure that students pay only when they are actually earning (Barr 2004).

Financial problems are still acute, and raising the current fee cap poses major problems for future governments because, short-term, it costs a great deal of money (in the form of higher loans and loan subsidies). However, the 2004 Act has been extremely important in rejuvenating the sector and contrary to the predictions of opponents (and in line with the predictions of supporters) had no negative impact on demand for university places by home students. University education remains overwhelmingly the preserve of the middle classes; but the barriers to entry are at school level, where, as discussed above, disadvantaged students consistently perform less well, and are far more likely to attend schools with low average attainment (Wolf 2002; Davies et al 2008).[17]

And so to skills

What of the 1996 aspiration to be a 'skills superpower'? Here, again, Labour made a Tory obsession its own, but more so. Like its predecessors, it has been convinced that the key to economic growth lies not just with education but with vocational 'skills' and piling up qualifications in the adult workforce. Successive ministers including, crucially, then-Chancellor Brown, concluded that employers were not training enough, that the country would fall behind India and China if it did not invest in more 'skills', and that the policy remedy was to move to an increasingly centrally planned system, which provided subsidies for employers to have their workers trained and certificated.

One of the 1997 government's first acts was to establish a wide ranging 'National Skills Task Force': targets for skills were renewed, increased, and tied to qualification levels. But the ink on the Task Force reports was barely dry before we were into the Treasury-based Leitch inquiry. This called for a 'demand led approach' while in fact setting new, higher central targets (Wolf 2007b). Command and control reign; for example in the decision to make education or training compulsory for all 16 and 17 year olds, a policy which many (including this author) have attacked as unlikely to motivate disaffected young people, unlikely to increase substantive attainment, but very likely to damage or destroy the youth labour market (Wolf 2007a; Ryan 2008).[18]

Early policies did give an important role to individual choice, notably through 'Individual Learning Accounts'. These matched individual contributions with state funds, and were an instant, enormous and expensive success. The Education Maintenance Allowance, which in effect pays 16 and 17 year olds to stay in school, also attempts to change individuals' choices rather than make certain activities compulsory. It was piloted and evaluated thoroughly in 1999 – the heyday of evidence-based policymaking. The evidence that EMAs encouraged some additional young people to stay in school, though with substantial dead-weight costs, led to their being rolled out nationally in 2004; and it now costs over half a billion pounds a year.[19]

Post-2000, however, there was a major shift of emphasis. After some fraud was uncovered – a direct result of rushing the policy into place before the systems were ready (House of Commons Select Committee 2002) – Individual Learning Accounts were closed. Increasing amounts of money were instead channelled towards workplace training and accreditation, through a programme with the self-explanatory label 'Train to Gain'. Further education colleges had to sign detailed contracts to 'deliver' set numbers of qualifications, in line with centrally set targets and priorities. Rules have proliferated governing what sort of qualifications are eligible for full or high rates of subsidy: these rules outlaw many choices, including most cases where adults might want to train for a new occupation, as opposed to progress within their current one. The entire system is overseen by a shifting set of quangos, agencies and government departments, whose structure is far more complex than that of either the school or the higher education sector, in spite of a much smaller total budget.

The combination of contracts with training providers and colleges which mean they get paid largely for completed qualifications, and an expensive, 'competence-based' assessment regime for most vocational awards means that the emphasis is on certification, not training or learning. Large sums of money have recently been moved out of adult education. In contrast to the late 1990s, when adult numbers grew rapidly, adult student numbers are in sharp decline, with the biggest losers students from lower-income groups (NIACE 2008).[20] Even so, the current Train to Gain budget is seriously under-spent, as employers and employees show a distinct lack of enthusiasm and interest in what has been planned for them. In this area, even more than for schools, the limitations of a top-down, micro-managed approach seem increasingly evident.

The last ten years have left us with an improved education infrastructure, more teachers, a larger share of GDP going into education, a population accustomed to formal pre-school provision, and revitalized universities. They have also shown how hard it is to raise standards for all, and how little 'zero tolerance for failure' can act as a guarantee of universal achievement. To give just two examples, hundreds of thousands of pupils each year fail to achieve a C grade in GCSE English or Maths, and almost half of those on free school meals fail to attain any grades above D at all.

This long tail of under-achievement is surely the top priority for education policy. This is not just for economic reasons. Not all future jobs will be highly skilled – quite the opposite (Brown and Hesketh 2004; Keep 2000). We can, quite evidently, continue to generate economic growth for decades on end while a substantial sub-group of our citizens remains effectively excluded from higher education and from much of the job market. The last ten years bear witness to this. So do the previous twenty. Change is a priority not on narrow economic grounds but because social justice and common citizenship make it intolerable that so many children are denied the opportunities for individual advancement and development.

The other major lesson of the last ten years is surely that neither central planning and 'hyper-accountability' (Mansell 2007), nor myriad initiatives and special programmes provide an effective strategy. The latter are wasteful and distracting, while a growing body of evidence shows that the former are increasingly counter-productive. Higher education, the greatest success story of the last decade, is also by far the least regulated and micro-managed education sector and the most responsive to its users.

The most important priority for a future government is thus not a new list of special measures, but a resolution to stay away from them. This is, of course, unlikely. Any junior minister out to make her name will want her own special initiative. However, even a reduction in the number and pace at which they appear would be welcome.

The second priority is to move towards a system that is genuinely more responsive to individual demands and needs. I say 'towards' because it is impossible for any education system to completely offset the advantages of family background and individual circumstance. But there are ways to get closer than at present.

On that basis, there are five major changes which a new government might usefully prioritize. Each is underpinned by the general objective of targeting more resources and help towards the most deprived, or of substituting choice and responsiveness for micromanagement and 'hyper-accountability', or both. Some of the changes (notably 1 and 2) have been discussed in detail by one or both of the main opposition parties, and accepted in principle. As with all policies for a system as complex as modern education, there are myriad details on which to disagree. But if a new government does not start with clear priorities and overall objectives, it will sink into exactly the sort of tail-swallowing incentives that now afflict New Labour.

Option 1: Adopt 'pupil premia' that ensure additional funds follow disadvantaged pupils

At present schools have a strong incentive not to take, or focus their efforts on, disadvantaged pupils, because they tend not to score highly on league-table statistics, and are often more demanding to teach. At national level, although funds follow pupils to some extent, the overall allocation of funds to and with LEAs remains complex and non-transparent (even to headteachers). LEAs have a strong incentive to spread funds out among all their schools. Nationally, schools with comparable levels of disadvantage and challenge may receive very different, and very unstable, levels of per-pupil funding.

A 'pupil premium' would mean that schools that enrolled a disadvantaged pupil would receive more for that pupil than for others. For additional impact, a higher proportion of funding should follow the pupil than at present.

There would then be positive advantages to enrolling disadvantaged pupils and to ensuring that the resources they bring are devoted to them. (Otherwise they may take themselves elsewhere.) Indeed, if the premium is large enough, the additional resources pumped into recipient schools will also make them less off-putting to middle-class parents.[21]

Option 2: Increase ease of entry of new schools and freedom to expand for successful schools, so increasing supply

This is a far less generally accepted policy than Option 1 (though it is also current Conservative policy, in a form reflecting the current Swedish model). However, if one accepts any of the arguments that individual choice and competition drive up quality, then it is clearly necessary for there to be something to choose between. Local education authorities, trying to serve, protect and respond to all their existing schools, see things differently: from an LEA perspective, empty places are 'spare capacity' which should be used up before one starts investing in more 'surplus capacity' elsewhere.

LEA planning was much easier in the past, before school choice. But while there are plenty of unhappy parents every year, who do not get their choice of school, this should not be taken as indicating any desire, by parents or children, for a return to no choice at all. The limited successes of the last decade's policies do not in themselves prove that greater autonomy and competition would be more effective; but the international evidence does suggest that it is on balance the right approach (Le Grand 2007b; Lim and Davies 2008).

Again, there are multiple alternatives, to be discussed and fought over. None of the current proponents of greater supply and freer entry are proposing a situation in which schools can opt into the state system and then charge fees on top. But the current situation, including the level of regulation imposed on new schools and the treatment of school capital, appears too stacked in favour of incumbents.[22]

Option 3: (Re-)introduce individual learning accounts for post-18 education

The current system of non-university post-compulsory education and training is the most centrally planned and least successful part of the country's education system. It subsidizes the in-house training of some of the country's largest companies, while at the same time large swathes of adult education are closing down for lack of any public support.[23] It sets rigid targets tied to notional 'levels' combined with a system of outcome-related funding that undermines standards and gives providers an extremely strong incentive to provide courses which require minimal new learning. Many of the qualifications it promotes have no discernible market value (Jenkins et al 2007; Wolf 2007a) and non-qualification-bearing courses have been squeezed out of funded provision.

Dismantling the whole infrastructure of targets, regulations and quangos which has grown up round this dysfunctional system will be very hard; and the best immediate option for a new government is simply to let it wither and die while by-passing it via a different funding mechanism. The original ILAs, introduced by an earlier Labour government, were not only rushed into place, but were also highly bureaucratic and circumscribed in their coverage. In order to develop an adult education and training system that is responsive to learners' demands, reformed ILAs should be gradually re-introduced, providing subsidies for individuals to use on the education and training of their choice.

A new system should require some matching of individual contributions and subsidy, paid into a special account. A clear organization model for such accounts exists in the form of the Charities Aid Foundation (CAF) which organizes precisely such accounts, into which individuals pay as and when they wish: to which the government adds money (gift-aid in CAF's case) and where payments can be made only to registered and approved recipients.[24]

Option 4: Re-allocate pre-school funding to the greater benefit of the most deprived families

As discussed above, current pre-school policies are complicated by their dual purpose – to improve pre-school education and to encourage parents into the workplace. It is now clear, from the empirical evidence, that the way funds are disbursed needs recalibrating. Too few of the most deprived households are benefiting; and if children from these backgrounds do not receive high quality pre-school education, they are almost bound to fall further and further behind.

Option 5: De-nationalize qualifications

Current government policy is driven, in all sectors except the universities, by 'stretching' quantitative targets, largely expressed in the form of qualification totals and qualification levels.[25] This distorts the offers which providers make to would-be learners (see Option 3 above). It also threatens to corrupt government itself. One of the prime purposes of government oversight is the 'weights and measures function' – ensuring that what people are offered is indeed what it says it is, and that they not receiving 'short weight'. But the pressure on governments to deliver targets which they pay for and control inevitably encourages decisions and reporting which are, in effect, deceptive, just as with any centrally planned system. Examples include counting all 'level 2s' as 'equivalent to five GCSEs' when reporting on 16 year olds' achievement.

Qualifications are currently given levels for one simple reason: the government has tied itself to quantitative targets *expressed* in terms of levels. But the problem this creates is greatly exacerbated because qualifications are now minutely regulated *and* have their content defined and developed by government agencies. In other words, government is policing its own products. On top of that, contractual payments to colleges and training companies are made for 'delivery' of particular qualifications, using payment-by-results, which undermines the quality and rigour of the assessment process (Colley and Jarvis 2007). With governmental careers made or broken by targets met or missed, the incentives are perverse and mutually reinforcing.

Until the 1980s, qualifications were developed by charitable organizations under light-touch regulation. There is no evidence to suggest that standards then were lower or less reliable, qualifications less useful to the labour market, or slower to adapt to change – indeed, the evidence suggest the opposite (Wolf 2001; Sturgis 2000). The progressive nationalization and quasi-nationalization of qualifications that started under the Thatcher governments, and was accelerated by Labour can and should be reversed.

This is, moreover, easily achieved. Ofqual is an independent assessment regulator only recently established by legislation. It has not actually replaced any of the myriad existing education agencies, although it has taken some functions from the Qualifications and Curriculum Authority. However, in principle there is no reason why one should not, now, de-nationalize the assessment industry,[26] abolish a cluster of agencies (including QCA) and restore to government, through Ofqual, the attainable and necessary task of checking quality, honestly.

Notes

1. Although the original idea of a University for Industry never worked, the institution lives on, transmogrified, as 'UfI', a provider of on-line basic IT, literacy and numeracy courses, available in 'learning centres' such as FE colleges and training providers.
2. The other *Options* priorities were: (1) A lack of accountability among schools and LEAs for how funds were spent, because of the lack of clarity in how funds were distributed. The lack of clarity remains (O'Shaughnessy and Leslie 2005), although schools' 'accountability' for results has increased and is now extremely high: see below. (2) An unfair post-compulsory funding system. And (3) a need to reform secondary qualifications. The latter has been a recurring preoccupation of governments since the war. Labour has been extremely 'busy' in this area, without actually achieving any substantial changes (see Wolf 2002; Allen and Ainley 2008).
3. The most dramatic example in recent years is Germany, which had always taken for granted that it had a superior education system until it performed (relatively) very badly in the first 2000 PISA survey; but France was also both shocked and infuriated by its apparently poor showing on the OECD's adult literacy study, and insisted on its results being omitted from the report. A later study, funded by the EC and carried out by the ONS did underline the fallibility of many of the measures used in IALS and, by extension, in other such studies (Carey 2000).
4. Alumni of the latter were markedly less likely to drop out of school or into crime as teenagers than their peers
5. It is important to emphasize that Sure Start is not a 'pre-school education' programme, but an attempt to change the whole area-wide environment, and so enhance the lives of children growing up in deprived communities. The evaluations

thus look at outcomes for a sample of children chosen because they live in the relevant community, not a sample of children attending particular Sure Start facilities. There has consequently been debate over whether such area-based evaluations are too insensitive to possible direct impacts on children receiving services.

6. If 'high performing schools' already have most children performing at or above the target level, any overall increase in proportions of the age-group performing 'at target' is virtually bound to translate into noticeable decreases in the gap between high- and low-performing groups of schools, on that particular fixed measure. See Glennerster (2002) for an analysis of 1997–2002.

7. Only 37 are likely to be complete by 2008, reflecting the difficulty of completing large infrastructure projects

8. Although most of these initiatives have been claimed as successes, improvements ascribed to them may in many cases have simply reflected the general upward trend in recorded attainment. See Bradley and Taylor (2007).

9. The tests for 14 year olds are now to be abolished in their current form, following a high profile and expensive administrative failure in 2008 (and a fiscal crisis).

10. Ministers may themselves have been unaware of this.

11. Michael Gove, the Conservative shadow DCSF secretary, has asked a series of Parliamentary questions on the proportions of individual pupils receiving free school meals attaining certain results/qualifications, as compared to the overall national average. These indicate that the gap has stayed the same or even widened at Key Stage 2. See Hansard 19 February 2007, 29 January 2008 and 10 July 2008 (or access via TheyworkForYou.com).

12. Labour also set up a General Teaching Council, but its powers are quite limited and have not created any major increase in autonomy for the teaching profession.

13. The Royal Society's response, during the 'consultation' on the new curriculum for trainee science teachers, was typical: 'the Society considers the extreme level of detail and prescription of the documents to be unhelpful', it stated.

14. 1,094 have been recruited to the programme since its launch in 2003–04, of whom 742 completed the programme. Around half of those stayed in teaching after their two-year programme was over. Written answer to a parliamentary question, by Lord Adonis, 25 June 2008.

15. Since the awards were to be made on headteachers' recommendations, the unions also argued that it would make it very difficult for teachers to behave independently and question anything in school, or probably government policy. Of course, any performance-related scheme alters the balance of power in favour of those awarding the bonus; and given the current difficulty of getting rid of any teaching staff, however poor, this was probably indeed one of the government's objectives.

16. Labour also, inexplicably, abolished grants for the poorest students, though retaining the loan system for maintenance costs.

17. There is some evidence that students from poorer households tend to apply to less selective universities than their grades would indicate (Sutton Trust 2007), but this is a minor problem compared to the problem of earlier under-achievement. The UK is also not at all unusual in the over-representation of middle class students (Bakker et al 2001).

18. The requirement to remain in part-time education and training extends even to young entrepreneurs with their own businesses. The then-Skills Minister, Phil Hope, explained in a letter to the *Financial Times* (21 May 2007) that this was an enormous improvement because it would mean that 'young entrepreneurs will

have opportunities that people like the Alan Sugars and Richard Bransons never had' and that 'Crucially, they will also have advice on choosing training to help develop their businesses.'

19. The EMA provides a depressing example of the demise of any pretence of evidence-based policy, as well as the temptation to make benefits wide-ranging and so electorally popular. The LSC website proclaims that the EMA has raised participation by 6 percentage points on the basis of an evaluation that asked young people whether they 'thought [sic] they would have stayed in learning without the EMA'. A follow-up evaluation by the IFS – which conducted the original pilot – suggests that the EMA, as implemented (as opposed to the pilot scheme), may in fact have increased attendance by well under 2 percentage points. The scheme currently pays 46% of young people, thus creating enormous dead-weight: it was originally conceived as a scheme for the poorest.

20. Middle-class students are more able to find alternative privately organized provision, e.g. through University of the Third Age.

21. For more detailed discussions see Astle (2007), Booth (2008), Freedman and Horner (2008).

22. The requirements for any recognized school – including one which does not aspire to charitable status – make opening one a very slow process, and involve a high level of expenditure on e.g. IT.

23. Adult education is not 'free' in the sense of not charging fees; but now receives effectively no support at all for much of traditional provision. Financially straitened and risk-averse colleges have responded by simply cancelling large parts of their provision.

24. I am greatly indebted to John Harwood for pointing out that the CAF model could be generalized to ILA provision.

25. In universities, enrolments by 'home' students are capped on an institution-by-institution basis.

26. Ofqual could also take responsibility for any Key Stage tests. Those at stage 3 have recently been, effectively, abolished, following a marking fiasco, but some form of periodic check on pupils' attainment is desirable and popular with parents.

7
Science and Technology Policy
Jonathan Grant and Joachim Krapels

In 1994, Gordon Brown won the Plain English Campaign's Foot in Mouth award for his 'New Economics' speech, where he analysed 'the growth of post neo-classical endogenous growth theory and the symbiotic relationships between government and investment in people and infrastructures'. The then Shadow Chancellor of the Exchequer was setting out why an incoming Labour government would invest in science and technology (S&T). In short, in an age where Britain was no longer a manufacturing nation, he argued it had to trade on ideas – particularly in science – and by doing so would see an increase in economic growth over and above the investment made.

A decade and a half later it is fair to say that S&T policy has never had it so good. The Labour government has overseen a 63% increase in government science expenditure, largely under the stewardship of what many would regard as the UK's best ever Minister for Science, Lord Sainsbury (BBC News 2006). The research undertaken using this funding is of high quality – of all G8 nations, UK researchers receive the most citations per paper and publish the most papers per researcher (King 2004). There has been a transformational change in the way that research is transferred to the market, with UK universities competing with US counterparts in terms of patents, licences and income (Sainsbury 2007). Recent evidence shows that in 2005 the UK had a net graduate immigrant 'brain-gain' of around 100,000 people (*The Times* 2008) and anecdotal evidence exists to illustrate that scientists are now preferentially migrating or returning to the UK, largely from the US (Universities UK 2007; Parliamentary Office of Science and Technology 2008).

This chapter explores the S&T policy options available to an incoming government. The chapter is split into three sections. First, we provide an overview of the structure of S&T policy and funding in the UK. The second section identifies some of the enduring and emerging challenges that an incoming government will face. In the final section, we conclude by proposing three policy options for incoming government. Throughout, we focus on

UK S&T policy, but it should be noted that science – and science policy – is a global endeavour.

The scientific machinery of government

The government's Science, Engineering and Technology (SET) budget[1] for 2004/05 was £8.99 billion, or 0.76% of GDP, and was set at £10.31 billion for 2007/08, or 0.74% of GDP (BERR 2008). As illustrated in Figure 7.1, the 2004/05 budget is split five ways, between the seven Research Councils[2] (the 'science budget'); the Higher Education Funding Councils (HEFCs) that support UK universities; civil government departments; Defence; and EU research and development (R&D). By comparison, the private sector spent £13.4 billion on R&D in 2005, and non-profits (largely in the biomedical and health sphere) £0.5 billion (ONS 2007b).

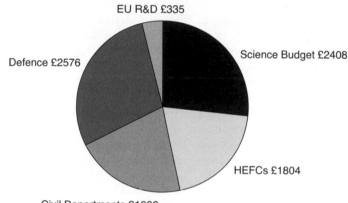

Figure 7.1   SET Budget (£ million), 2004/05 (Total, £8.99 billion)

Source: BERR (2008).

The Department for Innovation, Universities and Skills (DIUS) is responsible for developing, funding and managing the performance of science and research across the UK. It aims to ensure that the UK continues to develop a world-class research base that is responsive to users and the economy, that UK universities and public laboratories are sustainable and financially strong and that there is a sufficient supply of scientists, engineers and technologists. The Government Office for Science, headed by the Government Chief Scientific Adviser (GCSA) is located within DIUS, and is responsible to the Prime Minister and Cabinet for the quality of scientific advice provided to them on scientific and science policy issues.

Ninety years of science policy

The rise of S&T policy, in terms of size as well as prominence, is one of the defining characteristics of the last century. Following the First World War, Lord Haldane undertook a review of the function of government and identified the need for government to engage in, and fund, science (see Box 7.1). Victory in the Second World War demonstrated the contributions of research and, in the post-war period, it was widely believed that continued scientific progress would strengthen the British economy and ensure continued security. This belief was challenged in the 1970s and 1980s, but renewed by the first White Paper on science in 1993. Table 7.1 outlines the highlights of past SET policy, on the basis of time periods identified by Wilkie (1991).

Box 7.1   **The Haldane Principle**

The so-called 'Haldane Principle' stems from a distinction that Haldane proposed between 'research work for general use' and 'research work supervised by administrative departments'. In terms of the organization of government, the former was to be undertaken independently of administrative supervision, as 'science ignores departmental as well as geographical boundaries' (Ministry of Reconstruction 1918). The latter was to be conducted by government departments to support administrative decisions. The principle was put into practice when the Medical Research Committee was kept separate from the Ministry of Health when it was established by the Minister Christopher Addison in 1920.

John Major's Conservative government provided new impetus to S&T policy in 1993 with the publication of the first ever S&T White Paper, *Realising Our Potential* (DTI 1993). Its ambition was to harness the UK's strengths in science, engineering and technology via new links and partnerships between industry, government and the science base. Despite this renewed attention, government expenditure on SET declined during the first half of the 1990s. Only after the election of Labour in 1997 and the 1998 *Comprehensive Spending Review* (HM Treasury 1998) in which science emerged as a priority, did spending increase again.

The idea of the 'knowledge economy' gained prominence towards the end of the 1990s. Knowledge in general (i.e. the science base), and knowledge workers in particular, were seen as vital to the UK's competitiveness in an increasingly globalized economy (Warhust 2008). The transfer of scientific knowledge to industry through commercialization became a focal point of policymaking, and was outlined in the 1999 Baker report and the 2000 White Paper *Excellence and Opportunity* (DTI 1999, 2000). The latter contained the government's agenda for investing in science excellence and listed several substantial investment initiatives to foster academia–industry collaboration,

Table 7.1   UK Science Policy, 1945–92

	Period of Promise (1945–62)	Age of Reform (1963–78)	Delusion and Decline (1979–92)
Guiding principles	Strong belief in (basic or 'pure') science to solve problems and increase well-being. Guided by 'Haldane Principle'.	Introduction of customer-contractor principle. Government departments increasingly guide and determine research projects.	Continued constraints on spending and increased need for accountability and transparency.
Funding and facilities	Vast increases in resources. Large spending increases for basic science. Massive numbers of new research initiatives. Expansion of research facilities and student numbers.	From large budgets to decreases in resources. Restructuring of funding, less spending on basic science. Decrease in budget, advent of 'big science'.	Discontinuation of several large research facilities. Part restoration of changes initiated by the customer-contractor principle.
Influential reports and documents	Report of the Machinery of Government (Haldane)	Trend report Rothschild report	Rothschild report Priorities in Medical Research

Source: Wilkie (1991).

such as the Regional Innovations Funds and the Small Business Research Initiative. Further investments were announced in 2004, with the publication of the *Science and Innovation Investment Framework 2004–2014* (HM Treasury 2004). The Framework set the ambitious goal of increasing the 'knowledge intensity', measured as the ratio of R&D across the economy to GDP, from 1.9% to 2.5% by 2014 – an average annual increase of 5.8% in real terms.

The focus under the innovation framework was, however, wider than simply academic R&D. The importance of individual skills, especially the so-called STEM (science, technology, engineering and mathematics) skills in driving innovation, also received greater attention. As the Roberts review *SET for Success* noted, 'although not all innovation is based on scientific R&D, the need for human ingenuity in making discoveries and creating new products, services or processes means that the success of R&D is critically dependent upon the availability and talent of scientists and engineers' (HM Treasury 2001). The report further noted a 'disconnect' between the supply and demand of scientists and engineers, and called for a broad approach to tackle the shortages, ranging from improvements in secondary schooling to higher PhD stipends. Furthermore, the review highlighted that governmental supply-side interventions alone would not be sufficient, and that the private sector would have to create attractive employment opportunities for scientists and engineers in order for any strategy to work. Skills continued to be important drivers of innovation and national prosperity, and further nationwide programmes to enhance skills were promulgated by the Leitch reviews published in 2005 and 2006 (HM Treasury 2006a).

In 2007/08 the major themes of innovation, knowledge, skills and business links have come together in several new government bodies, most notably the Department for Innovation, Universities and Skills. DIUS was created in July 2007 following the appointment of Gordon Brown as Prime Minister. The Department incorporated responsibilities for science and innovation from the former Office of Science and Innovation at the Department of Trade and Industry, and for further and higher education from the former Department for Education and Skills.

The most recent publications of significance are the Sainsbury review, *The Race to the Top*, and the DIUS White Paper *Innovation Nation* (Sainsbury 2007; DIUS 2008). Of significance was Lord Sainsbury's proposal to reform the Technology Strategy Board (TSB) as a non-departmental public body and provide it with 'a new leadership role, working with the RDAs, the Research Councils, government departments and the economic regulators to co-ordinate public sector technological innovation activity, leverage public sector resources and simplify access to funds for business' (Sainsbury 2007).

Enduring and emerging challenges in science policy

The historical and contemporary overview allows us to identify and assess some of the inherent tensions that science policymakers are faced with. Some of these are new and some are old. Some have been managed successfully, others continue to challenge. In this section, we review the four enduring and emerging challenges that an incoming government must engage with in formulating a new science policy. They are: the supply of scientists, the funding of science, the translation of science into economic and social benefit, and the accountability of science.

The global 'war for talent'

The so-called 'war for talent' dominates much of today's business, management and leadership literature, with increasing global demand for highly educated and skilled knowledge workers. Although the uptake of places to study biological and mixed sciences has increased, the relative uptake of pure sciences (physics, chemistry) and engineering subjects has been weaker at both A-level and university (see Figure 7.2). There is also a growing concern over the falling popularity of SET courses at Masters and doctorate levels. Although engineering and technology remain static in absolute terms, there is a relative decline in mathematical and physical sciences at these levels. This could have a significant impact on the numbers of graduates opting to take teaching qualifications in SET subjects, thus perpetuating the cycle of a falling supply of scientists. The Sainsbury Review notes: 'The UK has a reasonable stock of STEM graduates, but potential problems lie ahead. There has been a 20-year decline in the number of pupils taking A-level physics.' Given the downturn in STEM students, problems could arise in the future, which could be exacerbated by a demographic decline in 18–20 year olds in ten years' time (Universities UK 2008; Office for Standards in Education, Children's Services and Skills 2008).

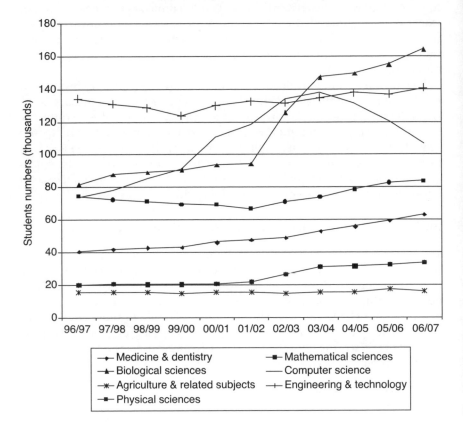

Figure 7.2   Number of Students per Subject Area

Source: Higher Education Statistics Agency (2008).

   These potential supply problems are compounded by the continuing demand for STEM skills from employers, and the fact that future innovation and technological development relies heavily on such skills. Projections suggest an increasing demand for STEM skills over the next ten years, and that supply in engineering and the physical sciences is not likely to increase to meet this demand (DfES 2006). A survey by the Institution of Engineering and Technology found that the engineering and technology sector is facing a growing recruitment crisis (Institution of Engineering and Technology 2007).

As Winston Churchill observed in 1943, 'the empires of the future will be empires of the mind' (Churchill 1943). For the UK to be a competitive knowledge-based economy, it needs a strong supply of scientists, engineers and technologists. However, by the government's own admission, 'progress towards meeting its ambitions is relatively slow' (HM Treasury 2006c). An incoming government will need to address this issue with some urgency. What makes this a particularly tough problem is the fact that the current skill shortage is counter-cyclical, occurring at a time where there is political and financial support for science.

Science funding

The notion that government should fund basic science stems from two seminal papers by RAND economists in the late 1950s and early 1960s. Nelson and Arrow argued that, as the private sector would not be able to capture all the economic externalities resulting from basic research owing to the public nature of knowledge, their total investments in basic research would be sub-optimal, and thus society would not reap all the potential benefits from such research (Nelson 1959; Arrow 1962). Hence, public funding of basic research would increase social benefits. More recently, studies have demonstrated the link between expenditures on research and productivity growth and social benefits (Guellec et al 2004; Coccia 2008). Both public and business funding of research have been shown to increase productivity and generate social benefits for the public good, with the exception of defence-related research. Furthermore, public funding of higher education appears to generate larger productivity gains than business funding, which is attributed to the focus (basic vs. applied science) of the research agenda pursued by each (Aiginger and Falk 2005). More recently, the Health Economics Research Group at Brunel University, RAND Europe and the Office of Health Economics have attempted to quantify the economic returns from medical research in the UK, and estimate an internal rate of return of around 9% from cardiovascular research (Buxton et al 2008).

Nelson and Arrow's early ideas have persisted over the last four decades and currently the amount of money a government spends on S&T is often used as a science policy barometer. Government expenditure on SET, which includes government expenditure on R&D (referred to as GOVERD), has increased from £5.97 billion in 1997 to £9.72 billion in 2007, an average annual increase of 4.87%. Behind these figures are two areas of concern for an incoming government. First, GOVERD as a percentage of total GDP has remained virtually the same, and even slightly declined, over the past decade, and is low compared to other competitor nations. Second, Business Expenditure on Research and Development (BERD), which is in decline as a percentage of GDP, is lower than in other competitor nations and is larger than GOVERD. The combined effect of these trends is that the total Gross Domestic Expenditure on R&D (GERD) has also declined as a percentage of GDP over the last ten years. These trends are illustrated in Table 7.2 and Figure 7.3.

Table 7.2   GERD as Percentage of GDP

	France	Germany	Japan	UK	US
2003	2.17	2.52	3.20	1.78	2.66
2004	2.15	2.49	3.17	1.71	2.59
2005	2.13	2.48	3.32	1.76	2.62(p)
2006	2.1(p)	2.53(p)	3.39	1.78	2.62(p)

Note: (p) = provisional.
Source: OECD (2008a).

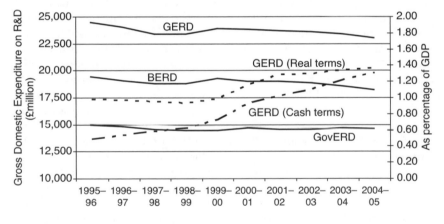

Figure 7.3   Expenditure on R&D

Note: Real terms are calculated using the GDP deflator at market prices; 2006 =100.
Source: BERR (2008).

Looking to the future, the 2004 Science and Innovation Framework and the 2007 Comprehensive Spending Review stated the aim of increasing the science budget by 17.4% in cash terms between 2007/08 and 2010/11, while the European Commission's agenda challenges Member States to spend 3% of GDP on GERD by 2010 (HM Treasury 2007a; European Commission 2002e).

Whether such commitments will be or should be maintained is debatable. The first question is what proportion of GDP a country should spend on science. As a previous Chief Scientific Adviser to the Government, Robert May, pointed out in 1998, we don't know: '[t]here are no theorems, no basic principles that answer these important questions' (May 1998). Recent studies into the optimal percentage of GDP to sustain long-term productivity growth suggest a value between 2.3% and 2.6%.

Perhaps of more practical concern for a new government is the risk of boom and bust in science funding. Given the downbeat short- and medium-term economic outlook, and the progressive increases in science funding in recent years, a plausible future is one where science funding is cut in real and cash terms. Indeed, this debate is beginning to emerge, and concerns have been noted in the 2008 House of Commons report on science budget allocations (House of Commons Innovation, Universities, Science and Skills Committee 2008). The committee foresees that increases in the science budget will fall short of the planned increases in spending.

This being the case, a key policy lever for S&T policy could be the government's £150 billion procurement budget. A proportion of this could be used to stimulate innovation and drive research, largely in the private sector (National Endowment for Science, Technology and the Arts 2007; HM Treasury 2007e). Innovative procurement has the potential to foster the development or invention of goods and services government requires through two mechanisms. The first is that government can support innovation by being an early user. As an early user, government is sending a signal of confidence to the wider marketplace about a new technology. In addition, early users can also be helpful in testing and improving emergent products. The second mechanism is where government guarantees future purchase of a technology or service. For example, the government could announce that it would buy a certain number of portable dialysis machines. This would then reassure the private sector and encourage them to invest in developing the necessary new technology. An interesting alternative to guaranteed purchases is the use of prizes, whereby the government (or other funder) stimulates innovation by offering a prize for, say, the first portable dialysis machine. Through all these mechanisms, innovation risk is being transferred from the private enterprise that develops and supplies a new technology to the public sector that requires such technology. Despite the acknowledged potential, implementation of innovative procurement is not an easy task, and more work needs to be undertaken to understand the context, application and success criteria in using procurement to stimulate innovation (Edler et al 2005).

An incoming government will also need to address how S&T research funding is allocated. A recurrent debate in the academic and lay literature is whether science policy should be mission oriented – 'let's land a man on the moon' – or driven by the curiosity of the researcher, in the belief that serendipity will lead to unpredictable but nevertheless beneficial outcomes.

Anecdotal examples support both schools of thought, but conclusive evidence is much harder to come by (Grant et al 2003).

Partly for this reason, Sir David Cooksey, in his HM Treasury-sponsored report on health and biomedical research in the UK, challenged the accepted interpretation of Haldane, arguing that 'it is clear ... that the establishment of research councils to conduct research at "arm's length from government" was a step beyond that recommended by Haldane' (Cooksey 2006). Although a seemingly arcane historical argument, the commitment to a 'hands off' interpretation of Haldane within the scientific community is widely held. Indeed it is in the clear interests of the scientific community to advocate for, and defend the existence of, unrestricted curiosity driven research funding. On the other hand, politicians need and want to see a return on research investment, and preferably rapidly. Both views have been eloquently articulated over the past 40 years. Arguably neither position is tenable. The scientists' argument is akin to 'trust me: I am a doctor', whilst the politicians' view underestimates the incremental and accumulative pace of scientific development, aspiring to paradigm shifting 'Eureka moments' which are both rare and unpredictable. The question remains whether the results achieved via 'Eureka moments' could have also been obtained via practically oriented research, and if so, if we can evaluate which type of research is more efficient.

Finally, there is a question whether our mental map of S&T is too narrowly focused on traditional manufacturing and industry, and the research that has traditionally supported it. Nelson and Arrow's classic arguments apply just as well to new kinds research that are relevant to financial services, the creative industries and other burgeoning service industries and new product areas. It is important that our definition of research does not inadvertently exclude new forms of inquiry and knowledge.

Lost in translation

In a modern economy, maintaining productivity growth, high standards of living and an equitable society depends on how efficiently knowledge is transferred to the market and end user (Grossman and Helpmann 1993). Yet a number of obstacles to translation exist due to 'market failure' and the 'stickiness of knowledge' (Szulanksi 2003), so typically technology and knowledge transfer is not efficient (Cohen and Levinthal 1990). Against this background, policies to promote technology and knowledge transfer in the UK have progressively become more prominent over the last decade.

One of the undoubted successes of the past decade has been technology transfer from higher education institutes to the market. Although difficult to produce a definitive estimate, almost £800 million of tax-payers' money has been invested in supporting numerous government schemes to promote technology transfer since 1999, and a further £429 million has been allocated to knowledge transfer to 2011 (Table 7.3). This investment has induced a significant cultural change that has legitimized the commercial exploitation of inventions by publicly funded researchers and research institutes and is beginning to see a financial return. The number of patents filed and granted, licensing agreements, spin-out and income from licensing agreements more than doubled between 2001/01 and 2005/06 (Sainsbury 2007).

Table 7.3 Knowledge Transfer Government Schemes

	Years Running	Total Funding (million)
Higher Education Innovation Fund (HEIF) 1,2 and 3	2001/08	£517
Public Sector Research Exploitation Fund, round 1, 2, 3, 4	2001/08	£80
University Challenge Seed Fund, round 1, 2	1999/2001	£60
Science Enterprise Challenge, round 1, 2	1999/2001	£43.9
Cambridge-MIT	2000–	£65
DTI Five Year programme to promote university links		£6
Total Expenditure	**1999/2008**	**£771.9**
HEIF 4	2008/11	£396
Extra for Centres for Knowledge Exchange (CKE)	2008/09	£8
Public Sector Research Exploitation Fund (from Science Budget)	2009/11	£25
Total Planned Expenditure	**2008/11**	**£429**
Grand Total	1999/2011	£1200.9

Source: BERR (2008).

While the government should be congratulated for its achievements in technology transfer, it has not been as focused (or successful) at transferring knowledge that has a non-commercial but valuable end-point. In a 2003 National Audit Office (NAO) report,[3] it was pointed out that

[g]etting research into practice is widely acknowledged to be a difficult process. For research with potential commercial outcomes, a number of schemes are available to help researchers realise the economic potential of their findings, such as seed funding for protocol and pre-market development. However, for research that aims to improve service delivery and inform policy, the outcomes are often not commercially exploitable. Yet, for non-commercial research, there is also a need to help researchers realise the social benefits of their findings. (NAO 2003)

The difficulty of getting research into practice has long been recognized. At least three recent literature reviews refer to numerous academic studies that have reported this problem over the past 30 years (Stone et al 2001; Hanney et al 2002; Innvaer et al 2002). More recently, the British Academy concluded that policymakers are not realizing the full potential of social science research (British Academy 2008). The 2003 NAO report, based on case studies and an extensive literature review, outlined the 'explanations for the perceived gap between policy and research'. A summary of the most important explanations is provided in Box 7.2. The British Academy report recommends a move to a 'co-production' model of policymaking where the boundaries between researcher and policymaker are consciously blurred through extensive exchanges and engagement through both policy and research processes.

Box 7.2   **Why Knowledge Is Not Transferred**

- Research results are not easily accessible
- Policy questions are poorly understood by the researchers
- Research results are poorly communicated by the researchers
- Research results are poorly understood by policymakers
- Research results have no direct, short-term relevance for policy.

Perhaps most damning is that this evidence was known and articulated as long ago as the 1970s. A charitable view would be that getting non-commercial research into practice is intractable, i.e. practice on a significant scale is not feasible. That said, an interesting thought experiment would be to consider the impact of over £1 billion invested in non-commercial research outcomes. This could include: supporting databases to identify and disseminate what works, such as the Cochrane Collaboration and the Blueprints for Violence Prevention project in the US; the establishment of knowledge brokering organizations such as the Canadian Health Services Research Foundation (see Box 7.3, and Conklin et al 2008); research funding for journalists and professional writers to make research results more accessible, such as that successfully used by the ESRC in its *Future of Work* programme (Wooding et al 2007); and, support for researchers to spend time in government, such as the recent ESRC *Placement Fellows Scheme*.

Box 7.3   **Canadian Health Services Research Foundation (CHSRF)**

The Canadian Health Services Research Foundation is a leader in what it describes as 'knowledge exchange'. Not a granting council, CHSRF was instead incorporated as an arm's length, not-for-profit foundation in spring 1997 to fund health services research but also to promote its use in Canada's health sector. The CHSRF was set up in response to federal government interest in improving the scientific basis for decisions made by health services managers and policy-makers, and also concerns about what had been a paucity of applied research within Canada's existing granting councils, particularly the medical research council.

From advocacy to accountability

Part of the implicit deal between the Treasury and the scientific community (as represented through DIUS and the Research Councils) was the need to demonstrate an economic impact – or return – for the additional investment. Although officials at the Treasury understood many of the challenges associated with evaluating research – notably the role of serendipity, the lengthy time lags between research investment and outcome, and the challenge of attributing gain to a specific investment – they also made it clear to the scientific community that some form of auditing was essential.

This resulted in a number of laudable responses. First the (then) Department of Trade and Industry (now DIUS) put together an 'Outputs Framework' responding to a series of Public Service Agreements between the Treasury and the DTI (DTI 2005). This framework was then cascaded down into the seven Research Councils, which were all required to respond against a broad set of targets using appropriate metrics. The first iterations of the output framework focused more on inputs and process than on outputs and outcomes (and in the language of the Treasury, 'economic impacts'). As a consequence, and with the support of the Treasury, the Research Councils commissioned Peter Warry to examine what economic impact there was and how it could be increased (Warry 2006). Concurrent with this official investigation of economic impact, in its 2006 report, *Medical Research: Assessing the Benefits to Society*, the Academy of Medical Sciences made a number of recommendations, including a clear statement that the 'research community should consider how it can better demonstrate the value and benefits of medical research to all its stakeholders' (Academy of Medical Sciences 2006). A related issue is understanding what works in science policy – that is 'researching research' (Smith 1987; Grant et al 2004; Marburger 2005). This agenda was endorsed by Cooksey and the Academy of Medical Sciences and is beginning to be implemented by various research funders (Cooksey 2006; AMS 2006).[4]

An incoming government must continue to demand, and support, the accountability of publicly funded science and scientists, not only to ensure value for money, but also to acknowledge that science is part of democratic society and thus needs the support of all stakeholders.

Policy options

The above discussion sets out the historical antecedents and contemporary issues around S&T policy in the UK that a future government will need to address. Two clear themes emerge. The first is that S&T policy is a relatively stable and enduring policy domain. Second, given the support for science over the past decade, it may prove difficult for an incoming government to develop a policy that is perceived to improve on the status quo.

Together these create an opportunity to take a more radical – and thus risky – approach to future S&T policy which could be transformational. In Box 7.4 we set out a series of policy options, under three strategic headings: *If it ain't broke, don't fix it*, *Unfinished business*, and *Mainstreaming evidence*. As is the norm with any options appraisal, we have stretched the policy frame by including a range of ideas that merit consideration by an incoming government. As our brief is to identify options – as opposed to making recommendations – we deliberately do not identify our preferred set.

Box 7.4   Policy Options for an Incoming Government

Option 1: *If it ain't broke, don't fix it*

- No strategic change, i.e. follow agenda set out in the *Race to the Top*
- See through existing initiatives such as the Technology Strategy Board
- 'Defend' existing S&T expenditure in government and business

Option 2: *Unfinished business*

- Focus on procurement as a tool to stimulate innovation (including reforming the Small Business Research Initiative)
- Put evidence at the heart of policymaking in government departments

Option 3: *Mainstreaming evidence*

- Establish translation agencies
- Unify and refocus RCUK into a single Haldane Fund for 'research for general use'

In drawing together these three options we suggest that the following are also likely, though not inevitable:

1. **There will be no significant increase in government expenditure on R&D, in absolute or proportionate terms.** The combination of recession-led public expenditure constraints and existing spending plans limit an incoming government's ability to significantly increase the science budget. While econometric models suggest that further increases in science spending in the UK would generate healthy returns, these of course need to be set alongside alternative options and priorities for spending in other areas (see other chapters in this volume).
2. **There will be a decline in the scientific human capital (i.e. knowledge workers) available to work on publicly funded R&D in the UK.** Although the 'brain gain' is likely to continue, it will not be large enough to offset the decline due to the continued competition for talent from the private sector and other well-funded public sector research systems.

3. **There will be continued demand for accountability.** The current system of performance management and overall accountability will bed down and raise further questions regarding the economic returns from research.

Option 1: if it ain't broke, don't fix it

The presumption for this option is that the current S&T policy is delivering and, crucially, will continue to deliver in the future so no radical overhaul is needed. This does not imply doing nothing. As we enter an economic downturn it will be important for an incoming government to protect existing R&D expenditure and not allow it to be cut or raided for other areas of government activity. As noted earlier in the chapter, the return from science expenditure is significant and must be seen as an investment for future economic growth and improvements in welfare. A greater challenge will be persuading the private sector to follow suit. In addition, Lord Sainsbury's 2007 review of government science and innovation policy made a number of recommendations which have been accepted by the current government. These will need to be executed to ensure that the current strategic direction is maintained.

Option 2: unfinished business

The purchasing power of government can be used to stimulate innovation in the private sector. The public sector spends around £150 billion a year on procurement and a small proportion of this could be used as an early and/or guaranteed future purchase of new technologies. Whilst there is a political consensus that an incoming government should use procurement as a policy lever in this field, the detail as to how such a policy will be successfully implemented is lacking. Formulating and implementing an effective policy that leverages the purchasing power of government to support private sector innovation will prove challenging but attractive to an incoming government.

This option also envisages a parallel effort to stimulate innovation in the public sector by putting evidence at the heart of policymaking. As noted in Figure 7.1, government departments spend £1.9 billion a year on SET. For this research to affect the way that policy is formulated and service is delivered, it needs to be embedded within the policymaking process. A commitment to evidence-based policymaking, the expansion of information platforms, interchange of researchers and policymakers between one-another's institutes, and a move to a 'co-production' model will all be essential ingredients of this policy mix.

Option 3: mainstreaming evidence

There is an element of *déjà vu* in trying to improve the use of evidence in policymaking. This was a clear theme in the early years of New Labour and captured in a number of documents, including *Modernising Government White Paper* (Cabinet Office 1999). The fact that this remains a challenge suggests that a more transformational approach may be required. Just as the Technology Strategy Board needed to be relaunched as an arm's length agency to improve technological innovation in the UK, it could be argued that translation agencies are needed to facilitate the use of evidence in policymaking. Whether this can be done by a single agency or a series of discipline-based agencies will need to be discussed. Either way, such agencies need to have a remit of synthesizing the existing and new knowledge base and translating and localizing it into a form that will help and inform the policymaking community. The closest example to these translation agencies is the Canadian Health Services Research Foundation (as described earlier in Box 7.3), which spends about half its budget on research and the other half on knowledge brokerage (Conklin et al 2008). A radical option for creating the funding for such agencies would be to abolish the Research Councils. A unified Haldane Fund could be established with a mission to undertake curiosity-driven research to enhance the research knowledge base of the UK. The fund would be exclusively dedicated to basic research or, in the words or Haldane, 'research for the general use' and would be formed from the basic research element of the Research Councils' budgets. The remaining, applied, element would be used to fund the translation agencies.

Notes

1. Throughout this chapter we refer to both the Science, Technology and Engineering (SET) budget and the government expenditure on Research and Development (GOVERD). The definition of the SET budget is provided by the Department for Business, Enterprise and Regulatory Reform (BERR), and is a subset of GOVERD. For the sake of international comparison we will often refer to GOVERD, however, the total expenditures on Science and Technology are more accurately reflected by the SET budget.
2. The seven research councils are: Arts and Humanities Research Council (AHRC), Biotechnology and Biological Sciences Research Council (BBSRC), Engineering and Physical Sciences Research Council (EPSRC), Economic and Social Research Council (ESRC), Medical Research Council (MRC), Natural Environment Research Council (NERC), Science and Technology Facilities Council (STFC).
3. Co-authored by Jonathan Grant.
4. For example, JG is a co-Director of a DH funded Policy Research Unit that examines S&T policy in the health domain and is also part of a collaboration investigating the economic returns from research funded by the Medical Research Council, Wellcome Trust and Academy of Medical Science.

8
Crime and Criminal Justice: Exploring the Policy Options

Mike Hough and Julian V. Roberts

Criminal justice remains one of the most contested domains of public policy. Crime and the response to crime attract a level of public and media attention that few other areas of public policy can match. This creates pressure upon politicians and policymakers who often have to devise or amend crime policies in reaction to some high-profile crime or in response to periodic tabloid campaigns. The sheer volume of criminal justice legislation during the years since the last *Options for Britain* volume was published (Halpern et al 1996) creates a challenge for scholars of criminal policy. Some areas of justice have changed in a totally unexpected way while others have remained unexpectedly unchanged.

For example, few if anyone in 1995 predicted: (i) the creation of the anti-social behaviour initiative, including the Anti-Social Behaviour Order (ASBO), the Acceptable Behaviour Contract (ABC) and the Dispersal Order; (ii) the abrogation (in the Criminal Justice Act 2003) of the ancient rule against 'double jeopardy' and the introduction of restrictions to the right to trial by jury; (iii) the decline in crime rates across a wide range of offences; (iv) the vertiginous rise in the size of the prison population; (v) the creation of not one but two statutory bodies to devise and promulgate sentencing guidelines; (vi) the widespread use of indeterminate sentences; and (vii) the inauguration of a Ministry of Justice separated from the Home Office – to name just a few developments during the last decade.

Since the early 1990s, criminal justice policymaking has become increasingly politicized. As the next general election looms, all political parties will gird themselves for the penal policy debate which is likely to prove one of the most heated areas of public policy. The government will point to its increasingly populist agenda in recent years to buttress its claim to represent the community's interests.[1] The opposition will likely assume a tougher approach to criminal justice, albeit one which will attempt also to be rather nuanced, in the way that Blair's 'tough on crime, tough on the causes of crime' conveyed a dual message about crime policy. Opposition politicians will also point to the government's limited success in assuaging public anxiety about crime, or in tackling issues such as knife crime that have assumed a high public and media profile.

The political stakes are high; crime and criminal justice are likely to play a determinative role in deciding the outcome of the election. An Ipsos Reid poll in 2007 asked respondents to rate the importance of a range of issues facing Britain. Crime and anti-social behaviour was the issue cited as being 'very important' by the largest percentage of respondents (57%), ahead of health care (54%), education (45%), or managing the economy (28%) (Duffy et al 2008). How the parties develop and present their criminal justice policies to the public will therefore have an important impact on the outcome of the election.

Regardless of its political orientation, the next government will have to choose between populist criminal justice policies or a more nuanced – and hence less politically attractive – approach to responding to crime and disorder. The experience in other jurisdictions suggests that if the next government is elected with a minority or a weak majority, criminal justice policymaking will continue to reflect short-term goals, and will remain essentially reactive in nature. One of the goals of the current chapter is to suggest and promote a longer-term approach to criminal policy development.

This brief chapter contains three parts. We start with an assessment of crime trends since 1997 – and set these in the context of slightly longer time-frames, and of public perceptions of the crime problem. We then examine some cross-cutting policy issues which the next government will need to address in its policies on crime control. Finally we examine five specific policy issues which need addressing.

Crime trends since 1997

Two thirds of the polled public in 2007 believed that there had been a lot more crime across the country in the previous two years (Duffy et al 2008). In fact, people respond that crime rates have been increasing whenever the question is posed – evidence of the effect of media coverage (Roberts and Hough 2005). Despite considerable public concern about crime, crime trends since 1997 show a clear downward trend. Figure 8.1 shows trends since 1981, and reveals three trend-lines, indexed to 1981 levels:

- British Crime Survey (BCS) trends for *'All BCS crime'* (bottom line)
- Crimes *reported* to the police, as measured by the BCS (top line, dotted)
- Crime statistics *recorded* by the police (middle line, until 2001/02).

The BCS provides estimates of crimes reported to the police as well as crimes that remain unreported. (The survey asks a large sample of the general population to state any crimes of which they have been a victim within the previous 12 months.) Victims are also asked whether they reported incidents

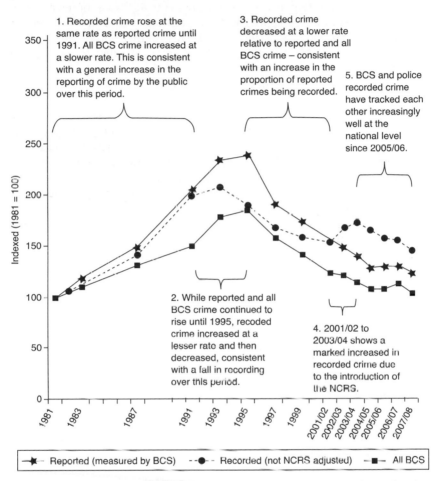

1. Recorded crime rose at the same rate as reported crime until 1991. All BCS crime increased at a slower rate. This is consistent with a general increase in the reporting of crime by the public over this period.

2. While reported and all BCS crime continued to rise until 1995, recoded crime increased at a lesser rate and then decreased, consistent with a fall in recording over this period.

3. Recorded crime decreased at a lower rate relative to reported and all BCS crime – consistent with an increase in the proportion of reported crimes being recorded.

4. 2001/02 to 2003/04 shows a marked increased in recorded crime due to the introduction of the NCRS.

5. BCS and police recorded crime have tracked each other increasingly well at the national level since 2005/06.

— ★ — Reported (measured by BCS)   – – ● – – Recorded (not NCRS adjusted)   — ■ — All BCS

1. BCS estimates for 1991 to 2007/08 are based on estimates of population and the number of households in England and Wales that have been revised in light of the 2001 Census. For more information please see the Glossary.
2. From 2001/02, reported and all BCS crime relate to interviews carried out in that financial year and incidents experienced in the 12 months prior to interview. Recorded crimes relate to incidents in the 12 months up to the end of September of that financial year. This is so that the recorded crime data are centred on the same period as reported and all BCS crime.

Figure 8.1   Crime trends in England and Wales from 1981

Source: Kershaw et al (2008).

to the police. The BCS does not provide a complete count of crime – were such an enterprise even possible – but it provides a reasonable guide to crimes committed against individuals and their personal property.

The 'All BCS crime' trend shows a steady rise until 1995, followed by an equally stable decline (Figure 8.1). According to the BCS, rates of most crimes have fallen since the mid-1990s, and the declines in burglary and vehicle crime rates have been particularly marked. This – rather optimistic – view of crime has been the subject of much political and media debate, as recorded crime statistics tell a different story.

Police recording practices have fluctuated considerably since 1997. The police started to record proportionately fewer crimes in the early 1990s – probably responding to Michael Howard's performance management regime which placed considerable emphasis on meeting crime reduction targets. This trend was reversed from 1998 onwards when a greater emphasis was placed on more comprehensive recording; and in 2002 the National Crime Recording Standard (NCRS) introduced an explicit policy of full recording, in particular taking victims' reports at face value. The upward turn in trends in recorded crime from 2001/02 to 2003/04 is therefore largely illusory.

In sum, we can be confident that most forms of crime have fallen over the last decade, although the causes of the declining rates remain hotly debated. However, there are exceptions to the pattern of lower rates, with evidence of increases in the number of:

- 'e-crimes' (e.g. identity theft, downloading pornography);
- theft or robbery of 'hot consumer products' such as iPods and plasma TVs;
- violence and disorder linked to the late-night economy;[2]
- crimes of violence related to gang culture or to drug markets.[3]

Some cross-cutting policy issues

Before addressing five specific policy challenges, we shall consider three sets of 'cross-cutting' policy issues that have implications for many areas of criminal policy. They relate to:

- the balance to be struck between exclusionary and inclusionary crime prevention strategies;
- the need to pursue public confidence and trust in justice;
- the balance to be struck between management driven by professional standards and management driven by numerical performance targets.

Exclusion or inclusion?

The nature and magnitude of the crime problem depends critically on the degree to which our politicians can counterbalance the tendency towards punitive 'tough on crime' policies with those that are genuinely 'tough on the causes of crime'. Our best guess is that many liberal market countries such as Britain will demonstrate an increasing tendency towards populist strategies that will aim – but fail – to restrain rising crimes rates. At the same time they will invest too little in strategies of social inclusion that may lead to a more stable social order. There are two broad policy responses to the crime problems created by socially marginalized groups: deploying *exclusionary* strategies (such as the mass imprisonment that characterizes the US) or *inclusionary* strategies designed to increase commitment to the law and to mitigate the impact of social and economic inequalities. Britain faces fundamental political choices ahead and it is essential to strike the right balance between these two approaches.

Exclusionary strategies attempt to reduce crime rates through narrowly instrumental measures that make it harder, riskier, or more costly for people to commit crime. Whilst incapacitative imprisonment best illustrates the paradigm, we would also include deterrent strategies involving formal policing as well as technological strategies involving forms of surveillance that support deterrent and incapacitative strategies (e.g. CCTV, DNA testing). There are also target-hardening solutions to crime, associated in particular with the design or management of the physical environment. In short, exclusionary strategies are designed to *thwart* the impulse to offend.

Inclusionary strategies by contrast *dissipate* the impulse to offend through strategies aimed at social inclusion and cohesion – whether this takes the form of economic inclusion, or re-inclusion into mainstream values. We shall not discuss strategies of economic inclusion here – but this is not to downplay their importance. Patterns of crime over the next 25 years are likely to be shaped substantially by changes in patterns of economic and social inequality. If the government fails to promote greater equality, increased crime is one likely consequence (cf. Wilkinson and Pickett 2009). Policies designed to contain income inequality can be justified in part by their crime preventive impact, but this justification will always be secondary to considerations of social justice.

Public trust in justice

More narrowly relevant for our purposes are those inclusionary strategies that aim specifically to stimulate normative commitment to the rule of law. Many of these strategies constitute forms of secondary prevention, in that they target known offenders and aim to rehabilitate these individuals. Other strategies are concerned with encouraging compliance with the laws across the broader population. Criminology has devoted most of its efforts to examining why people break the law; too rarely does it address the question why most people *obey* the law most of the time. An obvious but important point to remember is that they do so at least in part because they think it *wrong* to break the law. Any intelligent criminal policy has to reflect the fact there is an important element of normative compliance to crime control.

In general terms, policy needs to identify the 'drivers' of institutional legitimacy within criminal justice, and to consider how best to bolster the legitimacy of the institutions of justice. Theories of procedural justice suggest that treating people with fairness and respect are critical strategies for achieving this objective (Tyler 2003, 2007). A significant challenge is that much of the information that people receive about justice is filtered – and distorted – by the mass media. Effective strategies of community engagement are needed. The progress that has been made with neighbourhood policing is encouraging, but public ignorance about the courts is so pervasive (e.g. Roberts and Hough 2005) that it will be difficult to persuade people that sentencers are, for the most part, both rational and reasonably tough in their sentencing practice. We have argued elsewhere that some sort of institutional solution is needed to address public mistrust of the courts, such as the establishment of a sentencing commission with an explicit community engagement function (Jacobson and Hough 2008). Public criticism of sentencers is unlikely to be eliminated by this step – the tabloid newspapers will ensure that judges always remain targets for public obloquy – but it may at least undermine some populist attacks.

Professional standards or numerical targets?

One of the marked trends in justice policy since 1994 has been the way in which 'New Public Management' (NPM) has taken hold. Whilst the criminal justice system had somehow managed largely to evade the first wave of public sector managerialism imposed by government in the 1980s, this increasingly made itself felt on the police in the 1990s. Both Labour and Conservative governments have enthusiastically pursued forms of NPM. The favoured solutions included budgetary cuts, applying private sector management methods to the public sector, and increasing the degree of choice over the providers of these services. Crucially there has also been increasing emphasis on securing greater accountability to central government through performance management regimes that rely on quantitative performance indicators and target-setting.

The problems of institutional inflexibility that NPM was designed to address were real enough, but the problems associated with NPM across many areas of social policy have become increasingly apparent, in terms of the unintended consequences of poorly specified targets. Recently, there have been signs of a governmental retreat from micro-management, both in criminal justice and in other areas of social policy. In particular the 2008 Policing Green Paper (Home Office 2008b) set out plans for a form of policing governance that promises to place much less emphasis on targets set by central government, and places much more emphasis on locally set priorities, reflecting the preferences of local communities. There are also calls from both the main opposition parties to abandon national targets altogether – a move that would appear consistent with all the parties' ambitions for localism and civic renewal.

It remains to be seen whether this form of locally responsive decentralization is a more viable option than the NPM that we have seen for the last 15 years. Certainly these two do not represent the only options for criminal justice performance management. There are others, better suited to the highly complex environment of criminal justice. Part of the problem is that central government has been overly-concerned with the measurement of *outcomes*. One of the central tenets of New Public Management is that conventional bureaucracies lose sight of outcomes in their concern with process, and that performance management systems should instead have a clear outcome focus (cf. Osborne and Gaebler 1992). This is all very well if it is possible to specify outcome measures with subtlety and sensitivity. But after a decade and a half of attempts, it is clear that central government never quite managed to develop a set of measures that can be implemented with integrity whilst reflecting the complexity of the justice environment. If we are right in arguing that institutional legitimacy is a key ingredient for successful criminal policy, then policy needs to have a subtle appreciation of the ways in which the institutions of justice are perceived, and any quantitative performance indicators that are used will need to be deployed and interpreted more intelligently than has occurred to date.

In our view, there is a strong case for making principles of justice and professional standards the cornerstones of performance management in criminal justice. In other words, there should be a rather looser oversight by government – whether central or local – of criminal justice agencies. Performance monitoring might be seen not as a process of target-setting goal-achievement (or outcome achievement), but about monitoring policing or probation or court practice against professional and ethical standards. Whilst the justice system needs to remain outcome-focused, it does not make sense to deny the complexity of the justice environment, and to expect to see a simple relationship between activities and the achievement of desired outcomes. This would represent a reversion to principles of professionalism against which NPM was a reaction. If the professional judgement of criminal justice managers is to be given more weight in performance assessment, this has to be done in a way that is not at the expense of accountability. There will be a continued need for some forms of quantitative indicators and targets, but it is crucial that these should properly reflect the most important dimensions upon which local managers need to be held to account. It should be clear from what we have said above that *trust in justice* is precisely one such dimension.

Critical policy challenges

In this section we identify five important policy challenges: (i) Responding to violent crime; (ii) Addressing drug crime; (iii) Reducing re-offending rates;

(iv) Reducing the size of the prison population; (v) Correcting public misperceptions about crime trends.

Responding to violent crime

Public concern about violent crime has long been, and remains intense. Developing a persuasive and effective political response to this form of offending has proved elusive. Part of the difficulty is that the problems of violent crime break down into several different components; and part is that some of these sub-components are poorly measured either by police statistics or by the British Crime Survey. Both the BCS and police statistics indicate that the majority of the population face lower risks of violent crime than we did ten years ago. Few people would probably believe this, but it is hard to find any explanation for the downward trend in BCS violence since 1996 except that – *for the people covered by the survey* – the risks are indeed in decline.

Violence associated with alcohol use

Violence and disorder associated with binge drinking has been a staple of media news for several years. There is no doubt that patterns of leisure activity for young people have changed over the last decade or more, with higher levels of alcohol consumption in venues that are geographically and temporally concentrated: the 'late-night economy' of both large city centres and of smaller cities and towns has become increasingly visible. With it have come problems of violent crime and social disorder. The liberalization of licensing laws introduced by the Licensing Act 2003 does not appear to have further stimulated, or reduced, alcohol-related violence (Hough and Hunter 2008) but levels of alcohol consumption remain high.

The problem is best conceptualized as a crime of affluence. People have more disposable income than before, and the cost of alcohol has declined significantly in recent years. Relative to some other forms of violence, it is probably more amenable to prevention. Although the Licensing Act was seen at its introduction as relinquishing all controls over licensed premises, it actually provides local authorities, as the new licensing authorities, with extensive powers to intervene where licensed premises are causing problems. What is needed is the political will, at the local level, to use the new powers to take action where action is necessary. Beyond this, excessive alcohol consumption needs to be treated as a public health issue – as indeed the current administration is doing. The extent to which drinking cultures amongst young people are permeable to government initiatives may seem limited, but there have been considerable successes in the past, for example in relation to drunk driving. There is also extensive evidence that levels of alcohol consumption are sensitive to changes in price, though there are political costs and obstacles to tackling binge drinking though price control strategies.

Knife crime

Throughout 2008 knife crime has been increasingly visible in the media. This has had an impact on the public. When respondents who thought crime had been increasing were asked to identify the specific category of crime they had in mind, 'knife crime' was the most frequent category cited (Duffy et al 2008). There have been several high-profile murders, mainly involving boys and young men. Often, but not exclusively, victims and offenders have been members of rival gangs, or at least share a gang culture associated with deprived groups in inner cities. Some victims, however, appear to have been caught up in violent confrontations randomly, and in some cases, fights that might have ended simply with a bruise or two now result – because of the presence of knives – in severe injury or death. In contrast to violence associated with binge drinking, it makes no sense to think of these forms of violence as crimes of affluence. Indeed whilst it is something of a sociological cliché to say so, violence can serve as a means of securing status and respect within such sub-cultures, whose members have limited access to more conventional forms of achievement. Nor is there any reason to think that alcohol or drugs serve as facilitators.

Crimes of this sort are likely to prove more of a political challenge than alcohol-related violence. There is some scope to change young people's behaviour in carrying knives – which will reduce the severity of injuries arising from violent assaults – but the problem will remain that groups of young men who find themselves excluded from the opportunities of mainstream society are likely to play life by a different set of rules. To the extent that this is true, the solution is to be found in strategies targeting those groups, typically in poor inner city areas and often from minority ethnic groups, who have prolonged experience of social exclusion.

Addressing drug crimes and drug related acquisitive crimes

Illicit drug use has grown in most industrialized countries since the 1970s (see for example, EMCDDA 2008). There are signs that some forms of drug use have peaked, but it is unquestionable that the use of drugs of dependence, notably heroin and cocaine, is now at a very much higher level than 40 years ago. It is also clear that there is a strong association between dependent drug use and acquisitive crime.

The literature (summarized in McSweeney and Hough 2005; McSweeney et al 2008) suggests that 'lifestyle' and 'sub-cultural' factors are important in explaining why those who try illicit drugs are also more likely to get involved in other forms of law-breaking. The search for novelty and excitement and the enjoyment of the rewards of risk-taking are defining aspects of youth culture. It is hardly surprising that large minorities of the population engage in the – relatively controlled – risks of both recreational drug use and minor crime at some stage of their adolescence and young adulthood. For those whose offending – and drug use – is more persistent and less controlled, other explanatory factors also need to be called into play. In the first place, chaotic drug users and persistent offenders – in contrast to controlled drug users and occasional petty offenders – have limited social and economic resources, and limited exposure to legitimate 'life opportunities'. The majority come from deprived backgrounds, with inconsistent parenting, poor access to housing and health care, low educational attainment and limited employment prospects. *Controlled* drug use has no obvious association with social exclusion; how could it, given the scale of participation? *Chaotic* or *dependent* use, by contrast, shares that constellation of risk factors that also predict heavy involvement in crime – and exposure to many forms of social exclusion.

While social factors predispose people both to uncontrolled drug use and to involvement in persistent offending, reciprocal causal relationships can begin to emerge, whereby criminal involvement both facilitates and maintains drug use, and drug use maintains involvement in crime (McSweeney and Hough 2005). Whilst sub-cultural explanations of the close linkage carry some weight, the accounts of the offenders themselves are more consistent with a pathological perspective, where dependence provides the motive for acquisitive offending.

Both the current and the previous administration have pursued strategies which combine public health approaches with the use of the criminal justice system as a conduit for bringing treatment to drug dependent offenders. Examples of strategies include drug arrest referral systems, drug treatment and testing orders and drug treatment courts. Research demonstrates that this drug treatment approach brings benefits at the margin, but is far from a panacea. It is resource-intensive, and drop-out rates from treatment can be high – in common with treatment into which people enter voluntarily. Re-offending rates are high for these drop-outs. There are also risks that this strategy may displace from treatment those dependent users who do not fund their habit through crime. Nevertheless the approach is as effective – and as cost-effective – as the alternative approaches such as imprisonment (cf. McSweeney et al 2008). What is now required are new ways of ensuring retention in treatment programmes and compliance with treatment conditions. One approach is to extend the medical prescription of drugs such as heroin. At present, the majority of prescription services offer substitute drugs, notably methadone, which are less attractive (by definition) to dependent users than their drug of choice.

In the longer term, the social costs of illicit drug markets and illicit drug consumption may become so high that legalization and tight regulation may be the only realistic option. International (United Nations) conventions may well limit the room for manoeuvre in the short term, but an incoming government needs to give more serious thought to the viability of legalizing and regulating selected drugs.

Reducing re-offending

The United Kingdom has traditionally been one of the beacons of best practices in probation, with one of the best developed, and best resourced, systems in the world (Hamai et al 1995). It has been further developed by both the present and the previous administration. However the last decade has been an unhappy one for probation, with a series of government initiatives to reform and centralize the service to enable it to provide a still greater range of community penalties for offenders. From 2003 onwards the government has struggled to introduce a viable National Offender Management Service (NOMS) which was designed to provide greater coordination between probation and prison work. Plans for reform were adopted with insufficient thought, and implemented in ways that maximized confusion (Hough et al 2006). The most marked legacy of these reforms is a seriously demoralized probation service. Perhaps the most important lesson for the next administration is to avoid any further organizational upheaval. The probation and prison services need time to settle down into the new arrangements.

However, there are other issues to address. Thinking about work with offenders has become overly narrow. The dominant model is a technocratic one, in which 'offender managers' orchestrate the delivery of evidence-based interventions that address offenders' 'criminogenic needs'. Work with offenders might benefit from adopting a conceptually richer approach to work with offenders.

The effectiveness of prison and probation work with offenders is likely to be shaped by several interacting factors. These will certainly include the structured activities, or interventions, to which offenders are exposed, but other factors may be much more important such as:

- The overall approach to work with offenders pursued by the probation or prison staff
- The quality of the regime of the prison or the ethos of the probation team
- The personal qualities and skills of the staff
- The level of funding for the service
- The resources of other organizations upon which prison or probation staff can draw.

It is reasonable to expect that the interventions to which offenders are exposed will have *some* impact on their subsequent behaviour, but these are unlikely to be the major determinant of prison or probation outcomes. At present, the government has advocated an approach to working with offenders which we call the 'case-manager/interventions' model. According to this model, the most skilled of prison and probation staff assess offender needs and decide on a package of interventions tailored to this need. The interventions are then delivered by other staff whose work is orchestrated by the case-manager. Within this model, it is the programmes or interventions which are assumed to be the things that really make the difference to outcomes. The human qualities and social skills of staff can add value to the assessment process and to interventions, but only in a subsidiary way.

This is not the only model of practice with any currency, of course. The traditional approach is the casework model, where the 'craft' of the key worker is in managing a process of effective moral persuasion. In this model, caseworkers may well deploy interventions in support of their work, but they will not regard interventions as the primary means of effecting change. There is very little narrowly defined *evaluative* evidence against which to test current policy preferences for the case-manager/interventions model – though plenty of useful evidence exists against which to evaluate the model. In particular, when offenders are asked what style of probation support they want, they consistently stress the importance of working with the same supervising officer. The continuity of the human contact allowed offenders to place trust in their supervising officer, which in turn allowed them to talk openly about personal issues and ask for help (e.g. Partridge 2004). However the probation and prison services are reformed over the coming decade, it is essential that politicians and their civil servants give greater recognition to the fact that rehabilitation is a human process, achieved through a trusting collaboration between offender and staff.

Reducing the prison population

Although the public may disagree, one of the most pressing issues that a new government will need to tackle is the rising prison population. The largely unplanned and uncontrolled increase in prison numbers has tightly constrained the current government's room for manoeuvre in developing new and imaginative policies, as almost all 'new money' in justice budgets is consumed by the prison system. Whilst there is considerable consensus among policy experts and criminal justice scholars that something needs to be done about the prison population, there is considerable disagreement about the appropriate remedies. First, however it is necessary to document the problem.

The most significant trend in punishment has been the steep increase in the use of imprisonment as a sanction. Figure 8.2 shows that the prison population in England and Wales has risen over most of the post-war period. For much of this time, the growth reflected rising crime rates, and increasing court workloads. Since the early to mid-1990s, however, patterns have been distinctively different. The numbers of offenders sentenced by the courts have been stable. Crime rates have fallen, yet the prison population has almost doubled since 1992, rising more steeply than at any time since 1945.

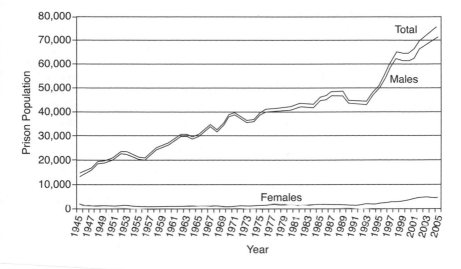

Figure 8.2   Growth in the Average Prison Population 1945–2005

Source: Carter (2007).

Relationship between sentence severity and crime rates

Readers who compare Figures 8.1 and 8.2 may be tempted to conclude that the steep increase in the use of imprisonment caused the sharp fall in crime rates. We caution against such an interpretation. This is not the place for a detailed examination of the evidence upon the incapacitative effects of custody – the preventive impact of keeping offenders out of circulation, in prison. The criminological consensus is that increasing the prison population can achieve some modest gains in reducing crime, but that this approach to crime prevention is both financially and socially costly (von Hirsch et al 1999). Cost-benefit analyses from the United States tend to support Michael Howard's dictum that 'prison works', but only at a price that makes it a very poor investment choice (e.g. Spelman 2005). Estimating the incapacitative benefits of imprisonment is an imprecise science, but the Halliday sentencing review (Home Office 2001d) suggested that a 15% increase in the prison population might achieve a reduction of only 1% in recorded crime.

Causes of growth in the prison population

The immediate cause of the growth in the prison population can be stated very simply: since 1992 the sentencing process has become tougher in all respects. Sentencers are more likely to pass custodial sentences in this decade than in the 1990s, and when they do, sentence lengths are likely to be longer.[4] The Parole Board has also become more reluctant to release prisoners on licence. Offenders are more likely to be recalled to prison following a breach of licence conditions, and are more likely to be sent to prison for breach of a community order.

Clearly, the next government will need to achieve more control over the prison population. As noted earlier in this chapter, the prison estate is currently at capacity. The government has had to resort to a number of short-term initiatives such as increasing the use of the home detention curfew scheme to prevent overcrowding. The use of such measures undermines public confidence in the criminal justice system and undermines the sentencing process.

This raises the issue of sentencing guidelines which has recently been the subject of much political, public and professional debate. At present, the Sentencing Guidelines Council issues definitive guidelines, following a protracted and rather inefficient consultation process.[5] By late 2009, the Council hopes to have issued definitive guidelines for a range of common offences. The accuracy of prison population predictions, and the size of the prison population, depend critically on the extent to which courts follow these guidelines. However, the only statutory obligation on courts is found in s. 172 and 174(2) of the Criminal Justice Act 2003. These provisions require courts to 'have regard to any guidelines which are relevant to the offender's case', and 'Where guidelines indicate that a sentence of a particular kind, or within a particular range would normally be appropriate for the offence and the sentence is of a different kind, or is outside that range, state the court's reasons for deciding on a sentence of a different kind or outside the range.'

These provisions represent a relatively mild degree of constraint upon sentencers. It would be surprising, therefore, if a significant proportion of sentences imposed were not outside the Council's guidelines, thus undermining efforts to contain or predict next year's prison population on the basis of guidelines with respect to the use of custody. Moreover, although the Sentencing Advisory Panel has been in existence for a decade now (since 1998), no statistics are collected which reveal the proportion of sentences falling within or beyond the Council's guidelines.[6] If the government is serious about wishing to be able to control the size of the prison population it will have to ensure that (i) a reasonable proportion of sentences fall within the sentencing guidelines; and (ii) a statistical database is available to continuously monitor judicial compliance with the guidelines.

Achieving the first objective will require a careful reconsideration of the statutory provisions relating to compliance with the guidelines, while the latter can only be achieved by considerable investment in developing an adequate sentencing database. At the time of writing (September 2008) we await the government's response to the report of the Sentencing Commission Working Group which was created to study the feasibility of adopting a US-style sentencing commission in England and Wales. In its final report the Working Group rejected such a reform, recommending instead that the government fuse the two statutory guidelines authorities into a single body, and make a number of other changes to ensure that sentencing becomes more predictable (Sentencing Commission Working Group 2008).

The policy options include the following:

- Increase the use of executive release from prison for the last part of custodial sentences
- Build more prisons, including so-called 'titan prisons'
- Institute an American-style tight sentencing guideline system
- Review the current guidance arrangements with a view to making sentencing patterns more consistent and predictable.

Reducing the size of the custodial population is only one challenge relating to prisons in this jurisdiction. There is a clear need to make correctional institutions more effective, in terms of programmes aimed at reducing re-offending. One way that this may be achieved is through the use of so-called 'titan' prisons, as proposed by Lord Carter (2007). Services including programmes addressing re-offending and substance abuse can be delivered more effectively in this way, although these larger institutions are not without their critics. The first step, however, in ensuring a more effective prison system is to conserve its resources for only those offenders who need to be incarcerated, and this can only be done by getting control over the size of the total population. Finally, it is important to note that reducing the size of the prison population is not simply a question of re-vamping the sentencing guidelines structures; the solution requires a more general approach. This will include promoting public and professional confidence in community penalties.

Addressing public concerns about crime

The last challenge we identify concerns the views of the public. As noted, for years now there has been a perceptions gap between public perceptions of crime trends, and actual trends. It is not suprising that the public believes crime is constantly rising. The public read about crime constantly in the newspapers, and have little faith in the traditional source of reliable information about crime statistics. A recent MORI poll found that approximately half the polled public would trust an independent public 'watchdog' most in terms of crime trends. In contrast, only 5% said that they would trust the Prime Minister or the Home Office (Duffy et al 2008). Creating such an agency would go a long way towards correcting public misperceptions about crime trends. This, in turn would relieve some of the pressure on politicians to 'do something about the crime problem'.

Conclusions

The predecessor to this chapter (Faulkner, Hough and Halpern 1996) concluded that more attention needs to be devoted to the policymaking process itself.

The authors argued that policymakers needed to pay more attention to the results of empirical research, and rather less attention to political fashion. Although much has changed in the past decade or so, this observation appears as valid now as a decade ago. We end by expressing the hope that the authors of the next *Options* chapter on this issue a decade or so from now will be able to tell a rather different story, one in which empirical research and long-range planning play a much greater role than at present.

Notes

1. See for example the report by Louise Casey (Casey 2008).
2. This said, implementation (in November 2005) of the 2003 Licensing Act does not appear to have triggered the surge in alcohol-related violence predicted as a consequence of liberalized licensing laws (see Hough and Hunter 2008).
3. Neither the BCS nor recorded crime statistics capture crimes of this kind adequately.
4. Straightforward comparisons of sentence length show no change for magistrates' courts since 1995 but a 20% increase in Crown Court sentence lengths. These comparisons mask the real trend, however, because the lowering of the custody threshold means that the average gravity of cases attracting imprisonment has fallen.
5. Before a definitive guideline is issued, the Council will consult widely on a draft guideline and this consultation will be preceded by advice from the Sentencing Advisory Panel.
6. Guideline schemes in the US permit far more accurate predictions of custodial populations.

9
Housing

Stephen Nickell

Housing in Britain: what has been happening?

Most people in Britain live in market sector housing, either as owner-occupiers or as tenants in the private rented sector. A relatively small minority (around 4 million) live in social housing which is subsidized from the public purse. Over the last decade, the real price of homes in the market sector has more than doubled. (See Figure 9.1.) This is a much more rapid increase than that in real incomes, so housing affordability has worsened dramatically over the same period.

For example, if we measure affordability for first time buyers as the ratio of lower quartile house prices to lower quartile earnings, this ratio has risen in England from 3.5 in 1997 to 7.25 in 2007. Furthermore, rises of a comparable

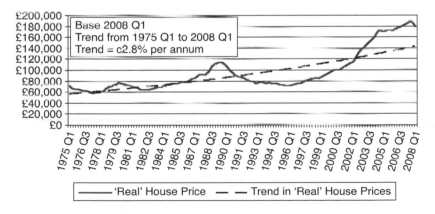

Figure 9.1   Long-term Trend in Real UK House Prices, Quarter 1 1975 to Quarter 1 2008

Source: Nationwide Building Society.

magnitude have occurred in all regions of the UK, although there remain large variations in this ratio, the highest levels being found in the South, the lowest in the North. (See Figure 9.2.) So what has been going on?

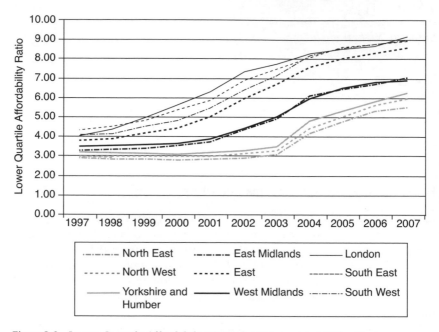

Figure 9.2   Lower Quartile Affordability Ratio by Government Office Region

Source: National Housing and Planning Association (2008a), Fig. 7.

Why has this happened?

Around the recent turn of the century, house building in the UK hit the lowest level since the war. Indeed, it was far lower than in the late 1930s. Furthermore, in the late 1990s, there was a large inherited backlog of social housing repairs. At the same time, the rate of growth in the number of households was rising steadily. For example, in the late 1990s, households in England were rising at around 160,000 per annum, with house building at around 135,000 p.a. By the early 2000s, house building did expand[1] but household growth rose even faster, with the gap between the latter and the former averaging around 50,000 p.a.

So why has the number of households been rising more rapidly in recent years? The main factors are: the significant increase in net migration into the UK in the late 1990s, which contributes around one third of the change; the continuing increase in life expectancy leading to a rapid rise in single person households among the elderly; and the steady rise in family breakdown. Single adult households are the fastest rising category.

So the first major reason for rapidly rising house prices has been an increasing gap between household growth and house building. On top of this is the fact that real incomes are steadily growing and that richer people tend to demand more housing services. The historical evidence suggests that the income elasticity of demand for housing exceeds the price elasticity of demand. In other words, as real incomes rise, house prices will rise more rapidly than incomes even if there is a perfect match between house building and population growth.

These have been the basic driving forces behind the house price boom but, in addition, we have seen historically low borrowing rates since the turn of the century. The fundamental factor here has been the world-wide decline in long-term real interest rates from around 4% in the mid-1990s to less than 2% in the 2000s. This has been caused by the excess of savings generated by the far Eastern economies as well as by the oil producing countries more recently. On top of this, fierce competition among mortgage lenders, with ready access to these savings using mortgage backed securities, has led to very easy access to credit for borrowers. A potential fourth factor has been the increase in incentives to invest in residential property driven by the sharp decline in equity markets in 2000–03; prospective capital gains; and the increasing use of buy-to-let mortgages. This has led many commentators to argue that there has been a housing market bubble, but the most complete analysis, to be found in Cameron et al (2006), suggests that the rise in house prices is perfectly consistent with the fundamental forces noted above and that there has been no significant bubble.

Recent events in the housing market

From mid-2007, the housing market in the UK has turned down, house prices are now falling and are expected to fall further. Since house building still lags far behind the increase in the number of households, what has happened? Basically, there has been a collapse in the availability of mortgages, particularly to first-time buyers, alongside a dramatic rise in mortgage rates. This has come about because the mortgage lenders are now more or less cut off from the money markets. A generalized lack of trust in mortgage backed securities, initiated by the sub-prime crisis in the US, has meant that the mortgage lenders now find it very difficult to access the continuing world-wide glut of savings because they are unable to use their mortgage assets as collateral. Since domestic retail deposits are not large enough to fund the flow of new mortgages required in a properly functioning UK housing market, mortgages are now severely rationed especially for first-time buyers, with a 60% fall in new mortgages for this group in the last year. This has led to a sharp fall in the demand for housing, a fall which has been accentuated by the very fact of declining house prices leading to first-time buyers holding back from the market. Nevertheless the number of people wanting to buy houses remains relatively buoyant, but since many cannot now raise a mortgage even if they have excellent credit records, this desire can no longer be acted upon.

The consequence is even more rapidly falling house prices, house builders unable to sell their new homes and a collapse in new housing investment with strongly adverse consequences for the wider economy. Despite the falling prices, this scenario is not particularly beneficial to first-time buyers because many can no longer access credit in order to buy the cheaper houses. Furthermore, those that can access credit find that more expensive mortgages more than offset the lower prices. This situation contrasts with the decline of the housing market in the early 1990s which was a *consequence* of a recession in the UK and rapidly rising unemployment. Currently, we are now entering a recession which is a consequence of the credit crunch and the declining housing market rather than the other way around. This will, of course, worsen the housing market situation even further.

So what are the prospects for the future?

Sooner or, more likely, later, the mortgage market will recover. The underlying forces driving housing demand upwards are projected to continue even more intensively over the next decade than they have done in the recent past. Household projections for England, based on the revised 2004 ONS Population Projections, suggest an average rate of increase in households of around 230,000 per annum up to 2020. Since the latest 2006 ONS Population Projections are considerably higher than those generated in 2004, it seems quite likely that the number of households will grow even more rapidly. This rate of increase in the number of households is considerably higher than the 200,000 per annum since the turn of the century and far higher than both recent rates of house building and current housing plans set out in the Regional Spatial Strategies. In the light of this, given that real incomes are also expected to grow, house prices are likely to continue to rise relative to incomes in the longer term provided that the mortgage market returns to normal and first-time buyers have reasonable access to credit (see NHPAU 2008a, 2008b for some recent projections). Of course, while the mortgage market remains highly restricted and the UK economy remains in recession, house prices will continue to be depressed. But lower levels of house prices generated by a mortgage famine and an economy in recession is no real solution to the long-term housing shortage and consequent affordability problem. For where are all the additional households supposed to live? The only serious way to resolve this problem is to generate higher rates of house building. Under existing structures, this seems unlikely to happen.

Does it all matter?

When house prices rise relative to incomes, property owners gain relative to the rest of the population. Non-property owners will have to spend a higher proportion of their incomes on somewhere to live via increased rents or increased mortgage costs. Basically, there is a large transfer of wealth from the young and the poor to the old and the wealthy. It is not clear that the former are less deserving than the latter and most would judge such a wealth transfer as socially undesirable.

More practically, as house building fails to keep up with increases in the number of households and prices rise relative to incomes, more people are driven into the private rented sector, driving up rents, and into the social renting sector, driving up waiting lists. Thus, between 2002 and 2007, there was a rise of over half a million households on the housing register compared with an increase of only 73,000 between 1998 and 2002. Furthermore, despite falling house prices, the demand for social housing is currently increasing still more rapidly. Overall, deprivation increases and the situation worsens in already deprived areas. There is more overcrowding and people are generally less well housed. Many key workers, such as nurses and teachers, are unable to find somewhere to live near where they work. All these problems increase the pressure for the spending of taxpayers' money in order to attempt to alleviate them. This is unlikely to be forthcoming, in part because the sums required are huge. To provide social housing for the extra half a million households on the housing register noted above would cost £50 billion at £100,000 per household, some 4% of GDP. This suggests that the only solution is to increase the rate of house building for the market sectors, making market housing cheaper relative to incomes, allowing more people into the market sector and reversing the process described above. Simply building more affordable housing just will not work, since it will never be done fast enough. Allowing more market housing to be built works because it reduces the demand for social housing.

Policy issues

A little history

The history of house building in England since World War II is encapsulated in Figure 9.3. Since the peaks of the 1960s, private sector house building has fallen somewhat but the rate of house building for social renting has more or less collapsed. In the 1960s and early 1970s, local authorities were building at the rate of more than 100,000 dwellings per year. Currently, houses for social renting are coming on stream at less than 30,000 per annum. Far less public money has gone into this sector since the mid-1980s and this has not been replaced by greater investment in private house building.

The planning system has been the main binding constraint on private house building. Restricting the supply of building land in the face of rapidly rising demand for housing has been a major factor in driving up house prices which are reflected in the extremely high values attached to building land, particularly in the South. (See Figure 9.4, p. 177.) In much of the South East,

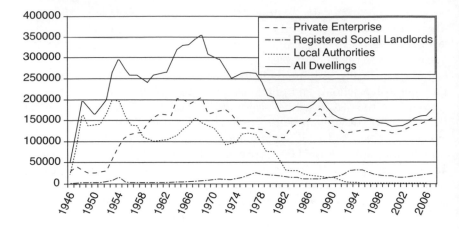

Figure 9.3   Dwelling Completions by Tenure in England

Source: DCLG.

building land in 2007 fetched £5 million per hectare, around 300–400 times the price of the same land for agricultural use. This shows what rationing can achieve.

Why did this happen?

After the war, public support for house building and development was widespread. During elections, political parties vied with each other in the grandiosity of their building plans. By the 1990s, this public support had evaporated. Concerns over the environment, the countryside, infrastructure, sustainable development and simple NIMBYism meant that the majority of people were not in favour of development, particularly in the South where increasing numbers wished to live following economic development.[2]

The impact of restricting the supply of land for house building did not emerge on the political agenda until the early 2000s, in part because the majority of people were benefiting from the house price boom and they were the older and richer members of society who carry more political weight in any event.

The local authorities, who control the supply of land for house building, have also seen a reduction in their incentives to allow development more generally. Their loss of control over, and direct access to, business rates and their overall loss of power in the 1980s were important in this regard. The upshot of all this was that, as we have already noted, by the turn of the century, fewer dwellings were being built in the UK than at any time since 1950 (see Figure 9.3).

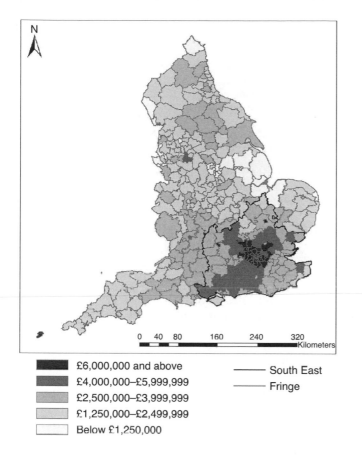

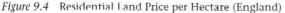

Figure 9.4   Residential Land Price per Hectare (England)

Source: Property Market Report (July 2007).

By 2003, the government recognized that the social and economic consequences of rapidly rising house prices and increasing numbers of less and less well housed individuals were problems to be addressed. They commissioned Kate Barker to write a report on housing supply (Barker 2004) and, as a result, set about adjusting the planning regime in order to increase the supply of housing. A good summary of their ideas may be found in the Housing Green Paper (DCLG 2007; see also Box 9.1).

Where are we now?

The basic mechanism by which central government, at least in England, attempts to influence the rate of house building is of the 'command and

---

Box 9.1 **The Housing Green Paper**

The Housing Green Paper attempted to address the need to accelerate the rate of house building in the UK while also pursuing environmental and social goals. It suggests a broad approach to achieving a goal of 240,000 houses built every year. Most of the work would involve a central government influence over the Regional Spatial Strategies. Other approaches fall into a similar 'command and control'-style approach, such as determining where 'New Growth Points' will be, use of the Housing Corporation to invest money in rural towns and villages, and a controversial scheme to build ten new 'eco-towns'. However, the paper also tentatively considers the use of incentives in order to influence decisions in a more decentralized way: in particular, a new Housing and Planning Delivery grant will provide a direct monetary incentive for local councils to 'deliver high levels of housing'. It also suggests a bill for a Planning Gain Supplement that will enable councils to benefit from the uplift in property prices that follow the granting of planning permission. This policy idea met significant opposition from developers and is likely to be drastically scaled back.

---

control' type. There are general rules governing new developments, such as the high proportion of new build on brownfield as opposed to greenfield sites,[3] at relatively high density. Then each region has to put forward a 'Regional Spatial Strategy' (RSS) along with local development frameworks. These RSSs set out the numbers of new houses to be built over a plan period along with an overview of where they are to be located. The latest planning guidance (Planning Policy Statement 3, PPS3) has a strong focus on ensuring an adequate supply of land for housing, in particular insisting that the prospects for market housing affordability must be taken into account in the planning process. Advice on affordability prospects is provided by the National Housing and Planning Advice Unit, a non-departmental public body. This body is also charged with providing advice to the government on the ranges of housing supply to be tested by the Regional Planning Authorities when the RSS plans are reviewed (see NHPAU 2008a for the latest such advice). By and large, since 2003 we have seen a sequence of plans, targets and advice indicating a desire to build an ever increasing number of houses, at least in part because official projections of household growth have been steadily rising over this period.

On top of this, there are a number of special policies involving further house building, notably plans for the Thames Gateway, ten new eco-towns and growth points. All these involve more or less continuous interaction between local authorities, regional assemblies, regional development agencies, and central government (Department of Communities and Local Government). This involves huge expenditure of time and energy which is accentuated by the fact that local authorities have little in the way of financial incentives to encourage house building in their locality. For example the Lyons Report on

Local Government (Lyons 2007) is much concerned with 'providing financial incentives for Local Authorities and communities to promote economic prosperity and residential growth ...'.

The consequences of this command and control system are often perverse. For example the encouragement of brownfield, high density building in England has led to a very significant increase in the proportion of new build in the form of flats, a significant reduction in the proportion of family homes and the gradual disappearance of back gardens in urban areas. This is despite the fact that family homes with back gardens are precisely what most households desire. But, overall, the key fact remains that unless local authorities have significant financial incentives to encourage development, no amount of command and control is likely to produce enough new homes to allow people in the UK to be properly housed.

Incentives for local authorities

Financial incentives for local authorities to allow development are not totally absent. At present, however, they have very little in the way of access to the 'planning gain' which typically arises from the granting of planning permission. So what sort of financial incentives currently exist? The obvious general incentive is that arising from the fact that the central government grant, which covers the vast majority of local authority expenditure, varies with population size. Thus more housing means more people means more money. The problem here is the delay because there is a long lag between the time the extra people arrive and the point when the extra money starts to flow. On balance, the net effect probably serves as a disincentive to allowing housing development. There are, however, a number of schemes – some existing and some proposed – which generate modest positive incentives.

Section 106 payments

These are made by developers to local authorities as a condition of planning permission. The idea is for the local authority, in return for granting planning permission, to negotiate some community benefits such as infrastructure, open space, and a proportion of low cost homes in the development. Since there has to be a separate negotiation for each development, the transaction costs are enormous and the sums generated are typically only a small proportion of the planning gain.

Housing and Planning Delivery Grant (HPDG)

This is a reward payment to local authorities that 'meet their agreed development time tables for new housing, based on the requirements set out in PPS3'. Thus it rewards the delivery of new housing and the identification of at least five years' worth of sites. Overall, however, the amounts are small and not likely to generate strong incentives.

Community Infrastructure Levy (CIL)

This is proposed and currently out for consultation. Originally, the notion of a tax on planning gain was floated,[4] known as 'planning gain supplement'. This was discarded as involving too much negotiation and being too costly to collect. The CIL allows the local authority to apply a levy (per roof or per square metre) on all new developments in order to fund new infrastructure. The local authority assesses infrastructure requirements and, after consultation, publishes a charging scheme with the levy being paid at the outset of development. The incidence of the tax is on the landowner and it must obviously differ between areas and between greenfield and brownfield sites. The existing plan is that the revenue cannot be used for general expenditure nor to remedy existing infrastructure deficiencies.

The basic problem facing local authorities, particularly in the South where housing demand is highest, is that the majority of their constituents are opposed to new development. So what they need is to generate enough money from new development to fund local improvements in services and the urban environment which will enable them to show the demonstrable benefits of new development to their constituents. The CIL could potentially operate in this way but, in the current proposal, the local authority is constrained to restrict expenditure to the provision of the infrastructure required by the new development and nothing else.

Overall, therefore, we have a system which has no real prospect of getting local authorities to be strong supporters of new housing development in the quantities required and in the places required (mainly the South) to house people properly. Without local authority support, it is unlikely that any amount of command and control from central government will succeed in generating the supply of new housing that is required.

Prospects for policy

In the light of the previous discussion, what policy changes might be helpful in ensuring that citizens are better housed than they are likely to be under existing arrangements? Responsibility for planning has to remain at local and regional level, and while we continue to have regional development agencies, they must also be involved. One of the basic problems is the fact that there are strong forces driving economic development towards the southern half of the UK. Economic development means jobs, people follow jobs, and demand for housing follows people. Generally speaking, the activities of the regional development agencies are not able to resist these trends. So restricting housing development in the South means higher house prices in the South, increased commuting, labour shortages and restricted economic development overall. On pure economic efficiency grounds, restrictions on housing development should be removed and southern towns would expand dramatically. This is the scenario envisaged in Leunig and Swaffield (2008) and Box 9.2. While this is a practical possibility, it seems unlikely, at the moment, that it would garner any strong political support.

Box 9.2 **Social Housing**
Tim Leunig

Social housing fails tenants and society in three ways: long waiting lists, unhappy tenants, and dreadful employment and education results. Nor is failure cheap: social housing is subsidized by between £6.6 billion and £14 billion a year (Hills 2007: 63).

Four million people are currently waiting for social housing (BBC News 2008). It would take 20 years to house them, and since new people join the list all of the time, many will die before they are housed (Hills 2007: 145, figure 12.8).

Social housing is 'objectively' in good condition, but social housing tenants are much more dissatisfied with their accommodation, landlord and area than are private tenants (Hills 2007: 71, figure 7.4; 72, figure 7.5; 73, figure 7.7; 97, figure 9.9). More than half do not feel safe alone outside after dark, and a truly shocking 18% of those living on flatted estates do not feel safe even in their own homes (Hills 2007: 96, figure 9.8).

Taking into account factors such as disability, lone-parenthood, and qualification levels, social housing tenants are only half as likely to be working as other people (Hills 2007: 102, figures 10.2 and 10.3). There is only a 1% chance that a social housing tenant and both their neighbours will be in full-time work (Hill 2007: 100, table 10.1).

After taking factors associated with poor school results into account, social housing children are twice as likely as other children to end up without qualifications (Sigle-Rushton 2004).

We need to change the balance between supply and demand, and improve satisfaction, education and employment rates.

Building 4 million more social houses requires £240 billion in subsidy (Hills 2007: 62). This is not realistic and never will be. A better solution, proposed by Steve Nickell in this chapter, is to build more market-priced houses. This will lower housing costs, reducing both demand for, and the cost of providing social housing. There can be no good outcome for social housing without more private house building.

Second, council tenants must be able to move more easily. At the moment, tenants who like space may well be allocated a smaller than average house, those liking quiet a noisy house, and so on. Social housing tenants are treated as commodities rather than as individuals with legitimate, individual preferences; no wonder dissatisfaction is high. Tenants could be given the right to require their landlord to sell the house they are currently living in, and buy them one that they prefer, to the same value. This would be a revolution in how social housing is run, and would revolutionize satisfaction levels.

Allowing people to move would break up monolithic estates in which worklessness and low educational attainment are normal. Young people need role models, and these are hard to provide when social housing is geographically concentrated and allocated by need. That leads to ghettos – something we must prevent emerging.

Nevertheless, if we are to have people better housed, the planning system has to ensure that houses are built in places where people want to live. And house prices, and hence the price of development land, are valid signals in this context. In order to inject these signals into the planning process, we should allow local authorities to access the planning gain from allowing development in a simple and systematic fashion. This suggests the following possible changes to the existing arrangements:

1. Reduce the extent and detail of the existing command and control framework including the elimination of Section 106 payments and the Housing and Planning Delivery Grant as well as relaxing the rules on brownfield development and density.
2. Use the Community Infrastructure Levy system to provide strong incentives for local authorities to favour housing development. This implies allowing CIL incentives to work, meaning that the rates – and revenue generated – would be much higher in areas where the value of land with planning permission is much higher than with its alternative use. The idea is to enable local authorities to extract a much higher proportion of the planning gain than is currently the case and to allow them to spend it on improving the lot of their constituents more generally, including the provision of subsidies to social housing. The planning rules about housing mix could be incorporated into the system. Or, perhaps better, instead of reverting back to Section 106 type negotiations about affordable housing, the local authorities could simply use CIL funds to ensure the supply of affordable housing on their own account. The general idea underlying this strategy is that instead of engaging in endless negotiation with developers, local authorities would simply tax developments, with the burden of the tax falling on development land prices.[5] The local authorities would then use the money as they see fit.
3. A more speculative alternative to the CIL system is that proposed in Leunig (2007). Here the local authority invites offers of land from landowners; that is, landowners state the price at which they would be happy to sell their land (in a sealed bid). The local authority then chooses what areas of this land it would like to see developed, buys it at the offered price, grants planning permission and then auctions this land to developers. The local authority keeps all or a high percentage of the money, which may be used to enhance local services and facilities, to provide infrastructure and to subsidize social housing.

Conclusions

The current system of planning and development in the UK generates new homes at a rate which has been well below the rate of increase of households for many years. This has helped to generate very rapid increases in house prices relative to incomes in the last decade as well as rapidly lengthening waiting lists for social housing. The fundamental problem has been the severe rationing of land for new house building by local authorities as they respond to opposition to housing development on the part of their constituents and the absence of any significant final incentives to encourage development. The policy options suggested in this chapter are geared to alleviate this situation by allowing local authorities to access the large financial gains accruing to landowners consequent on the granting of planning permission. The money can then be used to subsidize social housing and improve the locality more generally.

Of course, the ultimate decision on whether people in the UK are properly housed is political. And there is much political opposition, though this may shift as more people, especially the young, find themselves unable to achieve their housing aspirations. But most other rich countries seem to manage to build far more houses relative to their populations then we do in the UK. So it should not be that difficult.

Notes

1. Net additions to the housing stock, which includes conversions of existing buildings, expanded somewhat faster than house building, but this was, and remains, slower than the increase in households.
2. A good survey of the emergence of these ideas may be found in Barker (2007).
3. Brownfield sites are those where development has already occurred. These would include back gardens as well as old factory sites and the like.
4. It was proposed in the Barker Review and appeared in the 2007 Green Paper.
5. Of course, there is a limit to the tax in the sense that if it is so high that the development land price falls below the value of the land in its alternative use, then no development will occur. It is also worth noticing the push in the direction of zero carbon housing. The cost of this will also be a charge on the planning gain which will further limit what can be raised via CIL. In practice, instead of pushing towards zero carbon on new properties, a much bigger and more cost effective impact on carbon emissions could be achieved simply by providing free loft insulation to all existing properties, in part funded by CIL.

10
Economy and Environment: Tackling Britain's Transport Problem
Richard Wellings

Introduction

Transport has long been characterized by a significant level of state intervention, with the role of government increasing in the last ten years. This reflects the fact that transport is responsible for a quarter of UK carbon emissions and a high proportion of urban pollution such as carbon monoxide and particulates (DfT 2007a). At the same time, the movement of passengers and goods is crucial to the economy. Transport improvements can facilitate greater economies of scale, increase choice and competition, enhance labour mobility and enable a more specialized geographical division of labour. These are key drivers of rising productivity and economic growth.

The economic importance of transport is further demonstrated by the fact that it comprises the second largest area of household expenditure after housing, accounting for one sixth of spending (ONS 2007a). However, it would appear to have rather less political importance. Transport as a whole receives just 3% of government expenditure (DfT 2007a). Roads receive less than half this spending, despite accounting for over 80% of domestic freight and passenger traffic. Moreover, investment in transport has historically been exceptionally low in Britain compared with other industrialized nations. The UK has arguably the worst transport infrastructure of any major developed country. See for example International Road Federation (IRF 2006).

The economy and the environment are therefore the two key considerations of government transport policy. They are not necessarily in conflict. For example, traffic congestion increases pollution as well as imposing costs on road users. Nevertheless, government policy attempts to achieve a difficult balance – meeting environmental objectives while promoting economic efficiency. Policymaking is further complicated by the political market and the need to secure the support of special interest groups and voters.

The chapter begins by examining the policy aims set out ten years ago by the newly elected Labour government and how they have evolved. The success of these policies is then assessed in relation to the initial objectives, with regard to transport's economic and environmental role, and in the context of changing conditions and new problems. The final section draws on this analysis to suggest possible future directions for transport policy.

A new deal for transport

The election of a Labour government in 1997 cemented the environmentalist shift in transport policy that had begun in the early 1990s under the Conservatives (Dudley and Richardson 2003). Green concerns would now be a central consideration, along with egalitarian issues such as 'access' and 'mobility'. The new administration immediately imposed a moratorium on road building and the Department of Transport was merged with the Department of the Environment to form the Department of Environment, Transport and the Regions (DETR) in an attempt to ensure that environmental concerns played a more important role in policy development.

The new government set out its plans in the 1998 white paper, *A New Deal for Transport: Better for Everyone* (DETR 1998), which promised the development of an integrated transport system and set out a series of measures to encourage a modal shift from private cars to public transport. Tackling climate change had become a high priority within government, the UK hoping to beat its Kyoto target by achieving a 20% reduction in emissions by 2010, from the 1990 baseline. Yet environmental objectives would somehow have to be reconciled with the key role transport plays in the economy and the increasing cost of road congestion in particular.

The transport ten year plan

Despite the abandonment of some of the more radical plans, the broad vision set out in the white paper was translated into concrete policy objectives in the *Transport Ten Year Plan 2000* (DETR 2000). By 2010, the government should not only have met its obligations on CO_2 emissions. A series of ambitious targets, based on a 2000 baseline were also set out:

- reduce congestion on inter-urban trunk roads by 5%
- reduce congestion in large urban areas by 8%
- increase bus passenger journeys by 10%
- increase rail passenger traffic by 50%
- increase railfreight traffic by 80%

achievement from the environmental perspective. It is not clear, however, that government policies deserve all the credit for this outcome. For example, vehicle manufacturers have improved engine efficiencies. Consumers have also purchased more diesel cars, which have far greater fuel economy. But arguably such private decisions have been influenced heavily by government policies that have raised fuel costs (i.e. fuel duty) and have introduced Vehicle Excise Duty bands that discriminate against drivers of larger cars.

Efforts to reduce other forms of air pollution from transport appear to have been far more successful. Emissions of pollutants such as benzene, carbon monoxide, nitrogen oxides, lead, particulates and sulphur dioxide have all fallen dramatically in the last decade, in some cases by 90%. This reflects the introduction of improved technology, such as catalytic converters, and its gradual roll-out as old vehicles have been replaced. The EU made catalytic converters mandatory on new vehicles in 1993. While this regulation is likely to have imposed additional costs on road users, it has clearly contributed to reductions in certain forms of pollution.

Modal shift

Despite the policy effort, and considerable public transport expenditure, the last ten years have not been marked by a significant shift in travel behaviour (see Table 10.2). The private car remains the dominant mode of transport by a large margin. Having said this, the growth in car traffic appears to have declined markedly compared with previous decades (DfT 2007a, table 1.1), with annual growth of less than 1% compared with 2% in the 1970s, 4% in the 1980s and 7% in the 1960s. This is even more remarkable given that the number of registered vehicles has risen by around 2% per year in the last decade. The outcome cannot be explained by rising motoring costs, since these have generally declined as a share of household expenditure (ibid, table 1.13), at least until the recent oil price boom. Possible explanations include worsening congestion and government planning policies aimed at diverting economic activity to town centres and inner cities. It could also be partly a natural saturation effect.

Table 10.2   Modal Shift – Passenger Journeys (% of passenger-km)

	1997	2006
Cars, vans, taxis	86	85
Buses and coaches	6	6
Motor cycles	1	1
Rail	6	7
Air (UK)	0.9	1.2

Source: DfT (2007a).

Passenger rail

Rail passenger traffic has risen by a third since 1997 (Table 10.3), suggesting some success at encouraging travellers to use public transport. However, previous periods of relatively strong economic growth, such as the mid-1980s, have also been marked by increases in rail usage, which have subsequently been reversed during economic slowdowns. A large share of rail passenger traffic comprises London commuters, so the figures are heavily dependent on the capital's labour market, which grew significantly. Other factors may be increased congestion on inter-city motorways and more restrictive parking in city centres. Overall, it seems unlikely that the rise in patronage is entirely the result of government policy, although the regulation of most commuter fares after privatization may have boosted demand by rising at a lower rate than average earnings. It should also be acknowledged that substantial capital subsidies have contributed to capacity increases that have facilitated part of the growth in traffic – for example, the £8 billion modernization of the West Coast Main Line.

Table 10.3 Growth in Rail Traffic

Financial Year	Passenger (billion passenger-km)	Freight (billion tonne-km)
1997/98	42	16.9
1998/99	44	17.3
1999/00	46	18.2
2000/01	47	18.1
2001/02	47	19.4
2002/03	48	18.5
2003/04	49	18.9
2004/05	50	20.4
2005/06	52	21.7
2006/07	55	22.1

Source: DfT (2007a).

Although commuter trains produce about half as much CO_2 per passenger km as car travel (DfT 2007b), subsidizing rail may encourage people to live further away from their place of work, perhaps in rural and suburban areas. In some cases they will live in compact towns or suburbs where they can reach all the facilities they need on foot or by bike. In other cases, however, commuters will not only need to drive relatively long distances to the railway station but also for other activities, such as education, leisure and shopping. Thus it may not be the case that promoting rail necessarily reduces overall emissions and further research on these wider impacts would be valuable.

Furthermore, growth in rail travel may reflect government failure in other areas, such as education and anti-social behaviour. Demographic changes have arguably meant inner-city problems have spread out to previously 'respectable' outer zones of cities in the last decade. Thus the growth in commuting may partly reflect middle-class flight from urban problems. The distances travelled may also have been increased by planning controls that have prevented the organic growth of cities and pushed commuters into outlying satellite towns rather than new suburbs. Rail has, however, helped to maintain the centres of large cities as hubs of employment, shopping and entertainment – a key objective, rightly or wrongly, of government spatial planning policies.

Railfreight

Freight traffic has also increased by about a third since 1997/98 (Table 10.3), although once again this has not been the result of government transport policies to discourage road transport. Almost the entire increase is the result of closure of British coal mines and the shift to imported coal for electricity generation. Power stations were generally located inland, close to the coalfields themselves. The capacity of bulk terminals is also limited, so coal has had to be transported very long distances, often from Scotland to the Midlands, and this has accordingly inflated the railfreight figures. As additional terminal capacity is constructed in ports closer to the power stations, such as Hull and Immingham, the number of tonne-kilometres is likely to decline.

Bus travel

There has also been an increase of about 15% in passenger traffic on buses and coaches between 1998 and 2007. The rise in bus patronage has been concentrated in London, where the number of bus passenger journeys has increased by more than a quarter since 2000–01. Yet London buses have benefited from a large injection of Treasury cash and additional support from congestion charge revenues. Taxpayer-funded subsidies trebled between 2000 and 2007. The additional subsidies have helped keep fare rises below inflation. A series of concessionary fares have also been introduced, giving free travel to various groups such as under-18s, and thus it is unsurprising that usage has risen.

Air travel

Air passenger traffic at UK airports has risen by 60% in the last decade, while freight has risen by 20%. The airlines sector has been marked by high levels of entrepreneurship and competition that have been absent in other transport sectors. The growth of low-cost carriers such as EasyJet and Ryanair has offered cheaper fares and a greater choice of routes. However, to the extent that this development has stimulated additional demand, it may have conflicted with objectives on climate change.

Halting airport expansion has not been part of the government's environmental agenda. After an inquiry lasting over eight years, the construction of Terminal 5 at Heathrow was given the go-ahead in 2001 (and opened in 2008). Furthermore, the 2003 white paper, *The Future of Air Transport* (DfT 2003), recommended the construction of new runways at Stansted (2011/12), Heathrow (2015–20) and Gatwick (after 2019).

In many ways, aviation policy in the last decade has therefore resembled roads policy until the early 1990s. While state regulation has meant it has been impossible to 'predict and provide' in the manner of a private business, policy has nevertheless aimed to accommodate at least some of the rising demand for air travel. Environmentalists could therefore make a strong case that this approach is inconsistent in the context of a raft of demand management measures imposed on road users. At the same time, it has been argued that the aviation sector provides economic benefits that far exceed its relatively small environmental impact. See, for example, BAA (2008). Moreover, international competition, for example from Schiphol (Amsterdam), Charles de Gaulle (Paris) and even Dubai, moderates policymakers' room for manoeuvre. Accordingly there is evidence that Heathrow is suffering relative decline in its position as an international hub with potentially serious ramifications for London's global city status (DfT 2008a).

Traffic congestion

The government's ambitious congestion targets were abandoned in December 2002. While the plan had aimed for a 5% reduction on inter-urban trunk roads, a 15% rise was now expected by 2010 (DfT 2002). Indeed, it would appear that road congestion generally continued to increase gradually until 2007, by about 1% annually, although 2008 has seen a slight reduction from 2007 levels due to large rises in fuel prices and a concomitant fall in car traffic (DfT 2008b).

A scheme to charge drivers £5 to enter Central London commenced in 2003. After operating costs, the revenues have been used predominantly to support the capital's bus services. The London Congestion Charge was also backed with Treasury funding for both implementation costs and subsequent increases to bus subsidies, at a level that has dwarfed the income from the scheme. In 2006/07 total revenues were £213 million, and due to high operating costs, net revenues were £123 million (TfL 2007). Despite a rise in the charge to £8, the scheme has failed to achieve a permanent reduction in congestion, and traffic speeds in Central London in 2008 are generally lower than they were before the preparation and implementation phases of the project (DfT 2007a, table 7.12). Buses and taxis comprise a high proportion of traffic and yet are not subjected to the charge. The amount of roadspace has also been reduced by TfL in some central locations.

Future policy options

Government policy will be heavily constrained in the medium term. The economic slowdown and the level of government borrowing are likely to preclude any significant increase in state transport expenditure.[1] At the same time, high fuel prices could make it politically difficult to raise additional revenue from users. Accordingly, it seems unlikely that policy over the next ten years will begin to solve the long-term structural deficiencies that have given Britain a second-rate transport system.

It may, however, be possible for the government to proceed with its environmentalist agenda through incremental steps introduced at a local level. The draft Local Transport Bill 2007 aims to increase the powers of passenger transport authorities (PTAs) and passenger transport executives (PTEs) in other metropolitan areas, so that they can perform a comprehensive role similar to that of TfL, including the implementation of road pricing schemes in partnership with local councils. Yet the history of PTE-run bus services and the performance of Transport for London indicate that this model risks bureaucratic growth, inefficient expenditure, capture by special interests, lack of accountability and large rises in public subsidies. (On the PTEs see Hibbs 2000; on TfL see Wellings and Lipson 2008: 34.) And if local schemes require substantial central government support then clearly financial constraints could limit their scope, particularly if the focus is on expanding uneconomic public transport services rather than simply tackling road congestion. While there is evidence, for example White (2008), to suggest that PTEs and TfL may well be capable of increasing public transport ridership, a political decision must be made as to whether such gains represent value for money in the context of the likely resulting additional burden on taxpayers.

The European Union is also likely to play a growing role in UK transport policy. The government is committed to adhering to its EU target to reduce CO_2 emissions by 20% by 2020 (compared with 1990 levels). Road transport may be included in the EU emissions trading scheme, possibly from 2013 (DfT 2007c), although if fuel prices remain high this may have to be delayed for political reasons. It is also possible that the EU will intervene in the setting of transport tax rates. Already there would appear to have been an 'unofficial' policy of harmonization, with fuel duty and road tax rates converging in member states.

While the transfer of policy to local and European levels will constrain UK policy, there are benefits for the government to the extent to which it can avoid democratic accountability for unpopular measures.

Road pricing

Road pricing clearly has the potential to address many of the problems currently facing transport policymakers. Congestion can be reduced by varying tolls according to traffic levels (see Glaister and Graham 2004).

Charges could also be related to environmental impact, although setting appropriate rates is highly problematic. Perhaps most importantly, prices can be used to allocate transport investment more efficiently by providing information on the financial viability of any given project (Day 1998). Despite these theoretical benefits, the practical process of implementing widespread road pricing is fraught with difficulties.

Public opposition

First, charging faces a high level of public opposition. Almost 2 million people signed a petition against road pricing on the Downing Street website and surveys suggest that between half and three quarters of the public are opposed to the idea, depending on the specifics of the scheme (RAC Foundation 2006). Indeed, persuading the public to accept road pricing may be still more difficult if fuel prices remain at historically high levels. There may be fears that charges will in effect be an additional tax on top of fuel and vehicle excise duty. Nevertheless, there is some evidence that public support increases when it is made clear that a large share of pricing revenues will be used for transport improvements (ibid).

Setting rates

In a free market, private road owners would set rates to maximize revenues, probably by minimizing congestion to ensure a high throughput of vehicles.[2] However, in the context of political control the situation is less straightforward. Prices are likely to be set with regard to what is politically acceptable. Special interest groups – such as London's black cab drivers with the congestion charge – may have to be bought off with concessions. Economic benefits will inevitably be reduced by political expediency, and prices are unlikely to be set at an appropriate rate to maximize allocative efficiency.

Simplicity vs. complexity

There is a further tension between designing schemes that are sophisticated enough to ensure the efficient use of road space and ensuring they are predictable and easy for users to understand. Spatial and temporal boundary effects must also be considered. Traffic can be diverted to uncharged or low-cost routes, which may or may not be desirable. This problem can largely be avoided by deploying area-wide charging or cordons, yet such 'broad-brush' schemes tend to lack the kind of nuanced and flexible pricing that would maximize efficiency. Of course, congestion can also be experienced just before and after peak rate charges operate.

The public transport problem

While motoring is a significant net contributor to government revenues even if one includes external costs (see Sansom et al 2001), public transport receives substantial taxpayer subsidies, amounting to an estimated £14 billion in

2007/08 (DfT 2007a). There is a danger that road pricing will displace drivers onto already overcrowded peak-time trains and buses, leading to demands for expensive new capacity and increasing subsidy levels even further. The economic benefits of road pricing could be lost in this way. The problem can be avoided by phasing out government support and raising peak-time fares – applying the logic of road pricing to public transport – but such measures are unlikely to be politically expedient.

Equity issues

While in heavily congested locations the benefits of well-designed road-pricing schemes are likely to far outweigh the costs, there may be a redistributive effect, with some groups benefiting more than others. Some areas may suffer through the movement of businesses and jobs to locations with lower tolls. People on moderate incomes might find running a car prohibitive if they live in congested inner-city neighbourhoods. Social polarization could increase if motorists move to low-toll suburban and rural locations, leaving inner cities to welfare-dependent public transport users. Addressing such impacts through regeneration subsidies and planning controls could be extremely costly, and could reduce the economic gains from pricing. On the cost and effectiveness of regeneration policies, see Leunig and Swaffield (2008); on the economic cost of restrictive planning policies, see Evans and Hartwich (2007). See also Crafts (Chapter 1).

Running costs

It is also conceivable that road pricing could be hampered by high administrative burdens. For example, operating costs absorb about one third of the revenues from the London Congestion Charge. A complex national scheme would be particularly vulnerable to the kind of cost overruns seen in other ambitious public projects, such as the 'choose and book' computer system being developed for the National Health Service.

The way forward for road pricing

Public opposition could perhaps be addressed by making the benefits of road pricing more explicit by making the transport sector more responsive to consumer demand. Drivers paying road tolls could receive an improved service, in terms of upgraded infrastructure and faster travel times. This would mean spending a significant proportion of revenues on enhancing road capacity. Indeed, it would be possible to make such improvements before pricing was introduced, for example by using private finance to fund construction costs in return for a share of future toll revenues (Wellings and Lipson 2008). Yet in major urban areas it is debatable whether major road building would reduce public opposition, and whether, given the high costs, major infrastructure investment is economically viable in such locations.

Of course, it could be politically expedient to use a share of revenues for public transport enhancements where appropriate, particularly in the largest cities where there is a realistic prospect of drivers changing modes, although toll monies should certainly not be used to fund wasteful schemes with very poor rates of return. A high proportion of tram schemes come under this category (see Babalik 2000). Unfortunately, many policymakers would appear to favour trams and trains over buses, perhaps through some kind of romantic attachment (Hibbs 2006), despite their higher capital and running costs.

Most schemes planned for the near future, for example under the government's Transport Innovation Fund (TIF), would appear to offer few benefits for motorists and will spend revenues (boosted by Treasury subsidies) on public transport schemes which are nowhere near commercially viable. Demand management, redistribution and regeneration are the key elements, rather than improving the economic efficiency of local transport. This feeds motorists' perception that road pricing, in effect, will be just another redistributive tax, which will also cultivate growing and more powerful local transport bureaucracies.

For example, the Greater Manchester TIF package, subsidized with at least £1.5 billion from the Treasury, would have harnessed toll revenues to support new tram links to less well off areas such as Rochdale and Oldham, and expand bus services (see GMPTE 2008). But the proposal was massively defeated in a referendum in December 2008.

The future of rail

Rail currently absorbs around a third of the transport budget yet accounts for a small fraction of the market for mobility. The high level of subsidy combined with the high costs of increasing capacity, together with the economic slowdown and the level of government borrowing, mean that significant further increases in investment – beyond the already historically high levels – are unlikely. The record of the last ten years also suggests that the railways do not have the potential to bring about the wholesale modal shift desired by policymakers. Neither can they make a significant contribution to meeting climate change targets. The government appears to have recognized these limitations and is increasingly focusing on incremental enhancements to improve capacity and reliability. These measures may enable rail to increase its modal share and continue to serve important niche markets such as London commuters.

Rail passengers – as opposed to general taxpayers – are likely to pay a higher proportion of costs (DfT 2007b). In recent years, state subsidies have exceeded passenger receipts. Regulation has meant that average fares have risen more slowly than average incomes and operating costs. Future fare rises will have the benefit of reducing demand and therefore reducing the rationale for expensive uneconomic investment projects.

Significant taxpayer subsidy will be required, however, for London's £16 billion Crossrail scheme, which will be constructed between 2010 and 2017. Whether Crossrail delivers the promised benefits or avoids the severe cost overruns and delays that have plagued other large-scale projects will affect policymakers' appetite to implement other mooted plans, such as French-style high-speed lines to the northern cities and Scotland.

The UK's geography enables many of the largest cities to be connected along a single reverse S-shaped route from London to Glasgow. A high speed line would also free up capacity for freight on existing routes. However, experience with the Channel Tunnel Rail Link suggests that building such routes would require huge taxpayer subsidies, while the relative proximity of English cities means savings in overall journey time are likely to be fairly limited. It is also questionable whether high speed rail would be a more productive investment than, for example, increasing motorway capacity or making incremental enhancements to existing lines (see, for example, Eddington 2006).

Conclusion

The last ten years of transport policy have been characterized by ambitious objectives that have subsequently been watered down in the context of institutional, financial and political constraints. Although there have been isolated examples of radical initiatives, such as congestion charging in London, on the whole policy has differed little from previous periods. Despite the environmentalist rhetoric, road spending has increased significantly in the last five years, driven by economic imperatives. And while rail expenditure rose sharply following the renationalization of the infrastructure in 2001, this to a large extent reflected spending on renewals in the context of heightened safety fears. Although the substantial growth in rail traffic can be viewed as a significant achievement from the perspective of the government's policy aims, the environmental benefits have arguably been small when viewed from the perspective of the transport sector as a whole. Moreover, the economic gains from the growth of rail have perhaps been undermined by the heavy burden placed on taxpayers to fund the network.

In terms of the environmentalist agenda, specific transport interventions, such as increasing taxpayer support for public transport, may not be the most effective way of achieving reductions in carbon output at minimum cost. A carbon tax or the incorporation of transport into emissions trading schemes could be more efficient, but these options raise very difficult questions for government regarding motoring taxes and public transport subsidies. Road users may well be overtaxed vis-à-vis their environmental impact even at the high end estimates used in the Stern Report and certainly compared with domestic energy users who do not even pay full rate VAT. Adding, for example, emissions trading levies on top of fuel duty risks compounding existing misallocations of resources.[3] And if emissions trading encompasses public transport, should operators be compensated by government, even if this means effectively subsidizing carbon pollution?

For the economy, it is clear that recent policy has failed to deliver the step change in infrastructure provision needed for Britain to catch up with other developed countries. Government transport expenditure, particularly at the levels seen in the last five years, would probably have been sufficient to make a significant difference had it been allocated efficiently. Unfortunately, the institutional framework means that transport investment has been driven by politics rather than economics and expenditure has tended to be wasteful. For example, widening motorways by one lane in each direction costs a similar amount to building a brand new six-lane motorway (Archer and Glaister 2006). Structural reform would therefore help to improve the efficiency of Britain's transport sector.

Localism could provide part of the solution. If local transport investment had to be funded by councils (perhaps through road-pricing schemes) without recourse to Treasury support then there would be better in-built incentives to invest efficiently and in ways that promoted growth. Given current financial constraints, this proposal would of course require the radical reform of local government finance so that a far higher share of local expenditure was sourced from local taxation.

At a national level, there is a strong case for detaching infrastructure funding from political control and Treasury purse strings. On the railways this means passengers rather than taxpayers must fund a higher share of expenditure and the industry should be given more flexibility over service levels. The facilitation of structural reform – reintegrating ownership of track and train – should also be considered, as a possible method of reducing political intervention and lowering costs.

On the trunk roads, more extensive pricing could be the means to greater institutional independence – the Highways Agency could evolve into an autonomous body that raised toll revenues and invested them according to market demand (Newbery 1998). It could even be privatized, perhaps along the lines of the regulated utility industries. Individual private toll roads, like the M6 Toll,[4] are another way to bring substantial investment into the sector, particularly if road pricing is extended to existing trunk routes. Yet the widespread application of pricing-based solutions may not be possible, both economically and politically, if road user taxes remain at current levels. The Manchester referendum result points to the difficulty of gaining public support within the current fiscal framework.

The central role of HM Treasury in the allocation of transport resources may be one major obstacle to the institutional reform necessary to make the sector more responsive to consumer preferences. At the same time, politicians and DfT officials may also be reluctant to relinquish control. Yet transport is too important – for both the economy and the environment – to be determined by political expediency, interest group politics and limits on public sector spending. The whole sector can be freed from bureaucratic control and opened up to the kind of entrepreneurship and innovation seen in other spheres. This is essential if Britain is to get the efficient transport system necessary for her to prosper in an increasingly competitive world.

Notes

1. Assuming the absence of neo-Keynesian, 1930s-style policies that might attempt to boost employment by funding the construction of additional transport infrastructure. The economic wisdom of such measures is beyond the scope of this chapter.
2. It is debatable whether and to what extent price regulation would be required in this context to address competition issues.
3. Emissions trading levies are likely to be added at the fuel supply stage rather than incorporating individual vehicle owners into emissions trading. Nevertheless, as with fuel duty, the additional costs will be passed on to users.
4. On the problems faced by the M6 Toll, and its impact, see Wellings and Lipson (2008: 24–5).

11
Energy, Climate Change and the Environment

Federico Gallo,[1] Andrew Woods, Chris Hope,
Bryony Worthington and Adam Coutts

'We cannot solve the problems we have created with the same thinking
that created them.'

Albert Einstein

Introduction

Over the past 200 years most of the world has experienced an unprecedented rise
in standards of living. This has been driven by cheap fossil fuels, technological
innovation, an economic system that unleashes our creative potential and a
set of values that rewards the accumulation of material wealth.

Mainstream economics assumes that human ingenuity will continue to
deliver this economic growth in the future. However, this view clashes with
the fact that we live on a planet constrained by finite resources and there
is increasing evidence that we may be beginning to hit some of its limits.
Examples include fresh water (Rogers 2008), cheap fossil fuels (The Economist
2008b) and global warming (Flannery 2005; Stern 2006).

In this context, this chapter looks at two of the greatest challenges
facing mankind today, and the implications for the UK in the twenty-first
century:

- environmental degradation, of which climate change is but one
  example;
- and the increasing threat to the supply of energy resources.

The thinking behind this chapter is based on a first principles approach. Its
purpose is to offer a holistic view of the problem before discussing a policy mix

to address it. The first section states the problem. The second then identifies the underlying fundamental causes of the problem. The third section outlines future scenarios and challenges and proposes policy options to address these. The subsequent section reviews the actions that have been taken until now, and the fifth section explains the need to tackle this problem at a global level, and the difficulties behind reaching an international agreement. The penultimate section lists the available policy levers to control and influence the underlying driving forces. Finally, there is a conclusion.

What is the problem and who cares?

Our climate is changing. The price of oil and gas, as well as the cost of energy, are becoming increasingly volatile with our natural environment becoming degraded at an ever faster rate. Model forecasts indicate that our climate could change dramatically, with unimaginable consequences (Lynas 2007). This state of affairs is unsustainable. And, since the world's population is expected to reach 9 billion by 2050, this situation can only get worse.

However, as Figures 11.1 and 11.2 show, the public remains largely unconvinced by the potentially devastating impacts of climate change (MORI 2008a). In addition people are concerned with the ability of the government to take the necessary steps to tackling climate change (Figure 11.3). In relation to what they perceive as more immediate life-changing issues as the economy,

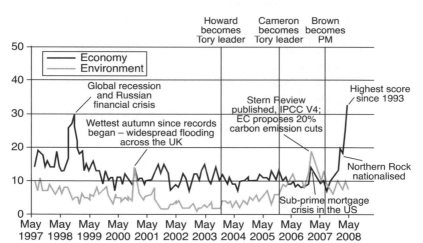

Q What do you see as the main/other important issues facing Britain today?
(Economy/Environment responses)

Figure 11.1   Economy vs. Environment

Source: MORI (2008a).

concern with climate change is relatively low down in the public's everyday worries. This is an issue we address below.

How concerned, if at all, are you about climate change?

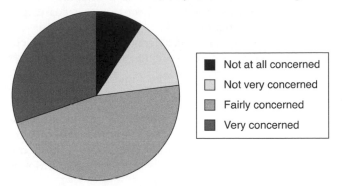

■ Not at all concerned
□ Not very concerned
▨ Fairly concerned
▨ Very concerned

Figure 11.2 Headline Concern About Climate Change

Note: Base: 1,039 GB adults aged 15+, interviewed f-2-f and in home, 23–29 May 2008.
Source: MORI (2008a).

How confident, if at all, are you that the Government will deal with climate change in the next few years? Are you ...?

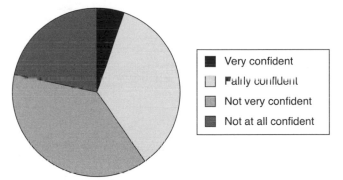

■ Very confident
□ Fairly confident
▨ Not very confident
▨ Not at all confident

Figure 11.3 Public Confidence That Government Will Deal With Climate Change in the Next Few Years

Note: Base: 1,039 GB adults aged 15+, interviewed f-2-f and in home, 23–29 May 2008.
Source: MORI (2008a).

The following subsections look specifically at three interconnected issues: energy resources, climate change, and the environment.

Energy resources and security of supply

It is becoming generally accepted that the era of cheap fossil fuels is over. Moreover, fossil fuel reservoirs are concentrated in small geographical regions, some of which are politically contentious regions such as Iran and Russia. The combination of scarcity and geographic concentration leads to the serious issue of security of supply. This can cause international tensions and sometimes even conflict. This is especially problematic for the UK which, until recently the world's sixth largest producer of oil and a net exporter, has now become a net importer.

Climate change

The balance of scientific evidence points clearly to the fact that man-made greenhouse gas emissions are significantly affecting the Earth's atmosphere. This is already causing global warming and climate change and, due to the inertia of the Earth's natural systems, further environmental deterioration is inevitable (IPCC 2007).

In order to avoid further damage to the Earth's systems, we need to reduce greenhouse gas (GHG) emissions to a sustainable level that is consistent with the capacity of the Earth to absorb them. The evidence suggests that stabilizing GHG concentrations at 450–500ppmv CO_2e (parts per million by volume of CO_2 equivalent) offers the best balance between projected risks and costs (Stern 2008). Figure 11.4 shows the typical pathways consistent

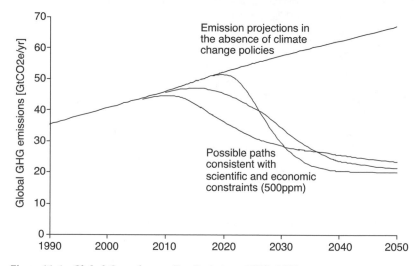

Figure 11.4   Global Greenhouse Gas Emissions 1990–2050

Note: In the absence of climate change policies, GHG emissions will keep rising. To avoid dangerous climate change, emissions will need to peak in the near future and then decline to a sustainable level.

Source: SiMCaP model.

with stabilization at 500ppmv CO_2e. A worrying trend to note however is that, as we improve our ability to measure and forecast the impact of global emissions, we find that emissions are growing faster than previously estimated (Garnaut 2008), and that their environmental impact is worsening (Hepburn and Stern 2008).

As the diagram indicates, and is also becoming generally accepted wisdom (Stern 2008), global emissions should fall to around 20GtCO_2e (20 gigatonnes of CO_2 equivalent) by 2050. Given that the UN forecasts the world population to be about 9 billion at this time, it follows that on average each person will be entitled to emit 2tCO_2e. Considering that current per capita emissions in the UK are around 10tCO_2e per person (Energy Information Administration 2005), the UK should aim to reduce its emissions by at least 80% by 2050.

The environment

We rely on our natural environment. It provides us with services that are free of charge and that we often take for granted. For example, forests and the oceans absorb the carbon we emit, bees pollinate our crops and microbes biodegrade most of our waste. However, the environment cannot cope with the damage we are currently inflicting upon it. As a general picture, it is estimated that over the past 30 years the world has lost 25% of its biodiversity (WWF 2008).

In order to secure our future we need to ensure that our economic system is sustainable. Currently this is not the case: it is estimated that our global ecological footprint – the demands we impose on the planet's ecosystems – is about 25% higher than the Earth's productive capacity (WWF 2008). In other words, we are living beyond our ecological means and we are putting the costs of our excesses on the shoulders of future generations.

Causes of the problem

This section explores the causes behind the exponential growth in demand for fossil fuels and natural resources.

Figure 11.5 illustrates the three forces behind the growth in GHG emissions (O'Neill et al 2001): demographic change, changes in levels of consumption, and changes in technology (GHG intensity).[2]

Figure 11.6 quantifies the individual contributions from these three forces: it presents their projected changes relative to the base year 1990.[3] The graph shows that, although GHG intensity in the UK is projected to improve by almost 80% by 2050, GHG emissions are actually expected to remain broadly constant. This is because the gains from GHG intensity are lost due to a growing population that is becoming significantly wealthier. This pattern is also true at a global level. In other words, GHG emissions are rising mainly due to our growing material wealth as well as to the increasing population. This is supported by a number of recent studies (Jackson 2008a, 2008b).

Studies also show that greenhouse gas emissions are sensitive to population growth in the long run. Some studies even suggest that population growth will be responsible for up to 50% of the growth of global CO_2 emissions from fossil fuels between 1985 and 2025 (Bongaarts 1992). This implies that we should try to understand better the interaction between climatology and demographics, including population growth and migration.

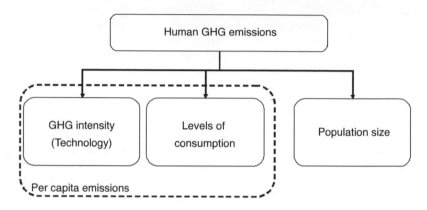

Figure 11.5   The Three Forces Behind the Growth in Greenhouse Gas Emissions

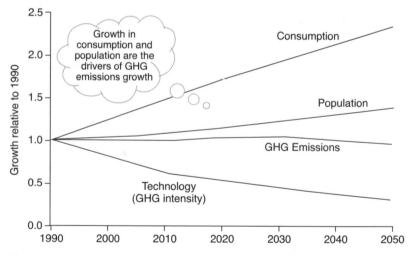

Figure 11.6   Projected Contributions to GHG Emissions Growth from Population, Levels of Consumption and Improvements in Carbon Efficiency in the UK

Note: The figures assume that no policies have been put in place to reduce GHG emissions – this is known as the 'business as usual' scenario.

Source: POLES.

Policy options

A comprehensive policy portfolio should make the most of all abatement opportunities. Current efforts focus heavily on technology innovation to improve GHG intensity; for example, replacing coal power plants with wind farms. Improvements in energy efficiency are driven mostly through regulation. However, policies aimed at addressing growth in population and levels of consumption do not feature in the current debate, even though the evidence shown in Figure 11.6 suggests that significant opportunities may exist in these areas.

This section explores in more detail the issues around stimulating renewable technologies, and addressing both the rise in consumption and population growth.

Stimulating renewable technologies

There are a number of technological solutions to assist with the challenges of energy supply and energy demand, which could lead to a major step change in carbon emissions, and which would provide greater security in terms of supply. In order to place these potential solutions in context, it is useful to observe that the present mix of primary energy is dominated by hydrocarbon, with coal, oil and gas representing over 80% of global supply, and the remainder is primarily derived from nuclear and hydroelectric. (See Figure 11.7.)

The potential impact of new technologies needs to be considered within the present context, in terms of understanding the timescale for implementation of the technologies and the materiality of the technologies.

First, we observe that over the next few decades, hydrocarbons are likely to represent a major part of the energy mix, owing to the present investments of

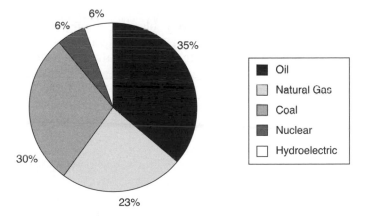

Figure 11.7   The Global Primary Energy Mix

Source: Data from British Petroleum (2008).

infrastructure centred on hydrocarbon power generation. In order to mitigate the emissions from such fuels, one technologically feasible solution is that of carbon capture and storage (CCS). Existing schemes such as that at the Sleipner field in Norway (Chadwick et al 2006) and the In-Salah field in Algeria (Friedmann 2007) have demonstrated the technical capability in the oil sector to re-inject substantial volumes of CO_2 into the subsurface, and to monitor the dispersal of this CO_2 using a range of technologies. The challenge now seems to rest in establishing an economic framework to promote widespread implementation of CCS technologies, with a prime target being coal and gas fired power stations, since these represent large, fixed sources of CO_2 emissions. Global-scale implementation of CCS has the potential to be a material part of the overall challenge of providing clean energy at scale, especially over the next few decades. On a longer timescale, there are numerous substitute technologies for oil, coal and gas, with applications in different sectors.

For power generation, nuclear power has enormous potential for expansion, with only 5.8% of global primary energy currently originating from it (British Petroleum 2007), although on an international scale, it requires some movement in public acceptance. Wind turbine technology, especially for onshore developments, can now produce power for 5–10 cents per kilowatt-hour although the challenge of scaling up the materiality of wind power globally is substantial given the present mix of world primary energy, and here is likely to meet the conflicting environmental challenge of locating suitable sites.

Solar energy, in its various guises, appears to be the longer-term solution for evolving from a hydrocarbon-based economy, from a technical perspective. Direct power generation through photo-voltaics costs between about 7–8 US\$ per watt (IEA 2005), while reflective solar concentrators also have the potential to generate very substantial quantities of power; with efficiencies of between 10% and 20% in conversion. Direct solar heating, through hot water systems, is also likely to have a major impact in reducing domestic hot water load, although for the medium term a part of the challenge lies in refurbishing existing building stock rather than with new build given the multi-decade life-time of most buildings.

Biofuels have received tremendous interest, and there are large-scale initiatives such as the bio-ethanol fuelled transport in Brazil from sugar-cane. Biomass for heat and power generation is also a practical technology. However, there remain technological challenges relating to improving the efficiency of conversion of incident solar radiation into plants through photosynthesis and ultimately to generate liquid fuels.

Promoting efficiency and reassessing consumption patterns

At the moment, we have three basic policy goals that would help to limit the extent of global warming: to shift the basis of our energy supply away from fossil fuels and towards renewable sources of energy; to reduce our energy consumption; or to do both of these things.

The historical experience is that improving energy efficiency has been a normal process at least since the 1880s, with or without government intervention. However, improvements in energy efficiency are nowhere near large enough to affect the overall dynamic of economic growth, and thus carbon emissions. It took more than 50 years at an average year-on-year growth of 7.25% for oil to account for 50% of total energy supply. No other transition has been achieved with equivalent rapidity and scale. For renewable technologies to provide 75% of world energy in 40 years' time, it would require a continual yearly growth of around 9–10% (Warde 2007).

The lesson for policymakers is thus that reduction of carbon emissions is only likely where the use of renewable energy is combined with direct measures to restrict overall energy use. A significant co-benefit of such a policy would be financial savings from energy efficiency – some models estimate that yearly saving of up to US$500 billion could be achieved by 2030, US$90 billion of which in the USA alone (Creyts et al 2007).

A reduction in energy consumption can be achieved in three ways: we can consume more efficiently; we can consume less; or we can do both of these things.

Consume more efficiently

Our socio-economic system is full of opportunities to achieve higher energy efficiencies. Buildings represent one of the main targets for reducing energy demand, while there are still considerable opportunities in the transport sector. Beyond simple improvements in the building stock, such as improved insulation, low-wattage lighting systems, and more energy efficient design of the heating and ventilation, there are technical solutions. Ground-source heat pumps, which use the ground as a thermal reservoir can be much more efficient than conventional heating systems, especially if combined with better building design, including appropriate levels of insulation and glazing, so that low temperature heating systems can be used. Perhaps the main challenge in buildings is the timescale and cost of refurbishment of existing building stock to bring about significant improvements in energy efficiency and the cost of embodied energy associated with new building projects.

Improvements in internal combustion engine design, combined with hybrid engine technologies continue to provide increments in energy efficiency, although these need careful assessment in terms of the cost of embodied energy and operating energy.

Behaviour change

Almost everyone, at an individual level, could reduce their environmental impact by making simple changes in their everyday lives: switching off the lights when not needed, using less water, reducing the thermostat, driving more efficiently and cycling. More significant changes involve replacing incandescent light bulbs with new energy efficient bulbs or insulating our homes. Policies could be designed with the goal of directly inducing behaviour change and culture change. This will require a better understanding of people's incentives and preferences.

Promoting personal responsibility and methods/mechanisms of inducing behaviour change amongst the population has been taken up across government – from health and education, to promoting more energy efficient behaviours. However, the actual practicalities of achieving a behavioural shift amongst the population poses great challenges for policymakers (Darnton 2008; Halpern et al 2004). Changing behaviour is complex, and environmental behaviours are very different from one another. As a recent report by Downing and Ballantyne (2007) notes, a distinction must be made in terms of conscious behaviours (e.g. buying a car) and subconscious behaviours (e.g. driving a car); between small behaviours likely to change rapidly and those requiring longer time horizons; and between isolated behaviours and interconnected 'sticky' behaviours that influence others (Downing and Ballantyne 2007). Given socio-economic differences between the population and therefore the differing capabilities (mainly financial and educational) to be able to adopt more environmentally or socially beneficial behaviours there is not a 'one size fits all' message that can be used to encourage change in the behaviour of individuals and families. Jackson (2005) offers a review of the research and evidence on consumer behaviour and behaviour change. Moreover, new models are being developed that could help identify the key drivers behind people's choices, and perhaps even potential tipping points to trigger structural changes (Gallo et al 2008).

Consume less

There is an emerging and rapidly expanding body of empirical evidence to suggest that, beyond a certain level, material wealth does not deliver consistent improvements in well-being: *'having more stuff does not always make us happy'* (Jackson 2006). There is also evidence on how the excessive choice available to consumers is proving detrimental to our psychological and emotional well-being (Schwartz 2005). Research also shows that relative wealth is more important than absolute wealth, and richer but more unequal societies may experience lower standards across a range of areas such as health and education (Wilkinson and Pickett 2007), and that it is this inequality that ultimately drives the social need to 'catch up' and, in part, the need for continuous economic growth in developed countries (Ariely 2008).

What has been done so far to tackle the problem

Figure 11.8 shows a chronology of key regional agreements related to tackling climate change. The Kyoto Protocol treaty is currently the most important international tool to reduce emissions of greenhouse gases: for the first target period (2008–12) signatory nations have agreed to reduce their aggregate emissions by 5.2% relative to 1990.

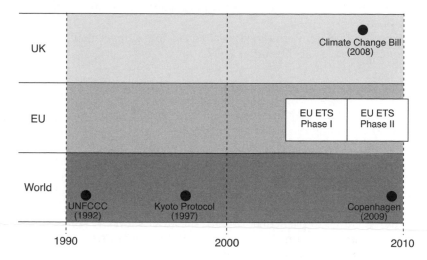

Figure 11.8 Chronology of Key Events Related to Climate Change in the World, EU and UK

The Kyoto Protocol established two important things: the assignment of greenhouse gas emission targets to developed countries, and arrangements for emissions trading of the six most important greenhouse gases (Flannery 2005).

More recently, first in Germany in 2007 and then in Japan in 2008, the G8 agreed on the need to reduce world emissions of GHG by 50% by 2050. However, no specific details were given on the base year, and no legally binding commitments were signed.

The EU has taken a lead role in combating climate change and has been a big supporter of an international carbon market. It established the EU Emissions Trading Scheme (EU ETS), which currently covers 40% of all EU25 GHG emissions. Moreover, the EU has committed to cut emissions by 20% by 2020 relative to 1990, and offered to increase this to 30% if major emitters agree on taking legally binding comparable targets (European Commission 2007a). This package also specifies a number of other goals, including support for twelve CCS demonstration projects.

The UK has also been taking unilateral action to reduce its emissions. A number of regulations require business to reduce emissions. An example is the Carbon Emissions Reduction Target (CERT) (DEFRA 2007). More concretely, the UK was the first country in the world to pass a Climate Change Bill with self-imposed legally binding emissions targets. The Climate Change

Act, which came into force on 28 November 2008, legally commits the UK to reducing greenhouse gas emissions by 80% by 2050. Moreover, in October 2008 the government set up a new Department of Energy and Climate Change to give a greater focus to solving the twin problems of climate change and security of supply.

It is expected that an international deal on tackling climate change will be agreed in Copenhagen at the end of 2009.

The next step: reaching an international agreement

We previously argued that the available scientific and economic evidence would require global greenhouse gas emissions to fall below $20GtCO_2e$ by 2050. The crucial next question is: how is this burden to be shared among the nations of the world? This section explores the issues around securing a global deal on climate change.

Climate change is a global problem. Action to reduce emissions by individual countries will be meaningless unless it is integrated into a coordinated international effort. In particular, due to the current level of emissions in the major developing countries, and especially in view of their forecasted growth, it is now accepted that industrialized nations do not have the power to solve the problem on their own.

Developed countries, which are responsible for the majority of the CO_2 emitted so far, have an opportunity to prove their commitment and demonstrate that low-carbon growth is possible. If the target is to be met, however, developing nations should eventually take steps of their own (perhaps by 2020 and with the aim of peaking global emissions before 2030). Stern (2008) proposes a number of key principles upon which a global deal should be based.

A global deal to tackle climate change should specify the abatement targets for all countries as well as the abatement mechanisms, such as the carbon market. This, in turn, would specify the national goals and put some constraints on the policy options that may be available to policymakers.

The political problems associated with reaching a deal – which include currently rich countries facing economically challenging times and rapidly industrializing countries who will not act unless those responsible for the historic stock of emissions do so first – are well known and are a major impediment to achieving progress.

One potential solution is to consider global emissions sector by sector as well as country by country. This can assist in solving the political problems since participants within sectors are more homogeneous (many are international companies) than the economies of countries. The sector that lends itself most readily to global regulation is the global power sector since it is the most easily regulated, is not exposed to international competition, and has the most cost-effective abatement solutions available to it to rapidly decarbonize.

It is such a significant source of emissions of CO_2 that it could force global emissions to start decreasing by 2020.

The policy levers

There is no 'silver bullet' that can solve this problem. Instead, the solution will require a 'policy mix', the details of which may vary over time and geography. Moreover, given the global nature of the problem, it may be necessary to implement policies that are not optimal but that ensure international cooperation. This section presents the main policy levers available to decision-makers.

Price-based policies

Carbon technologies would naturally begin to be phased out when green technologies become comparatively cheaper. Figure 11.9 illustrates schematically how carbon technologies, e.g. coal power plants, could become relatively more expensive than green technologies, such as wind farms, if the social cost of carbon is added to them (Box 11.1).

Monetary policies that could change the relative cost of green technologies include: cap and trade, taxation, and subsidies.

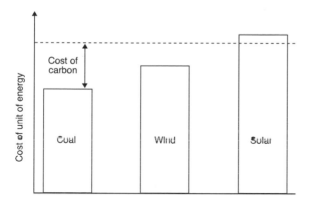

Figure 11.9 Adding the Social Cost of Carbon into the Cost of Energy

Cap and trade

Cap and Trade is a system that automatically incorporates a carbon cost to consumer goods through the market mechanism of supply and demand. The system is composed of two elements:

1. Regulation on emissions: individual players – states or sectors of the economy – receive legally binding limits on their greenhouse gas emissions (the cap).

2. Trade: players are allowed to trade carbon credits from the carbon market in order to meet their targets and minimize their costs (the trade).

Box 11.1   Social Costs of Carbon
Chris Hope

Fossil fuels would naturally be phased out only when their costs become higher relative to green technologies. This may occur naturally as fossil fuels run out and get more expensive while green technologies improve, are mass produced and become cheaper. However, given the urgency of climate change and security of supply, we have a problem of timing: we need to find ways to accelerate the transition from a carbon economy to a green one. One option is to incorporate the *social cost of carbon* into the cost of energy. This would ensure that the relative cost of fossil fuels becomes comparatively high, which would drive demand away from them.

The impacts of climate change affect not only those who emit greenhouse gases, such as carbon dioxide. Rather, any tonne of carbon dioxide that I emit spreads out throughout the atmosphere and mixes thoroughly with all the other tonnes that are emitted by other households, towns, countries and regions. Without intervention, there is essentially no incentive for me to cut my emissions, as I would bear all the costs of cutting them, but receive only a minuscule fraction of the benefits. Everyone else would feel the same, so greenhouse gases would continue to be emitted, as long as the activities that cause them, such as the burning of fossil fuel, remain useful or profitable to the individuals, households and companies who make the decisions.

What is the solution? There needs to be some way to estimate the impacts caused by the tonne of carbon dioxide that I emit – called its social cost – and to charge me for those impacts, in accordance with the principle that polluters should pay for the damage they cause.

How is the social cost of carbon measured? A model linking CO_2 emissions to concentrations, temperature rises, the impacts on GDP and the valuation of non-market impacts is required to calculate the social cost. Models that do this are called Integrated Assessment Models (IAMs), as they integrate the findings from science and economics to give results that are useful for policymaking. A successful model should account for the significant uncertainties involved (Parson and Fisher-Vanden 1997: 609). A leading example of this modelling approach to finding the social cost of a range of greenhouse gases is the PAGE2002 model (Hope 2006).

Using the PAGE2002 model, the Stern review reported a social cost of $85 per tonne of CO_2 (Stern et al 2006). This value is the mean result in year 2000 $US for a tonne of CO_2 emitted in 2001. It rises at 2–3% per year, as we get closer to the date when the most serious impacts of climate change are likely to occur, so in 2008 it is $100 per tonne of CO_2. What about our uncertainty about the climate sensitivity, the shape and scale of the impacts with temperature, and all the other inputs to the model? They lead to a wide 90% confidence interval for the social cost in 2008 of $25–300 per tonne of CO_2.

A key property of Cap and Trade is that, by changing the abatement targets, policymakers are able to indirectly influence the price of carbon, and therefore stimulate green technologies.

Cap and trade has a number of advantages. It can reduce costs, as abatement is carried out where it is cheaper. It provides a mechanism to incentivize developing countries to join an international market, as they could receive substantial financial flows. It allows us to fix the abatement targets in accordance with the science to ensure that we avoid dangerous climate change. It avoids the political problem of introducing a new direct carbon tax on consumers.

On the other hand, Cap and Trade has also a number of disadvantages. It requires agreeing and setting up a carbon market; this could be done at community, company or national level, but ultimately would require an international carbon market. This involves a large number of practical obstacles, most of which are yet unknown. A significant obstacle is the agreement of national targets.

Carbon tax

It is also possible to impose a carbon price directly through taxation. In this case policymakers control the price of carbon directly. A tax has several advantages. The carbon price would be predictable and stable. This would encourage businesses to make long-term investments in green technologies. Using a tax is theoretically sound, as the impacts from greenhouse gas emissions are the same wherever they are emitted. It is very straightforward to apply at the point of sale of fossil fuels, using well-established systems. It would provide substantial revenues that could be used to reduce other distortionary taxes and substantially reduce the costs of tackling climate change.

On the other hand, a tax loses direct control over the climate target, as this will depend heavily on consumers' response to the tax. A further disadvantage is that price changes do not produce a stable response, as people tend to accommodate to price changes over time (Ariely 2008). This may require adjustments in the level of tax over time, which may lead to political battles, but is also theoretically justified as the social cost of greenhouse gases increases over time.

Subsidies

Another policy option is to subsidize green technologies. This would involve lowering the cost of green technologies rather than increasing that of carbon technologies.

Subsidies can significantly boost the development of new technologies, reduce their costs and help bring them to market. One example is the development of solar energy in Germany, which is now the world leader in this area. Subsidies could also play a key role in the demonstration of new technologies. A typical example is that of carbon capture and storage: it is currently uneconomical but, given the widespread availability of cheap coal, it could allow us to build clean coal-fired power stations. Moreover, subsidies could be applied to special cases, for example to temporarily compensate big losers during the period of transition.

On the other hand, subsidies require governments to raise revenues elsewhere to pay for them. They can also be very uncertain for investors: they rely on government picking winners and, if the subsidies are removed, whole industries can suddenly become unviable. An example is the solar industry in the USA (The Economist 2008a). This could lead to market distortions that could be counter-productive in the long term.

Finance

There are several instances where carbon savings are missed due to the upfront costs. For example, the costs of running a nuclear power plant are low compared with the upfront costs of building it. Also, insulation of buildings can lead to significant savings on heating bills, but the initial cost of insulation can be very high. This means that there is an opportunity to design innovative financial tools that could help companies and individuals to spread the upfront costs over time.

Non-monetary policies

This subsection explores non-monetary policies that could influence consumer behaviour.

Regulation

Monetary tools may not always be ideal, and sometimes may not even work at all. To take an example, it is estimated that increased energy efficiency in the residential sector would not only lead to carbon reductions but also to financial savings. Some estimates suggest that worldwide savings could be $500 billion by 2030 (Creyts et al 2007). Regulation could be a concrete and reliable policy option to exploit this potential. For example, international standards have led to substantial improvements in energy efficiency in the automotive sector.[4] The UK is currently regulating energy suppliers to improve the energy efficiency of their residential customers (DEFRA 2007).

Information

Dealing with climate change is particularly challenging because, due to the delay in the Earth's response to our greenhouse gas emissions, the real effects could become apparent only when it is too late to avoid them. This raises the issue of public opinion: people may be reluctant to change their behaviour, let alone change their lifestyles, to avoid a threat that they do not perceive as real.

Government should actively engage with the public: it should inform and create awareness but should avoid creating climate change fatigue.[5]

Government should also provide advice on how best to reduce emissions. Moreover, government could change the terms of the debate by stressing the opportunities as well as the challenges associated with climate change.

Behaviour change

As Figure 11.6 shows, the key driving force behind the growth in greenhouse gas emissions is the growth in consumption. Imposing limits on consumption from above are politically impracticable. This means that there is an enormous potential in finding ways to incentivize the public to spontaneously change their behaviour towards more sustainable levels of consumption. This is a notoriously hard goal to achieve, but one worth pursuing. The major problem is that consumption patterns and behaviours are ingrained, with individuals torn between competing and conflicting mindsets (Hamilton and Denniss 2006). They may say they want to prevent climate change but, at the same time, as consumers they want to go on holiday and purchase the latest gadgets. People do recognize their collective responsibilities but at the same time fiercely guard their personal rights and freedoms (Downing and Ballantyne 2007).

We are not proposing that policy should aim to induce shame and guilt as proposed by McLean (2008) as a method by which to induce behaviour change. Different behaviours require different incentive structures. There is not a 'one incentive structure fits all' mode of behaviour change. It has to be nuanced but at the same time a mass social marketing approach, perhaps resembling that of the 1980s AIDS campaigns in the UK. Changing people's health or financial behaviours is different from getting them to adopt more energy efficient lifestyles. An individual can see an immediate benefit to their health and their bank account if they reduce their smoking and drinking and spending rates whereas adopting more energy efficient behaviours has no immediate financial effect or impact upon their health and well-being. It is up to the research community, with support from government, to find new ways of understanding these tensions and how and why individuals make certain social choices and how these are mediated by their socio-economic position. Government could support research aimed at developing tools that can identify policy levers to influence people's behaviour. Models based on discrete choice make use of survey data to estimate people's preferences in many circumstances, and are able to focus on specific socio-economic groups in space and time (see Box 11.2).

Carbon rationing

Carbon rationing could offer an alternative if time becomes an issue and changes are needed to take place quickly and reliably. In 1939 and 1940 the government introduced a rationing of consumption because it thought that the impact of tax rises would be too slow and inadequate; the public accepted that rationing was a temporary but necessary measure. The experience of the

Box 11.2   Designing Highly Cost-effective Policy Options by Identifying and Triggering Tipping Points
Gallo, Contucci, Gallo and Coutts

Ignacio Gallo and Pierluigi Contucci are developing a new family of mathematical models (Gallo et al 2008), based on a statistical mechanics extension of discrete choice theory. They offer a set of formal tools to systematically identify the incentives driving people's behaviour. An application example could be to predict the percentage of people choosing to buy new energy efficient light bulbs instead of the traditional incandescent versions. Through statistical evaluation of survey responses, these models can identify the key driving factors in the decision-making process; for example, the extent to which people imitate each other. In particular, these models allow us to incorporate the effect of social interactions and could help us identify 'tipping points' at a societal level. This knowledge could be used to trigger structural changes in our society. The results may provide tangible and deliverable evidence-based policy options to decision-makers.

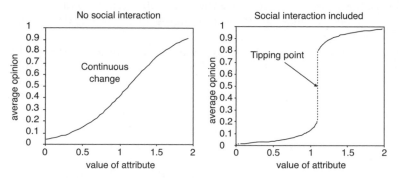

Figure 11.10   Social interaction at an individual level can give rise to structural changes or 'tipping points' at a society level, as 'herd behaviour' can trigger sudden and significant changes in mass behaviour. The ability to identify and perhaps trigger these tipping points could result in highly cost-effective policies whereby a small incentive could result in a sudden and significant change in behaviour at an aggregate level.

These models could offer an opportunity for the research community – in both the social and physical sciences – and decision-makers in the private and public sectors to work together towards preventing the potentially devastating social, economic and environmental effects of climate change.

Second World War indicates that the government must convince the public that rationing levels are fair, that the system is administered transparently (Roodhouse 2007).

If people are also allowed to trade their credits, this opens the possibility of a personal cap and trade system. It is important to note, however, that this may raise equity issues, and may be very hard to implement in the short term.

Conclusion: challenges and opportunities

This chapter discussed two of the major problems facing humanity in the twenty-first century: security of energy supply and a deteriorating environment, with particular focus on climate change. The problem was analysed using a first principles approach and identified three key driving factors in energy demand and greenhouse gas emissions: growth in both levels of consumption and population and greenhouse gas intensity in our technologies. It was argued that, although currently most attention is focused on technological solutions, the issues of consumption and population growth may offer new and unexplored policy opportunities. A list of policy levers to address these drivers was presented, and a number of concrete policy examples were discussed.

So far, our responses to these problems have not met the scale of the challenge, and have generally addressed the symptoms rather than the causes. Our relentless economic growth is inconsistent with the need to reduce greenhouse gas emissions, the impact of our activities on the environment as well as our dependency on fossil fuels. On top of that, it seems that the growth in wealth is not necessarily making us happier or healthier. So, in an increasingly resource-constrained world, we may need to reconsider our priorities and decide what we want our economic system to deliver. We should begin to honestly address the question of whether we are living within our ecological means or, on the contrary, we are demanding too much from the natural environment. We may need to rethink our relationship with the planet; but above all look beyond GDP as our measure of prosperity and success. It may not be necessary to reduce our standards of living, but we may need to increase them at a slower rate[6] that is consistent with sustainable development.[7] We could seek to reduce inequality rather than increase overall wealth.

The issue of climate change can also be a useful 'policy vehicle' by which to bring together a variety of government departments, agencies and private sectors to tackle this multidimensional and multidisciplinary problem which is pertinent to the effectiveness of all and to the future security and well-being of not just the British population but that of the world. However this inter-sectoral policy design and delivery will require strong leadership, particularly from those at national political level.

Any strategy should be realistic and take into account existing economic constraints; it should protect people's prosperity but should also aim to alleviate poverty. Overall, a sustainable long-term solution should take a more holistic and multi-sectoral approach that acknowledges the multifaceted nature and causes of the problem and makes use of all the available policy tools and options.

Acknowledgements

We would like to thank Ignacio Gallo and Pierluigi Contucci for their contribution on the models of behaviour change. We are grateful to Patrick Criqui and Alban Kitous from the University of Grenoble for sharing data from the POLES model, and Tim Jackson for his contribution on the topic of sustainable consumption. FG would also like to thank Sharvari Dalal, Lila Rabinovich, Jennifer Rubin and David Halpern for the helpful discussions.

Notes

1. The views expressed in this chapter are those of the authors and do not represent those of the British government.
2. GHG intensity is the amount of greenhouse gas emitted per unit of GDP produce, and depends on the technologies used to produce energy.
3. The forecasts assume that no new policies aimed at reducing GHG are introduced – this is known as the 'business as usual' scenario. This scenario does not account for the fact that rising energy prices could stimulate investment in cheap coal and tar sands, which would negatively affect the improvements in energy efficiency.
4. Experience suggests, however, that the gains made in efficiency have been lost by building bigger cars. Perhaps there is an opportunity to regulate car sizes as well as their energy efficiency.
5. Climate change fatigue refers to the fact that people who have been overloaded with news on global warming may lose interest in, or even become irritated by the issue of climate change.
6. The situation in developed countries is different: there exists a sincere need to improve living standards, and to lift millions of people out of poverty. Therefore, in an increasingly resource-constrained world, there is a need to consider more carefully the distribution of growth as well as growth itself.
7. Some studies go a step further and suggest that, in order to reduce GHG emissions, consumption in some sectors should actually decline (McMichael et al 2007).

12
Britain and the World: Options for UK Foreign and Security Policy

Malcolm Chalmers

Introduction

The change of government in 1997 was accompanied by a shift in UK foreign policy towards what Prime Minister Tony Blair sought to characterize as a more internationalist, and values-based, approach.

Eleven years later: achievements and failures in foreign policy

By 1997, UK foreign policy appeared to its critics to have become overly insular. Much of the government's political energy was consumed by internal divisions over Europe, while relations with the Democratic administration in the US had soured. The aid budget had stagnated, and the government appeared to view it as much as a means of export subsidy as of development assistance. The defence budget had fallen by 30% in real terms since 1985, and the UK had been fiercely criticized for its failure to react strongly to the onset of genocide in the Balkans and Rwanda. The only substantial overseas operational deployments were with NATO's Balkans force and the joint US/UK force policing Iraq's no-fly zones, in total some 6,500 personnel (IISS 1997: 72–3). In 2008, by contrast, smaller armed forces were deploying 14,000 personnel in Afghanistan and Iraq (IISS 2008: 431).

The Labour government that came to office in 1997 sought to develop a foreign policy that was more 'internationalist' and values-based. There were at least three main identifiable components to this new approach: first, energetic pursuit of new multilateral instruments for tackling security and conflict, often by working closely with NGO and business communities; second, a step-change in the level of commitment to international development, symbolized most of all by the establishment of the Department for International Development (DfID); third, and in part in response to the failures of the international community in Rwanda and Bosnia, a growing use of the UK military in humanitarian interventions.

On the first, the UK played an important role in extending an arms control remit as an instrument of humanitarian policy. Capitalizing on its improved relations with EU partners, the government played a leading role in securing agreement to the EU Code of Conduct on arms exports, as well as international agreement to the Ottawa Convention to outlaw anti-personnel landmines. Subsequently, it strongly supported plans for controls on small arms, and for a legally-binding Arms Trade Treaty.

In addition, despite US opposition and working closely with EU partners, the UK backed the establishment of the International Criminal Court, agreed in 1998. It initiated new proposals for an international regime to tackle 'conflict diamonds', and subsequently led the establishment of the Extractive Industries Transparency Initiative, designed to address the problems of conflict and corruption associated with resource-rich developing countries. The government gained considerable support for these initiatives from UK NGOs, who had pressed for the new regimes, and who continued to play a critical role in mobilizing political and media opinion.

UK development NGOs were also supportive of the second strand in the government's foreign policy reforms: the establishment of DfID, and the accompanying sharp increase in the priority attached to international development. Over the last decade, DfID has been accorded the highest spending priority of any major government department. Use of the aid budget as an instrument of trade promotion has ended, and the 'tying' of aid to UK producers has ceased. Moreover, with a continuing record of innovation across a range of policy areas, DfID has gained a reputation as one of the most pro-poor and least protectionist of the OECD donors. It is now a powerful Whitehall actor in its own right, exercising considerable influence in foreign and security policy, especially in relations with major aid recipients in sub-Saharan Africa and Asia. This is probably the greatest single achievement of the turn towards ethical internationalism on which Labour embarked after 1997.

The third key policy innovation was the increased use of the armed forces in 'humanitarian intervention'. The previous government had pioneered the use of military forces for humanitarian purposes, in defiance of previous non-interference norms, when it backed the creation of a 'safe haven' for Kurdish refugees in northern Iraq following the 1991 Gulf War. But neither the UK nor the US proved willing to take action to prevent or mitigate the 1994 Rwanda genocide. The UK, along with several other European countries, did deploy significant forces to Croatia and Bosnia during 1992–95 under a UN flag. But their limited remit prevented them from taking a more decisive role in ending the conflicts in the region, which claimed around 200,000 lives and led to 3 million refugees.

These failures were the context for the development of Labour's more interventionist approach after it took power. The 1998 Strategic Defence Review solidified the reorientation of the armed forces into a 'force for good', ready to intervene to protect populations from massacre and genocide. The government saw this as a natural counterpart to its active multilateralism and its increased commitment to international aid.

The turn towards interventionism was first evident in practice in the 1998–99 Kosovo crisis, as NATO countries sought to fashion a response to the growing conflict in that territory. Scarred by its previous failures in Croatia and Bosnia, the alliance launched an air campaign against Serbia in March 1999. Prime Minister Blair (together with France) urged a reluctant US to use the threat of ground forces in order to persuade President Milosevic to back down. As part of this campaign, Blair used his Chicago speech in May 1999 to set out an ambitious set of criteria for the use of military force in support of humanitarian objectives (Blair 1999). The UK went on to play a key role in urging the international community's acceptance of its 'Responsibility to Protect' those populations who were under threat of genocide or war crimes, in cases where their own governments were unable or unwilling to protect them.

This was, and is, a radical and direct challenge to a key principle of international order. In the single-superpower world of the late 1990s, however, the risks involved in adopting it appeared manageable, and the gains tangible. The NATO campaign against Serbia succeeded in forcing its withdrawal from Kosovo. A year later, President Milosevic was forced from office by a popular uprising against a rigged election, an event that soon triggered similar 'colour revolutions' in Ukraine and Georgia. Democratization, driven by domestic civil society movements and supported by the promise of EU membership and international democratization assistance programmes, appeared to be the wave of the future.

The record of the new interventionism in Africa was less impressive. The conflict in Kosovo distracted the attention of the major powers from the much larger inter-state conflict that broke out in August 1998 in the Democratic Republic of Congo, and involved the armies of eight African countries. Nor did the emerging interventionism mitigate the 1998–2000 Ethiopia/Eritrea war, which inflicted massive damage on two of the world's poorest countries. Emboldened by the success of Kosovo, however, in 2000 the UK reversed its previous hands-off policy and ordered military intervention in Sierra Leone to prevent the country's capital from being overrun by rebels. The subsequent operation has been widely praised for both its effectiveness in bringing Sierra Leone's civil war to an end, and for its cost-effectiveness in doing so with relatively limited resources.

The UK's success in Sierra Leone had wider implications. As well as showing that the government was prepared to back up its interventionist rhetoric with action, it provided an important precedent for subsequent international action in Liberia, and helped, for a while, to create a climate for more robust approaches to UN peacekeeping in other parts of Africa. By 2008, the continuing flaws in UN and African Union (AU) peacekeeping missions were all too apparent, as was the lack of commitment to those missions by NATO's most powerful member states. International intervention (diplomatic, developmental and military) can claim some of the credit in bringing an end to the conflicts that consumed West Africa during the 1990s. But these gains remain fragile, and conflict remains an ongoing reality in much of the Horn of Africa and the Great Lakes region.

Domestic politics and the new interventionism

The New Interventionism was consistent with New Labour's broader effort to move beyond traditional left/right divisions in UK politics and forge a new 'progressive' policy consensus. In opposition, Tony Blair and Gordon Brown were acutely aware of the contribution that the perception that Labour was 'soft on defence' (as a result of its commitment to unilateral nuclear disarmament) had made to its electoral unpopularity in the 1980s, and were determined to ensure that this would not be repeated. In its first years they were largely successful in this effort. The government's strong support for military intervention in Kosovo and Sierra Leone helped consolidate its image of being 'strong on defence', reducing the political costs of the tight budget settlements that the MoD received during this period.

The commitment to a stronger ethical dimension to foreign policy has fitted well within collective memories of Britain's experience as a global and imperial power (Deighton 2002: 120). An important consequence of this historical experience is the tendency, common to many parts of the national policy elite, to conceptualize the subject of foreign policy in terms of a wider unit than the UK itself. Two World Wars were fought by the British Empire, with colonies and former colonies making large contributions to overall Imperial Defence. In the aftermath of decolonization, political leaders of all parties still paid homage to an ill-defined 'international community', broader than the UK and its immediate EU and NATO partners, yet distinct from the UN and its constituent organs.

Attachment to this wider concept of community is in part the legacy of an imperial era, with family and personal memories of empire ensuring that the British elite remains more engaged in wider global affairs than most other European countries. The personal histories of officials in FCO and DfID, or officers in the armed forces – as well as the institutional memories of their bureaucracies – continue to be shaped by a time when Britain was the leader of the world's largest empire.

Britain's imperial and trading history has also left material legacies. In important respects, the UK economy is more globally integrated than most other economies of its size, with high levels of inward and outward investment, a leading economic sector – finance – that is heavily dependent on an open world economy, and with large numbers of UK citizens working abroad. The UK (and London in particular) is home to expatriate communities from across the world, and many foreign elites send their children to UK schools and maintain properties there.

One of the most important legacies of this historical experience is the widespread assumption that the UK, despite its relatively limited weight (1% of global population and 5% of world GDP) can significantly shape the direction of international events. Thus Prime Minister Blair emphasized that he saw the UK as a 'pivotal power' in the international system. Foreign Secretary David Miliband used a similar (if less state-centric) formulation when he described the UK as a 'global hub'.

This attitude is grounded in material capabilities. The UK has the world's second largest defence budget in cash terms. Moreover, by cutting the size of its forces sharply since 1990, it has been able to fund high levels of investment in equipment that have allowed it to make more progress in reorienting towards power projection than other, more personnel-intensive, European armed forces. It also possesses a range of political assets. Places on the UN Security Council and the G8 give it the right to participate in discussions with the biggest players across the range of international security issues. Its role as one of the world's five recognized nuclear weapons states, although a mixed blessing and the subject of continuing domestic controversy, reinforces its major power status, with a role to play in discussion of future nuclear arms control.

A loyal but junior ally

Since 2001, the reluctance of the Blair government to distance itself from the more controversial elements of US security policy meant that it shared in the Bush administration's growing unpopularity, in the UK as well as internationally. The UK's close relationship with the US gives it unparalleled access to US security information and decision-makers. Influence does not always follow, and its limits were already evident in the first year of the Bush administration, which was dominated by a belief that multilateral organizations and agreements placed unacceptable constraints on US national power. As the US moved to distance itself from arms control processes, it rejected the need for international agreements to combat climate change, and loudly proclaimed its lack of commitment to the UN. The UK could only watch from the sidelines.

In keeping with its policy of humanitarian intervention, and in solidarity with the US, the UK joined the US in its invasions of Afghanistan and Iraq. In both cases, however, the disproportion between the military forces of the two countries helped to ensure that the UK's ability to shape the occupations that followed was relatively limited. Historically, European countries have been able to exert their greatest influence over US interventions in cases where the US has been reluctant to commit, yet has not been opposed in principle. UK military operations in the Falklands in 1982, and subsequently in 2000 in Sierra Leone, were primarily national affairs, and their successes (as well as their flaws) were the UK's responsibility. Britain also exerted substantial influence over the 1999 Kosovo operation, which was organized by NATO and had substantial military commitments from European states. At crucial stages of this operation, it was a key diplomatic and military player. Collectively, European states played a central role in shaping the nature of the post-conflict peace settlement.

By contrast, in the operations in Afghanistan and Iraq, the opportunity for the UK to share in key decisions was significantly less. The US wanted the involvement of the UK and other states in order to show that a coalition of nations supported its actions. But it was committed to take action whether or not others did so, and it resisted any suggestion that US action be restricted by multinational committees (for example, through joint US/UK control of the misnamed Coalition Provisional Authority). For the US, the primary purpose of allied contributions was political more than operational. Commitments of forces on the ground, conducting difficult and dangerous tasks, can be of considerable political value to US diplomacy. But the US, now accounting for more than 50% of total global defence spending, is capable of filling the gap if allies decide not to take part. Thus, when it looked as if Tony Blair might fail to gain the support of the majority of his MPs for the Iraq invasion in March 2003, US Secretary of Defense Donald Rumsfeld indicated that the US would be happy to go ahead by itself, without the UK, if that would make it easier domestically for the UK government.

The UK's leaders and commentators have sometimes argued that, despite the relatively small size of its contributions, it brought a more experienced perspective, drawing on the lessons that had been learnt from a long history of imperial policing, for example in Afghanistan and Iraq. British officials harked back to Harold Macmillan's quip that Britain could contribute the wisdom of ancient Greece to the brash young superpower of Rome. The British, they argued, may not have the US's muscle, but they understood the world much better than their larger but clumsier ally.

While this argument played well in the UK, however, it was never welcomed in the US. Three decades after the end of Empire, few serving diplomats or officers have direct experience of imperial service. Moreover, the US has not stood still. Faced with some of the toughest conditions it has encountered since Vietnam, the US Army has embarked on a far-reaching programme of doctrinal and operational innovation, backed up with massive injections of new resources. By 2007, US force levels in Iraq (168,000 in November) dwarfed those of the UK (6,400) by a factor of 26 to 1 (IISS 2008: 426–31). While the US supplementary budget for the Global War on Terror (mainly Iraq and Afghanistan) totals $190 billion, the UK's equivalent budget was only £1.6

billion in 2006/07, rising to £3 billion in 2007/08 (IISS 2008: 21; Ministry of Defence 2008, table 1.19).

The limits to UK influence were also seen in relation to the Israel/Palestine conflict. Under Prime Ministers Blair and Brown, the UK has consistently argued that this conflict is one of the major sources of instability in the region and a key driver of disaffection in the Islamic world. Blair, in particular, devoted a great deal of personal effort to seeking to convince President Bush that the issue required more robust engagement by the US. Yet his arguments have largely fallen on stony ground, both in the US and in Israel. The UK's failure in this effort (which has been paralleled by the EU's lack of success, despite its role as the Palestinian Authority's biggest donor) does not reflect a lack of political will or (at least in the EU's case) of resources. Rather, it reflects the limits to what the UK and the EU can achieve in a situation where the US is the primary external actor involved.

The limits of intervention

One of the founding principles of New Labour's foreign policy since 1987 has been to avoid being portrayed as soft on national security. The UK had been the US's military partner in the confrontation with Iraq since 1990, and had fully participated in the large-scale bombing campaigns launched under the Clinton administration in 1999, despite the lack of UN authorization or NATO agreement, as well as in the 'no-fly zones'. The 2003 invasion, therefore, was in crucial respects a continuation of an existing policy, not a sharp departure from it. Blair was convinced that an attack on Iraq was necessary and morally justified. He was also aware that a decision not to do so would have been a fundamental change in direction, with far-reaching consequences for the UK's (and Labour's) foreign policy orientation.

Yet the failure to find weapons of mass destruction (WMD) in Iraq undermined general trust in the government, and is widely acknowledged as having played a key role in the subsequent erosion of Blair's political position. The strategic errors and incompetence that accompanied the US-led occupation also threw into question the assumptions underpinning Labour's embrace of 'humanitarian intervention'. The way in which military and detention operations were conducted, together with high levels of civilian casualties, undermined the moral case for intervention. Economic reform programmes greatly enriched US contractors and some Iraqi politicians, but failed to provide sufficient employment for demobilized Iraqi soldiers. Despite its best efforts, the UK government could not easily distance itself from these adverse consequences of the invasion.

At the height of the US's self-confidence in 2002–03, 'neo-conservative' commentators had begun to compare today's US with the British Empire, lauded the merits of democratic imperialism, and argued the need for new mechanisms (such as international trusteeship of failed states) through which the US and allies could build functioning, and friendly, states.

Yet the past history of colonialism also informed the perceptions of those in the states subject to intervention. In Afghanistan and Iraq, as in Iran and Palestine, this history reinforced the perception that today's interventions are part of a wider Western effort to reassert control over the region and protect Israel's interests. Western policymakers underestimate the power of such nationalist and anti-imperialist sentiments at their peril.

Military intervention can still have a role in foreign policy. But the US/UK experience in Afghanistan and Iraq has demonstrated its limits. At times, international forces may need to intervene to prevent sectarian conflicts within a country escalating into full-scale genocide. Yet even in the more benign circumstances of the Balkans, with all the economic and political carrots that EU membership can offer, expectations that integrated multi-ethnic democracies can be created by outsiders have had to be tempered. Intervention did help to halt the violence, reverse much of the mass displacement, and provide a degree of stability within which peaceful politics could re-emerge. Fourteen years after the Dayton agreement, however, Bosnia continues to be at risk of fragmentation. And the prospects for ending the current de facto partition of Kosovo seem limited.

Assessing the wisdom of the military interventions of the last 11 years also needs to take into account their impact on wider aspirations for strengthening international order, and in particular for relations with Russia and China. Both the 1999 Kosovo war and the 2003 invasion of Iraq took place despite the clear opposition of these two countries, and without UN authorization.

In the former case, NATO believed that there was an urgent need to protect Kosovo's Albanian population from expulsion and genocide. Despite the post-war UN resolution making clear that it would remain part of Serbia, however, the US and most EU member states recognized Kosovo as an independent state in 2008. There is a case to be made that this was simply an acceptance of the reality on the ground in Kosovo, and that further delay could threaten unrest. Yet it has also tipped the balance of international practice further in favour of self-determination for regions within states. It is a precedent to which Russia pointed in the aftermath of the Georgia war of August 2008, when it unilaterally recognized the independence of South Ossetia and Abkhazia.

Current and future trends

In March 2008, the government published its first National Security Strategy (NSS), one significant feature of which was the range of security challenges to the UK that it identified:

No state threatens the United Kingdom directly. The Cold War threat has been replaced by a diverse but interconnected set of threats and risks, which affect the United Kingdom directly and also have the potential to undermine wider international stability. These include international terrorism, weapons of mass destruction, conflicts and failed states, pandemics, and trans-national crime. These and other threats and risks are driven by a diverse and interconnected set of underlying factors, including climate change, competition for energy, poverty and poor governance, demographic changes and globalisation. (Cabinet Office, 2008)

The NSS is significant in part because it does not suggest that Islamic terrorism is the existential or overriding threat of our age, as the Bush administration has often argued in the past. Rather, it states:

While terrorism represents a threat to all our communities ... it does not at present amount to a strategic threat. But it is qualitatively and quantitatively more serious than the terrorist threats we have faced in the past, and it is likely to persist for many years.

The NSS represents a welcome recognition of the complexity of today's security challenges, and a useful step towards mapping their specific characteristics. History did not end in 1990, and some of the key structural determinants of conflict – such as inequality and climate change – have worsened in the two subsequent decades (Chalmers 2008). International cooperation will be central to responses to all these challenges.

Sometimes the security concerns of the future will be genuinely global, affecting all countries equally. Often, however, security risks affect some more than others, suggesting the continuing relevance of some international division of responsibility. Regions of particular interest to the EU will include (beyond Europe itself) sub-Saharan Africa, the Middle East and the former Soviet Union. During the next decade, the Middle East is likely to be a top priority, as a result of interrelated concerns over migration, terrorism and energy supplies, as well as the economic opportunities that are available to Europe if these concerns can be successfully managed. For both the EU generally and the UK specifically, the importance of sub-Saharan Africa will also grow. As transport costs fall and population pressures increase, spillovers from conflict, criminality and underdevelopment will increase further. Sub-Saharan Africa may see partial success in state-building and economic development, continuing the positive trends of the last decade. But setbacks are likely to try the patience of those seeking quick solutions.

The UK will have a particular interest in regions and countries where events can affect it directly as a result of its particular international links. The presence of large populations with close ties to Pakistan, Bangladesh and the West Indies gives the UK a stake in those countries that other EU member states do not have. The same is true for Commonwealth countries in sub-Saharan Africa, with whom the UK continues to have strong economic and political links. Just as recent crises in Sierra Leone and Zimbabwe have had larger migration effects on the UK than on other EU member states, so too would a major conflict within Nigeria or South Africa.

Incidentally, this should not be seen as an argument for the UK acting in a way that is particularly nationalist, compared with other EU member states. Most members have particular national interests in foreign policy – for example, Spain in South America and Morocco, Poland in Ukraine and Belarus, Greece in Cyprus and Turkey.

Looking forward over the next decade, perhaps the greatest strategic uncertainty is whether, after a period in which sub-state and transnational security challenges have dominated, interstate security dynamics may return to a more central place. The NSS was right to assert that the UK now faces no direct state threat. Yet it is worth noting just how unusual this state of affairs is in world history, and to consider at least the possibility that – in a world where growing economic interdependence exists in uneasy coexistence with political anarchy – this happy state of affairs may not last.

It is certainly not the case that interstate conflict has ended. The last decade has seen the armed forces of states fighting against each other in Congo, Iraq, Afghanistan and Ethiopia/Eritrea. Interstate conflict remains a very real possibility between China and Taiwan, Pakistan and Afghanistan, Pakistan and India, Russia and Georgia, and (again) Ethiopia and Eritrea. Nor can one rule out military conflict between Israel, the US, and Iran, with considerable potential to draw UK forces in Afghanistan and Iraq into renewed interstate warfare. There is a real possibility that, within the next decade, potentially hostile Middle Eastern states will be able to hit the UK with nuclear-armed ballistic missiles. Were this to occur, the current period could in retrospect appear to be a short interlude between two Cold Wars, rather than the beginning of an era in which the UK could focus its security policy on responding to sub-state and transnational security risks.

Indeed, while today's world can be characterized in part by the shift of authority from states to other actors (sub-state and supranational), the shift of economic power between states, and in particular towards China and other major developing states, is arguably just as unprecedented in its rapidity and potential consequences. China is already the world's largest emitter of greenhouse gases and, on some measures, its biggest exporter. It is the largest aid donor for a growing number of countries in Africa, Latin America and Asia, and its military budget continues to grow rapidly. It is a key player in international diplomacy in relation to North Korea, Burma, Sudan and Iran.

For 'realist' commentators, the rise of China could lead to a sequence of events similar to the late nineteenth century, when rising powers (the US, Germany and Japan) found themselves in growing conflict with the major status quo powers of their time. As a result, the democracies must brace themselves for a new Great Power confrontation, including a real possibility of military conflict. By contrast, liberals argue that the trend is for China to gradually become a 'responsible stakeholder', with whom Europe can work to deepen the role of international institutions. Both schools of thought agree, however, that relations between China and other major powers will be central in the international system of the mid twenty-first century.

Some key policy options

Highlighting national interests

Much discussion of UK foreign policy options focuses on the balance that should be struck between the special relationship with the US and the UK's role in the EU. At the height of the crisis surrounding the decision to invade Iraq in 2003, some argued that it was time for a fundamental reorientation towards a more definitively European stance (Dunne 2004; Wallace 2005). By contrast, some Eurosceptics, fearful of the long-term consequences of European integration for national sovereignty, believe that it is time to adopt a more Atlanticist security policy, even if this means being marginalized within the EU.

Yet this perennial debate, important though it is, can often obscure an equally important trade-off: that between national and common interests. The discourse of internationalism and responsibility plays well across the British political spectrum, in part because of the continuing legacy of the imperial period. Yet, both in narrative and in practice, it can risk undermining a clear formulation and articulation of specifically national interests. These do exist. The UK's interests are not identical with those of its fellow EU members, or with those of the US. The density of the UK's involvement in the EU, as well as in its bilateral relationship with the US, means that it should be willing to accommodate the priorities of its partners where at all possible, in the expectation that they will do the same. But unconditional loyalty can be counterproductive where it leads to the UK's own interests and views being discounted by others.

First of all, this means that UK security policy should give a high priority to specifically national security concerns. After the London bombings of 2005, there is little doubt that the UK faces an ongoing threat of domestic terrorism. Fortunately, the methods employed by those drawn to violent extremism have remained unsophisticated. But this could change, seriously escalating the threat. If this does occur, the risk would not only be the number of direct casualties (though these could be considerable) or physical damage. It could also likely deepen social tensions, undermining long-term efforts to promote social cohesion and risking a dangerous escalation in conflict from which jihadist recruiters could only benefit.

The government is already increasing the resources it provides to the security and police services for counter-terrorism. Further investments in improving the effectiveness of intelligence gathering, policing and border controls will undoubtedly be required. Additional resources will also be needed to address the political, social and economic factors that contribute to alienation. Currently, for example, the UK has only four Muslim MPs out of 646, despite Muslims constituting 3% of the total population. If they are to show that the Muslim community has a voice in democratic politics, all political parties need to do much more to ensure that their leading ranks reflect the multi-ethnic and multi-faith nature of UK society.

Second, it means that the UK should be ready to decline requests to participate in international stabilization missions where it does not agree with their aims, does not think that they are of sufficient priority for the UK, or does not believe that UK views will be taken sufficiently into account in their implementation. This last problem may be a particular issue in relation to US-led military operations, given the inequality of capabilities between the armed forces of the two countries. Even if the UK fully supports the initial aims of an operation, recent experience has demonstrated that the nature and objectives of military interventions change radically over time. Getting appropriate political and military mechanisms in place for controlling cooperative missions, therefore, is critical.

Third, in developing the narrative of UK foreign policy, leaders need to link foreign policy more clearly to national interests and values. It is not credible, for example, to argue that problems anywhere in the world are of equal concern to, or impose an equal responsibility on, the UK. Sub-global patterns of interdependence still matter. The EU has a particular interest in ensuring stability and preventing conflict within Europe, and the UK has a responsibility to contribute to the EU's efforts in this regard. In other parts of the world, however, European support for stability and conflict prevention is best pursued through cooperation with the relevant regional organizations, and/or through the UN. In parallel, the UK has a particular national interest in stability in countries with which it has close links, and where conflict could impact directly on its own security. A values-based policy cannot focus solely on UK interests. When deciding on the allocation of scarce resources, however, it is legitimate to focus UK efforts primarily in those areas where the UK has either a comparative advantage, or a comparatively greater interest, compared to its European and other partners.

Rethinking military intervention

Recent UK military operations in Iraq and Afghanistan have been characterized by initially unrealistic objectives, which have subsequently been exposed as being inconsistent with reality on the ground. With the UK's commitment to Iraq now likely to end in 2009, the main focus of attention is on Afghanistan, where the UK now deploys 8,000 troops, and where it is experiencing its most intense combat since the Korean War. Since the commitment in southern Afghanistan began in early 2006, 126 servicemen and women had lost their lives in that country as of mid November 2008. Many more casualties appear inevitable.

As of late 2008, there are good reasons for NATO to increase its troop levels in Afghanistan in order to build on its recent advances and to reduce the Taliban's capacity to hold population centres. Yet this short-term surge needs to be combined with a medium-term political strategy (over the next five years or so) that allows international military forces to be substantially reduced, and Afghan authorities to take primary responsibility for their own security. Opium cultivation will not be eliminated in this timescale, nor will the problems of corruption and warlordism. Yet these structural problems cannot be solved directly by the US or NATO, whatever levels of resources they are prepared to invest. The lead responsibility has to rest with Afghans themselves, working closely with those countries – such as Pakistan and Iran – that have the most direct interest in their country's stability.

This does not mean an end to UK engagement in either Afghanistan or Pakistan. Both countries should continue to be given a high priority in aid policy, including support for their security forces. But NATO needs to take account of the limited tolerance for foreign forces in both countries, and the reality that, even if its presence is necessary in the short term to hold the ring against a resurgent Taliban, it also fuels nationalist support for the insurgency. The government of Afghanistan continues to look for opportunities to reach out to 'local Taliban', and to isolate them from foreign fighters committed to international jihad. NATO should support these efforts. The UK's most important national interest in this region is to prevent its use as a safe haven for international terrorism. This objective is most likely to be achieved if those supporting such activity can be contained and defeated by local mechanisms of control.

This is not an argument for abandoning the commitment to humanitarian military intervention that formed an important part of the New Internationalism that characterized the Blair decade. It has played a positive role in Afghanistan, as it has done in Sierra Leone and Kosovo. Yet, in the US as well as in the UK, the experience of Iraq has raised the bar for any possible new interventions. And, even if withdrawal from Iraq is completed during 2009, the UK's heavy military commitment to Afghanistan will limit the forces available for taking on other responsibilities.

Yet the MoD is also struggling to balance the resources provided in support of existing stabilization operations and those needed to maintain future capabilities for a range of other possible contingencies. Most of the largest current procurement programmes – including the Typhoon aircraft, new attack and nuclear missile submarines, and large new aircraft carriers – have little relevance to counter-insurgency operations of the sort in which the armed forces are now engaged in Afghanistan. Given the range of possible future threats that might develop, however, the government is not yet prepared to reconsider its commitment to maintaining a wide range of different capabilities. The continuing risk of new nuclear threats from the Middle East, and uncertainty over the future strategic intentions of Russia and China, strengthens the case against giving up capabilities that might be needed in future interstate confrontations.

Given the UK's worsening fiscal position, a new government is unlikely to order a significant increase in defence spending. As a result, there is now an increasingly strong case for a major Strategic Defence Review to be held after the next general election, in order to bring political expectations and military resources more closely into line.

An analysis of the lessons from the interventionist policies of the last decade should be a central part of such a Review. Yet there is a danger of a new government swinging too far in an anti-interventionist direction. The original motivation for the Responsibility to Protect doctrine – the failure of the international community to respond effectively to genocide in Rwanda and Bosnia – remains as valid now as it did in the 1990s. There does need to be a serious re-examination of the criteria on which interventions are based, and a greater willingness to accept that military intervention is not always possible and can often be counterproductive. At the same time, the UK is one of a very small group of countries (with the US and France) that have an effective capacity to organize and lead such operations. In such circumstances, it would be a dereliction of responsibility, and against the UK's long-term interests, if the UK (and/or Europe as a whole) were to leave the US as the only power with such a capability.

Within a continuing commitment to maintain intervention capabilities, there should also be a review of whether the UK can meet this commitment in ways that are more effective, and which play more directly into its national comparative advantages. Two areas in particular are worth further consideration. First, there may be a case for the UK placing greater emphasis on participating in small-scale operations in which European states take a lead (currently in Lebanon, DRC and Chad), compared to its role in larger US-led operations. Both are important. At the margins, however, the UK may achieve more effect on the ground by increasing its commitment to operations where the US is unwilling to commit. Second, more priority should be given to helping to build indigenous security forces in countries at risk of instability and conflict. It is increasingly realized that security sectors that are inefficient and unaccountable are unable to contribute to stability, and indeed will usually undermine it. Experience in Iraq and Afghanistan is increasing the UK's capability for mentoring and training security forces. In relation to countries where UK combat forces are not currently deployed, however, this mission has been given a very low priority. The one exception to this is Sierra Leone, where UK training teams have played an important role in transforming the national military and police forces into a force for stability. There is also considerable potential for the UK to work to develop collective European capability in this field, working with the EU, NATO and the UN.

Reaching out to the emerging powers

Barring a major economic meltdown (admittedly a real possibility), Chinese power is set to continue to rise over the next decade. With an average annual growth rate close to 10% over the past two decades, China's GDP has been doubling every seven or eight years, changing the international balance of power at a pace never before seen in peacetime. Established international institutions, together with shared commitments to open markets, can help mitigate the potential for conflict over access to scarce resources that some fear may result. But, given the size of its population, China's rapid growth is much more significant than that of any of the rising powers of the past. Policymakers, both in China and in the West, will need to be highly innovative in their responses if they are to reform international politics at a rate that is commensurate with the shift in international economic power that has already begun.

It has been argued that one of the US's (and by association the UK's) main mistakes in the last decade has been an obsession with intervention in failed and failing states, at the expense of responding to the more important shifts going on at the level of global geopolitics. Yet the two issues cannot be so easily separated. The issue for policymakers is not whether, or by how much, to shift resources (money, people, high-level policy attention) from Africa and the Middle East to China and India. Both are important. Rather, it is to prepare for a world in which the effectiveness of strategies towards (for example) Iran, Zimbabwe or Afghanistan will increasingly have to take account of China's interests and policies. The rapid growth in Chinese trade and investment is propelling it to become more involved, despite its commitment to 'non-interference' as a principle. It is in the UK's interest that this trend continues, and that it does so in cooperation rather than competition with others.

If efforts to bring China into the 'club' of powerful states, and to strengthen its representation and role in global institutions, are to succeed, its leadership will have to recognize its own interest in the effective provision of global public goods, including security. But the Western powers will also have to adjust, taking greater account of China's interests in their deliberations, and changing well-established habits of cooperation. It will, for example, mean consulting China on difficult decisions from the beginning, not presenting them with positions already agreed by the US and Europe (still common in the United Nations Security Council). There is bound to be some continuing tension between democratic states and authoritarian ones over human rights and related issues. But human rights in China will not be improved by confrontation, or by excluding it from the G8 or other international organizations.

One of the hardest lessons that Europe and the US will have to absorb is that their collective ability to write the rules for international society is set to decline. There is still a tendency to think of the problem of engaging

China in terms of its being asked to join a club, and having to accept the established rules of that club when doing so. For a country as powerful as China, however, it may be more accurate to think of cooperation as being like a joint venture, in which each party brings different skills, and where mutual understanding of each others' interests is essential to success. In some areas, such as World Trade Organization membership, China has been prepared to accept the existing rules of the road, largely because (in the case of the WTO) the benefits to it of gaining assured access to global markets are so substantial. In other areas, however, it may be more determined to insist that the rules are adjusted to reflect its own interests.

This will lead to difficult debates on the best ways for the international community to manage processes of political change in weak states. China, with its particular concerns about 'splittism', places a strong emphasis – as does India – on the need to respect international norms of territorial integrity and non-interference. By contrast, some Western countries, including the UK, are more inclined to argue (as in the case of Kosovo) that self-determination and human security should take precedence over the rights of states to preserve their integrity.

If there is a way forward in reconciling different approaches to this problem, it is more likely to lie in the realm of practice than in debates about principles. For all their current enthusiasms for intervention, both the UK and the US recognize the dangers that secessionism and cross-border interventions pose to international stability, as was demonstrated most recently in Georgia. As China's recent impatience with North Korea and Sudan illustrates, moreover, it is increasingly aware of its own interests in the stability of neighbours and trading partners.

Cooperation with China will be vital to the success of European efforts to address underdevelopment and state weakness in sub-Saharan Africa. Increasing cooperation with Russia, China and India will also be increasingly critical for European policy in the wider Middle East. To obtain their cooperation, however, will require some difficult reorientation in the mechanisms currently deployed to contribute to security in this region. In the long term, for example, major Asian powers may question why an alliance of Atlantic powers should have the main responsibility for security in Afghanistan, without close cooperation with China, India and Russia. Similarly, given its increasing reliance on energy supplies from the Middle East, China might argue it has as much 'right' to establish military bases in the Indian Ocean and the Persian Gulf as do the US, UK and France.

Conclusions

Over the last decade, the UK has demonstrated that it remains an important power. It has been one of the key forces backing continuing innovation in multilateral regimes, and is on track to become one of the world's top two bilateral providers of development aid. Its record on military intervention, however, has been more mixed. Its achievements in this area are clearest in those interventions – Sierra Leone and Kosovo – where the UK was a primary driver or major shaper. Where the UK's role was as a junior partner to the US, especially in Iraq, the consequences for its interests and influence have been less clear and more controversial.

In debates about intervention, and on foreign policy more generally, the UK's relationships with its European partners and with the US will continue to be central. But relations with Asia's rising powers, and with China in particular, are likely to grow in importance. The UK's own independent weight in international discussions may decline, and it may become increasingly reliant on the EU for representation in global economic regimes. But the relationship with the US is likely to remain a central part of defence planning and policies.

The ambitious foreign policies of the last decade have left the next government with hard choices to make. If the UK economy continues to weaken, it may become harder, at least in the short term, for the government to devote additional resources to foreign and security policy. Yet it will still be under pressure to spend even more on domestic counter-terrorism, particularly if further attacks on British soil take place. All major parties are committed to increasing development aid to 0.7% of GNP by 2013, and aid spending is due to increase by £2.5 billion per annum over the three years to 2010/11. But it remains to be seen whether a new government (in contrast to most other major OECD states) will be prepared to honour this pledge.

The defence budget will be under severe strain, after a period in which major operational commitments have generated new demands on equipment and personnel. Unless major funding increases are awarded, the next government will therefore need to take hard decisions on the purposes and shape of the UK defence effort. On the one hand, there is considerable pressure to spend more on capabilities for sustained stabilization missions, similar to those in Afghanistan and Iraq. On the other, there is a reluctance to entirely abandon capabilities that might be required should major conventional war once again become a real possibility. The build-up of military strength by fast-growing Asian powers adds to this uncertainty, as does continuing concern over conflict in the Middle East and NATO relations with Russia. Much will depend on the assumptions made as to how far the UK can rely on allies for its future security. To the extent that the government believes that Europe needs its own capabilities for independent military action, the demands on UK military planning become greater and more difficult to fulfil. If the UK is willing to place its faith in the long-term reliability of the US, however, it may have more flexibility to focus on near-term requirements at the expense of longer-term insurance capabilities.

13
Diversity and Extremism

Varun Uberoi and Shamit Saggar

When the first *Options for Britain* (Halpern et al 1996) was written there wasn't a chapter on the policy issues that relate to governing Britain's culturally diverse citizenry. This might seem strange. After all, the Rushdie Affair had raised deep moral questions about the nature and extent of freedom of speech as well as public order issues. The latter was also a huge concern when riots tore through various places like Brixton, Toxteth and Handsworth. And the failure of the police investigations into the murdered black teenager, Stephen Lawrence suggested that discrimination was a problem in the Metropolitan police force. But these are all issues of the 1980s and early 1990s and by the mid-1990s, when the first *Options* was written, things seemed to have changed. The riots had abated and the furore over Salman Rushdie's *Satanic Verses* had given way to a reasoned discussion about the moral issues raised by its publication (Parekh 2000: 304). Equally the British Social Attitudes surveys show that in 1987 just under 40% of respondents were prepared to say that they were either 'very prejudiced' or 'a little prejudiced'. But from 1994 the figures for those who were prepared to say that they were either 'very' or a 'little' prejudiced consistently fell to 25% in 2001 (Creegan and Robinson 2008: 130). Indeed, Ipsos MORI's polling shows that 'immigration and asylum' was not even an issue that would help respondents to decide who to vote for in the two years running up to the 1997 election. This is not to say that this area had become problem free, but we can see why the editors of the first *Options* decided not to allocate the limited space available in their volume to a chapter on diversity-related issues.

More than a decade on, the story is very different. The 2001 riots in Oldham, Burnley and Bradford, as well as the few riots that have occurred since have re-introduced the threat of public disorder. Whilst post-war immigration was extensive, the net inflow of migrants only began in the early 1990s, rose to 171,000 in 2000, declined to 151,000 in 2003, rose to 222,600 in 2004, and then rose even further after the new accession countries joined the EU

(Vertovec 2007: 1028). By 2006 immigration had become a major national concern. Hence an Ipsos MORI poll showed that for 52% of respondents, 'immigration and asylum' will be an issue that helps them to decide who to vote for in the next election. Equally, those who are prepared to say that they are either 'very prejudiced' or 'a little prejudiced' rose from 25% in 2001 to 35% in 2005 (Creegan and Robinson 2008: 130). In short, what in the mid-1990s seemed like a subject that could be put on the political back-burner has become an area that politicians cannot ignore. In part this is because few at the time would have predicted that a small percentage of certain British minorities might pose a terrorist threat, yet today this is what many fear (Pew 2005: 3).

A chapter on the governance of Britain's culturally diverse citizenry has become unavoidable in a volume of this nature. This chapter highlights what the government has done in this area over the past decade and what the priorities for the next one should be. We proceed in three stages. First, we describe some developments in this area since 1997. Second, we identify two of the most salient challenges that policymakers in this area face. Finally, we identify some measures that any UK government (regardless of its political persuasion) has at its disposal to address these challenges.

1997–2008: A short history

In this section we summarize what we regard to be the most important developments in this area, beginning with immigration and asylum. The net inflow of migrants began to occur in the early 1990s but since 2004 and the accession of eight Central and Eastern European countries into the EU, immigration from these countries has increased from approximately 50,000 in 2004 to 72,000 in 2005 and 96,000 in 2006 but has dropped a little since. Figure 13.1 illustrates the changing nature of immigration into the UK from 1991 to 2006.

The numbers seeking asylum also increased rapidly between 1997 and 2002, but has declined since, as the Home Office's data in Figure 13.2 show. Indeed, the dramatic increase in the numbers seeking asylum during Labour's first term was one reason why the government introduced the 1999 Immigration and Asylum Act. The Act introduced vouchers (as opposed to cash benefits) for asylum seekers and a one-stop appeal service at which all asylum appeals would be considered. Amid criticism that the vouchers humiliated and stigmatized asylum seekers the Home Office disbanded the voucher system in 2002, but the government continued to fear being perceived as weak on asylum seekers. Hence various 'kites' were flown in the press, like plans to send in the Royal Navy to intercept traffickers and using the Royal Air Force to deport asylum seekers (Schuster and Solomos 2004: 280). Equally, reports of 'illegals' basing themselves at the Red Cross camp at Sangatte, northern France, and then coming into the UK through the Channel Tunnel led to the then Home Secretary lobbying the French government for Sangatte's closure. This was eventually achieved in March 2003 only after 1,200 of the 1,600 people in the camp were allowed to enter the UK (Schuster 2003: 519). Indeed, in 2002 a new Nationality, Immigration and Asylum Act was introduced which, *inter alia*, established detention centres for asylum seekers, simplified the procedures for their removal, and prevented them receiving benefits unless they applied for asylum as soon as is 'reasonably practicable'

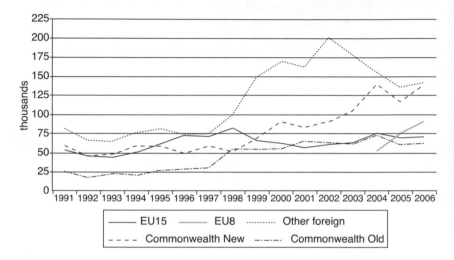

Figure 13.1   Net In-migration by Citizenship, Non-British Citizens, 1991–2006

Source: Pollard et al (2008: 17). Data from ONS.

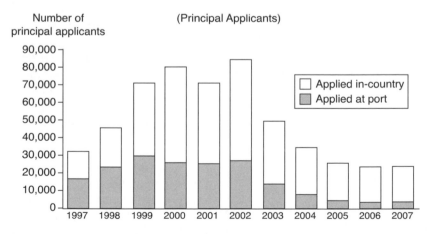

Figure 13.2   Applications for Asylum in the UK by Location of Application

Source: Home Office (2008: 17).

after entering the UK (Section 55 of the Nationality, Immigration and Asylum Act, 2002).

Also in Labour's second term we see the beginnings of a process of 'managed migration' that involved the introduction of schemes like the Highly Skilled Workers Programme and the Seasonal Agricultural Workers Programme. These schemes utilized migrants to fill labour shortages and are reminiscent of migration policies from the 1940s and 1950s. In Labour's third term, this process culminated with the introduction of a Canadian style points-based immigration system. The system is comprised of five tiers. Tier 1 relates to highly skilled migrants, Tier 2 relates to skilled migrant workers with a job offer, Tier 3 relates to low-skilled workers needed to fill specific shortages, Tier 4 relates to students, and Tier 5 relates to temporary workers who are allowed to work in the UK for a limited period. Unlike in Canada, the top two tiers are the only ones that can lead to citizenship, but even then citizenship is only possible if the necessary 75 points are obtained and these points are allocated according to age, qualifications, previous earnings and so on (Home Office 2006b: 15).

Moving on to multiculturalism and Britishness, both are often pitted against each other without any explanation of what either is and both have become prominent issues of discussion since 1997. Multiculturalism has come to mean many things and unlike Canada or Australia, Britain has never had a formal policy of multiculturalism. But the fact that Britain has had measures that aim to ensure that minorities are neither discriminated against (race relations legislation) nor disadvantaged by their cultural difference (legal exemptions for minority religious practices) as well as measures that help to explain why cultural diversity is valuable (multicultural education) suggests that Britain has had a policy of multiculturalism in all but name and this has become controversial. Hence the then Chair of the Commission for Racial Equality and now chair of the Equalities Commission Trevor Phillips has said that he would like to 'kill off' multiculturalism because it 'suggests separateness' (*The Times*, 3 April 2004). Many seemed to agree with Phillips' claim, but it is difficult to know where, when and how the government's policy of multiculturalism suggested separateness. Indeed, the most well-developed understandings of the British policy of multiculturalism have always criticized such an approach and helped to explain how a policy of multiculturalism can unite (CMEB 2000: 45; Swann 1985: 7). Yet despite the problematic nature of this criticism, many think that it sounded the death knell of the British policy of multiculturalism which, according to some, is currently being replaced by a policy of integration and cohesion as was the case in the Netherlands (Joppke 2004: 253–82; Vasta 2007: 2; Schuster and Solomos 2004: 267). Yet this also seems implausible because the vast majority of the most significant measures that comprise the government's policy of multiculturalism remain unchanged.

Of course, the government's policy of multiculturalism is criticized for other reasons, but one of the most significant criticisms is that this policy is said to undermine the British national identity and those who assert this are making an empirical claim (Uberoi 2008a). In order for their empirical claim to be thought of as true it must be supported by empirical evidence, but evidence is seldom offered. Those who make this claim sometimes cite others but they too usually offer no evidence to substantiate this claim and when evidence is offered, it seems unconvincing. This is because whilst one can point to data which suggest that people's British identities are declining in salience whilst their English, Scots and Welsh identities are increasing in salience (Heath and Roberts 2008) it is very difficult to show that a policy of multiculturalism is causing this. After all, globalization, supranational institutions and devolution are just some of the other factors that may be doing so instead.

But the British national identity is increasingly discussed for other reasons also. Indeed initially, Tony Blair seemed keen to distance himself from the Conservative conception of Britain. Hence while John Major in 1993 was prepared to say that 'fifty years from now Britain will be ... un-amendable in all its essentials', Tony Blair in 1995 described Britain as a 'young country' (*Independent*, 25 April 1993; Blair 1995). As a result of devolution, discussions about Britishness became more intense. Fear of the 'Break up of Britain' intensified to some extent because, as said earlier, studies have shown that people's British identities are currently decreasing in salience and their English, Scottish and Welsh identities are growing in salience. But in 2000 a very different discussion about Britishness erupted.

The Commission for Multi-Ethnic Britain published its report and, *inter alia*, suggested that there was a need to 'rethink the national story' (CMEB 2000: 14). This is because Britain is no longer the largely mono-cultural society that it once was. Britain is, so the Commission argued, a Habermasian post-nation – a 'community of communities' – and if Britishness is to be effective as a common identity that fosters cohesion, it must reflect this fact. The right-wing press attacked the report, and the government, after endorsing the report, subsequently distanced itself from it. However a year later, after riots in Oldham, Burnley and Bradford, the government seemed far more amenable to the idea of 're-thinking the national story'. Those who investigated the causes of the riots claimed that there had to be an 'acceptance that we are never going to turn the clock back to what was perceived to be a dominant or mono-culturalist view of nationality' (Home Office 2001a: 18). However, a more civic national identity was required because, as the then Minister of State for Public Order John Denham claimed, it was 'a means to unite people and express the common goals and aspirations of the whole community. A uniting identity can have a powerful effect in shaping attitudes and behaviour which are conducive to community cohesion' (Home Office 2001b: 19). Whereas the year before the government seemed unwilling to re-think the national story, the idea had now become more appealing.

In subsequent years, Gordon Brown took up the importance of Britishness and some say that he did so to detract attention from his Scottish background

(Bechhofer and McCrone 2007: 251). It is unclear if this is true. But what is clear is that the government has liberalized regulations over when the British flag can be flown from government buildings and is proposing a Bill of Rights and Duties as well as a Statement of Values, both of which are designed to help explain what it means to be British (Ministry of Justice 2007). This is also one reason why the government introduced compulsory citizenship ceremonies for new citizens that are designed to 'reflect our national character' (Home Office 2003). It is also the main reason why Jack Straw and John Denham both argue for 'an inclusive British history' to be taught to school children (Straw 2007: 4; Denham 2005: 7).

Finally, of course there is the crucial issue of tackling racial discrimination. The figures we cited earlier indicate that this had decreased during Labour's first term in office, but has risen since. Indeed, perhaps for many the main anti-discrimination issue that the government addressed was one that it campaigned on at the 1997 general election: setting up an inquiry into the death of the murdered teenager Stephen Lawrence. The inquiry was established in Labour's first hundred days in power and was led by Sir William MacPherson, who examined both the initial police investigation and the re-investigation of the 1993 murder. MacPherson uncovered police incompetence and institutional racism and recommended extending the 1976 Race Relations Act to all police officers and Chief Officers of Police. The latter were to be made 'vicariously liable' for the discriminatory practices of their officers. Home Secretary Jack Straw accepted the recommendation and proposed extending the 1976 Act to all public services (Hansard, 24 February 1999).

Hence the Race Relations Amendment Act 2000 was enacted. It would not only make Chief Officers of Police vicariously liable for acts of discrimination carried out by their officers, but it also extended the provisions of the 1976 Act to outlaw both direct and indirect racial discrimination in public authorities. 'Public authorities' were deliberately broadly defined, the Home Secretary was given powers to extend the list of public authorities and many (but not all) public authorities were given a general duty to promote race equality (Home Office 2000).

We have briefly discussed four developments that relate to governing Britain's diverse citizenry, but where do the most salient current challenges for policymakers in this area lie? If our policymakers happened to be trained economists or demographers, they might expect our answer to be the changing nature of UK immigration. If, however, our policymakers were political theorists and sociologists they might well expect our answer to be the changing nature of discrimination, or debates about multiculturalism and Britishness. But our only honest answer to this question can be *none of the above*. This is not because the issues discussed so far are unimportant or because any government could or should ignore them. It is because the two most salient challenges now appear to be the rise in hostility towards British Muslims and the fact that a small percentage of the latter seem willing to engage in acts of terrorism.

Indeed, these seem like the most salient current challenges not only because peace is the first *desideratum* of government and thus policy makers have to understand the causes, nature and extent of extra-political activity. Nor is it only because increased hostility towards British Muslims is immensely unjust and causes the same upset that it once did for British Catholics, Jews and various other minorities. It is also because it is more difficult to tackle the current terrorist threat if the hostility that British Muslims face is not being tackled also, and this point is brought into sharp focus if we ask two simple questions. First, what types of Muslims are more likely to see sense in violent Islamism: those who have seldom encountered hostility from non-Muslims or those who frequently do so? Second, what types of Muslims are likely to help the authorities to identify and stop potential terrorists within their own community – those who feel that the authorities are on their side in fighting the hostility that they encounter or those who think that the authorities are unconcerned by their plight?

Adequately tackling the current terrorist threat entails, *inter alia*, tackling the hostility that British Muslims face and this is not just a logical observation because the way in which the Irish were once mistreated helps to illustrate the point. Such mistreatment occurred in many ways and at many times, but the practice of internment 'led to 'hundreds of young men in working class nationalist communities joining the IRA' (Hillyard 2005). Equally, 'Stop and Search' powers alienated 'the very communities from which the police require good intelligence' (ibid). Of course the current terrorist threat and the former Irish one are different in nature. Equally, 'internment' and 'Stop and Search' are examples of the state introducing measures that mistreat a particular group and we are *not* suggesting that the state is introducing measures that mistreat British Muslims. But the reactions to both internment and 'Stop and Search' described above illustrate how members of a group can react to a level of external hostility: it can create sympathy for those in their ranks who claim that they are willing to fight for them. And at the very least such sympathy may make intelligence gathering amongst British Muslims harder and at most, it may radicalize more of them. Reducing the hostility that British Muslims face is thus intricately linked with the current fight against terrorism. But how rife is this hostility, how extensive is the threat of violent Islamism and what have the government attempted to do about both? It is to these questions that we now turn.

Hostility towards Muslims and terrorism

British Muslims have been campaigning for many years about the unfairness that resulted from case law decisions that affected the way that the 1976 Race Relations Act was interpreted. In a series of cases, judges sought to clarify and broaden what was meant by 'ethnic origin' in the 1976 Act in a way that meant some religious groups (Jews and Sikhs) were protected under the Act but others (Muslims) were not (Meer 2008). This resulted in a level of inequity for Muslims at a time when equalities legislation was needed most for them. Indeed, whilst it is hard to find scholarly data on the subject, the surveys that exist show that to some extent before, but certainly after 9/11, British Muslims experienced very high levels of discrimination. Hence in 1999, the Islamic Human Rights Commission (IHRC) conducted a survey of British Muslims in which 35% of respondents said that they had experienced discrimination. In 2000, this figure rose to 45% and in 2001 the Forum Against Islamophobia and Racism conducted a survey which showed that 80% of its respondents had experienced discrimination. Equally, in 2004 the IHRC also found that 80% of its respondents had suffered discrimination (IHRC 2004: 22–3).

In his study of 104 public polls of attitudes towards Muslims since the Rushdie Affair, Clive Fields documents the rise of Islamophobia in Britain. He points out that after the 7/7 bombings, 24% of respondents in one poll felt that Western liberal democracy and Islam were inherently contradictory. Another poll revealed that one in ten respondents were convinced that British Muslims felt no loyalty to Britain. A third poll revealed that 17% of respondents believed that British Muslims sympathized with terrorists (Fields 2006: 456–8). Indeed, results from the latest Pew Global Attitudes Survey, shown in Figure 13.3, illustrate that there was clearly a worsening perception of Muslims in Britain and many other countries in 2005, all of which collectively suggests that after 7/7 British Muslims have encountered great hostility.

Indeed, partly to do battle with this 'anti-Muslim wind' the government created 'religiously aggravated offences' in the Anti-Terrorism, Crime and

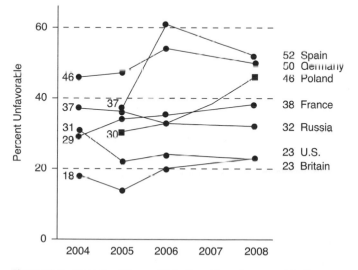

Figure 13.3 Negative Views of Muslims Have Increased in Europe

Source: Pew Global Attitudes Project, at http://pewglobal.org/reports/display.php?ReportID=262

Security Act in 2001 (Modood 2003). Equally, the government was obliged in December 2003 to transpose the EC Employment Directive that applies to 'religion or belief' into UK Law. This had the effect of prohibiting discrimination in employment that is based on religion and belief. In 2006, the controversial Racial and Religious Hatred Act was passed whereby 'a person who uses threatening words or behaviour, or displays any written material which is threatening, is guilty of an offence if he intends thereby to stir up religious hatred' (Racial and Religious Hatred Act 2006, Section 1). Clearly then the government has introduced many measures that will, it is hoped, help to tackle the hostility that British Muslims face.

Turning to the threat of extra-political activity, as Blick, Choudhury and Weir (2006: 14) state, 'it is very hard to judge the scale of home grown involvement in terrorist activity, as the authorities ... publish official estimates and release information in an unsystematic and ad-hoc way'. Indeed they also rightly point out that official statements often utilize very different figures (ibid). Equally, quantifying the extent of the security threat is made even more difficult by the fact that the definitions of 'terrorist' and 'extremist' are unclear, so it is difficult to know if the right things are being measured. However, *some limited* insight can be offered by examining the polling data that is available. A recent Gallup World Poll suggested that 5–10% of Muslims surveyed in Britain, France and Germany felt that violence was justified to pursue a noble cause however subjectively it was defined. Interestingly, roughly the same amount of the general public (one in ten) felt the same way (Saggar 2009: 15). Following the Danish Cartoon Affair – which could well have influenced responses – a poll for *The Times* revealed that some 7% of a weighted sample agreed that 'there are circumstances in which I would condone suicide bombings on UK soil'. This approximates to some 100,000 Muslims. In another poll taken after the Danish Cartoon Affair, a fifth of respondents had 'some sympathy with the feelings and motives of those who conducted the London attacks'. Following 7/7 the Federation of Islamic Student Societies conducted a poll of young Muslims in Further and Higher Education. 72% of respondents said that they would contact the police straight away on learning of a suicide bomber within their ranks; 8% said that they would try to talk the suicide bomber out of it before informing the police. 10% gave no response; 2% said that they were mistrustful of the police, another 2% said that they would 'never grass on a Muslim', and a further 6% said that they would not inform the police but could not say why (Saggar 2006: 314–15).

It must be remembered that the polls cited above are very crude indicators as many of them were conducted in the midst of highly controversial events. Yet they do suggest a problem that the government was aware of before the al-Qaeda attacks on the United States on September 11, 2001. Hence the Terrorism Act 2000 accepted that 'terrorism may have religious or ideological as well as political motivation' and expanded the list of proscribed organizations to those beyond the conflict in Northern Ireland (Home Office 2000: 4). In the aftermath of 9/11, the Anti-Terrorism, Crime and Security Act was passed, which gave 'enforcement agencies' the power to 'seize terrorist cash' anywhere in the UK, to 'freeze their assets at the start of an investigation rather than when they [potential terrorists] are about to be charged'. The Treasury was also given the power to freeze the assets of any overseas government or individual that has taken, or is likely to take action 'to the detriment … of the UK' (Home Office 2001c: 3). Likewise the Home Secretary was given the power to detain indefinitely any foreign resident suspected of terrorist activity, who could not be deported for fear of suffering torture or degrading treatment. The Law Lords declared this power to be disproportionate in 2004 thus resulting in the Prevention of Terrorism Act 2005 which introduced 'derogating' and 'non-derogating' control orders. Both can be imposed on those who are suspected of terrorism but the former derogate from the European Convention of Human Rights and the latter do not. Partly in reaction to the London bombings the year before, the Terrorism Act 2006 was passed and, *inter alia*, it made encouraging terrorism and disseminating terrorist publications an offence. More controversially it also increased the length of time that a suspected terrorist can be detained and questioned by the police without charge from 14 to 28 days – although all periods of detention beyond two days must be approved by a judge (Home Office 2006a).

Indeed, beyond legislation and at the level of institutions, non-security and crime-related issues have been made the purview of the Department of Justice; while the Home Office has become the focal point for counter-radicalization initiatives. The budgets for MI5 and the police anti-terrorism units have increased significantly and an anti-terrorism strategy called CONTEST has been introduced which comprises four Ps. The first P is Prevention which addresses long-term goals that can help to prevent terrorism, such as resolving the conflict between Israel and Palestine. The second element of this strategy is called Pursuit and it aims to pursue terrorist networks, their funders and their supporters in various communities. The third element is called Protection and activity that falls under this category aims to protect Britain's infrastructure and maintain its border security. The final element is Preparedness and activity pursued under this category aims to have contingency plans in place if the worst should happen (Blick et al 2006: 32). In addition to tackling the hostility that British Muslims face, the government has also done a great deal to address the threat that a very small percentage of Muslims may pose. But can anything more be done about both? In the next section we explore some possibilities.

Tackling hostility towards Muslims and terrorism

As we have already seen, the government has done a great deal to address the current hostility that British Muslims face; but legislation in this area, when it does work, takes a very long time to do so. Equally, whilst the Race Relations Amendment Act imposes a positive duty to promote race equality, it only applies to public authorities. It is also unclear whether race is understood by these public authorities to include all religious groups, including Muslims. This is not to criticize this or the other pieces of legislation described above. They can send a powerful message about the sort of behaviour that is and is not acceptable (Uberoi 2008a). But such messages take time to filter through. Hence after passing the 1976 Race Relations Act, racism was not immediately and drastically reduced; nor would we expect the Racial and Religious Hatred Act to curb hostility towards Muslims immediately. More and better multicultural education and religious education, a code of ethics for the media to prevent Muslims being stereotyped may help, but again will take time to be effective (Stone 2004: 73–80). Indeed, beyond what has been done already, it seems there is little that any government can do in the short term to address the hostility that British Muslims increasingly face.

But certainly what any government can do is not make things worse. There was a saying when one of the authors (VU) worked at the Home Office: 'Talk Right and Act Left'. What was meant was that it is sometimes necessary for members of the government to say certain things to show that they are against political correctness and against being excessively accommodating to minorities just to prevent criticism from the right-wing media and to win support from white working-class voters. But what matters is policy, and this is designed to help minorities. This phrase was never, at least in the author's experience, used in relation to British Muslims, but it neatly captures what the government seems to be doing. Legislation has been introduced to punish those who discriminate against Muslims and to set a normative tone about what sort of behaviour is acceptable, but at the same time some rather unhelpful and inaccurate rhetoric is evident. Hence, Jack Straw claimed in 2007 'the trend towards greater segregation is most marked in areas with large Asian, principally Muslim, population' (Straw 2007). Likewise when he was Home Secretary David Blunkett said 'it is a worrying trend that young second generation British Muslims are more likely than their parents to feel that they have to choose between feeling part of the UK and feeling part of their faith' (Blunkett 2003).

Such rhetoric is partly problematic because it is untrue. Ludi Simpson refutes the trend towards greater segregation that Straw discusses when he shows that there has been a 'decrease in the unevenness of residence between each ethnic group and the rest of the population. This decrease in unevenness has occurred for all groups, *but is greatest for the mainly Muslim Pakistani and Bangladeshi groups for whom concern about segregation has been voiced most loudly*' (Simpson 2007: 409, emphasis added). This is not to say that many British Pakistanis and Bangladeshis do not live largely in concentrated urban areas but that increasingly there is more dispersal with what Simpson calls 'more mixed areas' (2007: 420). Likewise, it is difficult to know on what basis

Blunkett claims that young British Muslims are more likely than their parents to feel that they have to choose between feeling part of the UK and feeling part of their faith. This is a big empirical claim and it seems untrue when we consider the data which shows that the vast majority of Muslims have little difficulty 'feeling part of the UK'. A good indicator of this is whether they feel attached to Britain. Heath and Roberts have shown that 'controlling for age, we find no evidence that Muslims or people of Pakistani heritage were in general less attached to Britain than were other religious or ethnic groups'. Indeed, Heath and Roberts' data suggest that 85% of Muslims feel that they belong either 'very strongly' or 'fairly strongly' to Britain (Heath and Roberts 2008: 13). Both Straw's and Blunkett's claims thus seem inaccurate and both need to be careful because they seem to be painting an inaccurate picture of British Muslims which just re-enforces stereotypes.

However, such rhetoric is also problematic because it is occurring at a time when, as we have seen, British Muslims are encountering great hostility. Although there is little that the government can do in the short term – beyond what it already has – it is crucial that it does not make things worse for a group that already feels under pressure. Indeed, such 'talking right' is not only in breach of the normative tone that is being created by their 'acting left' but it is also counterproductive. This is because on the one hand representatives of the state (politicians) seem to be presenting factual errors about a group that results in them being painted in a negative light. On the other hand representatives of the state (the security forces) also need the help of that very same group to fight terrorism. Needless to say the former does not seem like the best strategy to achieve the latter.

However, what can be done about the small percentage of Muslims who are prepared to undertake extra-political activity? There are no quick fixes and many in Westminster and Whitehall now accept that counter-terrorism policy will have unintended consequences. A good example of this is the fact that if counter-terrorism policy is effective, then the chance of an attack will be reduced, but this is likely to reduce vigilance amongst the public at a time when it is most needed. There are also many things that contribute to the radicalization of young Muslims that government cannot easily control: for example relations between Israel and Palestine. In short most accept that it will be a 'long war' (Cabinet Office 2008).

Three things may, however, help to reduce the terrorist threat. The first is based on an observation made in a government memo that found its way into the public domain from the then Permanent Secretary to the Home Office, John Gieve, to the then Cabinet Secretary Andrew Turnbull. The memo suggested that both Muslims and non-Muslims are at risk of being radicalized and that this is also true of so-called 'high achievers'. But 'case histories' apparently show that amongst those most at risk of radicalization are Muslims who underachieve and possess a non-terrorist criminal background

(Gieve 2004). Government intelligence is far from perfect, but they are likely to know of many more case histories in this area than any outsider can. Equally, the claim that underachieving Muslims are those most at risk from radicalization seems intuitively plausible. After all, this is a group with low educational attainment and little direction in life hence they may lack the educational training to question those so-called 'jihadis' who claim to offer them such direction.

Indeed, when thinking about who these underachieving Muslims might be we must note that it is those of Pakistani and Bangladeshi origin who are most likely to under-achieve. They have the 'lowest percentages of all ethnic groups in higher managerial professions', they also have the highest percentages of those classified as having 'never worked or long-term unemployed' and the 'highest percentages with no educational qualifications' (Peach 2005: 29). British Muslims of Indian, Ismaili or Middle Eastern descent perform considerably better. This suggests that government should target their efforts on preventing underachievement amongst those of Pakistani and Bangladeshi origin. Indeed even in this minority within a minority, we see some recent educational improvement amongst Bangladeshi girls, which suggests that the measures needed should possess the precision of a sling-shot. This is easier said than done but such underachievement is problematic for any government that wants a society to be more socially just and, as we have seen, underachievement amongst these groups is likely to make them more prone to radicalization. This is not to suggest that the best way for an underachieving group to obtain more government assistance is to engage in extra-political activity. But it is to say that underachievement amongst those of Pakistani and Bangladeshi origin seems to make them more prone to radicalization and this is one of many reasons why the government should attempt to reduce underachievement amongst these groups.

Our second measure focuses on what some call the 'circle of tacit support' or the 'moral oxygen' of those young Muslims who are prepared to undertake extra-political activity. Many of them receive financial and logistical support from others, they also benefit from those who turn a blind eye and those who recognize that what is being done in the name of Islam is wrong but are unprepared, as one of our earlier polls showed, to 'grass on a Muslim'. Of course, it is impossible to gauge how widespread this circle of tacit support is. The polls referred to earlier give us some understanding, but it may be a distorted one as many of them were taken in periods of heightened passions. However we do know from other conflicts how important it can be to break this circle of tacit support for intelligence gathering purposes and earlier we explained why reducing hostility towards Muslims can help with this process (Saggar 2006).

But it is also necessary for those who are part of this circle to accept that they occupy the position of the classic 'fence-sitter' as they are partly convinced, partly not, by the righteousness of the actions of terrorists and yet they are helping their cause. Indeed these so-called fence-sitters are not only helping the cause of terrorists, they are also harming the reputation of British Muslims as loyal British citizens. But who are the types of people that can break this circle of tacit support? It is doubtful that the government can, as they are viewed with at least some degree of suspicion after the invasion of Iraq and Afghanistan, the Forest Gate debacle and so on.[1] The leadership necessary to convince some Muslims of the harm that can be caused through their fence-sitting must come from within the Muslim community. Some may retort that it is not one community and this is not the place for a conceptual discussion about what a community is. All that is meant is that those who are most likely to convince British Muslims of how harmful it is to be part of the circle of tacit support are other British Muslims and thus Muslim leadership on this issue must be encouraged. Of course, it is hard to lead groups whose members are heterogeneous and in some cases have divergent interests. It also takes time to build up the credibility necessary to do so, but all this highlights the significance of a group like the Muslim Council of Britain (MCB). As an umbrella organization that reflects the views of approximately 350 other organizations, over time it may well cultivate an ability to circulate an understanding of the dangers involved in fence-sitting.

Of course many have criticized the MCB in recent years because they think that it is not representative of British Muslims and that government shouldn't deal with organizations that claim to represent groups; instead it should deal with citizens (Mirza et al 2007: 83). Others suggest that leaders of the MCB are sympathetic to the extremist views of leading members of the Muslim Brotherhood and worry about the MCB's influence at the Foreign and Commonwealth Office (FCO) (Bright 2006).

Taking each of these criticisms in turn, the notion that the MCB is unrepresentative of British Muslims misses the point and perhaps strangely, Edward Heath's autobiography helps to make it. This is because Heath recounts as Prime Minister, the discussions that he had with Vic Feather who was the then General Secretary of the Trades Union Congress (TUC). Heath says of Feather, 'I knew that he was not really in a position to deliver: the General Secretary of the TUC has no troops' (Heath 1998: 329). Feather was not important to Heath because he represented all trade unionists, or because he could control them, but because he apparently understood the 'psychology' of trade unionism (ibid). Likewise the MCB is important now *not* because it represents, or doesn't represent, all British Muslims but because it might, over time, become an effective means to warn against the dangers of fence-sitting. As an organization that is comprised of Muslims who work in the interests of Muslims, the MCB has a credibility when talking to British Muslims that the government doesn't. There are, of course, other Muslim organizations that could be used but if the MCB's reach is limited, it is certainly broader than those of other organizations.

Yet those who believe that the government should engage specifically with citizens and not with organizations like the MCB will disagree. The logic of their position dictates that government should communicate the dangers of fence-sitting directly to individual Muslim citizens. But how would this occur and why would those who are willing to fence-sit on the dangers of terrorism be at all receptive to the government? As said earlier, foreign policy interventions have made many British Muslims suspicious of government and undoubtedly this is true of those most willing to fence-sit. Those most likely to be successful in convincing fence-sitters of the dangers of their position are going to be Muslims themselves and the MCB or an umbrella organization like it is thus needed.

Yet what if the MCB's leadership has sympathy for the views of certain extremists? This is certainly what some suggest and it is unclear if it is true. What is clear, however, is that it is not unusual for a government to work with those who have some extremist views, and if it was unusual then the current Northern Ireland peace process would be inexplicable. But a quick look on the MCB's website shows that it has been more than willing to work with the government in denouncing terrorism and suggesting ways to fight extremism. Presumably this is exactly what warning people about the dangers of fence-sitting requires, but of course some suggest that it is this cosiness with government and in particular the FCO that is the problem.

It is difficult to know if this cosiness really existed, but more importantly it is difficult to understand why specifically it is a problem. If the MCB was dictating FCO policy then one might see the point, but it is difficult to demonstrate that this occurred. Also claims that minority civil society organizations are dictating policy are not new and historical studies suggest that the story is usually much more complex (Uberoi 2008b). Equally, it is noticeable that the government ignored the MCB's calls not to invade Afghanistan or Iraq which seems to suggest that the MCB isn't dictating policy at the FCO and in sum the criticisms levied against the MCB seem unconvincing. It is regrettable, therefore, that it seems to have fallen out of favour in government at a time when it, or an umbrella organization like it, is needed most. A positive step then would be to promote, perhaps using financial means, either the MCB, or an umbrella organization like it to help communicate the dangers of fence-sitting in this area.

Our third and final measure is a call for research into *former* violent Islamists like Ed Hussein, Majid Narwaz and others. These people have renounced their former beliefs and declared them to be a perversion of Islam, not a reflection of it. Indeed many such people have come to form the Quilliam Foundation that aims to curb extremism and such people represent an interesting data set. Rather like studying former criminals helped criminologists to understand the path that people take to and from crime, so too studying former violent Islamists can help us understand the path that people take to and from violent Islamism. Indeed, it may help us to understand how to stop people getting on that path and how you bring those already on it back from the brink. And criminologists have shown how such a study might be undertaken. By interviewing many former criminals, obtaining their life stories and then analysing these life stories criminologists were able to detect the similar and divergent factors that attracted people to and eventually repelled them from crime (Maruna 2000). We don't have a large sample of former violent Islamists, but doing similar life-story interviews with as many former violent Islamists as possible could help us to understand the similar and divergent factors that attracted people to and eventually repelled them from violent Islamism. Indeed a good place to start is with those like the members of the Quilliam Foundation who are willing to talk to outsiders (as is illustrated by their interviews with the press). Of course, the government may not want to fund such a study directly, due to the suspicion that potential interviewees have of the state, but the Dutch government have sponsored a similar study and the Economic and Social Research Council is already funding work in this area (Buijs et al 2005).

Conclusion

In conclusion, governing Britain's diverse citizenry is a complex task that involves many areas of activity. From immigration and asylum, multiculturalism and Britishness, to tackling racism, hostility towards Muslims and extremism, this policy area is as broad-ranging as any of the more traditional ones that relate to crime, education and so on. Certainly in financial terms not nearly as much goes into diversity-related issues as other areas, but finance is a crude means of assessing the significance of an issue. The risk of not acting is perhaps a better measure. The risks attached to not addressing the hostility that British Muslims face and of not curbing extremism are large. Whilst there is little more that government can do to curb the hostility that Muslims currently face – save not making things worse – we hope that we have identified a few measures which can, over the long term, help to curb extremism.

Notes

We are grateful to Dr Nasar Meer for his comments on an earlier draft of this chapter.

1. In June 2006 the police raided two houses in Forest Gate, East London, shot a man in the shoulder and arrested another man. Both men were released and neither was ever charged. The Independent Police Complaints Commission, whilst ruling that the raid was necessary in relation to the intelligence that the police had, upheld a small number of complaints against the operation and gave a written warning to one policeman. See http://news.bbc.co.uk/1/shared/bsp/hi/pdfs/13_02_07_forest_gate.pdf

14
Communications and Media Policy

*Damian Tambini**

Communications policy 1997–2008

The 1997 government was elected with a clear set of policy objectives for the communications sector. Many of the key planks of policy, such as the setting up of Ofcom and reform of the BBC, had been developed by the Labour Party in opposition. (See Collins and Purnell 1994; Collins and Murroni 1996; for a review see Freedman 2002.) After a decade, the government appears to have delivered on many of these plans. Despite major reforms in the sector however, the overall challenge for the next decade is similar to that of 1997: to respond to rapid technological change brought about by digitization. But as the pace of change intensifies, media and communications policy will move up the list of government priorities. Governments can no longer ignore the pressing need for decisions on high speed broadband for example, and urgently need to address the crisis of public broadcasting. Policymakers also need to deal with the consequences of recent initiatives such as the setting up of Ofcom.

Those designing a new framework for UK communications need to be proactive, not merely reacting to current challenges. Whilst there are urgent matters to address, such as Channel Four and broadband, policy should be based on clear and stable guidelines about the fundamental values and long-term objectives, particularly the desired role of the state, commerce and public accountability in media and communications, and it should acknowledge that the public interest in communications cannot be protected merely by encouraging more competitive markets.

The central product of New Labour communications policy was the Communications Act of 2003. In the decade leading up to the drafting of the Communications Act, and since, the sector has seen rapid and profound changes: the number of internet connections per 100 population rose from

---

* In November 2008 Damian Tambini was appointed as a member of the Communications Consumer Panel. This chapter was written before his joining the panel and represents a personal view. It should not be seen as representing a Consumer Panel or Ofcom view.

close to zero at the beginning of the 1990s to 19.3 in 2002 and 30.4 by 2007. But the real challenge for institutions comes with the convergence between the internet and broadcasting. The narrowband internet has rapidly evolved into a broadband medium capable of delivering television-like services. The number of broadband connections per 100 population rose from 2.3 in 2002 to 26.0 in 2007 and continues to rise. At the same time, the takeup of digital television rose from close to zero in the mid-1990s to 38.5% of homes in 2002 and 86.3% of homes in 2008 (Ofcom 2008a).

Government faced the difficult task of introducing a new regulatory framework during this period of rapid change. The policy aims, according to the Communications White Paper of 2000, were to: (i) Make the UK home to the most dynamic and competitive communications and media market in the world, (ii) Ensure universal access to a choice of diverse services of the highest quality and (iii) Ensure that citizens and consumers are safeguarded (DTI/DCMS 2000).

The centrepiece of the resulting legislation was the establishment of a new 'converged' communications regulator, Ofcom. The new regulator replaced five separate regulators for radio, spectrum, television, broadcasting standards and telecoms. The new regulator was designed to be strong (with the resources and research capacity to provide an evidence base for policymaking) and 'converged' – working across the entire communications sector.

Communications policy since the 2003 Communications Act has been developed in a complex matrix between central government, DCMS and BERR (DTI), and Ofcom. Parliamentary Committees have had occasional influence on outcomes (notably the scrutiny committee on the 2003 legislation itself) but have otherwise lacked influence. Increasingly, Ofcom research and reviews have led communications policymaking.

There were four main planks to policy during the period 1997–2008:

- using competition to regulate the provision of networks including the use of the electromagnetic spectrum;
- the switch to digital broadcasting;
- a managed migration of advertising-funded public service broadcasters into the digital era;
- continued support for the BBC.

In this chapter I examine these policy areas in turn and then I outline some key challenges and options.

Competition: spurring rollout of telecoms networks and services

Oftel, the telecoms regulator prior to Ofcom, was essentially a competition regulator, dealing with the problem of having a large and powerful incumbent operator and regulating the range of potential abuses of its market power. Ofcom's activities in telecommunications regulation continued this basic framework, applying interconnection, access, pricing and quality of service regulation, as the UK attempted to evolve away from a system dominated by one player, to a more pluralistic competitive market for telecoms networks and services.

Broadband became a political issue around the turn of the millennium, due to the difficulty of obtaining it in rural areas, including some marginal seats. Government urgently sought a means to increase availability, and the policy of 'local loop unbundling' was the main response. This means opening up the local telephone exchange, usually run by BT, to competing providers of broadband who use the 'local loop' of existing copper wiring to provide broadband services to consumers. By regulating the relationship between BT and these competitors, it was hoped it would be possible to spur competition and provision of high quality services. The policy has been effective, with the UK rising in OECD comparative tables on provision of broadband. In 2008, the OECD reported that the UK had experienced one of the highest global rises in broadband access over the previous six years. Broadband subscriptions in the UK are now almost 30 per 100 people, which compares favourably with similar economies around the globe, particularly in Europe (OECD 2008c: 8, 10).

Ofcom's 2004 Telecoms Review considered taking a step further and recommending that effective competition could only be achieved by breaking up the former monopoly. But the option was rejected in favour of continuing with one dominant player and regulating behaviour through the 'BT undertakings' – chiefly a commitment to separating out the wholesale arm of BT.

The main 'converged' area of policy was spectrum management, as it concerns a resource that is crucial both to broadcasting and to telecommunications. Historically, spectrum (the 'airwaves') has been an under-used resource, and economists have argued that markets for spectrum rather than central planning would lead to efficient outcomes (Coase 1959).

Ofcom has called for a market-oriented approach to spectrum. In preparing the policy framework for the award of the biggest and most valuable spectrum band in recent history however, Ofcom's resolve was tested. It reserved interleaved spectrum for a range of wireless services, and planned to release some spectrum in packages that would be suited for local TV (Ofcom 2007). While Ofcom had initially proposed a pure market approach to the introduction of High Definition Television (HDTV) it eventually agreed to a substantial regulatory intervention to clear one area of spectrum to allow for HD to be provided in a new, more spectrum efficient manner. The decision illustrated the tension between Ofcom's commitment to the digital switchover project, and its duties to ensure spectrum efficiency and protect consumers. The extent to which Ofcom is prepared to pursue markets in spectrum, and to use it as a tool for social goals is a key question for the future. In an October 2008 speech to the thinktank *Polis* at the London School of Economics, the Conservative Shadow Culture minister called for spectrum to be planned in order to foster the development of local TV, indicating a possible future direction of Conservative policy.

Digital switchover

Satellite broadcasting upset the cosy oligopoly of UK public sector broadcasters (PSBs) during the 1990s, introducing a new kind of television: more commercial, and with a lower level of public service obligations. Thus began the gradual displacement of the old system of public service by a more commercial 'multichannel' offering. The 1996 Broadcasting Act introduced digital terrestrial broadcasting in the UK by making available spectrum which was first licensed by OnDigital, later ITV Digital. OnDigital offered a pay TV package in competition with SKY's satellite service. It was not until 1999 that the government publicly committed to managing the transition to an all digital television broadcasting system. Culture Secretary Chris Smith set out the affordability and access conditions that would need to be met for the government to support the switch off of analogue television broadcasts. Since then, a new DTT provider, Freeview, has emerged from the ashes of the bankrupt ITV Digital, and the government has coordinated a managed transition and set out a detailed timetable for switching off the analogue signals through a stakeholder policy coordination group, Digital UK. It is envisaged that all analogue TV broadcasts will have ceased by 2012.

Digital switchover is a huge policy intervention, which involves a very significant level of public funding. Crucially it also uses the BBC as an instrument of public policy: which is reflected in the BBC's new general duty to 'Build Digital Britain'. The Corporation is charged not only with a key role in managing Freeview, but has duties to promote Digital, provide new digital services and also to subsidize the 'targeted help' for those who have difficulty switching for economic or other reasons.

The principal driving force behind spectrum policy is the spectrum benefit. Digital broadcasting takes up less space in the airwaves than analogue broadcasting. It is possible to cram up to six digital channels (or up to three high definition channels) into the space released by switching off one analogue channel. Whether looked at in terms of the public value that could be generated by alternative services, or in terms of the cash the Treasury could raise by selling that spectrum, there is a broad consensus that ceasing analogue broadcasts is efficient (DTI 2002). But the policy of digital switchover was not only about spectrum efficiency, it was about enhanced services – increasing the channel choice and interactivity available to UK viewers, and providing some kind of competition to the dominant pay TV operator, Sky.

Managing public service broadcasting and broadcast regulation

The policy of migrating to digital television in order to cease using valuable spectrum to broadcast to analogue sets has largely been successful. By late

2008, almost 90% of the main television sets in UK homes (and almost 70% of all sets) were equipped to receive digital TV. This rapid migration to enhanced digital services with radically increased channel choice has formed the backdrop for a fundamental paradigm shift in broadcast regulation, and rapidly reduced PSB audiences.

The Communications Act implemented a 'tiered' approach to broadcasting regulation, based on a sliding scale of rights and obligations. Culture Secretary Chris Smith introduced it in the Commons:

> We propose a new three-tier approach to the regulation of broadcasting ... In the first tier, all broadcasters will be subject to basic rules on minimum content standards, impartiality in news, provisions on the protection of minors and access for people with disabilities. ...
>
> The second and third tiers will apply to public service broadcasters. In the second, regulated by Ofcom, those obligations that are readily measurable will be included: independent and original programme production quotas; requirements for regional productions and programming; and the availability of news and current affairs in peak time. (...) In the third tier – where the general public service provision of high-quality varied schedules will rest – we propose to rely primarily on transparent self-regulation, but with backstop powers in place in the event of failure. (House of Commons Debate, 12 December 2000, c 482–3)

This 'tiered approach' formed the basis for Ofcom's and the BBC's approach to PSB, but in two subsequent reviews Ofcom has surveyed an increasingly ragged and declining PSB system. ITV and Channel 4 look very vulnerable to a drip-drip dissolution of their public service remit.

Supporting the BBC

Histories will dwell on the events of the 'Gilligan affair'[1] as the moment when the New Labour halo slipped and finally fell. To the government's credit, it appears that it managed to keep policy on the BBC separate from the politics of the relationship between BBC journalists and government advisers. New Labour courted the BBC and there was a long list of personnel swaps between the Corporation and the government. Notably James Purnell, who was the lead policy adviser to the PM during the development of the Communications White Paper and later became Culture Minister and Work and Pensions Secretary, previously spent two years at the BBC as a strategy adviser. Ed Richards worked in BBC Strategy before replacing James Purnell at No.10 and then led No.10's input into the Communications Bill before moving to Ofcom where he is now Chief Executive. And John Birt, the BBC Director-General responsible for introducing internal market reforms during the 1990s, was later a key Downing Street policy adviser.

Following the Davies Review of 1999 the BBC was granted a generous above inflation licence fee settlement which effectively led to a year by year increase in fees until 2006. This was largely seen as an attempt to give the BBC the ability to respond to the challenges of digital and to reverse what had been a gradual reduction in licence fee in real terms under all but the last two years of the previous government. During the negotiations on the licence fee and BBC Charter from 2006 onward, the BBC had asked for a significant increase to fund new digital services but amid a general decline in television revenues this was not granted and the BBC's licence fee will decline in real terms.

Equipping the BBC to adapt to digital is a complex undertaking, however. One danger was that uncertainty about which markets the large, publicly funded BBC would enter creates disincentives for others to invest. This was the case for example in relation to the BBC's ambitious online education plans at the turn of the century. As a result, the new regulatory framework included an attempt to 'beef up' the BBC's regulation and the introduction of a test of both the market impact and the 'public value' of new services which the BBC Trust must carry out before the BBC can launch new services.

More radical solutions have been considered for reform of the BBC and continuing public service broadcasting in the UK in the longer term. Variations on 'decentralized funding models' for public service content have been devised. A more likely scenario would be the sharing of the BBC licence fee among various public service communications providers.

Other issues: content regulation on the internet

Whilst there were during the 1990s widespread concerns about inappropriate internet content and the challenge of child protection, the UK government in general favoured a competitive, open approach to the internet. Following a global debate about whether internet content should fit within a 'regulated broadcasting' or a 'free press' framework, a more liberal approach became the norm in the UK as elsewhere. It was accepted that censorship was undesirable and ineffective.

This liberal approach to internet content reflected in part a desire not to 'break' this miraculous new technology through over-regulation, and in part a desire not to discourage investment in this important new sector in the UK. There was a consensus that policymakers should stand back and rely on a vibrant marketplace to deliver public access to new services. Whilst politicians have remained constantly aware of public uneasiness about children and new internet and gaming technology, the recommendations of the major policy reviews, such as that chaired by Tania Byron which reported in 2008, have generally shied away from radical control measures favouring industry self regulation with government oversight (Byron 2008). The internet therefore stayed outside the scope of detailed content regulation, though the implementation of the 2005 EU Audiovisual Media Services Directive does now extend more regulation to internet delivered media services.

In addition, a range of communications related policy reviews have taken place such as the Gowers Review of Intellectual Property and the Byron Review on children and digital media. These policy reviews have largely adopted a 'steady as she goes' approach, though they have put on the table some more radical policy options should their awareness raising and self-regulatory recommendations not deliver in the public interest.

Communications policy: the major challenges

Ofcom

The setting up of Ofcom has been a success. The regulator has established legitimacy with the public and regulatees. There have been no disasters, and research and decisions have been widely praised. However, the model of a regulator operating with wide discretion and balancing a range of interests and objectives does present a number of problems that will need to be addressed in the next policy cycle. Ofcom has encountered difficulties in managing the fundamental trade-offs between speed, effectiveness and accountability, and particular difficulties in dealing with decisions with a significant political/ideological element. Spectrum management is an example of an area where duties, procedures and methods can only take Ofcom so far. In setting the framework for access to the airwaves freed by digital switchover for example, the regulator has to balance social objectives such as access to rural broadband on the one hand, with alternatives such as promoting competition in spectrum markets or access to PSB services on the other. Technocratic procedures alone cannot provide answers to these complex normative dilemmas.

Questions have been raised about the degree of openness and transparency in Ofcom's deliberations. Part of this is simply the difficulty of navigating the volume of Ofcom publications. But there may be a more fundamental issue: bringing together the various regulators under one roof may in fact have reduced transparency by internalizing inter-regulator relations. And whilst Ofcom is usually exhaustive in its production of evidence, it is not always clear why decisions have been taken when the regulator inevitably exercises judgement and discretion. The balance between accountability and effectiveness of decisions was the subject of a speech made by Ofcom's Peter Philips on 4 July 2007. Philips' conclusion was somewhat simplistic: 'the loss of direct democratic accountability is OK so long as the job is done well. But we should be cautious. Trust can break down between government and regulator' (see http://www.ofcom.org.uk/media/speeches/2007/07/iea0407).

Some of the problems with the new regulatory system are thus becoming obvious. Whilst a strong independent regulator, acting within a set of general objectives, may be an effective model for the energy sector for example, the cultural and democratic complexities of the communications sector may require a more effective accountability mechanism. 'Doing the job well' is likely to be more contested than Ofcom officials wish.

State and market in communications: what is the long-term objective?

Policymakers need to ask some prior questions about the 'natural state' in communications: is regulation a temporary condition to be imposed only when the market fails to work its magic, or is a significant degree of enforced public accountability and regulation a permanent – even desirable – part of the communications landscape?

The history of electronic communications policy in the UK can be written in terms of the rise and subsequent retreat of public intervention. State monopoly provision – telephony through the Post Office and British Telecom, and broadcasting through the BBC – has been gradually displaced by competitive commercial provision. And whilst commercial providers have historically been tightly regulated in terms of the services they can offer, the quality thresholds they must meet and prices charged, this regulation is in rapid – and apparently inevitable – decline.

The shift to digital technology appears to be a final nail in the coffin of state intervention in the provision of electronic communications. For many, this is good news: we have long favoured freedom of the press in the UK. It is a small step to argue that digital should enable a similarly liberal policy framework based on the value of free expression for all electronic media including broadcasting: as long as there is a basic respect for the law, each editorial decision should be a private matter.

It could be argued therefore that the future of government policy in electronic communications appears to be a process of managed retreat and the onward march of liberal progress: competition – rather than public provision – appears to be an effective way of rolling out new electronic communication services (Sauter 1997), and driving up quality (Mulgan 1990), and in a world of unbridled choice of audiovisual content there seems little place for a public body like the BBC to choose on behalf of consumers. In the era of choice and open media, public service providers must provide what consumers want in order to maintain audience. So why not let the market provide it and charge per view or per subscription?

The framework initiated by the Communications Act 2003 and implemented by the new regulator Ofcom conformed to this deregulatory impulse – up to a point. Ofcom has tended when exercising discretion to favour less regulation, self regulation and consumer choice, rather than proposing new interventions. When they have mooted significant new interventions – as with the proposed public service publisher or the break-up of BT – they have retreated.

This deregulatory thrust departs from historical norms in the UK approach to communications. Since the Sykes Committee Report concluded in 1923 that since broadcasting was so powerful 'control of it ought to remain with the state' (Broadcasting Committee Report 1923), the tendency has been to assume that broadcasting belongs outside of the market. Subsequently the notion of public service broadcasters (PSBs) independent from the government of the day has emerged. Not only the BBC, but all broadcasters in the UK have ultimately been considered public servants: using a public resource (spectrum) in return for delivering information, education and entertainment. Given current trends, this will not be the case in the future.

It is worth at this point making a simple observation about the UK media system. Namely that in general, UK PSB has been hugely successful, and has resulted in a broadcasting system that is the envy of the world. So whilst competition may be right for networks, competition alone is more likely to be wrong for content, which creates difficulties in a converged regulatory system. The electorate might tolerate the privatization of a post-Big Brother Channel 4: but is unlikely to forgive botched reform – or neglect – of the BBC. The shift to digital and the rise of broadband offer the possibility that, apart from the BBC, broadcasting will shift to an entirely commercial system. Policy has to ride two horses: the need to provide the most modern communications environment possible, but at the same time to maintain institutions – such as independent domestic production and public service content – from the old media world.

Communication and media policy: the options

Reform the regulator?

Delegation of powers to independent bodies has been a key theme of New Labour reforms. This gives the appearance of removing ideology and low politics from decision-making, introducing technical rigour ('what works') in its place and at the same time of reducing political risks associated with regulatory failure. Delegation can also provide flexibility in fast changing circumstances: give the regulator some broad objectives and leave the details of implementation to them.

Because the regulator may only take decisions within its statutory powers and according to its duties, and because its decision-making lacks democratic accountability in the conventional sense, Ofcom tends to rely on technocratic policymaking tools (such as market failure analysis and cost benefit analysis) where 'objective' evidence can be brought to bear to justify decisions. Regulatory decisions do not arise from the raw data however. Welfare economics, market failure analysis and cost benefit analysis are hugely powerful tools for the production of policy advice, but only if conflicting public interests and outcomes can be expressed in a common currency.[2] In this view, markets are the most efficient way of distributing goods and providing consumers with what they want, and public intervention should take place only when markets demonstrably fail. For example the government has conducted a detailed cost benefit analysis for the switch to digital and the Ofcom Consumer Panel together with BERR have collaborated on a project looking at the costs and benefits of the switch to a fibre-based telecoms network and the likelihood that the market will provide it (Plum Consulting 2008).

Officials at the regulator are acutely aware that Ofcom risks exposure to expensive judicial review. Whilst there is no evidence to date that this has occurred, current structures may lead to a danger that the regulator could be tempted to take positions that accommodate and compromise with regard to the stakeholders that have the resources to judicially review a decision.

The principal way in which public interest issues have been incorporated into economic analysis in communications policy, in Ofcom and in government, has been in terms of notions of 'Public Value', 'broader social value' or 'externalities' (e.g. Ofcom 2007). These economic frameworks can be incorporated into research on costs and benefits through, for example, the argument that costs and benefits might include those that are indirect or difficult to measure, or the argument that markets might fail because overall social welfare might include value that is not recognized in individuals' decisions to consume. The BBC pioneered the notion of 'Public Value' in relation to its own services, and developed some innovative new survey methodologies to measure the extent to which people thought that the BBC was good for society, as well as being good for them personally (BBC 2004). The other objection to such technocratic procedures is that they are inherently anti-democratic – because they express what are ultimately judgement calls in a language that only a few specialists can understand.

In practice, some policy decisions do require political, normative input, and accountability to the public or politicians. A decision on broadband not only requires policy guidance on what degree of social exclusion of rural communities is tolerable; it requires a balancing of the pros and cons of various options of intervention to assist rollout of high speed broadband. Governments might impose regulation through defining standards for new build (or even renovated) housing; or for new telephone connections; or they might choose to dedicate significant public investment (EC State Aid rules permitting). The balancing of these various options, in a fast changing environment, will require clarity: hopefully policymakers will have a clear idea of what degree and types of intervention are favoured, and to what extent equity (e.g. rural–urban parity) should guide policy. The crucial point is that such judgements must be legitimate, and in a democracy legitimacy is generally provided by a link to elected authority. Because of the obvious need for independence from government, Ofcom has faced difficulties in securing legitimacy for judgements.

It has not been possible in this short chapter to do full justice to the range of policy issues that will have to be addressed, including press, competition and ownership policy, and the implementation of the new EC telecoms package. The aim rather has been to focus on some of the key areas, and cross-cutting themes. There are a range of options available to those who wish to reform Ofcom:

- Improve accountability to Parliament. Current accountability to Parliamentary committees has been very weak, due in part to the lack of specificity in terms of Ofcom's reporting duties, and in some cases to a lack of preparedness on the part of the MPs. A survey of MPs' views of Ofcom conducted in 2007 showed a low level of awareness about the work of Ofcom (Taylor 2009). Whereas the endemic problem of lack of support and resources to select committees cannot be resolved, communications policymaking could be improved by obliging Ofcom to provide specific access to select committee members on a cross-party basis, and organizing joint public hearings on specific policy issues.
- Improve transparency, and accountability to the public. Ofcom does some exemplary work in terms of its audience research, outreach and use of innovative public involvement in its policymaking. Audience preference is seen as the key justification of communications policy intervention. But more could be done in terms of formal public involvement and opening the process of decision-making to public scrutiny.
- Clarify the duties. Ofcom officials privately complained after the passage of the 2003 legislation that they view the duties of Ofcom as too many and too complex. This is partly due to nervousness about the new regulator, and also due to a perceived lack of accountability for key decisions of policy. The general duties are perhaps too general, and the specific duties too specific.

Join the broadband race? Public investment in Next Generation Access (NGA)

There is a widespread belief that the UK is falling behind in the race to roll out high-speed broadband. The rollout of the current broadband network has been rapid. However, game and video traffic is already testing its capacity, and many argue that it is necessary for a completely renewed fibre optic network to be built. Should the UK join Korea and Japan in investing public money in the rollout of a key public infrastructure which many argue will promote economic growth, deliver public services and provide a platform for key consumer-oriented services? Or should this be left to the market to provide? If it is left to the market, should network providers such as BT and

Virgin be allowed to charge content providers (including the BBC) to carry their traffic?

A government-sponsored review (Caio 2008) estimated that the cost of deploying the next generation of ultra high speed broadband in the UK would be between £24.5 billion and £29 billion for the fastest fibre network or around £5 billion for a slower and less reliable alternative. The same government review recommended that the government should – for the time being – avoid making a major intervention (e.g. providing public funding or regulatory holidays), but should look to the market to provide and intervene only by providing incentives and altering new building regulations.

Should the state fund new communications networks? The general response of government – at least prior to the financial crisis of 2008 – was that if there is demand for the service, we can rely on private investment to roll it out. But there could be important equity issues raised – particularly the divide between rural and urban access, since ultra high speed broadband is being rolled out in the most affluent, densely populated areas first. Also there may be market failures to take into account, for example the important economic 'externalities' or value not realized by individual consumers but by others. High speed broadband could lead to investment and – according to some economists – jobs and improved 'competitiveness'. It may have implications for the efficiency of delivering public services. Two government-sponsored reports on this issue (Caio 2008; Plum Consulting 2008) have appeared. And as with the shift to digital television (or from coal to sea gas) there is an important policy coordination role for government to play. The shift to next generation broadband could require telecoms companies to dig up many of the roads in the UK.

Thus far, BERR and the stakeholders involved have adopted a 'wait and see' stance. A future government will have to review the rollout of the infrastructure and will have to make a call on the following issues:

- If there is a demand for high speed broadband, won't private investment supply it? (Should market failure, or network effects be taken into account?).
- Would high speed Broadband be important in the delivery of improved government services such as health and education? And might cost savings be made?
- If public funds are not provided to subsidize rollout of the infrastructure, might network providers be permitted to seek other sources of funding such as charging content providers for distribution, or should principles of net neutrality be respected and such discrimination be outlawed?
- What are the equity issues involved? If there are likely to be enduring inequalities of access, quality and speed between rural and urban areas, how long-term will these be, and what will be their implications for economic development, access to services, and social exclusion?

And these are of course only a few of the issues involved. Around the world, policymakers tend to take a 'new is better', 'more is better' approach to technology, but given the scale of the investment required and the implications for equity, and for all other media, decisions on NGA will need to be taken with caution. And it is likely that broadband policy will impact regional development policy: it is accepted that improved access to faster, more reliable broadband can be a factor in attracting inward investment to a region. A South Yorkshire consortium of local authorities with the regional development agency has secured EU and private funding for a plan to connect 600,000 homes and small businesses in the region with an optical fibre network. Without targeted intervention, might a market-based strategy result in disproportionate access to ultra high speed broadcasting in the densely populated South East, a pattern likely to exacerbate regional economic imbalances?

A new framework for public service broadcasting?

For the first time, the complete collapse of the existing public service broadcasting system is being contemplated. In the UK, public service included all television broadcasters, according to a sliding scale of rights and responsibilities that is codified in the 2003 Act. The BBC has the broadest and most exacting public service obligations as it is publicly funded, but even the commercial TV channels 3, 4, and 5 have been very tightly regulated in return for the permission to use the scarce public resource of the airwaves. But now that television is not reliant on terrestrial broadcasting to reach audiences, and broadcasters must increasingly pay market rates for distribution, the obligations that accompany the right to broadcast are being torn up.

ITV for example, has argued consistently since the formation of Ofcom that its public service obligations are becoming too expensive to meet now that it no longer enjoys a near monopoly of television advertising and audiences are in decline. Ofcom has accepted that ITV may decide to 'hand back' its public service licence – and along with it its public service obligations, and become a purely commercial broadcaster. It has therefore used its discretion to vary ITV's licence obligations, for example its obligation to produce regional and educational programming. The potential impact of this on the public became clear in 2008 when a locally organized protest to defend a regional ITV news programme from closure resulted in 13,000 responses to an obscure Ofcom consultation.[3] Media policy can feature in the public consciousness when something people treasure is taken away from them. Not only local citizens but local MPs (for obvious reasons) have an affection for local TV news services. In a purely market system, these are unlikely to be funded to the same extent. It is the broadcast licensing system that sustains them.

Given the threat to commercial public service broadcasting, there is a distinct possibility that the BBC will be the only public service broadcaster in the country, which leads us to wonder where this great march of liberalization might be taking us (Gardam and Levy 2008). Perhaps competition, choice and freedom of expression will only get us so far. In order to confront some of the fundamental choices facing communications policy it is necessary to ask a prior question: what kind of communications infrastructure will best serve liberal democracy in Britain, and what role, if any, will policy play in reaching that goal? As policymakers establish a view on desirable end points, and fundamental values, this is the question that should be foremost in their minds. It has not always been in the past.

The notion of Public Service Broadcasting probably ranks among the UK's most influential policy exports during the twentieth century. Ofcom now accepts that the status quo is not an option (Ofcom 2008b), and the policy framework for delivering PSB needs to be entirely redesigned if PSB is not to wither away. Whilst the regulator has at various points tried to lead the debate by suggesting new funding models and even new institutions – the so-called Public Service Publisher – Ofcom in its policy-development and advice function has been constrained by the technocratic approach described earlier. The options on the table for saving the UK public service system – sharing BBC licence fee income being the most favoured – are inadequate to the challenge. Fundamental decisions will need to be taken about the desirable balance between public, private and hybrid models. In recent years the UK has been served well by a broadcast system that managed to balance services across three tiers of public service. It is likely that a significant new intervention would be needed to continue this. The idea will have to come from government, not Ofcom.

Conclusions

No policy area is a blank canvas, and no government can simply define its blueprint for the future and set out a legislative timetable to deliver it. Politics intervenes. Social, demographic, commercial, attitudinal and technological changes, together with the need to implement European and other international obligations open policy windows, close them, and shape the timetable. And there are unintended consequences of early decisions. Once legislation is contemplated a bill can become a 'Christmas tree', offering enticing branches for policy entrepreneurs to hang additional reforms and obligations on. So the Communications Act of 2003, whilst largely concerned with implementing the 2002 EC Directive package of telecoms reforms (European Commission 2002a–d), contained a range of other measures including setting up Ofcom, liberalizing the regime for providers of telecoms services, and reforming the approach to commercial public service broadcasting. These reforms, which have been largely successful, have set the framework for regulation of communications into the new digital age, but the fundamental decisions – particularly on the future balance between public and market provision – will be taken with the next Communications Act.

Communications policy is, however, one area where Europe looks to the UK for a lead. It did so with the development of the European 'mixed system' of broadcasting and again with the liberalization of telecoms. But even given this room for manoeuvre, the new system may be arrived at more through accident than by design. The interactions between disparate policy areas are simply too complex. Across Europe, the current norm is a mixed economy of electronic communications providers, but there is little clarity on whether this mixed economy remains the policy goal.

Whilst it appears obvious that the citizen is best served not only by a choice of commercial providers, but by a choice between commercial and public service providers, the long-term future of this mixed model is uncertain. One of the failings of New Labour was its tendency to follow the policy cycle. With some notable exceptions, such as the setting up of Ofcom, policy has been pragmatic and sensible, but sometimes piecemeal and reactive. Another failing was a preference for dodging some of the fundamental normative questions and opting for pragmatic compromises with lower levels of political risk. During the next decade in communications policy, fences will be more uncomfortable places to sit. Policy – or at least good policy – will inevitably contain an element of pragmatism, but if the public interest is to be protected, it must be guided by a more decisive vision for where the direction of travel should be leading us.

Future policymakers should start by providing a clear vision of the desirable end point in terms of the desired balance between state, public and market provision. Policymakers should also avoid distraction by second order institutional scuffles. Arguments about money and institutions should be resolved as part of a larger strategy, and in terms of the fundamental objectives, not piecemeal. Crucially, policymakers must resist the power of media owners. Owner power is in decline in the age of new media, and journalists and the public can be encouraged to balance that power. By courting media owners and their editors, politicians increase the power of those owners.

Notes

We are grateful to Varun Uberoi and David Levy for their comments on earlier drafts of this chapter

1. Following a 2003 BBC news report alleging misleading Downing Street 'spin' of the rationale for the war in Iraq, the BBC was subject to sustained public criticism from the government. After a government-appointed Commission of Inquiry, the Chairman and Director-General of the BBC resigned.
2. The problem of incommensurability in policy analysis is fundamental here. Cost benefit analysis in policymaking requires that values of policy outcomes are expressed according to a common unit of value. However, the value of some policy outcomes may be contested, immeasurable, and/or incommensurable with one another. Compare Boardman et al (2006) and Sunstein (1994).
3. http://ofcompsbreview.typepad.com/ofcompsbreview/2008/04/when-a-picture. html

15

The Constitution

Roger Gough and Guy Lodge

Introduction

For a Prime Minister who gave little apparent priority to the subject, Tony Blair left behind an extraordinary legacy of constitutional change. The Labour government put into effect:

- The Human Rights Act 1998 (HRA)
- The creation of devolved institutions in Scotland, Wales and Northern Ireland
- The creation of the Mayor of London and the Greater London Authority
- Use of referenda to establish devolved institutions in Scotland and Wales
- The removal of all but 92 hereditary peers from the House of Lords and the establishment of a (non-statutory) independent appointments commission
- The Freedom of Information Act 2000
- Introduction of (various forms of) proportional representation for the elections to the European Parliament, devolved institutions in Scotland, Wales, Northern Ireland and the London Assembly
- Bank of England independence
- Reforms designed to 'modernize' the House of Commons
- The Local Government Act 2000, which overhauled the leadership model of local authorities, including an option (subject to a local referendum) to introduce directly elected mayors
- The Political Parties, Elections and Referendums Act 2000 reforming party finance

- The Constitutional Reform Act 2005 which made the Lord Chief Justice head of the Judiciary, and which created a Supreme Court and an independent Judicial Appointments Commission
- Experiments with new forms of participatory democracy, e.g. citizens' juries.

If constitutional reform was not high on Blair's priority list, neither was it on the voters': with the exception of demands for devolution in Scotland (and to a much lesser extent in Wales) there were no real public pressures for action. However, on devolution and the HRA (the latter much more of an elite interest) Blair inherited commitments from his predecessors. Other measures were either a response to specific issues (such as the attempts to develop new forms of local government leadership) or to the dynamics created by the government's own programme (such as the creation of the Supreme Court).

In his first weeks in office, Gordon Brown brought forward constitutional proposals in the Green Paper *The Governance of Britain*, while Conservative thinking has been seen in front bench pronouncements and in the work of the Democracy Task Force, chaired by Ken Clarke. Future administrations, whether Labour or Conservative, will have to respond to the consequences of the Blair reforms. Many of the changes are contested or incomplete. Many create their own, often unpredictable dynamic: thus asymmetric devolution gave rise to the English Question, while the Human Rights Act has further empowered the judiciary. Meanwhile, low turnouts, falling party membership and public cynicism about politics indicate a severe problem of trust and engagement. Whatever its other merits, constitutional reform has so far failed to reverse this trend.

Before returning to these broader themes, this chapter addresses four key areas that have seen significant change:

- The HRA and the 'judicial branch'
- Devolution and the Union
- Parliament
- Central-local relations

The Human Rights Act and the 'judicial branch'

Important changes in the judiciary, leading to much greater assertiveness, had taken place over several decades prior to 1997. Judicial review had been growing since the 1960s, and as its use accelerated the doctrines underlying it became more expansive. EU membership provided an occasion for judges to strike down – or 'disapply' – legislation that violated EU directives (notably in the 1990 *Factortame* case). The European Convention on Human Rights (ECHR) had a growing impact on jurisprudence, even though it was not incorporated into domestic law. While clashes with ministers – especially over immigration cases – grew, some judges argued for more radical doctrines (such as Lord Justice Laws' doctrine of 'constitutional' statutes in the *Thoburn* 'metric martyrs' case, or Lord Woolf's 1994 argument that 'ultimately there are even limits on the supremacy of Parliament which it is the courts' inalienable responsibility to identify and uphold').[1]

These trends continued after 1997, frequently to ministers' exasperation (as with the successful judicial review launched by Greenpeace regarding the government's energy review). However, the Labour government also made a decisive contribution to strengthening the judicial role in politics through the 1998 Human Rights Act. The Act incorporated the ECHR into British law and made clear its comprehensive application to public administration. Judges cannot strike down legislation under the HRA, but they can issue a declaration of incompatibility; the combination of moral pressure and the prospect of a challenge before the European Court with domestic courts having already ruled against them makes ignoring such a declaration an unappealing option for ministers. Thus, while parliamentary sovereignty has not been directly challenged, ministers have always complied with declarations of non-compatibility.

The HRA has not been successfully embedded in our political culture or public consciousness. It has been associated – especially in the press – with the claims of unpopular minorities, European usurpation of British legal and democratic traditions and unwarranted judicial activism. It came into effect a year before the 9/11 attacks and has become entangled with issues of terrorism and national security, which have accounted for almost half the declarations of incompatibility issued so far. The then Labour Home Secretary, David Blunkett, complained that he was 'fed up with having to deal with a situation where parliament debates issues and the judges then overturn them' (King 2007: 141).

The Conservative leader, David Cameron, pledged to scrap the HRA and bring forward a British Bill of Rights. Cameron's proposal ran into criticism, but also struck a political chord: that the HRA was an alien implant and that something more aligned to domestic traditions was needed. *The Governance of Britain* raised the possibility of a British Bill of Rights and Duties (the latter part responding to concerns over a demanding 'rights culture'), although as a supplement to the HRA rather than as a replacement.

The 2005 Constitutional Reform Act formally separates the judiciary from both the executive (by putting the Lord Chief Justice rather than the Lord Chancellor at the head of the judiciary, and creating a new Judicial Appointments Commission) and the legislature (by transforming the Law Lords into a Supreme Court, with its separate building, staff and budget). Executive–judiciary relations – previously managed by the Lord Chancellor's 'roles of linchpin and shock-absorber' – are now governed by a Concordat negotiated in 2003–05 (McDonald 2007: 137–41). The new Supreme Court will come into being in October 2009. On paper, it is merely the Law Lords in new guise; however, it is far from clear whether its separate status will encourage different behaviour on the part of the judges, or what direction that might take. It is possible that, building on the trend towards judicial activism and identifying with an international community of active Supreme Courts, the new Court could be more assertive, which could potentially strain executive–judicial relations; alternatively, the judges' loss of the protection of the Lord Chancellor might make them more cautious.

Options

- **Augmenting the HRA with a British Bill of Rights and a statement of Duties.** The former would repackage the ECHR so that it reasserted the compatibility of the HRA with the common law tradition and with its antecedents in British history. More radically it could add specific 'British' rights over and above those set out in the ECHR, encompassing, for instance, social and economic rights. Such a move would, however, be contentious given fears over the litigation it would provoke and further judicial encroachments on areas of political debate. A statement of civic duties might also offset public concerns about a 'rights-based culture'. However, since the existing legislation would still stand, existing areas of contention (such as immigration and counter-terrorism) would remain.

- **HRA repeal – with or without a new Bill of Rights.** David Cameron's view on the HRA has been stated enough times to be taken seriously. A Conservative government might seek to follow the line that Cameron first set out in 2006, repealing the HRA and replacing it with a 'British Bill of Rights' (probably, in view of the current state of the debate, with some duties too). It would be a challenge to ensure that this Bill of Rights did what was wanted of it, notably to produce 'common sense' outcomes that were more acceptable in political and media terms than has on occasion been the case with the HRA. There are also potential conflicts with the devolved administrations if human rights policy is shifted. In addition, Cameron has pledged to remain a signatory to the ECHR, so any British Bill of Rights would need to be consonant with the Convention. If not, it would be for the judges to resolve such matters – which would, paradoxically, serve to strengthen the power of the judiciary. If the British Bill of Rights proved too difficult, the result might be a return to the status quo ante that applied from 1966 (when British citizens were first able to take cases to the Strasbourg court) until the advent of the HRA. Under either scenario, at least some of the sources of recent political–judicial conflict would be likely to remain.

- **Leaving the ECHR.** This, by far the most radical option, is not the official position of any party, and might call into question Britain's role in the EU (given the EU's requirement that member states respect fundamental rights). The policy would certainly be consistent, avoiding some of the contradictions in earlier options, but with a price in international standing that any British government would be extremely reluctant to pay. There might also be unintended consequences: would a British government that withdrew from the ECHR feel the need to bring forward its own Bill of Rights to demonstrate its liberal and human rights credentials, setting off an unpredictable domestic debate?

- **The status quo – consensus of exhaustion?** Any of the policy options above could be implemented – so long as leaders are willing to commit the requisite time and political capital in the issue. However, the HRA and ECHR may simply not be high enough on the political priority list to justify this – in which case grudging acceptance of the status quo, HRA and all, may seem the most plausible option.
- **Politicians and judges: a new equilibrium** ... The political–judicial relationship under the Concordat and with the Supreme Court in existence has yet to be tested. Judges have sometimes argued that it is parliament's inability to restrain the executive that has made them more assertive. If this is so, a strengthened parliament – perhaps working through an enhanced Joint Committee on Human Rights – might take the heat out of ministerial–judicial clashes. Better links and dialogue between parliament and the judges could play a role, such as joint sessions between Supreme Court justices and a specially constituted Select Committee, post-confirmation hearings for new Supreme Court justices, or indeed full parliamentary confirmation hearings. The latter would be deeply unwelcome to much of the judiciary, and would raise the spectre of the highly divisive confirmation hearings seen in the US, although it is uncertain whether this would be replicated.
- **... or a crisis.** If a new equilibrium is not found, and the trends of ministerial arbitrariness and judicial activism continue – the latter reinforced if the Supreme Court looks to some of its international peers and takes an expansive view of its role – then there is the significant possibility of a crisis in relations. The tensions between a 'political' view of the constitution, focusing on the electoral accountability of those who make laws, and those who see themselves as the guardians of fundamental rights and the rule of law could boil over. Under these circumstances, politicians would look for the weapons that they have to hand, the judicial budget perhaps chief among them.

Devolution and the union

Devolution for Scotland and Wales in 1997–99 was among the earliest and most sweeping of New Labour's reform measures; it is effectively irreversible; but the current arrangements also look far from stable. Much of this reflects the circumstances in which devolution was brought about, and the attitudes of the two main (Union-wide) parties. The Conservatives refused to take account of the movement of opinion – especially in Scotland – until they had been wiped out as a parliamentary force. For Labour, the imperative to head off the nationalist challenge overrode other considerations.

Funding remains a central issue. Allocations under the celebrated (and largely misunderstood) 'Barnett formula' bear little resemblance to any needs-based assessment, privileging Northern Ireland and Scotland, and underfunding Wales and England.[2] It also gives administrations in both Holyrood and Cardiff little control over their total funding, leaving them vulnerable to an involuntary squeeze if spending is cut in England.

Grievances resulting from the Barnett formula link to the wider 'English Question'. The Union's largest nation is the only one with no Parliament or Assembly of its own, and its affairs are consequently entirely conducted through the Union (Westminster) Parliament. The result is 'what those with short memories call the West Lothian Question'[3] (since it also bedevilled Gladstone's attempts at Irish Home Rule): the asymmetry arising from the ability of non-English MPs to vote on English matters while the affairs of the other countries are dealt with by the devolved assemblies. (In this, as in other respects, Wales is currently a half-way house.)

The West Lothian Question highlights the partisan dimension to territorial politics in the UK. Although the Conservatives are ideologically committed to the Union, only four out of their 193 MPs come from outside England. They may well improve this position at the next general election (with even some Northern Ireland representation through an electoral pact with the Ulster Unionists); however, there are limits to their potential breakthrough in Wales and (especially) Scotland. Labour, by contrast, hold the majority of Westminster seats in both Scotland and Wales, with 67 of their 350 MPs from outside England. For the Conservatives, there is the risk of attempting to govern the rest of the UK as a predominantly 'English party'; for Labour, it is that a future election could leave them governing England on the basis of their lopsided majorities in Scotland and Wales.

Thirdly, the institutional support for the settlement, and for relations between the different governments within the Union, remains very limited. This arguably mattered less when governments in Westminster, Holyrood and Cardiff were all of the same complexion; that has already broken down, and still sharper divergences are possible in future. (How might Nationalist or perhaps Labour politicians in Scotland or Wales react to the return of the Conservatives in London?) Although policy coordination takes place as required at an official level, there is little common political or strategic approach.

Already, in both Scotland and Wales there are pressures for changes to the settlement. In Scotland, this does not only come from the nationalists: the Calman Commission, supported by the unionist parties and by the British government, is examining the operation of the 1998 Scotland Act (Muscatelli 2008; Calman 2008). The Government of Wales Act 2006 strengthened the

Assembly and Executive somewhat and opened the prospect of the Assembly acquiring full legislative powers after a referendum. The Labour–Plaid Cymru coalition has established the All Wales Convention to consider issues related to the referendum.

Pressures for change are less threatening to the Union than are indifference and the lack of a compelling rationale. Although polling shows pro-Union majorities in all four nations, Scotland and England, in particular, have drifted apart; the Holyrood institutions' wide-ranging policy remit has made the Scottish media's focus more introspective, while the London-based media has largely ignored Scotland (Fraser 2008). While in the past empire, security, prosperity and the welfare state have all provided instrumental benefits that reinforced emotional commitment to the Union, a contemporary equivalent has proved hard to develop. Gordon Brown's efforts to appeal to shared 'British values' have so far failed to differentiate themselves from the common values of modern liberal societies. The banking and economic crisis of late 2008 gave pro-Union Labour politicians the opportunity to argue that Scotland was better off within a larger financial system; it remains to be seen how durable this argument proves.

Options

- **Tackling Barnett.** The intellectual consensus against the existing formula is now strong, while public awareness and unease about spending disparities is growing (Curtice 2008). There are plausible alternatives combining greater fiscal freedom for Scotland (and, in time, Wales) with a needs-based redistribution formula (see McLean, Lodge and Schmuecker 2008). The former would have to be part of the package: Scotland would gain something (greater financial discretion and effective self-government) in return for a less generous grant regime. The timing and politics of shifting to a new system will remain difficult, though the prospect of Barnett crunch as spending is held down across the UK might ease the transition.
- **Answering West Lothian?** This is the point of sharpest party difference. The Conservative leadership has given a sympathetic response to the modified version of 'English Votes for English Laws' (with MPs from outside England excluded from the Committee and Report stages of English bills) put forward by Ken Clarke's Democracy Task Force. Labour remains opposed to change. Each stance has its difficulties. Critics of the Conservative approach argue that there will be difficulties in defining the territorial extent of legislation, that this will have implications for the role of the Speaker, and that political conflict might arise whenever a UK government lacked a majority within England; Labour can be seen as still refusing to address the question, which could prove difficult to sustain.

- **The English Question: other answers?** Neither an English Parliament nor regional government is likely to provide resolution. The first faces the problem of England's overwhelming predominance within the Union, and its lack of mass support. The second was scuttled by a decisive 'no' vote in the North East referendum in 2004. Decentralization to existing English local government is more promising, and worth doing for its own sake (see next section); however, it is unlikely to embrace the scale of legislative autonomy already available to Scotland and in future probably to Wales too.
- **Devolution and the electoral system.** Advocates of Proportional Representation for Westminster argue that it could ease many of these problems by reducing the stark differences in representation of parties within the UK's different nations. Yet this could only ever be a secondary argument for a change to the electoral system. In addition, the Conservatives remain strongly committed to the status quo, while the reform option to which Labour is more open, the Alternative Vote, is non-proportional and thus of limited relevance to redressing the balance within the nations.
- **Legislative powers for Wales: a problem for the parties.** The Government of Wales Act 2006 gives the Assembly enhanced legislative powers under an Order in Council mechanism (Legislative Competence Orders – LCOs), and allows for full primary legislative powers after a referendum. There is a powerful logic to clarifying Wales' ambiguous status, but conflicts between the Assembly and the Welsh Affairs Committee over the scope of LCOs suggests that further devolution could be a divisive issue within both the Conservative and Labour parties.
- **The Union: strengthening the mechanisms.** Options include: a Department of the Nations to consolidate the work of the Scottish, Welsh and Northern Ireland offices (for which there is in any case a strong efficiency argument); a revival and strengthening of the Joint Ministerial Committee as a starting point of enhancing joint working between governments; and a statement of Union-wide guarantees and examination of the Union dimension in devolved areas such as health. There has also been interest across the political spectrum in recasting a reformed Lords as a chamber of the nations; however, the question of English representation would be problematic, and so far the parties' interest in Lords reform remains focused on a directly elected chamber.

Parliament

For many parliamentary reformers, the two greatest prizes – changing the electoral system of the House of Commons, and replacing the House of Lords with an elected second chamber – remained unfulfilled after more than a decade of Labour in power. Nonetheless, there has been significant change in Parliament – some of it reflecting the law of unintended consequences.

Electoral reform of the Commons never got very far. The Jenkins Commission reported briskly by September 1998, advocating a semi-proportional 'AV [Alternative Vote] plus' system which maintained the single member constituency. The Blair government did not, however, act on the recommendation and references in subsequent Labour manifestos followed a Cheshire Cat trajectory. Although ministers, including Justice Secretary Jack Straw, have shown some interest in AV, the issue has remained on the back burner. Nonetheless, for elections outside Westminster, Labour has been an innovator, using the Supplementary Vote for the London mayoralty and the Additional Member System (AMS) for the Scottish Parliament, Welsh Assembly and London Assembly.

When the Blair government expelled most of the hereditary peers in 1999, Conservative critics charged that it was creating a pliant second chamber. Whatever the government's intentions, the result was the exact opposite: the Lords' confidence has been enhanced by shedding their association with hereditary privilege, while the removal of the hereditary peers means that no one party holds a majority, which puts additional pressure on the government of the day to win the support of the Lords in order to carry its legislation. In the 2001–05 Parliament, the government was defeated on 245 occasions, double the level seen in the first Blair term, and covering issues as disparate as animal health and terrorism (Cowley and Stuart 2005). This has carried over into the succeeding parliamentary term: it was the Lords who dispatched government proposals for holding terrorist suspects for 42 days without charge, although unease on the government's Commons benches undoubtedly deterred ministers from seeking to confront the Upper House.

An elected Lords was supposed to follow the expulsion of the hereditaries (just as it was supposed to follow the 1911 Parliament Act). Since 1997, there have been 'four white papers … along with a Royal Commission, two joint Parliamentary committees, and two votes in parliament' on Lords reform (Russell 2008: 268). This activity has yet to yield an outcome. It has, however, produced a shift in opinion. Early proposals were for a largely appointed Upper House, and in its votes in 2003 the Commons rejected all the reform options. However, Commons votes in March 2007 showed majorities for both an 80% and 100% elected Upper House. A subsequent Justice Ministry White Paper, *An Elected Second Chamber* (July 2008), indicated a fair degree of cross-party consensus (at least between the party leaderships); however, action has been deferred until (at least) the next parliament.

Efforts to improve the working of the Commons had mixed effects. There were significant changes under the ambiguous rubric of 'modernization'. However, even with a committed reformer such as Robin Cook as Leader of the House, measures that helped the executive get its business through (such as timetabling) fared better than those which enhanced scrutiny (such as removing Select Committee appointments from the control of the whips). Nonetheless, there have been some modest (and patchily utilized) but useful reforms: Westminster Hall debates, extra payments for chairs of Select Committees, the Prime Minister's appearances before the Liaison Committee, the replacement of Standing Committees with Public Bill Committees (with their ability to call expert witnesses), the growth of pre-legislative scrutiny and the prospect of systematic post-legislative scrutiny. Meanwhile, the long-term trend towards more frequent rebellions against the party whip, which began in the 1970s, has reached new highs: the 2001–05 Parliament was the most rebellious of recent times, and the trend has continued since the 2005 election.

Options

- **Commons voting reform**. A move to a fully proportional system still looks unlikely; past experience of hung parliaments gives little indication of the Liberal Democrats' ability to enforce it on reluctant bigger parties. A move to AV is a slightly stronger possibility; Labour might see it as an anti-Conservative device, and the Liberal Democrats as a staging post to a more proportional system (though neither assumption would necessarily hold true). The Conservatives remain firmly committed to a powerful single-party executive, and a voting system that supports that.
- **PR for the second chamber**. This is a concession that the Liberal Democrats might have a better chance of extracting in a hung parliament; it could be slightly more acceptable to the major parties, especially Labour. The Conservative Front Bench is so far opposed – this remains one of the points of contention between the two parties – but it is perhaps less of a sticking-point than PR for the Commons. Arguably, this would undermine the legitimacy of a first past the post Commons (especially given the use of other electoral systems elsewhere in the UK); however, Australia uses a non-proportional system (AV) for its lower house and a proportional one for its upper house. There could be a distinction between the role of one chamber (to provide a clear government) and that of the other (to scrutinize legislation with no party holding a majority).
- **An elected second chamber**. In spite of the formal cross-party consensus in favour of an elected second chamber, and the Commons votes of March 2007, this does not seem imminent. For any government, it offers no particular political benefit while draining parliamentary time and necessitating use of the Parliament Act. There are still many sceptics within the Commons and strong opposition to change within the Lords (both propositions apply particularly to the Conservatives). The relatively feisty appointed chamber that has emerged unexpectedly since 1999 may thus prove to be a durable 'temporary' expedient. Indeed gradualist

measures to strengthen the semi-reformed Lords such as the removal of the remaining hereditaries, putting the Independent Appointments Commission on a statutory footing, and the introduction of a retirement age may well be adopted if consensus on more fundamental change cannot be reached. The only circumstances in which radical change might emerge are as part of a cross-party deal in a hung parliament, or as a result of a 1909–11-style confrontation with the Commons.

- **A (somewhat) stronger Commons.** *The Governance of Britain* included a number of measures – supported by broad cross-party consensus – to enhance the role of the Commons in relation to treaties, commitment of troops, public appointments and its own recall and dissolution. However, measures with more effective rather than symbolic significance – such as greater control by the Commons over its own timetable through a cross-party business committee, or the election of Select Committee chairmen by the full House – have been advocated in various reports but not taken up. Not even these measures would overturn the powerful position of the executive (nor were they intended to do so), but they would enhance the Commons' capacity for more effective challenge and scrutiny.

Central–local relations

In opposition, Labour had been critical of the centralism of the Thatcher and Major governments: rate-capping, unilateral restructuring of local authorities and the transfer of functions to quangos. In practice, however, Labour has demonstrated a Jekyll and Hyde approach to local government. Dr Jekyll

- reinstated London-wide government
- modified the restrictive *ultra vires* regime by giving local government a 'power of well-being'
- encouraged stronger and more visible local leadership through elected mayors and a leader and cabinet model
- enhanced local government's 'convening' role in local partnerships.

However, when it came to

- a reversion to rate-capping
- an onerous and elaborate regime of targets and performance management
- increasing use of ring-fenced grants; and
- continued, sometimes increasing reliance on quangos and agencies

Mr Hyde was firmly in control.

While some ministers were genuinely committed to strengthening local authorities, and 'localism' became a fashionable buzzword across political parties, it encountered – and still encounters – a set of formidable road blocks.

The first impasse concerned finance. Local government remained a one club golfer, solely dependent on a highly visible property tax. By 2003, double-digit council tax increases had led to a reintroduction of capping. Neither the 2003–04 Balance of Funding Review nor the review by Sir Michael Lyons produced significant changes to council tax, and the modest proposals in the latter's final report (council tax revaluations, and changes to banding) had politicians of both major parties running for cover. The only potentially significant change being taken forward is for Supplementary Business Rates. Meanwhile, tax accounts for only a quarter of local authority spending, one of the lowest shares in the OECD, while the transfer of education funding to a specific grant tightened the screws further.

Structures were a second roadblock. The drive towards directly elected regional authorities – never wholeheartedly supported within government – came to a halt with its heavy rejection in the North East, the area supposedly most receptive to it, in November 2004. What remained was a predominantly technocratic structure to which a variety of planning and economic development functions had been passed, and which the *Review of Sub-National Economic Development and Regeneration* (HM Treasury 2007f) proposed to enhance. The government also toyed with extending the 1990s Conservative push towards unitary authorities; the resulting piecemeal reviews chipped away at the 1974 two-tier structure without comprehensively replacing it.

A third factor was the government's focus on public services, and the distrust by both ministers and civil servants of local government's capacity to deliver them effectively, combined with the resistance of media and public opinion to local variation (the 'postcode lottery' argument). Best Value, introduced in 2000 as a supposedly flexible replacement for Compulsory Competitive Tendering, became an extraordinarily intense and over-prescriptive performance management system. In 2002 it was supplemented by Comprehensive Performance Assessment, which aimed to scrutinize and enhance councils' leadership capacity. While CPA was widely credited with aiding a drive for improvement in local government, the system of 'upwards accountability' was increasingly criticized for its cost, distortions and stultifying impact on local initiative (see, e.g., Gutiérrez-Romero, Haubrich and McLean 2008).

The centralizing drive peaked around 2004, and there have since been signs of a cautious reappraisal. The Lyons Review stressed local government's 'place-shaping role'; while cautious in its specific recommendations, it reinforced a growing critical consensus about the pervasiveness of central control. The White Paper *Strong and Prosperous Communities* (2006) and subsequent legislation in 2007 reduced target-setting, scaled back specific grants a little and strengthened local government's leadership role of public service agencies through a mutual 'duty to cooperate'.

In spite of these signs of progress, policy remains deadlocked. There is little progress on finance; there are now 'only' 198 national indicators that local government must track; while the SNR, mingling warm words about the role of local government in economic growth with further transfers of functions to the regional tier, is a reminder of the centre's at best ambivalent thinking.

Options

- **Constitutional protection for local government.** The *Governance of Britain* Green Paper (July 2007) had relatively little to say about local government, but proposed a 'Concordat' governing central–local relations, which was duly delivered in December. The then chairman of the Local Government Association (LGA) argued, convincingly, that the relationship should be formalized further through a cross-party 'constitutional convention' (Milton 2007: 11).
- **Finance: greater autonomy and buoyancy.** Although neither major party is currently willing to go beyond limited measures related to business rates, more wide-ranging options are available. The LGA has argued for a 'combination option': a reformed council tax, relocalized business rates and some element of income tax, perhaps initially via assignment of part of the tax take (an option favoured also by Lyons) and with scope for local rate variation in the longer term. Similar proposals have been put forward elsewhere; without greater financial independence, policy autonomy will remain elusive.
- **Regions, sub-regions, city regions.** 2005–07 saw intense debate within government over the respective merits of city regions (in many ways, a throwback to the Redcliffe-Maud report of 1969) and of the emerging regional structure. The LGA, meanwhile, argued for sub-regions (which could embrace city regions) as a key organizing unit: natural economic areas, crossing local authority boundaries and so requiring cooperation, but smaller than the government regions (LGA 2007). The SNR reflected an uneasy equilibrium between these concepts; the Conservatives, by contrast, are likely to pare back regions and focus on sub-regions.
- **Regaining powers.** The LGA used its sub-regional analysis to argue for a variety of powers – relating to skills, employment, infrastructure, economic development and other areas – to be devolved to councils working together at this level. In Further Education and youth policy, the government has undertaken a modest (and highly qualified) return of functions to local authorities. Planning represents a point of difference between the parties, with the Conservatives committed to reversing the transfer of strategic planning to the regions under the 2004 Planning and Compulsory Purchase Act. To the degree that local authorities take

back powers, it eases some of the accountability muddle inherent in the wide range of local partnerships; however, a significant role for partnerships is likely to continue, with both parties committed to Local Area Agreements (LAAs). There may be scope to make these more truly local and to enhance local government's leadership role.

- **Mayors.** The institution of a London mayor looks durable: both Ken Livingstone and his successor Boris Johnson have made the job a highly visible part of the political landscape. However, there has been limited success in promoting the mayoral model elsewhere under the 2000 Local Government Act, though this is largely because the Act effectively handed local authorities a veto over the mayoral policy. Given local government's strong opposition to mayors it is hardly surprising that only a dozen mayors have been introduced (and one is due to be scrapped), mostly in medium-sized towns. However, the clear delegation of responsibility to visible leaders makes mayors attractive to ministers. The *Communities in Control* White Paper (July 2008) made clear ministers' wish to encourage adoption of elected mayors. The Conservatives are also sympathetic, with the leadership responding positively to the proposal by Michael Heseltine's Cities Task Force for elected mayors with wide-ranging regeneration powers in major cities (DCLG 2008; Conservative Party Cities Task Force 2007). Thus, in spite of reservations about concentrations of power, diminution of the role of councillors (already an issue with the Leader and Cabinet system) and difficulties in applying it outside urban areas, the mayoral model is likely to continue to spread. Indeed they may be key to encouraging a more radical transfer in power from the centre to the locality.
- **Participatory democracy.** Alongside their enthusiasm for directly elected mayors, national politicians have sought 'double devolution' – from local councils to communities, as well from the centre to local councils (curiously, they have sometimes seemed more enthusiastic about the former than the latter). *The Governance of Britain* (Ministry of Justice 2007) encouraged initiatives in participatory budgeting, citizens' juries and an enhanced role for local petitions; these and other measures were central to the subsequent *Communities in Control* Green Paper. The Conservatives, meanwhile, have shown interest in local referendums, including on larger council tax increases. Both the government (in the Policing Green Paper) and the Conservatives have supported directly elected police chiefs, which would enhance local accountability but raises the question of conflicting mandates with that of the local authority. Although developments towards more participatory politics have been incremental (and often merely reflect practice among many local authorities), there is likely to be further movement in this direction under governments of either party.

- **Guidance and performance management.** There is clearly a strong case for further reduction in central guidance and performance management, not only in the regime of targets, indicators and inspection, but also in what Sir Michael Lyons called 'softer and less direct controls such as guidance, central encouragements and conditions on grant' (Lyons 2007: 79). This presents challenges for both major parties, but especially for Labour, given the party's traditional attachment to a strong central state as a guarantor of social justice. Against this, the continuing divergences apparent from any Ofsted or Audit Commission report make clear that an overstretched central state cannot deliver the same outcomes everywhere. The experience from highly egalitarian countries such as those in Scandinavia suggests that local choice and variation, backed by national minimum standards, can produce outcomes that would meet Labour aspirations (Lodge 2007).

Conclusion: power and participation

No grand design lay behind Labour's constitutional reforms. One implication of this ad hocery is that the cumulative impact of the various reforms (some of which are still on-going) is hard to judge. Nonetheless, it is clear that over the next decade governments will have to work with the consequences of the reforms for the way that power is exercised in the UK. They will also confront a continuing issue that the reforms failed to resolve: the decline in political participation.

Power

How far has the traditional British constitution, based on parliamentary sovereignty and majoritarianism, been usurped by one now characterized by a stronger separation of powers, and more effective checks and balances? How far have British governments engaged in 'power-shedding'? (King 2007: 355.)

There have been major changes. The HRA has strengthened the role of the judiciary in the constitution and reinforced the more assertive role of judges. Devolution limits the reach of Westminster in the affairs of Scotland, Wales and Northern Ireland on devolved matters. The removal of the hereditary peers, combined with the absence of single-party control, have made the Lords more willing to challenge and defeat the government. The last ten years have also seen the expansion of independent regulators (such as an independent Bank) and arms-length constitutional bodies (e.g. the Electoral Commission and the Information Commissioner), which have added further constraints on the executive. In turn, the reforms are likely to generate further changes: there are points of tension around the English Question, the judiciary's relations with the executive (and perhaps the legislature) and possibly the House of Lords.

In two respects, however, there has been much less change. In England, Whitehall has significantly tightened its grip over local government and large swathes of the public services. Centralization in this domain has greatly outweighed the power government has ceded to the devolved institutions. Secondly, Britain retains powerful single-party government whose relationship to the Commons is little changed. International comparisons and recent events highlight the concentration of power in the executive branch. Whereas the US Treasury Secretary, Hank Paulson, had to battle through Congress for approval of the bank bailout, Gordon Brown was able to commit billions of pounds without recourse to any parliamentary vote.

Participation

Labour's 1997 manifesto argued that 'there is a crisis of confidence in our democracy' and that what was needed to deal with this was a large dose of constitutional reform. Yet the reforms have coincided with a *rise* in political disaffection and disengagement – political participation is at an all-time historic low (Thornberry, Muir and Kearns 2007: 280).

Some apparent disengagement may reflect short-term conditions. Turnout fell significantly in the 1997 and 2001 general elections, and revived only marginally in 2005, but this may well be because Labour's electoral hegemony was barely challenged by the Conservatives, and because economic conditions were benign. Economic downturn and pressure on public finances will raise what is at stake and thus may affect turnout. Equally, the revival of the Conservatives will intensify political competition; the 2008 US election and the 2007 French presidential election suggest that this could push up turnout.

However, the evidence of declining political participation is much clearer when it is broken down by age and socioeconomic class, and paints a worrying picture of rising inequality over the last forty years. The turnout gap between the highest and lowest income groups in 1964 was 7%; by 2005 it had nearly doubled to 13% (Keaney and Rogers 2006). Similarly, the gap in participation between the 18–24 age group and those over 65 has grown from 8 percentage points in 1970 to 40 percentage points in 2005 (ibid). This rise in political inequality raises important questions for policymakers about the relative influence of different groups in British political life – although the answer may be as much political as constitutional.

For some constitutional reformers, the failure of the post-1997 programme to deliver the new politics that they sought is evidence that it was too piecemeal and did not go far enough. However, international evidence does not support the claim that a proportional electoral system or an elected second chamber would have any real impact on boosting political participation. Effective responses are likely to be found much closer to citizens' daily lives.

The recognition that citizens can most effectively engage with the political process at the local level lay behind the Blair/Brown governments' rhetoric of 'double devolution'. There has also been growing interest across the spectrum in more participatory forms of democracy, whether in citizens' juries and participatory budgeting on the left, or referendums and direct election of officials on the right (Carswell and Hannan 2008). So far, however, there has been no real movement on the first part of this equation; local government's (precarious) role in the constitution has continued to be undermined, while the steady expansion of local partnership bodies has helped to generate a profound accountability muddle that has further confused the public. If participation is to be meaningful, both these trends need to be reversed. An effective approach to political engagement could be to link some of the 'new democratic processes' with the dog that did not bark in the post-1997 reforms: a programme of decentralization and empowered local government in England.

Notes

1. R. v. Secretary of State for Transport ex parte Factortame Ltd (No. 2) [1991] 1. A.C. 603; Thoburn v. Sunderland City Council, [2002] 3 WLR 247; McDonald (2007) pp. 183–4 (Craig Parsons), and 146 (Kate Malleson).
2. In 2007–08 Northern Ireland and Scotland received 21% above the UK average spend per head, while Wales and England received, respectively, 8% and 3% below the UK average spend per head (McLean, Lodge and Schmuecker 2008).
3. The phrase is that of the constitutional lawyer Brigid Hadfield, quoted by McLean (2005).

Conclusion

David Halpern and Iain McLean

Politics can be a thankless task. If you solve a problem, it is soon forgotten. Instead, you are judged by your failures, your ability to take on new challenges; and by the resonance of your message with the values, aspirations and fears of the public. As one ex-Minister commented, 'elections are won by parties that own the future'.

The good news is that the great challenges of the past generally have been overcome, though often leaving in their wake new problems for the next generation and government to address. Britain's problems with inflation and industrial unrest in the 1970s were overcome, not least by the tough medicine of the Thatcher years, but left in their wake major concerns over unemployment that dominated much of the 1980s. As unemployment fell in the mid-1990s, public concerns came to focus on public services, and particularly health and education. These concerns dominated the 1997 election, and helped sweep Labour to power (see Figure 16.1).

After a decade of heavy investment, public services were no longer a dominant concern among the public. By the mid-2000s, public concerns about defence and terrorism (including the War in Iraq); race and immigration; and crime and anti-social behaviour had come to the fore. These concerns played a big part in the 2005 election (see also Halpern 2009).

At the time of writing, and in the wake of the global slowdown, public concerns have remerged around the economy in a way that has not been seen since the early 1990s. These new concerns have further displaced the public's previous concerns about public services, and to some extent those over immigration and terrorism. Concerns about crime, however, remain strong.

The history of public concerns tells a powerful story of the changing landscape of British politics and policy, but does not tell the whole story of the challenges that face governments and societies.

Continuity and change: 1996 vs. 2009

When *Options for Britain I* was published, Britain was approaching what turned out to be a decisive shift in politics. A Conservative government had been in

Most important issues facing Britain in election years (% public see as key issue)

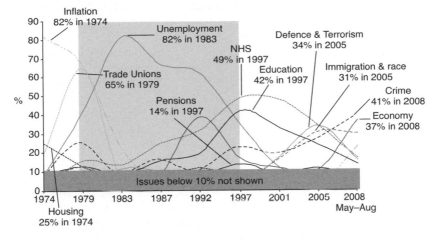

Figure 16.1 Public Concerns in the UK, 1974–2008

Notes: Light grey area indicates period of Conservative government; lines based on average concerns in election years. Separate code for 'economy' starts from 1987.

Source: Data from Ipsos MORI.

power for 17 years, and a youthful opposition leader was agitating for change. Today, the Labour government faces what looks like a similar challenge, with low popularity in the polls and a tough election approaching. The outcome, of course, is by no means certain. An election result much like 1992 is highly possible, when John Major hung on to power in the face of similarly negative polls and public concerns about the economy. It is also conceivable that Labour will learn the trick of its Scandinavian sister parties to reinvent and refresh itself and hold power for another generation. Or it could be wiped out, and the hour-glass of British politics turned once again.

What is certain is that the political landscape of the coming election will be very different to that of 1997. In retrospect, the public-service-dominated politics of the late 1990s and early 2000s had a simplicity very different to that of today. During that period, the political virility of parties' commitments to public services could be roughly measured by the scale of their financial pledges to the public sector. Of course, both sides talked about 'reform', but against the background of the self-evidently low spending on public services in Britain compared with other European countries at the time, money did a lot of political talking. That argument is not so easy to run today. Spending on public services in the UK has moved decisively towards the European average, and away from the lower levels of the USA. In as far as 1997 was a choice, Britons chose the European model. But the public are far from convinced by the case for more spending above current levels, and the global downturn has greatly reduced room for manoeuvre. Instead parties will have to argue more around their competence to run public services, rather than their commitment to fund them, though doubtless this will play at the margins too.

In retrospect, and on the evidence presented in the chapters in this volume, the dominant issues of 1996–97 also look surprisingly 'domestic'. A cursory glance at changing public concerns, or even a comparison of chapter titles in the two *Options* volumes, hint at the change. Though we might be 'cheap-talk' environmentalists (see Introduction and Chapters 10 and 11), there is no doubt that global environmental limitations are pressing into political and everyday awareness in a way very different to even a decade ago. Terrorism is no longer a matter of conflict in Northern Ireland (though this still simmers) but of global ideological conflict. Energy security is a familiar phrase in a nation that has rapidly switched from an exporter to one dependent on often unstable and distant parts of the world. A discussion on 'Britain in Europe' that dominated debate a decade ago has been decisively broadened to 'Britain in the World', in terms of our interests, interdependencies, and institutions. And if any doubt remained, the credit crunch has decisively reminded or informed us all of just how interdependent our world has become.

This all said, political scientists can point to continuities too. Analyses of transitions across governments show that, behind the rhetoric of change, the continuities across governments are often greater than the differences (Hogwood 1992; Halpern and Wood 1996; Halpern 2009). Blair did not throw out the labour market reforms of Thatcher, and even where policy initially seemed to mark a sharp divide with previous Conservative reforms – such as in education and health – government often quietly found its way back to a similar path.

Old hands might highlight the current financial crisis, and the responses to it, as a return to 'business as usual'. The current government, perhaps quite rightly, is planning to stimulate the economy in a manner that Keynes would have been proud of. In so doing, debt will increase and taxes will rise (and/or spending fall) after the next election. If the stimulus package is successful, the government will surely hope to be re-elected. If it fails, it will saddle its successor with debt and difficult and unpopular decisions. We may like to think of ourselves as more economically and analytically sophisticated than those who have gone before us, but this is surely a pattern that politicians and commentators would recognize from many previous governments.

How did Labour do?

All of our authors were asked to assess how Labour had done since 1997: what did it seek to do, and did it work? It is difficult to do justice to such a large exercise in a few words: the conclusions vary across and within policy areas, and are subject to debate. Our view then, should be taken as a personal and tentative one.

Let us start with the successes – areas where we might at least award the government something in the range 'A+' to 'A–', or at least a B+. These include:

- **Science and technology policy.** Though not an issue of much interest to the public, the Labour government's performance on science policy, and particularly in relation to the universities, has been a quiet but marked success. The aspiration to be 'world class' is over-used, but is appropriate in this area. The strong performance was partly based on policies commenced before 1997, but unlike in some other areas of policy, this was built on smoothly with an effective combination of investment and further reform. The strong performance in this area should also pay dividends in future growth, if econometric models are to be believed (Guellec and van Pottelsberghe de la Potterie 2004; and Grant and Krapels, Chapter 7). [A+]
- **Health.** As we have seen, public concerns about the NHS were a powerful force in both the 1997 and 2001 elections. After something of a faltering start, it is fair to say that the Labour government has significantly delivered on health, though at a hefty price. As Appleby and Coutts show, satisfaction with the NHS is running at historic highs, with improvements in morbidity, waiting times and a historically unusual absence of conflict with professionals. But the price has been high, and questions hang over how the NHS will handle the inevitable slowdown in investment and the settling in of current reforms. [A]
- **Northern Ireland.** Again, though not a high priority in the public mind, the achievement of an uneasy peace in Northern Ireland has been one of the quiet successes of the last 12 years. It required considerable focus, and some credit to the government is due as well as the determination and courage of many on the ground. However, there is a real danger that those in Westminster will think this is a 'job done', focus lost, and history will repeat itself. In particular, there is a need to maintain the hard slog of building stable and mature institutions, parties and economy that will be self-sustaining for generations to come. [A]
- **Constitutional reform.** Pre-97, constitutional experts warned Labour not to attempt too much legislation on constitutional matters. However, armed with such a large majority (and self-imposed fiscal constraints that limited action in other areas), the incoming government launched a remarkable set of 'modernizing' measures. These include the creation of the Scottish Parliament, Welsh Assembly, Mayors and the incorporation of the ECHR into UK law. Some have argued that these changes, and their ramifications, will stand out long after the post-97 Labour government's other achievements and disappointments have faded in the memory. But despite their scale, the reforms were curiously 'British' – in a Heath Robinson sense – in that a number of obvious gaps and inconsistencies

remain, with patches that will have to be added by later governments to address the new problems created by the settlements. [A–]

- **Economic growth.** For much of the last 12 years, the UK economy has experienced a strong growth rate, with GDP per capita overtaking that of a number of historic rivals. Equally impressively, income growth has been relatively evenly spread across the rich and poor, in marked contrast to the 1980s. The growth was premised on a fairly benign international context, but was helped by a mix of good fiscal and monetary policy, policies to get people into work, economic immigration and so on – but also by increased private debt and asset price inflation. Given the recent downturn, subsequent scholars may revise this positive grade, but some credit will still be due for more than a decade of strong, and even, growth and low inflation (see Weale and Crafts chapters). [A–, tentatively revised to a B+]

The areas above were ones that our authors broadly rated as successes. A number of others are best described as being 'mixed'. In a crude sense, these might be thought of as meriting a rating in the range 'B+' to 'B–'.

- **Crime.** This is a controversial area, but surely merits rating as a broad success. By all measures – except the public's answer to the question 'do you think crime has fallen?' – crime and fear has fallen dramatically (Hough and Roberts chapter). In fact, in terms of the scale of improvement, one could argue that the reduction in crime dwarfs the scale of improvement in other hard outcomes such as health or educational attainment. However, there are a number of qualifications that suggest that Labour cannot take all the credit. The fall clearly began before 1997, and appears to be common across a number of countries. Also, there is good evidence that much of the spending and political impetus (across all parties) is largely causally irrelevant to the decline, and has more to do with being seen to respond to public concern. Still, on objective facts alone, plus the contribution of more helpful policies such as neighbourhood policing, target hardening, drug treatment and youth redirection, it has to be rated as a clear overall success. [B+]
- **Education.** This is often highlighted as one of the post-1997 Labour government's early successes, particularly in relation to primary school education. However, viewed in the round over 12 years, the track record in education policy and achievement is perhaps best described as 'positive but with significant areas of concern'. Education policy has been characterized by considerable internal contradiction over the period. Coherence may be over-rated, but the scale of the differences in approach across primary, secondary, further, higher and adult education and training drawn out by Wolf are striking and also seem to correspond with the differential performance across the sector.

Educational attainment remains shockingly uneven across social groups. Great hopes are now pinned on the ambitious expansion of early years interventions and support, but this, like other areas of educational policy, has been dogged by dogma, rather than ruthless evidence-based spending. Nonetheless, educational attainment has generally improved, even though international comparisons suggest that it has a long way to go to be world-class in depth. The improvement and investment has certainly been enough to help remove education from the top of public concerns since 1997, meriting a decent, if not outstanding overall grade. [B]

- **Foreign policy.** This has been an area of marked contrasts, certainly in terms of political controversies and public attitudes. In Chalmers' measured review, and through the discussions at *Options* conferences, we begin to get a more rounded sense of the post-1997 administration's performance in this area incorporating but dominated by the rawness of feelings around the invasion of Iraq. Outside the shadow of Iraq, there have been some marked successes. The substantial expansion in the aid budget (including its loosening from more narrow trade objectives) has been another quiet success that has brought both real relief and considerable respect for the UK in the donor community. Chalmers also highlights the relative successes the UK has had as a leader of humanitarian military interventions, in contrast to its relative failure when serving as a junior partner of the USA. [B–]

- **Poverty, mobility and inequality.** One of the classic divides across the political spectrum is the extent of focus on inequality and poverty. The post-1997 administration sought to navigate a mid-line between Labour's historic desire to reduce poverty and inequality and the public's appetite for redistribution. As mentioned above, perhaps the government's biggest success in this area was to achieve income growth that was more evenly spread than in the previous administration, particularly in the face of global forces that have been sharpening the tendency for 'winner takes all'. Both pensioner poverty and child poverty were reduced, especially in the middle years of the administration, and the success of getting more people into work saved billions of pounds that could be better spent elsewhere. However, as Kenway and Blanden highlight, the drive to reduce poverty and increase mobility has been hard going, and in some respects disappointing. There are real concerns about 'in-work poverty'; inequality has not reduced; and – though there are promising signs in the most recent data – a transformation in social mobility has yet to materialize. Perhaps most worrying, there has been stubbornly little change in certain groups of particular concern, notably numbers on incapacity benefit and 'NEETs' (young people not in employment, education or training). Certainly judged against the administration's own high hopes, this is a policy area characterized by a mix of hard won successes, but also notable disappointments. [B–]

Finally, are there policy areas where the Labour administration can be said to have been genuinely weaker, at least in comparison with its relative success in other areas. Again, in crude terms, these might be viewed as 'C's.

- **Environment.** As noted above, though much talked about by policy-wonks for decades, this is an issue that has finally forced itself on the mainstream policy agenda in recent years (see Gallo et al chapter). That said, we mostly remain 'cheap-talk' environmentalists, and the issue has yet to surface in any significant way in the public's sense of everyday concerns. This is not unique to the UK – there is not a single European country within which concern about the environment has made it into the public's top three concerns. But other governments seem to have made more progress over the last 12 years in quietly and concretely progressing the agenda, such as through the promotion of renewable energy generation. The UK has now made bold and arguably world-leading commitments with some imaginative thinking around carbon trading and policy, but this is an area notoriously littered with good intentions. Rated on action alone, the post-97 administration has at best a moderate record in this area. [C+]
- **Transport.** Never the most exciting area, but still important, transport has been repeatedly identified as one of the UK's weak links in recent years. As Wellings explains, this has been characterized by modest pledges on which government has failed to deliver. Policy has also oscillated over the last 12 years in an area that desperately needs long-term planning. This is a policy area that requires boldness and imagination to navigate through the complex tensions between public, business, environmental and fiscal constraints. There is no reason, in principle, why in 15–20 years we could not all be driving electric vehicles, charged by renewables overnight; on generous and free-flowing roads; with efficient and comfortable public transport. It may be that policy is now starting to fall into place, but on the basis of the last 12 years, this has not been an area of great success. [C]
- **Housing and planning.** Of all the major policy areas, housing and planning is one with arguably one of the weakest records. The UK has consistently failed to build enough housing (see Nickell chapter), and planning and infrastructure is consistently identified as a brake on UK growth (Crafts chapter). But, as Nickell shows, there is no great mystery as to why: the incentives in our planning system work strongly against development. Politically fraught though this area is, most other countries do seem to have found more successful ways of balancing

appropriate local controls and sensitivity to growth with the demand for housing and improved infrastructure. [C–]

In sum, it is a pretty respectable record. Ironically, if it were not for the hyperbole of claims often made along the way, the public would be more impressed. But as Bok observed in his classic study of government and public sector performance, improvements in outcomes don't necessarily translate into public affection or trust (Bok 2001).

Options and choices

An incoming, or incumbent, government faces a wide variety of challenges. Each of these brings with them policy choices and options, not only for the government but for society more widely.

The Prime Minister and Cabinet will find their red boxes populated by issues coming from at least four different sources (see Figure 16.2). First there will be the need to respond to public concerns, the changing flux we have already seen in Figure 16.1. Second there will be 'external imperatives' or threats that need to be dealt with regardless of whether the public are currently tuned into them. Third, there will be host of 'boring but important' issues that will flood in from officials, administrative concerns about failing and underperforming sectors and institutions that need to be fixed. Finally, the government will have its party-based political objectives that it wishes to deliver on, that get its activists out of bed in the morning and that motivated its drive for power. In the last few pages, we will use this framework to briefly consider some of the key choices that face the Prime Minister(s) of 2009–15.

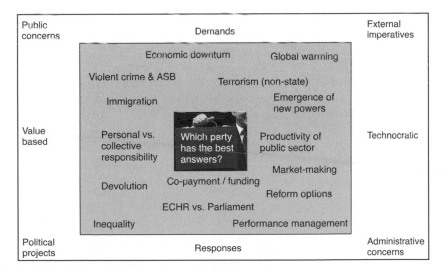

Figure 16.2   A Conceptual Map of the Issues Facing the UK in 2008–09

Public concerns – economy, crime and immigration

Public concerns frame the imperatives that elected governments must deal with to survive, though it is worth noting that political parties themselves help to shape these concerns (Heath and Roberts 2008).

The economy

At the time of writing, the pre-budget report of 2008 and the responses of the Opposition to it have tentatively defined the choices facing Britain in the coming years – the gamble on spending now versus pain later. One view, at least hinted at by Weale, is that in reality governments don't have much of a choice about economic policy and, short of messing it up completely, much of what they do has little impact on overall growth rates. But it is clear that there are at least some choices here. These include:

- Avoiding (or embracing) a retreat into protectionism. To date, there remains a political consensus to avoid protectionism. But this view is not shared across countries (including sections of the EU and US), and the temptation to break ranks may resurface as an election nears, especially if jobs are at risk.
- In the medium to long term, certain investments are thought to have an impact on growth rates, such as in research and development, education and infrastructure. There is always a difficult political judgement to be made between investing now for benefits that may not be seen for five to ten years at least, versus forms of spending that give a feel-good payback within the parliamentary timetable.
- There may also be less conventional options that a bold administration might consider. Econometric models previously suggested that joining the euro-zone would boost growth over a 50-year period, but a killer argument against was the impact it would have on inflating fixed asset prices. At a time of falling asset prices, perhaps the option should be considered again? Other options include fostering citizen-produced information about products and services in order to oil the working of markets and enhance growth (Halpern 2009); or, as set out by Wren-Lewis in this volume (Box 2.1), creating an independent fiscal council to help steer governments to responsible fiscal habits and protect sterling.

Crime

Whether rational or not, public concern about crime remains a powerful issue in British politics, and seems set to remain so for the foreseeable future. There are several options, most of which are not incompatible.

- We could maintain our current trajectory of prison building, tougher sentences and even tougher talking. The evidence is that this does work a bit, but at enormous cost. Still, we are a relatively rich country, and this is a real option.

- The evidence suggests that there is a considerable range of efficacy in our criminal justice responses. For the politically bold, a systematic shift of the criminal justice system and wider public service resources into the more effective forms of intervention could significantly reduce crime at current levels of spending. This includes interventions such as drug treatments in prison, treating alcohol as a public health issue, strengthening the human side and discretion in relation to probation, and perhaps the wider legal prescription of heroin (see Hough and Roberts chapter).
- The best long-term option, perhaps surprisingly, may be to go 'tough on pro-social behaviour and the causes of pro-social behaviour', to adapt a familiar phrase.

Immigration and cohesion

Public concern about immigration, and particularly around flash-point issues such as reputed special treatment of asylum seekers, has reached all-time highs in recent years. It may be that the economic downturn and the exiting of migrant workers will take the sting out of this issue, though history also warns that times of hardship can also unleash deep ethnic hostilities. The efficacy of options is particularly unclear in this area. They may include:

- Talking down the issue. Uberoi and Saggar essentially suggest that this issue may have been blown out of proportion, or at least inadvertently aggravated, by political posturing and commentary. This suggests that simply taking out some of the heat from the issue may also help address it.
- A counter view is that a tougher regime of points-based immigration controls (even at the cost of slower economic growth) twinned with more active efforts at integration, such as through the new citizenship ceremonies and exams, will be necessary.
- Another option, possibly complementary to either view above, is to focus efforts on relieving the everyday difficulties that many disadvantaged groups face, be it discrimination experienced by Muslims; low aspirations on the part of young whites; or anti-social behaviour or underperforming schools experienced by disadvantaged communities regardless of race.

External imperatives – environment and security

There are important issues that every government faces that are not matters of great public concern, but probably should be. These include grave threats to the state and the nation which, through effective government, will hopefully never come to pass.

The environment

Environmental degradation and climate change can now credibly be argued to be perhaps the greatest threat facing humanity, as Sir Nicholas Stern reported in 2006. Its devastating impacts are not restricted to direct effects, but to the dangers arising from mass migrations and war arising from the effects of climate change in nations thousands of miles away. The policy options are increasingly well rehearsed, and their relative contributions clearly made in the chapter by Gallo et al. These include:

- Various systems for carbon pricing, taxing and trading. Most of these proposals rest heavily on international cooperation. As such, environmental concerns introduce a new urgency to the need to strengthen international governance structures to the point that we can, as a species, take more intelligent action to address this problem that faces us all, yet none can take on alone. One suggestion in the chapter, that tax and trading schemes might start with an early focus on particular sectors, notably energy generation, seems especially promising.
- Push the technology. We are relying heavily on technological advances to do much of the heavy lifting, and to reduce the pain of transition to a low-carbon economy. This can be catalysed by a mixture of regulation, investment, and perhaps the canny use of prizes and government procurement.
- Changing behaviour. There is growing interest in how much stimulating behaviour change can supplement the other options above. However, the policy talk is, for the most part, some way ahead of the slog involved in building and operationalizing an evidence-base to achieve such change. This could be an area where a small marginal investment could pay a big policy return.

Security

Interestingly, environmental and more 'traditional' security concerns have become increasingly entwined over the last decade, and will become even more so in the years to come as growing economic powers come into conflict over dwindling resources. Chalmers gives some clues about the more promising options that face us:

- The UK continues to 'punch above its weight'. One option could be for us to give up on this idea, and to cut our defence and other spending. However, this does not seem to be an option that anyone is attracted to, especially given the pressure to sustain or even increase our spend on security service activity; the stabilizing of failed states (in an age of increasing availability of Weapons of Mass Destruction); and the grey area in between.

- Focus efforts on smaller, UK-led, interventions. Chalmers offers the thesis that these have generally been more successful, at least within the narrower but legitimate terms of UK national interest.
- Ensure that the growing economic powers of the coming decades – notably China and India – feel real ownership and commitment to the framework of international institutions on which our future security (and economy) rests. This may require current Western nations to give considerable ground, but is likely to be a price worth paying.
- A lot of security issues concern countries and places that have become settled enough to have slipped off our political radar. Northern Ireland is becoming one such area close to home, but there are many others limping out of, or into, civil war and conflict. A major objective and option is to seek to invest effort in such places before they re-explode into conflict – a trick easier to say than to do.

Administrative concerns – public services, governance

Many of the issues discussed in this book are 'administrative concerns', in that the public don't necessarily care that much about them – at least directly – and nor do they fundamentally threaten our survival as a nation. They are what we might call 'boring but important'.

Public services

As this book has shown, public services are no longer the top of the political agenda in the way that they were when its predecessor was written in the mid-1990s. But that does not mean that there is not much to do, and to be learned. Interested readers are referred to other ongoing projects for more detailed thoughts and policy proposals, such as the current Public Services Trust all-party Commission, due to conclude in early 2010. But a few observations are worth making:

- There seems to be a sense that, despite its arguably more painful road, health policy is now in better shape than educational policy.
- Productivity in the public sector remains a major issue. A common theme across the contributors to this volume, and in the conferences that preceded it, is that the fashion for top-down direction is now correctly giving way to more subtle 'social market'-based allocative mechanisms. These are not pure markets, but have some of the properties of markets, albeit in more regulated environments. This means voucher-based (or equivalent) mechanisms in health and education that create powerful forces to gradually drive up quality and performance. Wolf's critical comments on the performance of Further versus Higher Education performance is perhaps the clearest illustration of this point.
- There are clearly politically salient options about who the public service providers of the future will be. Across parties, there is increasing

interest in the role that can be played by the third and private sectors in education, health and welfare provision. Some of these options will inevitably threaten the interests of big public sector providers (though could also be an opportunity to others). For the most part, our authors have been fairly neutral on this point, with a soft implication that the status of who provides doesn't matter, but this does not mean that the public and providers will feel so relaxed.

- Who pays? The shadow of co-payment hangs over a number of the discussions of public service provision in the book. Appleby and Coutts point to the fiscal pressures on health, but also the importance of behaviour change and personal responsibility. Similarly, Wolf is upbeat about the role of tuition fees with grants and loans in higher education, and Wellings explores various forms of co-payment in transport. The combination of a tighter fiscal environment and growing aspirations for service provision means that debate about co-payments will only intensify.

Transport, housing and the local environment

It is striking that the clutch of policy areas that arguably made least progress over the last 12 years have strong connections between them. Policy options for this cluster of issues include:

- Reform the incentives within the planning system. In essence, the key change is to ensure that more planning gains go back to those who are most affected by any development. Nickell points to a number of options, the simplest of which is to allow local councils to retain additional revenues arising from development such as housing (but also potentially business too).
- With transport and congestion, it is difficult to get away from the hard reality that the UK's infrastructure requires further major investment. In principle, an attractive option is the greater use of congestion charging, but the practical and political challenges remain substantial. The idea of wholesale privatization of the road network is raised as a radical option, but it would lead to pressure on the Treasury to correspondingly reduce road tax and fuel duty – it would be no free lunch. In principle, transport infrastructure could be a short-term winner of the current drive to pump revenue into the economy, but the long timescales of such schemes impose practical constraints, again further aggravated by the slowness of the planning system.
- A larger question hangs over this area, which is the autonomy and responsibility of local and regional government. The UK is now an extreme outlier in terms of how little tax revenue is raised locally, and the corresponding weakness of local discretion. All parties now talk of

the need for greater devolution to local government, and to neighbour-hoods and citizens beyond. However, this enthusiasm tends to wane once in power in Westminster.

Governance

The first post-devolution Secretary of State for Wales, Ron Davies, repeatedly said, 'devolution is a process, not an event'. He was right. The same is true about all the other constitutional changes started since 1997.

- On devolution, the 2007–11 terms of the devolved parliaments will speed up the process of 'cohabitation', as the French call it. Governments of different parties will have to learn to coexist, unless Scotland becomes completely independent. This is likely to see more use of the hitherto unused intergovernmental institutions created in 1997–98. It is also likely to see progress towards solving those notoriously tough problems, finance ('Barnett formula') and representation ('West Lothian Question').
- The human rights genie is out; and it will be hard for politicians of any party to put it back, even though they are under populist and tabloid pressure to do so. In any country including the UK, the human rights that attract most attention are those of despised, and sometimes despicable, minorities. But that is the point of having *human* rights in the first place.
- On parliament, the semi-reformed House of Lords created in 1999 will continue to challenge governments more effectively than ever since 1909, when the old unelected house failed through overreach, though it continued to harass governments of the left. The new house will harass governments both of the left and the right. This may force governments to become serious about an elected upper house, with appropriate (and different) electoral systems for the two houses.
- Although Lodge and Gough had no room to talk about monarchy or established churches, their position may, as a consequence of upper house reform, become more interesting.

Political choices – equality, means and the division of power

Although the continuities may be larger than the differences, governments are also motivated by political and ideological projects. In this book, we have encouraged authors to refrain from political judgements, and rather to leave these to politicians and parties. Some of these choices include:

- The scale of commitment to redistribution, both direct and indirect? The argument is often made, especially on the left, that it is economically rational or even essential to improve the position of the poorest. As an economic argument, the case is far from proven – as illustrated by the experience of the USA. But morally and politically it is a perfectly defensible argument. With the recent decision by the Labour government to increase the top rate of income tax, the longstanding choice around redistribution may become more overt once again. In the meantime, parties will continue to argue about which types of policies will indirectly benefit the poor and disadvantaged.

- Personal responsibility and the role of government? All parties now concede that 'government cannot do it all'. However, they continue to differ in views about how far key problems should be taken on by the state and its agencies versus left to personal responsibility. Debates about obesity provide a new battleground for this old issue. For example, is the answer state-funded exercise, or is it just for the state to ensure that people are well informed (such as through clear food labelling) and for individuals to make their own choices?

- Who should 'deliver'? Both left and right have become rhetorically wary of the 'big state' that both prescribes and directly delivers services. Within the current Labour government, the stated objective is 'the strategic state'; while in the Conservative opposition the phrase 'post-bureaucratic state' is favoured. But behind the language, there clearly exists a real difference of view about the capability of the state to deliver mass programmes and the most appropriate means by which the society's objectives can be achieved. In broad terms, the right favours a scaled-back state leaving more room for a vibrant third and private sector to fill the gap, while the left holds to a more extensive and continuing role for the state.

- Socially liberal or prescriptive? Cutting across left and right, there are big differences of view about the extent to which the state should actively prescribe lifestyle and habits. Issues such as the regulation of gambling, alcohol and drug use tend to split the parties laterally. Over time, policy positions tend to move with the assessment of social harms. Hence the argument gradually tipped in favour of a smoking ban as the effects of secondary smoke became clearer. But the argument is much harder to call where the social harms are less clear. Instead this becomes a matter of judgement about lifestyle and identity, as well as tapping into a view about the value of soft social institutions and habits that help form the identity of a culture and nation.

- How much immigration? We have already rehearsed the issue of immigration as a public concern, as well as a factor in economic growth. It is also an administrative issue in as far as it is possible to control and affect (not least links to the question of Identity Cards). But its profile has also made it a big political question too. As one Minister recently put it, 'for the public, Britain still has to feel like home'. More aggressive policy lines are possible, such as tougher restrictions in the points system, or on marriages to non-English speaking partners or overseas spouses under a certain age. These tougher lines may strain relations with business leaders and existing minority communities, and they might even be counter-productive in terms of creating a shared sense of British identity, but they could also be very popular.

- Environment vs. growth? All parties are 'green' now. But there clearly are trade-offs around moving more aggressively on climate change and other environmental (and quality of life) issues now versus leaving them until technology and international agreements are in a more advanced state. The Stern report advises that early moves will be cost effective, but that doesn't necessarily imply a substantial investment in political capital and trade-offs.

- Power. Finally, there are always issues about the distribution of power. How high a price are Westminster politicians prepared to pay to keep decisions under their own control, as opposed to in Scotland, Wales, Northern Ireland? How far will parties embrace democratic innovations and more radical forms of devolution? How far should we cede power to supranational bodies, such as the EU, NATO, or WTO, in order to get some leverage in a bigger world? Most fundamentally, how prominent in a party's political vision is the idea that power should be ceded back to individuals or communities, versus a belief that the voice of the collective needs strengthening?

And finally …

If there is one thing that the reader should take away from this book, it is that there are real choices that face us as individuals and nations.

We felt that it was important to set out how the UK government had performed, and how the world had changed, since we first did this exercise in the mid-1990s. Our sense is that it was not a bad performance, though often not down to government alone. But we have also identified many areas where mistakes were made and gaps remain; where valuable time and impetus was lost while policy followed a gentle circle; and where rhetoric far outstripped delivery.

We have strongly encouraged contributors to avoid party political judgements and steers. It is unlikely that we succeeded entirely, but at least our all-party advisory group ensured that if there were biases, they went in no one direction. The intention is to now leave it to the reader to make their own judgements about which parties are best prepared for, and have the best answers to, the challenges our contributors have identified.

References

Academy of Medical Sciences (2006) *Medical Research: Assessing the Benefits to Society*. London: AMS.

Acheson, D. et al (1998) *Independent Inquiry into Inequalities in Health Report*. London: HMSO.

Adam, S., Bozio, A., Emmerson, C., Greenberg, D. and Knight, G. (2008) 'A Cost-benefit Analysis of Pathways to Work for New and Repeat Incapacity Benefit Claimants', DWP Research Report No. 498, Leeds, Corporate Document Service.

Afonso, A., Schuknecht, L. and Tanzi, V. (2005) 'Public Sector Efficiency: An International Comparison', *Public Choice*, 123: 321–47.

Aiginger, A. and Falk, M. (2005) 'Explaining Differences in Economic Growth among OECD Countries', *Empirica*, 32(1): 19–43.

Allen, M. and Ainley, P. (2008) *A New 14+: Vocational Diplomas and the Future of Schools, Colleges and Universities*. Cambridge: Radicaled Wordpress.

Ambler, T. and Chittenden, F. (2007) *Deregulation or Deja Vu? UK Deregulation Initiatives 1987/2006*. British Chambers of Commerce.

Anderson, J. and van Wincoop, E. (2004) 'Trade Costs', *Journal of Economic Literature*, 42: 691–751.

Angrist, J. and Lavy, V. (1999) 'New Evidence on Classroom Computers and Pupil Learning', NBER Working Paper 7424, National Bureau for Economic Research.

Appleby, J. and Phillips, M. (2009) 'The NHS: Satisfied Now?' *British Social Attitudes 25th Report*.

Appleby, J. and Maybin, J. (2008) 'Topping up NHS Care', *British Medical Journal*, 337, November.

Archer, C. and Glaister, S. (2006) *Investing in Roads: Pricing, Costs and New Capacity*. London: Imperial College.

Ariely, D. (2008) *Predictably Irrational: The Hidden Forces That Shape Our Decisions*. London: HarperCollins Publishers.

Arrow, K. (1962) 'Economic Welfare and the Allocation of Resources for Invention', in R.R. Nelson (ed.) *The Rate and Direction of Inventive Activity*. Princeton: Princeton University Press.

Astle, J. (2007) *The Surest Route: Early Years Education and Life Chances*. London: CentreForum.

Astle, J. and Ryan, C. (eds) (2008) *Academies and the Future of State Education*. London: CentreForum.

Atkinson, A. (2004) 'Evaluating the Impact of Performance-related Pay', Centre for Market and Public Organisation Working Paper 04/113, University of Bristol.

Autor, D. and Dorn, D. (2008) *Inequality and Specialization: The Growth of Low-skilled Service Jobs in the United States*. MIT Press.

Autor, D., Levy, F. and Murnane, R. (2003) 'The Skill Content of Recent Technological Change: An Empirical Exploration', *Quarterly Journal of Economics*, 118: 1279–333.

BAA (2008) *Economic Benefits of Heathrow: At the Heart of the UK Economy*. London: BAA. Available at: http://www.heathrowairport.com

Babalik, E. (2000) 'Urban Rail Systems: A Planning Framework to Increase Their Success', unpublished PhD thesis, University of London.

Badinger, H. (2005) 'Growth Effects of Economic Integration: Evidence from the EU Member States', *Review of World Economics*, 141: 50–78.

Baily, M.N. and Kirkegaard, J.F. (2004). *Transforming the European Economy*. Washington: Peterson Institute for International Economics.

Bakker, S. and Wolf, A. (eds) (2001) 'Examinations and Entry to Higher Education: Pressure and Change in a Mass System', *Assessment in Education*, 8(3), Special Issue.

Baldwin, R. (2006) 'The Euro's Trade Effects', European Central Bank Working Paper No. 594.

Barber, M. (2007) *Instruction to Deliver: Tony Blair, Public Services and the Challenge of Achieving Targets*. London: Politico's.

Barker, K. (2004) *Delivering Stability: Securing Our Future Housing Needs*. HM Treasury.

Barker, K. (2006) *Barker Review of Land Use Planning, Final Report*. London: The Stationery Office.

Barker, K. (2007) 'Planning Policy, Planning Practice, and Housing Supply', *Oxford Review of Economic Policy* Conference on Housing Markets, Said Business School, Oxford, September.

Barr, N. (2004) 'Higher Education Funding', *Oxford Review of Economic Policy*, 20(2): 264–83.

Barrell, R. and Kirby, S. (2008) 'The Budgetary Implications of Global Shocks to Cycles and Trends in Output', *ESRI Budget Outlook*, October. http://www.esri.ie/publications/latest_publications/view/index.xml?id=2574

Barrell, R. and Pain, N. (1997) 'Foreign Direct Investment, Technological Change and Economic Growth within Europe', *Economic Journal*, 107: 1770–86.

Barrell, R., Gottschalk, S., Holland, D., Khoman, E., Liadze, I. and Pomerantz, O. (2008) 'The Impact of EMU on Growth and Employment', European Commission. Economic Paper No. 318. http://ec.europa.eu/economy_finance/publications

BBC (2004) *Building Public Value*. London: BBC.

BBC News (2006) 'Sainsbury Earned Science Respect', http://news.bbc.co.uk/2/hi/science/nature/6135762.stm

BBC News (2008) '"1m More" on Housing Waiting List', http://news.bbc.co.uk/1/hi/uk/7403896.stm

Beaven, R, Bosworth, D., Lewney, R. and Wilson, R. (2005) 'Alternative Skills Scenarios to 2020 for the UK Economy', http://www.hm-treasury.gov.uk/d/alternative_skills_scenarios_execsummary.pdf

Bechhofer, F. and McCrone, D. (2007) 'Being British: A Crisis of Identity?', *Political Quarterly*, 78(2): 251–60.

Berkman, L. and Kawachi, I. (2000) *Social Epidemiology*. New York: Oxford University Press.

BERR (Department for Business, Enterprise and Regulatory Reform) (2008) *SET Statistics – Science, Engineering and Technology Indicators*. London: BERR.

Better Regulation Task Force (2005) *Regulation: Less is More*.

Bhidé, A. (2008) *The Venturesome Economy*. Princeton: Princeton University Press.

Black, D. (2008) *Working for a Healthier Tomorrow. Review of the Health of Britain's Working Age Population*. London: The Stationery Office.

Blair, T. (1995) '"The Young Country" Speech to Labour Party Conference, 3 October 1995', in T. Blair, *New Britain, My Vision for a Young Country*. London: Fourth Estate.

Blair, T. (1999) 'Doctrine of the International Community', Speech delivered to Economic Club of Chicago, 24 April. http://www.number10.gov.uk/Page1297

Blanchflower, D. and Oswald, A. (2004) 'Well Being Over Time in Britain and the USA', *Journal of Public Economics*, 88: 1359–86.

Blanden, J. (2008) 'How Much Can We Learn From International Comparisons of Social Mobility', Paper given at Sutton-Carnegie Summit on Social Mobility, New York.

Blatchford, P. (2002) *Pupil–Adult Ratio Differences and Educational Progress over Reception and Key Stage 1*. London: DfES.

Blatchford, P. (2003) *The Class Size Debate: Is Small Better?* Buckingham: Open University Press.

Blatchford, P., Russell, A., Bassett, P., Brown, P. and Martin, C. (2005) *The Role and Effects of Teaching Assistants in English Primary Schools (Years 4–6) 2000–2003*, Research Report 66. London: DfES.

Blick, A., Choudhury, T. and Weir, S. (2006) *The Rules of the Game: Terrorism, Community and Human Rights*. York: Joseph Rowntree.

Bloom, N. and van Reenen, J. (2007) 'Measuring and Explaining Management Practices Across Firms and Nations', *Quarterly Journal of Economics*, 122: 1351–408.

Bloom, N., Griffith, R. and van Reenen, J. (1999) 'Do R&D Tax Credits Work? Evidence from an International Panel of Countries 1979–1994', IFS, Working paper 99/8.

Blundell, R., Dearden, L., Goodman, A. and Reed, H. (2000) 'The Returns to Higher Education, Evidence from a British Cohort', *Economic Journal*, 110: F82–F99.

Blundell, R. and MaCurdy, W.T. (1999) 'Labour Supply: A Review of Alternative Approaches', in O. Ashenfelter and D. Card (eds) *Handbook of Labour Economics*. Vol. 3A.

Blundell, R., Duncan, A., McCrae, J. and Costas, M. (2000) 'The Labour Market Impact of the Working Families Tax Credit', *Fiscal Studies*, 21: 75–104.

Blunkett, D. (2003) Heslington Lecture, 'One Nation, Many Faiths: Unity and Diversity in Multi-faith Britain', 30 October.

Boardman, A.E. et al (2006) *Cost Benefit Analysis: Concepts and Practice*. Upper Saddle River, NJ: Pearson/Prentice Hall.

Bok, D.S. (2001) *The Trouble with Government*. Cambridge, MA: Harvard University Press.

Bongaarts, J. (1992) 'Population Growth and Global Warming', *Population and Development Review*, 18(2): 299–319.

Booth, P. (ed.) (2008) 'Supplement on the Pupil Premium', *Economic Affairs*, 28(2).

Bourles, R. and Cette, G. (2006) 'Les évolutions de la productivité "structurelle" du travail dans les principaux pays industrialisés', *Bulletin de la Banque de France*, 150: 23–30.

Boyle, S. and Appleby, J. (2000) 'Blair's Billions: Where Will He Find the Money for the NHS?', *British Medical Journal*, 320(7238): 856–67.

Bradley, S. and Taylor, J. (2007) 'Diversity, Choice and the Quasi-market: An Empirical Analysis of Secondary Education in England', Working Paper 2007/38, Lancaster University Management School.

Bradshaw, J., Middleton, S., Davis, A., Oldfield, N., Smith, N., Cusworth, L. and Williams, J. (2008) *A Minimum Income Standard for Britain: What People Think*. York: Joseph Rowntree Foundation.

Brewer, M. (2007) 'Supporting Couples with Children through the Tax System', chapter 12 of *Institute for Fiscal Studies Green Budget 2007*. London: IFS.

Bright, M. (2006) *When Progressives Treat With Reactionaries: The British State's Flirtation with Radical Islamism*. London: Policy Exchange.

British Academy (2008) *Punching Our Weight: The Humanities and Social Sciences in Public Policy Making*. London: British Academy.

British Chambers of Commerce (2008) *Burdens Barometer 2008*.

British Petroleum (2007) *BP Statistical Review of World Energy*.

British Petroleum (2008) *BP Statistical Review of World Energy*.

British Social Attitudes (1997) *14th Report: The End of Conservative Values?*. BSA. National Centre for Social Research.

Broadberry, S. (2006) *Market Services and the Productivity Race, 1850–2000*. Cambridge: Cambridge University Press.

Broadberry, S. and O'Mahony, M. (2004) 'Britain's Productivity Gap with the United States and Europe: A Historical Perspective', *National Institute Economic Review*, 189: 72–85.

Broadberry, S. and O'Mahony, M. (2007) *Britain's Twentieth-Century Productivity*.

Broadcasting Committee Report (1923) (Chairman: Sir Frederick Sykes). London: HMSO.

Brown, G. (2008) Speech to the Specialist Schools and Academies Trust, 23 June.

Brown, P. and Hesketh, A. (2004) *The Mismanagement of Talent: Employability and Jobs in the Knowledge Economy*. Oxford: Oxford University Press.

Buijs, F.J. et al (2006) *Home Bred Warriors: Radical and Democratic Muslims in the Netherlands*. Amsterdam: Spinhuis.

Buiter, W.H. (2003) 'Ten Commandments for a Fiscal Rule in the E(M)U', *Oxford Review of Economic Policy*, 19: 84–99.

Buxton, M., Hanney, S., Morris, S., Sundmacher, L., Mestre-Ferrandiz, Garau, J.M., Sussex, J., Grant, J., Ismail, S., Nason, E., Wooding, S. and Kapur, S. (2009) *Medical Research: What's it Worth? Estimating the Economic Impact of Medical Research in the UK*. London: Medical Research Council, Wellcome Trust and Academy of Medical Sciences.

Byron, T. (2008) *Safer Children in a Digital World: The Report of the Byron Review*. London: Department for Children, Schools and Families.

Cabinet Office (1999) *Modernising Government White Paper*. London: HMSO.

Cabinet Office (2004) *National Alcohol Harm Reduction Strategy*. London: HMSO.

Cabinet Office (2008) 'The National Security Strategy of the United Kingdom: Security in an Interdependent World', Cm 7291, HMSO, March.

Caio, F. (2008) *The Next Phase of Broadband UK: Action Now for Long-term Competitiveness*. London: BERR/HMSO. http://www.berr.gov.uk/files/file47788.pdf

Calman, K. (2008) *The Future of Scottish Devolution within the Union: A First Report*. Edinburgh: Commission on Scottish Devolution. http://www.commissiononscottishdevolution. org.uk/uploads/2008-12-01-vol-1-final--bm.pdf

Cameron, G., Muellbauer, J. and Murphy, A. (2006) 'Was There a British House Price Bubble?' CEPR Discussion Paper 5619.

Carey, S. (2000) *Measuring Adult Literacy: The International Adult Literacy Survey in the European Context*. London: Office for National Statistics.

Carswell, D. and Hannan, D. (2008) *The Plan: Twelve Months to Renew Britain*. London: Direct Democracy.

Carter, Lord P. (2007) *Securing the Future: Proposals for the Efficient and Sustainable Use of Custody in England and Wales*. London: HMSO.

Casey, L. (2008) *Engaging Communities in Fighting Crime*. London: Cabinet Office.

Cassen, R. and Kingdon, G. (2007) *Tackling Low Educational Achievement*. York: Joseph Rowntree Foundation.

Cave, B. and Coutts, A. (2006) *Health Impacts of the Draft Spatial Strategy for London*. Greater London Authority and Mayors Office for London.

Cebulla, A., Flore G. and Greenberg, D. (2008) 'The New Deal for Lone Parents, Lone Parent Work Focussed Interviews and Working Families' Tax Credit: A Review of Impacts', DWP Research Report No. 484, Leeds, Corporate Document Service.

Centre for Economic Performance (2006) 'Incapacity Benefit Reform: Tackling the Rise in Labour Market Inactivity', Paper No. CEPPA005, March.

Chadwick, A., Noy, D., Lindeberg, E., Arts, R., Eiken, O. and Williams, G. (2006) 'Calibrating Reservoir Performance with Time-lapse Seismic Monitoring and Flow Simulations of the Sleipner CO_2 Plume', in *GHGT-8: 8th International Conference on Greenhouse Gas Control Technologies, Trondheim, Norway, 19–22 June 2006*. Oxford: Elsevier.

Chalmers, M. (2008) *Global Inequality and Security Policy: A British Perspective*, RUSI Whitehall Paper 70. Abingdon: Routledge.

Cheshire, P. and Hilber, C. (2008) 'Office Space Supply Restrictions in Britain: The Political Economy of Market Revenge', *Economic Journal*, 118: F185–F221.

Cheshire, P. and Sheppard, S. (2005), 'The Introduction of Price Signals into Land Use Planning Decision-making: A Proposal', *Urban Studies*, 42(4): 647–63.

Chrystal, K.A. and Mizen, P.D. (2001) 'Goodhart's Law: Its Origins, Meaning and Implications for Monetary Policy', Prepared for the Festschrift in honour of Charles Goodhart to be held on 15–16 November 2001 at the Bank of England. http://cyberlibris.typepad.com/blog/files/Goodharts_Law.pdf

Churchill, W. (1943) 'The Price of Greatness is Responsibility', Speech given at Harvard University. http://www.winstonchurchill.org/i4a/pages/index.cfm?pageid=424

Cincera, M. and Galgau, O. (2005) 'Impact of Market Entry and Exit on EU Productivity and Growth Performance', European Commission Economic Papers No. 222.

CM 7120 (2007) *Planning for a Sustainable Future*. London: The Stationery Office.

CMEB (Commission for Multi-Ethnic Britain) (2000) *The Future of Multi-ethnic Britain*. London: Profile Books.

Coase, R. (1959) 'The Federal Communications Commission', *Journal of Law and Economics*, 2: 1–40.

Coccia, M. (2008) 'What Is the Optimal Rate of R&D Investment to Maximize Productivity Growth?' *Technological Forecasting and Social Change*, in press.

Cohen, W. and Levinthal, D. (1990) 'Absorptive Capacity: A New Perspective on Learning and Innovation', *Administrative Science Quarterly*, 35: 128–52.

Colley, H. and Jarvis, J. (2007) 'Formality and Informality in the Summative Assessment of Motor Vehicle Apprentices: A Case Study', *Assessment in Education*, 13(3): 295–314.

Collins, R. and Murroni, C. (1996) *New Media, New Policies*. London, IPPR.

Collins, R. and Purnell, J. (eds) (1994) *Managing the Information Society*. London: IPPR.

Commonwealth Fund (2007) *International Health Policy Survey in Seven Countries*. http://www.commonwealthfund.org/surveys/surveys_show.htm?doc_id=568326

'Competition in OECD Countries: Taking Stock and Moving Forward', OECD Economics Department Working Paper No. 575.

Conklin, A., Hallsworth, M., Hatziandreu, E. and Grant, J. (2008) *Briefing on Linkage and Exchange: Facilitating Diffusion of Innovation in Health Services*. Santa Monica: RAND.

Conservative Democracy Task Force (2008) *Answering the Question: Devolution, the West Lothian Question and the Future of the Union*. London: Conservative Party.

Conservative Party (2008) 'Reconstruction: Plan for a Strong Economy', October.

Conservative Party Cities Task Force (2007) *Cities Renaissance: Creating Local Leadership.* London: Conservative Party.

Conway, P. and Nicoletti, G. (2006) 'Product Market Regulation in the Non-Manufacturing Sectors of OECD Countries: Measurement and Highlights', OECD Economics Department Working Paper No. 530.

Conway, P., Janod, V. and Nicoletti, G. (2005) 'Product Market Regulation in OECD Countries: 1998 to 2003', OECD Economics Department Working Papers No. 419.

Cooksey, D. (2006) *A Review of UK Health Research Funding.* London: HMSO.

Cottarelli, C. and Escolano, J. (2004) 'Assessing the Assessment: A Critical Look at the June 2003 Assessment of the United Kingdom's Five Tests for Euro Entry', IMF Working Paper No. 04/116.

'Countries, 1998–2003', OECD Economics Department Working Paper No. 419.

Cowley, P. and Stuart, M. (2005) 'Parliament', in A. Seldon and D. Kavanagh (eds) *The Blair Effect 2001–5.* Cambridge: Cambridge University Press, pp. 20–42.

Cowling, K. (1989) 'The Strategic Approach', in Industrial Strategy Group, *Beyond the Review: Perspectives on Labour's Economic and Industrial Strategy.* London: The Labour Party.

Crafts, N. (2006) 'Regulation and Productivity Performance', *Oxford Review of Economic Policy*, 22: 186–202.

Crafts, N. (2007). 'Recent European Economic Growth: Why Can't It Be Like the Golden Age', *National Institute Economic Review*, 199: 69–81.

Crafts, N. and O'Mahony, M. (2001) 'A Perspective on UK Productivity Performance', *Fiscal Studies*, 22: 271–06.

Creegan, C. and Robinson, C. (2008) 'Prejudice and the Workplace', in *British Social Attitudes, the 24th Report.* London: Sage, pp. 127–38.

Creyts, J., Derkach, A., Nyquist, S., Ostrowski, K. and Stephenson, J. (2007) *Reducing U.S. Greenhouse Gas Emissions: How Much Will It Cost?* McKinsey and Company.

Crisp, R. and Fletcher, D.R. (2008) 'A Comparative Review of Workfare Programmes in the United States, Canada and Australia', DWP research report 533.

Curtice, J. (2008) *Where Stands the Union Now?* London: IPPR.

Darnton, A. (2008) 'Practical Guide: An Overview of Behaviour Change Models and Their Uses', Government Social Research Unit, HM Treasury.

Darzi, A. (2008) *High Quality Care for All: NHS Next Stage Review Final Report*, Department of Health. London: HMSO.

Davies, P., Slack, K., Hughes, A., Mangan, J. and Vigurs, K. (2008) 'Knowing Where to Study', Staffordshire University for the Sutton Trust.

Day, A. (1998) 'The Case for Road Pricing', *Economic Affairs*, 18(4): 5–8.

DCLG (Department of Communities and Local Government) (2007) *Homes for the Future: More Affordable, More Sustainable*, Command Paper 7191.

DCLG (Department of Communities and Local Government) (2008) *Communities in Control: Real People, Real Power*, Cm 7427. London: The Stationery Office.

Dearden, L., Reed, H. and van Reenen, J. (2006) 'The Impact of Training on Productivity and Wages: Evidence from British Panel Data', *Oxford Bulletin of Economics and Statistics*, 68: 397–421.

DEFRA (Department for Environment, Food and Rural Affairs) (2007) *Household Energy Supplier Obligations.* http://www.defra.gov.uk/environment/climatechange/uk/household/supplier

Deighton, A. (2002) 'The Past in the Present: British Imperial Memories and the European Question', in Jan-Werner Muller (ed.) *Memory and Power in Post-War Europe.* Cambridge: Cambridge University Press, pp. 100–20.

Denham, J. (2005) 'Who Do You Want to Be', *Fabian Review*, Spring: 6–9.

DETR (Department of Environment, Transport and the Regions) (1998) *A New Deal for Transport: Better for Everyone*. London: The Stationery Office.

DETR (Department of Environment, Transport and the Regions) (2000) *Transport Ten Year Plan 2000*. London: The Stationery Office.

Devereux, M. (2007) 'Developments in the Taxation of Corporate Profit in the OECD since 1965: Rates, Bases and Revenues', Oxford Saïd Business School Working Paper No. 07/04.

DfES (Department for Education and Skills) (2006) *The Supply and Demand for Science, Technology, Engineering and Mathematics Skills in the UK Economy*. London: DfES.

DfT (Department for Transport) (2002) *Delivering Better Transport: Progress Report*. London: The Stationery Office.

DfT (Department for Transport) (2003) *The Future of Air Transport*. London: The Stationery Office.

DfT (Department for Transport) (2007a) *Transport Statistics Great Britain*. London: The Stationery Office.

DfT (Department for Transport) (2007b) *Delivering a Sustainable Railway*. London: The Stationery Office.

DfT (Department for Transport) (2007c) 'Road Transport and the EU Emissions Trading Scheme', Department for Transport Discussion Paper. http://www.dft.gov.uk/pgr/sustainable/climatechange/euemistrascheme

DfT (Department for Transport) (2008a) *Adding Capacity at Heathrow Airport*. London: The Stationery Office.

DfT (Department for Transport) (2008b) *Road Traffic and Congestion in Great Britain: Quarter 3 2008*, http://www.dft.gov.uk/pgr/statistics/datatablespublications/roadstraffic/traffic/qbtrafficgb/2008/q308

Dietz, S., Hope, C., Stern, N. and Zenghelis, D. (2007) 'Reflections on the Stern Review: A Robust Case for Strong Action to Reduce the Risks of Climate Change', *World Economics*, 8(1): 121–68.

DIUS (Department for Innovation, Universities and Skills) (2006) *Prosperity for All in the Global Economy: World Class Skills*. London: The Stationery Office.

DIUS (Department for Innovation, Universities and Skills) (2008) *Innovation Nation*. London: HMSO.

DIUS and DWP (Department for Innovation, Universities and Skills, and Department for Work and Pensions) (2007) *Opportunity, Employment and Progression: Making Skills Work*, Cm 7288. London: The Stationery Office.

DoH (Department of Health) (1989) *Working for Patients*, Cmnd 555. London: HMSO.

DoH (Department of Health) (1992) *The Health of the Nation: A Strategy for Health in England*. London: HMSO.

DoH (Department of Health) (1999) *Saving Lives: Our Healthier Nation White Paper and Reducing Health Inequalities: An Action Report*. London: HMSO.

DoH (Department of Health) (2000) *The NHS Plan: A Plan for Investment, a Plan for Reform*. London: HMSO.

DoH (Department of Health) (2002) *Delivering the NHS Plan: Next Steps on Investment, Next Steps on Reform*. London: HMSO.

DoH (Department of Health) (2003) *Tacking Health Inequalities: A Programme for Action*. London: HMSO.

DoH (Department of Health) (2004) *Choosing Health: Making Healthy Choices Easier*. London: HMSO.

DoH (Department of Health) (2007a) *Health Profile of England*. http://www.dh.gov.uk/en/Publicationsandstatistics/Publications/PublicationsStatistics/DH_079716

DoH (Department of Health) (2007b) *Tackling Health Inequalities: 2007 Status Report on the Programme for Action*. London: HMSO.

DoH (Department of Health) (2008a) *A First Class Service: Quality in the New NHS*. London: HMSO.

DoH (Department of Health) (2008b) 'Waiting Time Model', Freedom of Information Request, Reference DE00000176152.

DoH (Department of Health) (2008c) *Healthy Weight, Healthy Lives: A Cross Government Strategy for England*. London: HMSO.

DoH (Department of Health) (2008d) *High Quality Care for All: NHS Next Stage Review Final Report – Summary*. London: HMSO.

Dormont, B., Oliveira Martins, J., Pelgrin, F. and Suhrcke, M. (2008) 'Health Expenditures, Longevity and Growth', OECD Working Paper series.

Dorsett, R. (2007) 'The Effect of Pathways to Work on Labour Market Outcomes', *National Institute Economic Review*, 202: 79–89.

Dorsett, R. (2008) 'Pathways to Work for New and Repeat Incapacity Benefit Claimants: Evaluation Synthesis Report', DWP Research Report 525, Leeds, Corporate Document Service.

Downing, P. and Ballantyne, J. (2007) *Tipping Point or Turning Point? Social Marketing and Climate Change*. Ipsos MORI.

DTI (Department of Trade and Industry) (1993) *Realising Our Potential: A Strategy for Science, Technology and Engineering*. London: HMSO.

DTI (Department of Trade and Industry) (1999) *Creating Knowledge Creating Wealth: Realising the Economic Potential of Public Sector Research Establishments*. London: HMSO.

DTI (Department of Trade and Industry) (2000) *Excellence and Opportunity: A Science and Innovation Policy for the 21st Century*. London: HMSO.

DTI (Department of Trade and Industry) (2002) *A Cost Benefit Analysis of Digital Switch Over*. London: DTI.

DTI (Department of Trade and Industry) (2005) *Science Budget Allocation 2005–06 to 2007–08*. London: HMSO.

DTI / DCMS (Department of Trade and Industry / Department for Culture, Media and Sport) (2000) *A New Future for Communications* (Communications White Paper). London: HMSO.

Dudley, G. and Richardson, J. (2003) *Why Does Policy Change? Lessons from British Transport Policy 1945–99*. London: Routledge.

Duffy, B., Wake, R., Burrows, T. and Bremner, P. (2008) *Closing the Gaps*. London: MORI.

Dunne, Timothy (2004), 'The Atlanticist Identity in British Security Strategy', *International Affairs*, 80(5), October: 893–909.

DWP (Department for Work and Pensions) (2007) *Opportunity for All Indicators Update*, October 2007. London: DWP.

DWP (Department for Work and Pensions) (2008a) *Households Below Average Income 1994/95 to 2006/07*, table 4.3tr, via http://www.dwp.gov.uk/asd/hbai/hbai2007/excel_files/chapters/chapter_3tr_hbai08.xls

DWP (Department for Work and Pensions) (2008b), *No-one Written Off: Reforming Welfare to Reward Responsibility*, Cm 7363. London: The Stationery Office.

Eddington, R. (2006) *The Eddington Transport Study, The Case for Action: Sir Rod Eddington's Advice to the Government*. London: The Stationery Office.

Edler, J., Rolfstam, M., Hommen, L., Tsipouri, L. and Rigby, J. (2005) *Innovation and Public Procurement. Review of Issues at Stake*, Study for the European Commission ENTR/03/24. Karlsvule: Fraunhofer.

Egerton, M. and Parry, G. (2001) 'Lifelong Debt: Rates of Return to Mature Study', *Higher Education Quarterly*, 55: 04–27.

EMCDDA (2008) *2008 Annual Report: The State of the Drugs Problem in Europe*. Lisbon: EMCDDA.

Emmerson, C., Frayne, C. and Love, S. (2006) 'The Government's Fiscal Rules', Institute for Fiscal Studies.

Energy Information Administration (2005) *International Energy Annual 2003*. Table H.1cco2 (World Per Capita Dioxide Emissions from the Consumption and Flaring of Fossil Fuels, 1980–2003). http://www.eia.doe.gov/pub/international/iealf/tableh1cco2.xls

European Commission (2002a) Directive (2002/21/EC) on a common European Framework.

European Commission (2002b) Directive (2002/19/EC) on access and interconnection

European Commission (2002c) Directive (2002/20/EC) on the authorization of electronic communications networks and services.

European Commission (2002d) Directive (2002/22/EC) on universal service and users' rights relating to electronic communications networks and services.

European Commission (2002e) *More Research for Europe: Towards 3% of GDP*. Brussels: EC.

European Commission (2006) 'Public Finances in EMU – 2006', *European Economy*, 3.

European Commission (2007a) *The EU's Contribution to Shaping a Future Global Climate Change Regime*. http://ec.europa.eu/environment/climat/future_action.htm

European Commission (2007b) State Aid Scoreboard Autumn 2007.

Eurostat (2007) *Europe in Figures*, Statistical Office of the European Commission.

Eurostat (2008) *Taxation Trends in the European Union*.

Evans, A. and Hartwich, O.M. (2007) *The Best Laid Plans: How Planning Prevents Economic Growth*. London: Policy Exchange.

Evans, M., Harkness, S. and Ortiz, R.A. (2004) *Lone Parents Cycling between Work and Benefits*, Research Report 217, Sheffield, Department for Work and Pensions.

Farmer, M. and Barrell R. (1982) 'Why Student Loans are Fairer than Grants', *Public Money*, 2(1): 19–24.

Faulkner, D., Hough, M. and Halpern, D. (1996) 'Crime and Criminal Justice', in D. Halpern et al (eds) *Options for Britain: A Strategic Policy Review*. Aldershot: Dartmouth.

Feinstein, L. (2003) 'Inequality in the Early Cognitive Development of British Children in the 1970 Cohort', *Economica*, 70: 73–98.

Feinstein, L. (2004) 'Mobility in Pupils' Cognitive Attainment during School Life', *Oxford Review of Economic Policy*, 20(2): 213–29.

Fields, C. (2006) 'Islamaphobia in Contemporary Britain: The Evidence of the Opinion Polls 1988–2006', *Islam and Christian-Muslim Relations*, 18(4).

Fitzgibbon, C. (1999) 'Is Ofsted Helpful?', in C. Cullingford (ed.) *An Inspector Calls*. London: Kogan Page.

Flannery, T. (2005) *The Weather Makers: The History and Future Impact of Climate Change*. Melbourne: Text Publishing.

Francesconi, M. and van Der Klaauw, W. (2007) 'The Socioeconomic Consequences of In-work Benefit Reform for British Lone Mothers', *Journal of Human Resources*, 42(1): 1–31.

Frankel, J. and Romer, D. (1999) 'Does Trade Cause Growth?', *American Economic Review*, 89: 379–99.

Fraser, D. (2008) *Nation Speaking Unto Nation: Does the Media Create Cultural Distance between England and Scotland?* London and Newcastle: IPPR/IPPR North.

Freedman, D. (2002) *Television Policies of the Labour Party 1951–2001*. London: Sage.

Freedman, S. and Horner, S. (2008) *Social Funding and Social Justice: A Guide to the Pupil Premium*. London: Policy Exchange.

Friedmann, S.J. (2007) 'Geological Carbon Dioxide Sequestration', *Mineralogical Society of America*, 3(3): 179–84.

Gallo, F., Contucci, P., Coutts, A. and Gallo, I. (2008) 'Tackling Climate Change Through Energy Efficiency: Mathematical Models to Offer Evidence-based Recommendations for Public Policy', *Journal of Quality and Quantity – Special Issue Mathematics and Society*.

Gardam, T. and Levy, D. (2008) *The Price of Plurality: Choice, Diversity and Broadcasting Institutions in the Digital Age*. Oxford: Reuters/Ofcom.

Garnaut, R. (2008) *The Garnaut Climate Change Review*. Cambridge University Press.

Gieve, J. (2004) Undated letter to Andrew Turnbull entitled 'Relations with Muslim Community', http://www.globalsecurity.org/security/library/report/2004/muslimext-uk.htm

Glaister, S. and Graham, D. (2004) *Pricing Our Roads: Vision and Reality*. London: IEA.

Glennerster, H. (2002) 'United Kingdom Education 1997–2001', *Oxford Review of Economic Policy*, 18(2): 120–36.

GMPTE (Greater Manchester Passenger Transport Executive) (2008) 'Greater Manchester TIF Package Unlocks up to £3 billion of Investment', press release, 9 June.

Goldberg, H. (ed.) (1996) 'The IEA Studies' *Assessment in Education*, 3(2), Special Issue.

Goodhart, C. (2008) 'The Boundary Problem in Financial Regulation', *National Institute Economic Review*, 206: 48–55.

Goodman, A. and Sianesi, B. (2005) 'Early Education and Children's Outcomes: How Long Do the Impacts Last?' *Fiscal Studies*, 26(4): 513–48.

Goos, M. and Manning, A. (2007) 'Lovely Jobs and Lousy Jobs: The Rising Polarisation of Work in Britain', *Review of Economic Studies*, 89: 118–33.

Gowers Review of Intellectual Property (2006) London: HM Treasury.

Grant, J., Green, L. and Mason, N. (2003) 'From Bedside to Bench: Comroe and Dripps Revisited', HERG Research Report No. 30, Brunel University.

Grant, J., Hanney, S. and Buxton, M. (2004) 'Academic Medicine: Time for Reinvention. Research Needs Researching' [letter], *British Medical Journal*, 328: 48.

Greer, S.L. (2004) *Territorial Politics and Health Policy: UK Health Policy in Comparative Perspective*. Manchester: Manchester University Press.

Gregg, P. and Harkness, S. (2003) 'Welfare Reform and Lone Parents Employment in the UK', Centre for Market and Public Organisation Discussion Paper 03/73, Bristol.

Griffith, R. and Harrison, R. (2004) 'The Link between Product Market Regulation and Macroeconomics', European Commission Economic Papers No. 209.

Griffith, R., Harrison, R. and Simpson, H. (2006) 'Product Market Reform and Innovation in the EU', Institute for Fiscal Studies Working Paper No. 06/17.

Griffith, R., Redding, S. and van Reenen, J. (2001) 'Measuring the Cost Effectiveness of an R & D Tax Credit for the UK', *Fiscal Studies*, 22: 375–99.

Griffiths, R. and Durkin, S. (2007) 'Synthesising the Evidence on Employment Zones', DWP Research Report 449, Leeds, Corporate Document Service.

Griffiths, V. (2007) 'Experiences of Training on an Employment-based Route into Teaching in England', *Journal of In-Service Education*, 33(1): 107–23.

Grossman, G. and Helpmann, E (1993) *Innovation and Growth in the Global Economy*. Cambridge: MIT Press.

Grout, P. and Stevens, M. (2003) 'The Assessment: Financing and Managing Public Services', *Oxford Review of Economic Policy*, 19: 215–34.

Guellec, D. and van Pottelsberghe de la Potterie, B. (2004) 'From R&D to Productivity Growth: Do the Institutional Settings and the Source of Funds of R&D Matter?', *Oxford Bulletin of Economics and Statistics*, 66(3): 353–78.

Gust, C. and Marquez, J. (2004) 'International Comparisons of Productivity Growth: The Role of Information Technology and Regulatory Practices', *Labour Economics*, 11: 33–58.

Gutiérrez, R., Haubrich, D. and McLean, I. (2008) 'The Limits of Performance Assessments of Public Bodies: External Constraints on English Local Government', *Environment and Planning C: Government and Policy* 26: 767–87.

Halpern, D. (2008) 'Options for Britain II: Summing Up', Presentation in Cambridge, 7–8 July.

Halpern, D. (2009) *Living Together: A Policy Wonk's Notes on a Better Society*. London: Polity Press.

Halpern, D. and Wood, S. (1996) 'Introduction: The Policy-making Process', in D. Halpern, S. Wood, S. White and G. Cameron, *Options for Britain: A Strategic Policy Review*. Aldershot: Dartmouth, pp. 1–28.

Halpern, D., Bates, C., Mulgan, G. and Aldridge, S. (2004) 'Personal Responsibility and Changing Behaviour: The State of Knowledge and Its Implications for Public Policy', UK Cabinet Office, Prime Minister's Strategy Unit.

Halpern, D., Wood, S., White, S. and Cameron, G. (1996) *Options for Britain: A Strategic Policy Review*. Aldershot: Dartmouth.

Hamai, K., Ville, R., Harris, R., Hough, M. and Zvekic, U. (eds) (1995) *Probation Round the World*. London: Routledge.

Hamilton, C. and Denniss, R. (2006) *Affluenza: When Too Much is Never Enough*. Australia Institute.

Hanney, S., Gonzalez-Block, M.A., Buxton, M.J. and Kogan, M. (2002) 'The Utilisation of Health Research in Policy-making: Concepts, Examples and Methods of Assessment', *Health Research Policy and Systems*, 1(2).

Haskel, J. and Sadun, R. (2007) 'Entry Regulation and Productivity: Evidence from the UK Retail Sector', Ceriba working paper, at http://www.ceriba.org.uk

Hasluck, C. and Green, A. (2007) 'What Works for Whom?', DWP Research Report 407, Leeds, Corporate Document Service.

Heath, A. and Roberts, J. (2008) 'British Identity, Its Sources and Possible Implications for Civic Behaviour', http://www.justice.gov.uk/reviews/research.htm

Heath, E. (1998) *The Course of My Life*. London: Hodder and Stoughton.

Hepburn, C.J. and Stern, N. (2008) 'A New Global Deal on Climate Change', *Oxford Review of Economic Policy*, 24(2): 259–79.

Hibbs, J. (2000) *Transport Policy: The Myth of Integrated Planning*. London: IEA.

Hibbs, J. (2006) 'Railways and the Power of Emotion', in J. Hibbs, O. Knipping, R. Merkert, C. Nash, R. Roy, D.E. Tyrrall and R. Wellings, *The Railways, the Market and the Government*. London: Institute of Economic Affairs, pp. 21–45.

Higher Education Statistics Agency (2008) http://www.hesa.ac.uk/index.php?option=com_datatables&Itemid=121&task=show_category&catdex=3

Hills, J. (2007) 'Ends and Means: The Future Roles of Social Housing in England', CASE Report 34, February.

Hills, J. and Stewart, K. (2005) 'Conclusion: A Tide Turned but Mountains Yet to Climb?' in *A More Equal Society*. Bristol: The Policy Press.

Hillyard, P. (2005) 'The War on Terror, Lessons from Ireland', European Civil Liberties Network, http://www.ecln.org/essays/essay-1.pdf

Hirsch, D. (2006) *What Will It Take to End Child Poverty? Firing on All Cylinders*, Joseph Rowntree Foundation, http://www.jrf.org.uk/bookshop/eBooks/9781859355008.pdf, p. 13.

HM Treasury (1998) *Modern Public Services for Britain: Investing in Reform. Comprehensive Spending Review: New Public Spending Plans 1999–2002*. London: HMSO.

HM Treasury (2000a) 'Prudent for a Purpose: Working for a Stronger and Fairer Britain', March.

HM Treasury (2000b) 'Productivity in the UK. The Evidence and the Government's Approach', http://www.hm-treasury.gov.uk/media/D/C/ACF1FBA.pdf

HM Treasury (2001) *SET for Success: The Supply of People with Science, Technology, Engineering and Mathematics Skills*. London: HMSO.

HM Treasury (2003) *UK Membership of the Single Currency: An Assessment of the Five Economic Tests*, Cm 5776.

HM Treasury (2004) *Science and Innovation Investment Framework 2004–2014*. London: HMSO.

HM Treasury (2005) 'Supporting Growth in Innovation: Enhancing the R&D Tax Credit', http://www.hm-treasury.gov.uk/media/F/7/RDtax_credit.pdf

HM Treasury (2006a) *Leitch Review of Skills, Final Report*, paras 35–42. http://www.hm-treasury.gov.uk/leitch

HM Treasury (2006b) *Prosperity for All in the Global Economy – World Class Skills: Final Report*. London: HMSO. http://www.hm-treasury.gov.uk/leitch

HM Treasury (2006c) *Science and Innovation Investment Framework 2004–2014: Next Steps*. London: HMSO.

HM Treasury (2007a) *Meeting the Aspirations of the British People: 2007 Pre-Budget Report and Comprehensive Spending Review*. London: HMSO.

HM Treasury (2007b) *Productivity in the UK 7: Securing Long-term Prosperity*.

HM Treasury (2007c) *PSA Delivery Agreement 18: Promote Better Health and Well being for All*.

HM Treasury (2007d) *Tax Ready Reckoner and Tax Reliefs*.

HM Treasury (2007e) *Transforming Government Procurement*. London: HMSO.

HM Treasury (2007f) *Review of Sub-national Economic Development and Regeneration*. London: HMT, BERR and DCLG. http://www.hm-treasury.gov.uk/d/subnational_econ_review170707.pdf

HM Treasury (2008a) *Ending Child Poverty: Everybody's Business*, http://www.hm-treasury.gov.uk/media/3/F/bud08_childpoverty_1310.pdf, p. 25

HM Treasury (2008b) *Pre-budget Report*. Cm 7484. The Stationery Office. http://www.hm-treasury.gov.uk/prebud_pbr08_repindex.htm

Hogwood, B. (1992) *Trends in British Public Policy: Do Governments Make Any Difference?* Buckingham: Open University Press.

Hoj, J. (2007) 'Competition Law and Policy Indicators for the OECD Countries', OECD Economics Department Working Paper No. 568.

Hoj, J., Jimenez, M., Maher, M., Nicoletti, G. and Wise, M. (2007) 'Product Market Competition in OECD Countries: Taking Stock and Moving Forward', Economics Department Working Paper No. 575, OECD, September.

Home Office (2000) *Terrorism Act 2000, Explanatory Notes*. London: The Stationery Office.

Home Office (2001a) *Community Cohesion: A Report of the Independent Review Team*. London: Home Office.

Home Office (2001b) *Building Cohesive Communities: A Report of the Ministerial Group on Public Order and Community Cohesion*. London: Home Office.

Home Office (2001c) *Anti-Terrorism, Crime and Security Act, Explanatory Notes*. London: The Stationery Office.

Home Office (2001d) *Making Punishments Work: Report of a Review of the Sentencing Framework for England and Wales* (The Halliday Report). London: Home Office.

Home Office (2003) Press Release, 'Plans for Citizenship Ceremonies Welcomed', December 9.

Home Office (2006a) *Terrorism Act, Explanatory Notes*. London: The Stationery Office.

Home Office (2006b) *A Points Based System: Making Migration Work For Britain*, Cm 6741.

Home Office (2008a) *Control of Immigration: Statistics United Kingdom*. London: Home Office.

Home Office (2008b) *From the Neighbourhood to the National: Policing Our Communities Together* (The Policing Green Paper). London: Home Office.

Honohan, P. (2008) 'Risk Management and the Costs of the Banking Crisis', *National Institute Economic Review*, 206: 15–24,

Hoorens, S., Gallo, F., Cave, J.A.K. and Grant, J.C. (2007) 'Can Assisted Reproductive Technologies Help to Offset Population Ageing? An Assessment of the Demographic and Economic Impact of ART in Denmark and UK', *Human Reproduction*, 22(9): 2471–5.

Hope, C. (2006) 'The Marginal Impact of CO_2 from PAGE2002: An Integrated Assessment Model Incorporating the IPCC's Five Reasons for Concern', *Integrated Assessment*, 6(1): 19–56.

Hope, C. and Newbery, D. (2008) 'Calculating the Social Cost of Carbon', in M. Grubb, T. Jamasb and M. Pollitt (eds) *Delivering a Low Carbon Electricity System: Technologies, Economics and Policy*. Cambridge: Cambridge University Press. Chapter 2.

Hough, M. and Hunter, G. (2008) 'The 2003 Licensing Act's Impact on Crime and Disorder: An Evaluation', *Criminology and Criminal Justice*, 8: 239–60.

Hough, M., Allen, R. and Padel, U. (eds) (2006) *Reshaping Probation and Prisons: The New Offender Management Framework*. Researching Criminal Justice Series Paper No. 6. Bristol: Policy Press.

Hough, M., Jacobson, J. and Millie, A. (2003) *The Decision to Imprison: Sentencing and the Prison Population*. London: Prison Reform Trust.

House of Commons Committee on Work and Pensions (2007) *Benefits Simplification: Seventh Report Session 2006/07*, HC 463-I. London: The Stationery Office.

House of Commons Innovation, Universities, Science and Skills Committee (2008) *Science Budget Allocations: Fourth Report of Session 2007–08*. London: House of Commons.

House of Commons Select Committee on Education and Skills (2002) *Individual Learning Accounts*. London: House of Commons.

House of Lords (2008) *The Economic Impact of Immigration*, HL Paper 82-I. http://www.parliament.the-stationery-office.com/pa/ld200708/ldselect/ldeconaf/82/82.pdf

'Housing Market', *Oxford Review of Economic Policy*, 24: 59–78.

Howard, J. and Taylor, M. (2007) *A Higher Degree of Concern*. London: Royal Society.

IEA (International Energy Agency) (2005) *Solar Power and Chemical Energy Systems*. Solar PACES Annual Report.

IFS (Institute for Fiscal Studies) (2004) *The Green Budget*.

IHRC (Islamic Human Rights Commission) (2004) *British Muslims, Expectations of the Government, Social Discrimination Across the Muslim Divide*. London: IHRC.

IISS (International Institute for Strategic Studies) (1997) *The Military Balance 1997/98*. Oxford: Oxford University Press.

IISS (International Institute for Strategic Studies) (2008) *The Military Balance 2008*. Abingdon: Routledge.

Initiatives, 1987–2006. London: British Chambers of Commerce.

Inklaar, R., Timmer, M. and van Ark, B. (2007) 'Mind the Gap! International Comparisons of Productivity in Services and Goods Production', *German Economic Review*, 8: 281–307.

Innvaer, S., Vist, G., Trommald, M. and Oxman, A. (2002) 'Health Policy-makers' Perceptions of Their Use of Evidence: A Systematic Review', *Journal of Health Services Research and Policy*, 7(4): 239–44.

Institution of Engineering and Technology (2007) *Engineering and Technology Skills and Demand in Industry*. London: Institution of Engineering and Technology.

IPCC (Intergovernmental Panel on Climate Change) (2001) *Working Group I Report, Climate Change 2001. The Scientific Basis*. Cambridge: Cambridge University Press.

IPCC (Intergovernmental Panel on Climate Change) (2007) *Fourth Assessment Report. Working Group I Report: The Physical Science Basis*. Cambridge: Cambridge University Press.

IRF (International Road Federation) (2006) *World Road Statistics 2006*. Paris: IRF.

Jackson, T. (2005) 'Motivating Sustainable Consumption: A Review of Evidence on Consumer Behaviour and Behavioural Change', in *A report to the Sustainable Development Research Network*.

Jackson, T. (2006) *The Earthscan Reader in Sustainable Consumption*. London: Earthscan.

Jackson, T. (2008a) 'What Politicians Dare Not Say', *New Scientist*, 200(2678).

Jackson, T. (2008b) 'The Challenges of Sustainable Lifestyles', in *State of the World: Innovations for a Sustainable Economy*.

Jacobson, J. and Hough, M. (2008) *Creating a Sentencing Commission for England and Wales: An Opportunity to Address the Prisons Crisis*. London: Prison Reform Trust.

Jenkins, A., Greenwood, C. and Vignoles, A. (2007) *The Returns to Qualifications in England: Updating the Evidence Base*. London: Centre for the Economics of Education, London School of Economics.

Johansson, A., Heady, C., Arnold, J., Brys, B. and Vartis, L. (2008), 'Taxation and Economic Growth', OECD Economics Department Working Paper No. 620.

Joppke, C. (2004) 'The Retreat of Multiculturalism in the Liberal State: Theory and Policy', *The British Journal of Sociology*, 55(2).

Jorgensen, D.W. (1989), 'Capital as a Factor of Production', in D.W. Jorgensen and R. Landau (eds) *Technology and Capital Formation*. Cambridge: MIT Press, pp. 1–35.

Joseph Rowntree Foundation (1994) 'The Effects of the 1986 Social Security Act on Family Incomes', *Social Policy Research*, 54. http://www.jrf.org.uk/knowledge/findings/socialpolicy/SP54.asp

Keaney, E. and Rogers, B. (2006) *A Citizen's Duty: Voter Inequality and the Case for Compulsory Turnout*. London: IPPR.

Keep, E. (2000) 'Creating a Knowledge-driven Economy: Definitions, Challenges and Opportunities', SKOPE Policy Paper No. 2, University of Warwick, SKOPE.

Kershaw, C., Nicholas, S. and Walker, A. (2008) *Crime in England and Wales 2007/08. Home Office Statistical Bulletin 07/08*. London: Home Office. http://www.homeoffice.gov.uk/rds/pdfs08/hosb0708.pdf

Khomen, E. and Weale, M. (2008) *Are We Living Beyond Our Means? A Comparison of France, Italy, Spain and the United Kingdom*. National Institute Discussion Paper No. 311. http://www.niesr.ac.uk/pdf/100408_94720.pdf

King, D.A. (2004) 'The Scientific Impact of Nations', *Nature*, 430(6997): 311–16.

King, A. (2007) *The British Constitution*. Oxford: Oxford University Press.

Kirsanova, T., Leith, C. and Wren-Lewis, S. (2007) 'Optimal Debt Policy, and an Institutional Proposal to Help in its Implementation', European Economy Economic Papers No. 275, April.

Kneller, R. and P.A. Stevens (2006) 'Frontier Technology and Absorptive Capacity: Evidence from OECD Manufacturing Industries', *Oxford Bulletin of Economics and Statistics*, 68: 1–21.

Kneller, R., Bleaney, M. and Gemmell, N. (1999) 'Fiscal Policy and Growth: Evidence from OECD Countries', *Journal of Public Economics*, 74: 171–90.

Knott, D., Muers, S. and Aldridge, S. (2007) 'Achieving Cultural Change: A Policy Framework', The Strategy Unit, Cabinet Office.

Krueger, A.B and Meyer, B.D. (2002) 'Labor Supply Effects of Social Insurance', in A.J. Auerbach and M. Feldstein (eds) *Handbook of Public Economics*, 4.

Labour Party Manifesto (1997) http://labour-party.org.uk/manifestos/1997/1997-labour-manifesto.shtml

Le Grand, J. (2007a) 'Narrowing Health Inequalities in the UK: Next Decade Challenges', Lecture to the Fabian Society, Health Inequality Forum, November.

Le Grand, J. (2007b) *The Other Invisible Hand: Delivering Public Services Through Competition and Choice*. Princeton: Princeton University Press.

Leunig, T. (2007) *In My Backyard: Unlocking the Planning System*. London: CentreForum.

Leunig, T. and Overman, H. (2008) 'Spatial Patterns of Development and the British Housing Market', *Oxford Review of Economic Policy*, 24(1): 59–78.

Leunig, T. and Swaffield, J. (2008) *Cities Unlimited*. London: Policy Exchange.

Lewis, W. (2004) *The Power of Productivity*. Chicago: University of Chicago Press.

LGA (Local Government Association) (2007) *Prosperous Communities II: vive la devolution!* London: LGA.

LHC (London Health Commission) (2008) 'Health Impact Assessment', http://www.londonshealth.gov.uk/hia.htm

Lim, C. and Davies, C. (2008) *Helping Schools Succeed*. London: Policy Exchange.

Lishman, B. and Woods, A.W. (2006) 'The Control of Naturally Ventilated Buildings Subject to Wind and Buoyancy', *Journal of Fluid Mechanics*, 557: 451–72.

Lodge, G. (2007). 'Central–Local Relations: Why It Is So Hard To Let Go', in Richard Brooks (ed.) *Public Services at the Crossroads*. London: IPPR.

Lynas, M. (2007) *Six Degrees: Our Future on a Hotter Planet*. London: Fourth Estate.

Lyons Inquiry into Local Government (2007) *Place-shaping: A Shared Ambition for the Future of Local Government, Final Report*. London: The Stationery Office.

Machin, S., McNally, S. and Silva, O. (2007) 'New Technology in Schools: Is There a Pay-Off?' *Economic Journal*, 115(552): 1145–67.

Manning, A. and Petrongolo, B. (2008) 'The Part-time Pay Penalty', *Economic Journal*, 118(526): F28–F51.

Mansell, W. (2007) *Education by Numbers: The Tyranny of Testing*. London: Politico's.

Marburger, J. (2005) 'Wanted: Better Benchmarks', *Science*, 308: 1087.

'Market Reforms and Productivity in the OECD', OECD Economics Department Working Paper No. 460.

Marmot, M. (2004) *The Status Syndrome: How Social Standing Affects our Health and Longevity*. New York: Henry Holt & Co.

Marrano, M.G. and Haskel, J. (2006) 'How Much Does the UK Invest in Intangible Assets?' Queen Mary College Working Paper No. 578. http://www.econ.qmul.ac.uk/papers/doc/wp578.pdf

Marsden, D. and Belfield, R. (2006) 'Pay for Performance Where Output is Hard to Measure: The Case for Performance Pay for Schoolteachers', Centre for Economic Performance Discussion Paper 747, London School of Economics.

Marshall, P. (2007) *Tackling Educational Inequality*. London: CentreForum.

Martin, R., Sunley, P. and Nativel, C. (2001) 'Mapping the New Deal: Mapping Local Disparities in the Performance of Welfare-to-Work', *Transactions of the Institute of British Geographers*, 26(4): 484–512.

Maruna, S. (2000) *Making Good, How Ex-convicts Reform & Rebuild Their Lives*. Washington, DC: American Psychological Association.

May, R. (1998) 'The Scientific Investment of Nations', *Science*, 281(5373): 49–51.

McDonald, A. (ed.) (2007) *Reinventing Britain: Constitutional Change under New Labour*. London: Politico's.

McIntosh, S. (2006) 'Further Analysis of the Returns to Academic and Vocational Qualifications', *Oxford Bulletin of Economics and Statistics*, 68(2): 225–51.

McKee-Ryan, F. et al (2005) 'Psychological and Physical Well-being During Unemployment: A Meta-analytic Study', *Journal of Applied Psychology*, 90(1): 53–76.

McKinsey Global Institute (1998) *Driving Productivity and Growth in the UK Economy*. London.

McLean, I. (2005) 'Barnett and the West Lothian Question', Paper for ESRC Conference, December. http://www.nuff.ox.ac.uk/Politics/papers/2005/BarnettandtheWestLothianQuestion.pdf

McLean, I. (2006) *Adam Smith, Radical and Egalitarian: An Interpretation for the 21st Century*. Edinburgh: Edinburgh University Press.

McLean, I. (2008) 'Climate Change and UK Politics: From Brynle Williams to Sir Nicholas Stern', *Political Quarterly*, 79(2): 184–93.

McLean, I., Lodge, G. and Schmuecker, K. (2008) *Fair Shares? Barnett and the Politics of Public Expenditure*. London and Newcastle: IPPR/IPPR North.

McMichael, A., Powles, J., Butler, C. and Uauy, R. (2007) 'Food, Livestock Production, Energy, Climate Change, and Health', *The Lancet*, 370(9594): 1253–63.

McSweeney, T. and Hough, M. (2005) 'Drugs and Alcohol', in N. Tilley (ed.) *Handbook of Crime Prevention and Community Safety*. Cullompton: Willan Publishing.

McSweeney, T., Turnbull, P.J. and Hough, M. (2008) *The Treatment and Supervision of Drug Dependent Offenders: A Review of the Literature Prepared for the UK Drug Policy Commission*. London: UK Drug Policy Commission.

Meade Committee (1978) *The Structure and Reform of Direct Taxation*. London: Institute for Fiscal Studies.

Meer, N. (2008) 'The Politics of Voluntary and Involuntary Identities: Are Muslims in Britain an Ethnic, Racial or Religious Minority?' *Patterns of Prejudice*, 42(1): 61–81.

Melhuish, E. and NESS Research team (2008) *The Impact of Sure Start Local Programmes on Three Year Olds and Their Families*. London: DCSF.

Metcalf, H. and Meadows, P. (2008) 'Outcomes for Basic Skills Learners: A Four-year Longitudinal Study', in S. Reder and J. Bynner (eds) *Tracking Adult Literacy and Numeracy Skills*. Routledge, forthcoming.

Millar, J. (2008) 'Making Work Pay, Making Tax Credits Work: An Assessment with Specific Reference to Lone-parent Employment', *International Social Security Review*, 61(2): 21–38.

Milton, S. (2007) *Central, Nervous System: Can Localism Help Gordon Relax?* London: Localis.

Ministry of Defence (2008) *UK Defence Statistics 2008*. London: The Stationery Office.

Ministry of Justice (2007) *The Governance of Britain*, Cm 7170.

Ministry of Reconstruction (1918) *Report of the Machinery of Government*. London: Ministry of Reconstruction.

Mirza, M., Senthilkumaran, A. and Ja'far, Z. (2007) *Living Apart Together*. London: Policy Exchange.

Modood, T. (2003) 'Muslims and the Politics of Difference', in S. Spencer (ed.) *The Politics of Migration*. Oxford: Blackwell Publishing.

Modood, T. (2007) *Multiculturalism*. Cambridge: Polity.

Molyneux, P., Kemp, V. and Coutts, A. (2006) 'Housing and Health', The Health and Social Care Change Agent Team, National Health Service. http://www.changeagent-team.org.uk/_library/docs/housing/housingandhealth/sustaininghealth.pdf

MORI (2006) *Understanding Public and Patient Attitudes to the NHS*. Ipsos MORI.

MORI (2008a) *Public Attitudes to Climate Change, 2008: Concerned but Still Unconvinced*. Ipsos MORI.

MORI (2008b) *Understanding Public and Patient Attitudes to the NHS*. Ipsos MORI.

Mulgan, G. (1990) *The Question of Quality*. London: BFI Publishing.

Mullis, I.V.S., Martin, M.O. and Foy, P. (with Olson, J.F., Preuschoff, C., Erberber, E., Arora, A. and Galia, J.) (2008) *TIMSS 2007 International Mathematics Report: Findings from IEA's Trends in International Mathematics and Science Study at the Fourth and Eighth Grades*. Chestnut Hill, MA: TIMSS & PIRLS International Study Center, Boston College.

Muscatelli, A. (chair) (2008) *First Evidence from the Independent Expert Group to the Commission on Scottish Devolution*. Edinburgh: Heriot-Watt University.

NAO (National Audit Office) (2001) *Department of Health: Inpatient and Outpatient Waiting in the NHS*.

NAO (National Audit Office) (2002) *Innovation in the National Health Service: The Acquisition of the Heart Hospital*.

NAO (National Audit Office) (2003) *Getting the Evidence: Using Research in Policy Making*. London: HMSO.

NAO (National Audit Office) (2006) *Sure Start Children's Centres*. London: The Stationery Office.

NAO (National Audit Office) (2007) 'Helping People from Workless Households into Work'. HC 609. http://www.nao.org.uk/publications/nao_reports/06-07/0607609.pdf

NAO (National Audit Office) (2008) *The Administrative Burdens Reduction Programme, 2008*. London: The Stationery Office.

National Commission on Education (Great Britain) (1993) *Learning to Succeed*. London: Paul Hamlyn Foundation.

National Endowment for Science, Technology and the Arts (2007) *Driving Innovation Through Public Procurement*. London: NESTA.

National Evaluation of Sure Start Research Team (2008) *The Impact of Sure Start Local Programmes on Three Year Olds and Their Families'*. Accessible via http://www.ness.bbk.ac.uk/impact.asp

National Health Service Confederation (2006) *Lost in Translation: Why Are Patients More Satisfied With the NHS Than the Public?*

Nelson, R.R. (1959) 'The Simple Economics of Basic Science Research', *The Journal of Political Economy*, 67(3): 297–306.

Newbery, D. (1998) 'Fair and Efficient Pricing and the Finance of Roads', 53rd Henry Spurrier Memorial Lecture, given at the Royal Society of the Arts, 5 May.

NHPAU (National Housing and Planning Advice Unit) (2008a) 'Affordability Still Matters', NHPAU, July. http://www.communitities.gov.uk/nhpau

NHPAU (National Housing and Planning Advice Unit) (2008b) 'Meeting the Housing Requirements of an Aspiring and Growing National: Taking the Medium and Long-term View', NHPAU, June. http://www.communities.gov.uk/nhpau

NIACE (National Institute of Adult Continuing Education) (2008) *Counting the Cost: The NIACE Survey on Adult Participation*. Leicester: NIACE.

Nickell, S. (2005) 'What Has happened to Unemployment in the OECD since the 1980s?', unpublished presentation to Work and Pensions Economics Group, HM Treasury.

Nicoletti, G. and Scarpetta, S. (2003) 'Regulation, Productivity and Growth', *Economic Policy*, 36: 9–72.

Nicoletti, G. and Scarpetta, S. (2005) 'Regulation and Economic Performance: Product Market Reforms and Productivity in the OECD', OECD Economics Department Working Papers No. 460.

Nordhaus, W.D. (2007) 'A Review of The Stern Review on the Economics of Climate Change', *Journal of Economic Literature*, 45(3): 686–702.

O'Mahony, M. (1999) *Britain's Productivity Performance 1950–1996*. London: National Institute of Economic and Social Research.

O'Mahony, M. and Robinson, C. (2007) 'UK Growth and Productivity in International Perspective: Evidence from EU KLEMS', *National Institute Economic Review*, 200: 79–86.

O'Neill, B., MacKellar, L.F. and Lutz, W. (2001) *Population and Climate Change*. Cambridge: Cambridge University Press.

O'Shaugnessy, J. (ed.) (2007) *The Leadership Effect*. London: Policy Exchange.

OECD (Organization for Economic Cooperation and Development) (2006) *OECD Employment Outlook 2006*. OECD Publishing.

OECD (Organization for Economic Cooperation and Development) (2007a) *Babies and Bosses*, Vol. V.

OECD (Organization for Economic Cooperation and Development) (2007b) *Social Expenditure Database*.

OECD (Organization for Economic Cooperation and Development) (2007c) *Revenue Statistics, 1965–2006*.

OECD (Organization for Economic Cooperation and Development) (2007d) *Economic Survey of the United Kingdom.*

OECD (Organization for Economic Cooperation and Development) (2008a) *Main Science and Technology Indicators. 2008 Release 01.*

OECD (Organization for Economic Cooperation and Development) (2008b) *Tax Database.*

OECD (Organization for Economic Cooperation and Development) (2008c) 'The Future of the Internet Economy. A Statistical Profile'. OECD Ministerial Meeting, Seoul, Korea.

OECD (Organization for Economic Cooperation and Development) (2008d) *Jobs for Youth: United Kingdom.*

Ofcom (2007). *Digital Dividend Review*. At http://www.ofcom.org.uk/consult/condocs/ddr/statement/

Ofcom (2008a) *Communications Market Report*. Annual. At http://www.ofcom.org.uk/research/cm/

Ofcom (2008b) *Second Review of Public Service Television Broadcasting. Phase 2 Report*. At http://www.ofcom.org.uk/tv/psb_review/psb_2review/psbreview2.pdf

ONS (Office for National Statistics) (2005) *General Household Survey*. London: ONS.

ONS (Office for National Statistics) (2007a) *Family Spending, 2007*. London: ONS.

ONS (Office for National Statistics) (2007b) *Gross Domestic Expenditure on Research and Development 2005*. London: ONS.

ONS (Office for National Statistics) (2007c) *Public Service Productivity: Education*. London: ONS.

ONS (Office for National Statistics) (2008a) *Economic and Labour Market Review*, June 2008. Newport: ONS.

ONS (Office for National Statistics) (2008b) *Labour Market Statistics First Release*, October 2008. Newport: ONS.

ONS (Office for National Statistics) (2008c) *Public Service Productivity: Healthcare*. Newport: ONS.

Office for Standards in Education, Children's Services and Skills (2008) *Success in Science*. London: HMSO.

Osborne, D. and Gaebler, T. (1992) *Reinventing Government*. New York: Plume.

Page, B. (2008) 'Does Britain Need Fixing?', *Prospect*, October.

Parekh, B. (2000) *Rethinking Multiculturalism*. Basingstoke: Palgrave Macmillan.

Parliamentary Office of Science and Technology (2008) *International Migration of Scientists and Engineers*. London: POST.

Parson, E.A. and Fisher-Vanden, K. (1997) 'Integrated Assessment Models of Global Climate Change', *Annual Review of Energy and Environment*, 22: 589–628.

Partridge, S. (2004) *Examining Case Management Models for Community Sentences*. Home Office Online Report 17/04. London: Home Office.

Peach, C. (2005) 'Britain's Muslim Population: An Overview', in T. Abbas (ed.) *Muslims in Britain, Communities Under Pressure*. London: Zed Books.

'Performance in International Perspective', in N. Crafts, I. Gazeley and A. Newell (eds) *Work and Pay in Twentieth-century Britain*. Oxford: Oxford University Press, pp. 301–29.

Perron, P. (1989) 'The Great Crash, the Oil Price Shock and the Unit Root Hypothesis', *Econometrica*, 57: 1361–401.

Pew (2005) 'Support for Terror Wanes Among Muslim Publics. Islamic Extremism: Common Concern for Muslim and Western Publics', http://pewglobal.org/reports/pdf/248.pdf

Pew (2008) 'Unfavourable Views of Jews and Muslims on the Increase in Europe', http://pewglobal.org/reports/pdf/262.pdf, accessed 20th November 2008.

'Planning Decision-making: A Proposal', *Urban Studies*, 42: 647–63.

Plum Consulting (2008) 'A Framework for Evaluating the Value of Next Generation Broadband. A Report for the Broadband Stakeholder Group'. http://www.broadbanduk.org/component/option,com_docman/task,doc_view/gid,1009/Itemid,63/

Pollard, N. et al (2008) *Floodgates or Turnstiles*. London: IPPR.

Powell, E. (1970) Election Speech, 11 June 1970, in E. Powell, *Reflections of a Statesman, The Writings and Speeches of Enoch Powell*. London: Bellew.

Propper, C. and Wilson, D. (2003) 'The Use and Usefulness of Performance Measures in the Public Sector', *Oxford Review of Economic Policy*, 19: 250–67.

RAC Foundation (2006) *Road User Charging*. London: RAC Foundation for Motoring.

Ravitch, D. (1983) *The Troubled Crusade: American Education 1945–1980*. New York: Basic Books.

Riley, R. and Weale, M.R. (2006) 'Immigration and its Effects', *National Institute Economic Review*, 198: 4–9.

Roberts, J.V. and Hough, M. (2005) *Understanding Public Attitudes to Criminal Justice*. Maidenhead: Open University Press.

Rogers, P. (2008) 'Facing the Freshwater Crisis', *Scientific American*, 299(2).

Roodhouse M (2007) *Rationing Returns: A Solution to Global Warming?* http://www.historyandpolicy.org/papers/policy-paper-54.html

Rotberg, I. (ed.) (2004) *Balancing Change and Tradition in Global Education Reform*. Lanham, MD: Scarecrow.

Russell, M. (2008) 'Parliament: Emasculated or Emancipated?' in Robert Hazell (ed.) *Constitutional Futures Revisited*. Basingstoke: Palgrave Macmillan, pp. 267–84.

Ryan, C. (ed.) (2008) *Staying the Course: Changes to the Participation Age and Qualifications*. London: Social Market Foundation.

Saggar, S. (2006) 'The One Per Cent World: Managing the Myth of Muslim Religious Extremism', *The Political Quarterly*, 77:3.

Saggar, S. (2009) *Pariah Politics: Understanding Western Radical Islamism and What Should be Done*. Oxford: Oxford University Press.

Sainsbury of Turville, Lord (2007) *The Race to the Top: A Review of Government's Science and Innovation Policies*. London: HMSO.

Sansom, T., Nash, C., Mackie, P., Shires, J. and Watkiss, P. (2001) *Surface Transport Costs and Charges: Great Britain 1998*. Leeds: Institute for Transport Studies.

Sauter, Wolf (1997) *Competition Policy and Industrial Policy in the EU*. Oxford: Oxford University Press.

Schuster, L. (2003) 'Asylum Seekers: Sangatte and the Tunnel', *Parliamentary Affairs*, 56: 506–22.

Schuster, L. and Solomos, J. (2004) 'Race, Immigration and Asylum: New Labour's Agenda and its Consequences', *Ethnicities*, 4(2): 267–300.

Schwartz, B. (2005) *The Paradox of Choice: Why More Is Less. How the Culture of Abundance Robs Us Satisfaction*. New York: Harper Perennial.

Sentencing Commission Working Group (2008) *Sentencing Guidelines in England and Wales: An Evolutionary Approach* (Gage Report). London: Sentencing Commission Working Group.

Shayer, M. (forthcoming) 'Thirty Years On: A Large Anti-Flynn Effect? (II): 13 & 14 Year Olds. Piagetian Tests of Formal Operations Norms 1976–2006/7', *British Journal of Educational Psychology*.

Shayer, M., Ginsburg, D. and Coe, R. (2007) 'Thirty Years On: A Large Anti-Flynn Effect?' *British Journal of Educational Psychology*, 77(1): 25–41.

Sigle-Rushton, W. (2004) 'Intergenerational and Life-course Transmission of Social Exclusion in the 1970 British Cohort Study', CASE Paper 78.

Simpson, L. (2007) 'Ghettos of the Mind: The Empirical Behaviour of Indices of Segregation and Diversity', *Journal of the Royal Statistical Society*, 170(2): 405–24.

'Sleipner CO_2 Plume'. 8th Greenhouse Gas Control Technologies conference (GHGT-8), Trondheim, June 2006.

Smith, R. (1987) 'Comroe and Dripps Revisited', *British Medical Journal*, 295(6610): 1404–7.

Social Justice Policy Group (2007) *Breakthough Britain: Ending the Cost of Social Breakdown*. Centre for Social Justice.

Solow, R.M. (1957) 'Technical Change and the Aggregate Production Function', *The Review of Economics and Statistics*, 39(3): 312–20.

Spelman, W. (2005) 'Jobs or Jails: The Crime Drop in Texas', *Journal of Policy Analysis and Management*, 24: 133–65.

Stern, N. (2008) *Key Elements of a Global Deal on Climate Change*. The London School of Economics and Political Science.

Stern, N. (2006) *The Economics of Climate Change*. Cambridge: Cambridge University Press.

Stone, D., Maxwell, S. and Keating, M. (2001) 'Bridge Research and Policy: An International Workshop Funded by the UK Department for International Development', Radcliffe House, Warwick University, 16–17 July 2001.

Stone, R. (2004) *Islamophobia, Issues Challenges and Action*. Stoke on Trent: Trentham Books.

Strategy Unit (2008) 'Getting On, Getting Ahead: A Discussion Paper: Analysing the Trends and Drivers of Social Mobility', Cabinet Office, UK Government.

Straw, J. (2007) Cyril Foster Lecture, Oxford, 25 January.

Stuckler, D., Meissner, C. and King, L. (2008) 'Can a Bank Crisis Break Your Heart?', *Globalization and Health*, 4(1): 1–12.

Sturgis, J. (2000) 'The English Examining Boards: Their Route from Independence to Government Outsourcing Agencies', Unpublished PhD thesis, University of London.

Sunstein, C.R. (1994) 'Incommensurability and Valuation in Law', *Michigan Law Review* 92–3: 779–861.

Sutherland, D., Price, R., Joumard, I. and Nicq, C. (2007) 'Performance Indicators for Public Spending Efficiency in Primary and Secondary Education', OECD Economics.

Sutton Trust (2008) *Report to the National Council for Educational Excellence*.

Swann (1985) *Education for All: The Report of the Committee of Inquiry into the Education of Children from Ethnic Minority Groups*. London: HMSO.

Sylva, K., Melhuish, E., Sammons, P., Siraj-Blatchford, I. and Taggart, B. (2004a) *The Continuing Effects of Pre-school Education at Age 7 Years*. London: Institute of Education.

Sylva, K., Melhuish, E., Sammons, P., Siraj-Blatchford, I. and Taggart, B. (2004b) *The Final Report: The Effective Provision of Pre-school Education (EPPE) Project*. London: Institute of Education.

Symeonidis, G. (2008) 'The Effect of Competition on Wages and Productivity: Evidence from the United Kingdom', *Review of Economics and Statistics*, 90: 134–46.

Szulanski, G. (2003) *Sticky Knowledge: Barriers to Knowing in the Firm*. London: Sage Publications.

Taylor, Rufus III (2009) PhD Thesis. University of Oxford Law Faculty.

TfL (Transport for London) (2007) *Central London Congestion Charging: Impacts Monitoring*, Fifth Annual Report, http://www.tfl.gov.uk

The Conference Board (2008) *Total Economy Database*, January 2008.

The Economist (2008a) 'Freezing the Sun: A Double Blow for Solar Energy', http://www.economist.com/world/unitedstates/displaystory.cfm?story_id=11637342

The Economist (2008b) 'A Special Report on the Future of Energy', 387(8585).

The Times (2008) 'Influx of Migrants Brings a "Brain Gain" for the UK', http://www.timesonline.co.uk/tol/news/politics/article3406153.ece

Thomas, A. (2007) 'Lone Parent Work Focused Interviews: Synthesis of Findings', DWP Research Report 443, Leeds, Corporate Document Service.

Thornberry, E., Muir, R. and Kearns, I. (2007) 'Power Politics: Who Runs Britain?' in Nick Pearce and Julia Margo (eds) *Politics for a New Generation: The Progressive Moment*. Basingstoke: Palgrave Macmillan.

Timmer, M. and Ypma, G. (2006) 'Productivity Levels in Distributive Trades: A New ICOP Dataset for OECD Countries', Groningen Growth and Development Centre Research Memorandum No. GD-83.

Turner, D., Boone, L., Giorno, C., Meacci, M., Rae, D. and Richardson, P. (2001) 'Estimating the Structural Rate of Unemployment for the OECD Countries', OECD Economic Studies No. 33, 2001/II171.

Tyler, T.R. (2003) 'Procedural Justice, Legitimacy, and the Effective Rule of Law', in M. Tonry (ed.) *Crime and Justice*. Chicago: University of Chicago Press.

Tyler, T.R. (ed.) (2007) *Legitimacy and Criminal Justice*. New York: Russell Sage Foundation.

Uberoi, V. (2008a) 'Do Policies of Multiculturalism Change National Identities', *The Political Quarterly*, 79(3): 404–17.

Uberoi, V. (2008b) 'Multiculturalism and The Canadian Charter of Rights and Freedoms', *Political Studies*, October 2008: 1–26.

UNICEF (2007) *Overview of Child Wellbeing in Rich Countries*. Report Card 7.

United Nations (2006) *World Population Prospects. The 2006 Revision*. Volume 1: Comprehensive tables.

Universities UK (2007) *Talent Wars: The International Market for Academic Staff*. London: Universities UK.

Universities UK (2008) *The Future Size and Shape of the Higher Education Sector in the UK: Threats and Opportunities*. London: Universities UK.

van Ark, B., O'Mahony, M. and Timmer, M. (2008) 'The Productivity Gap between Europe and the United States: Trends and Causes', *Journal of Economic Perspectives*, 22: 25–44.

Vasta, E. (2007) 'Accommodating Diversity: Why Current Critiques of Multiculturalism Miss the Point', COMPAS Working Paper, No. 53.

Vertovek, S. (2007) 'Super Diversity and Its Implications', *Ethnic and Racial Studies*, 30(6): 1024–51.

Vinokur, A.D., Schul, Y., Vuori, J. and Price, R.H. (2000) 'Two Years After Job Loss: Long Term Impact of the JOBS Programme on Reemployment and Mental Health', *Journal of Occupational Health Psychology*, January 5(1): 32–47.

von Hirsch, A., Bottoms, A., Burney, E. and Wikstrom, P.-O. (1999) *Criminal Deterrence and Sentence Severity*. Oxford: Hart Publishing.

Wallace, W. (2005) 'The Collapse of British Foreign Policy', *International Affairs*, January 81(1): 53–68.

Wanless, D. (2002) *NHS Funding and Reform: The Wanless Report*. London: HMSO.

Wanless, D., Appleby, J., Harrrison, A. and Patel, D. (2007) 'Our Future Health Secured? A Review of NHS Funding and Performance'. Kings Fund.

Warde, P. (2007) 'Facing the Challenge of Climate Change: Energy Efficiency and Energy Consumption', http://www.historyandpolicy.org/papers/policy-paper-65.html

Warhurst, C. (2008) 'The Knowledge Economy, Skills and Government Labour Market Intervention', *Policy Studies*, 29(1): 71–86.

Warry, P. (2006) *Increasing the Economic Impact of Research Councils: Advice to the Director General of Science and Innovation, DTI from the Research Council Economic Impact Group*. London: DTI.

Weale, M.R. (2008) Commentary on chapter 8, *Mirrlees Review of UK Taxation*. Institute for Fiscal Studies.

Wellings, R. Lipson, B. (2008) *Towards Better Transport: Funding New Infrastructure with Future Road Pricing Revenues*. London: Policy Exchange.

White, M. and Riley, R. (2002) 'Findings from the Macro Evaluation of the New Deal for Young People', DWP Research Report 168, Leeds, Corporate Document Service.

White, P. (2008) *Factors Affecting the Decline of Bus Use in the Metropolitan Areas*. London: University of Westminster/PTEG.

Wilkie, T. (1991) *British Science and Politics since 1945*. Oxford: Blackwell.

Wilkinson, R.G. and Pickett, K.E. (2007) 'The Problems of Relative Deprivation: Why Some Societies Do Better Than Others', *Social Science and Medicine*, 65(9): 1965–78.

Wilkinson, R. and Pickett, K. (2009) *The Spirit Level: Why More Equal Societies Almost Always Do Better*. London: Penguin Press.

Winckler, V. and Kenway, P. (2006) *Dreaming of £250 a Week: A Scoping Study on In-work Poverty in Wales*. New Policy Institute and Bevan Foundation.

Wolf, A. (2001) 'Qualifications and Assessment', in R. Aldrich (ed.) *A Century of Education*. London: RoutledgeFalmer, pp. 206–27.

Wolf, A. (2002) *Does Education Matter? Myths about Education and Economic Growth*. London: Penguin.

Wolf, A. (2007a) *Diminished Returns: How Raising the Leaving Age to 18 Will Harm Young People and the Economy*. London: Policy Exchange.

Wolf, A. (2007b) 'Round and Round the Houses: The Leitch Review of Skills', *Local Economy*, 22(2): 111–17.

Wooding, S., Nason, E., Klaustzer, L., Rubin, J., Hanney, S. and Grant, J. (2007) *Policy and Practice Impacts of Research Funded by the Economic and Social Research Council: A Case Study of the Future of Work Programme, Approach and Analysis*. Santa Monica: RAND.

World Bank (2008) *Doing Business 2008*. Washington DC: World Bank.

WHO (World Health Organization) (2008) 'Closing the Gap in a Generation: Health Equity Through Action on the Social Determinants of Health', Social Determinants of Health Commission, Final Report.

WWF (World Wildlife Fund) (2008) *2010 and Beyond: Rising to the Biodiversity Challenge*, http://www.wwf.org.uk/filelibrary/pdf/2010_and_beyond.pdf

Wren-Lewis, S. (2003) 'Changing the Rules', *New Economy*, 10: 73–8.

Ypma, G. (2007) 'Productivity Levels in Transport, Storage and Communication: A New ICOP 1997 Dataset', Groningen Growth and Development Centre Research Memorandum No. GD-85.

Notes on Contributors

Iain McLean is Professor of Politics, Oxford University; Research Director, Oxford University Public Policy Unit; and a fellow of Nuffield College. His current policy research is on UK devolution and the constitution. He is a member of the Independent Expert Group, Commission on Scottish Devolution.

Varun Uberoi is a Post-Doctoral Fellow in the University of Oxford's Department of Politics and International Relations. His research focuses on how unity can and is being fostered amongst the culturally diverse citizens of modern polities.

Adam Coutts is a Post-Doctoral Fellow in the University of Oxford's Department of Politics and International Relations. His current research focuses on the health impacts of non-health sector government policies. He is also working on models of behaviour change.

David Halpern is Director of Research at the Institute for Government.

John Appleby is Chief Economist, The King's Fund.

Jo Blanden is Lecturer in Economics, University of Surrey.

Samantha Callan is Chairman of the Early Years working group at the Centre for Social Justice.

Malcolm Chalmers is Professor of International Politics at the University of Bradford, and was recently Special Adviser to Foreign Secretaries Jack Straw MP and Margaret Beckett MP.

Nicholas Crafts is Professor of Economic History, University of Warwick.

Martin Evans is Senior Research Fellow in the Department of Social Policy and Social Work, University of Oxford.

Federico Gallo is a visiting researcher at the BP Institute, Cambridge University.

Roger Gough is a Cabinet Member of Kent County Council and secretary of the Conservative Party's Democracy Task Force.

Jonathan Grant is President, RAND Europe.

Susan Harkness is Senior Lecturer, Social and Policy Sciences, University of Bath.

Chris Hope is a Reader in Policy Modelling, Judge Business School, Cambridge University.

Mike Hough is Director, Institute for Criminal Policy Research, King's College, London.

Peter Kenway is Director and co-founder of the New Policy Institute.

Sir David King is Director of the Smith School of Enterprise and the Environment at the University of Oxford, and a senior scientific adviser to the United Bank of Switzerland.

Joachim Krapels is a Research Assistant, RAND Europe.

Tim Leunig is a Reader in Economic History at the London School of Economics.

Guy Lodge is Senior Research Fellow in Democracy and Power at the Institute for Public Policy Research.

Stephen Nickell is Warden, Nuffield College, Oxford, and co-winner of the IZA Prize in Labor Economics 2008.

Julian V. Roberts is Professor of Criminology at the University of Oxford.

Shamit Saggar is Professor of Political Science at the University of Sussex and the Non-executive Chairman of the Board of the Legal Complaints Service of the Law Society of England and Wales.

Asheem Singh is a Senior Researcher at the Centre for Social Justice.

Damian Tambini is Senior Lecturer in the Department of Media and Communications, London School of Economics.

Martin Weale is Director of the National Institute for Economic and Social Research.

Richard Wellings is Deputy Editorial Director at the Institute of Economic Affairs. He is the co-author of the Policy Exchange report *Towards Better Transport*.

Alison Wolf is Sir Roy Griffiths Professor of Public Sector Management, King's College, London.

Andrew Woods is a Professor and Director of the BP Institute, Cambridge University.

Bryony Worthington is founder and director of Sandbag.org

Simon Wren-Lewis is Professor of Economics and a fellow of Merton College, Oxford.

Index